If I Can Do It Horseback

A Cow-Country Sketchbook

NUMBER FOUR

The M. K. BROWN *Range Life Series*

If I Can Do It Horseback

A Cow-Country Sketchbook

by JOHN HENDRIX

introduction by
WAYNE GARD

illustrations by
MALCOLM THURGOOD

UNIVERSITY OF TEXAS PRESS • AUSTIN

Requests for permission to reproduce material from this work
should be sent to:
  Permissions
  University of Texas Press
  P.O. Box 7819
  Austin, TX 78713-7819
  http://utpress.utexas.edu/index.php/rp-form

Library of Congress Catalog Number 63-17617

ISBN 978-0-292-73827-0, paperback
ISBN 978-1-4773-0717-5, library e-book
ISBN 978-1-4773-0718-2, individual e-book

Publisher's Foreword

The collection and publication of a group of articles such as these of John Hendrix, originally appearing in *The Cattleman*, demand from the publisher a frequently difficult decision. Shall the articles be printed exactly as they first appeared, or shall they be edited and combined to form a unified book? In presenting the articles in this book the publisher has followed the latter course.

John Hendrix wrote the articles over a period of approximately twenty years. Inevitably, he returned to certain subjects a number of times during that period. Such articles have been combined to give a unified treatment of the subjects. The publisher has also eliminated the repetitions which occurred, again inevitably, in articles written on the same subjects during many years: in the course of those years Mr. Hendrix explained the meaning of the phrase "belly deep to a camel" five times, and "bog a blanket" three times; he repeated certain favorite anecdotes and discussed certain interesting customs or facts wherever they seemed to fit the subject of a particular article. The publisher's changes, for the most part, have been confined to the elimination of these repetitions and of certain topical references which are no longer meaningful, and to minor grammatical alterations made necessary by the integration of two or more articles on the same subject. No attempt has been made to bring Mr. Hendrix's discussions up to date, and the reader should remember that many people mentioned as living have passed away since the original publication of the articles, and that some customs and techniques mentioned are now outdated, while others discussed as innovations are now common practice (using machine-driven earth-movers to build tanks, for instance).

The publisher wishes to express thanks to Mr. Henry Biederman, editor of *The Cattleman*, for making these articles available for publication and for providing helpful answers to a number of editorial queries; to Mrs. Biederman for her aid in preparing the manuscript; and to Mrs. John Hendrix for her cooperation throughout.

Contents

Introduction

Recent attention to oil and other resources should not obscure the great role that cattle have played in the development of Texas and other sections of the Great Plains. Early Spanish settlers brought with them large herds from Mexico—cattle for meat, sheep for warm clothing, horses for travel. When the Anglos came they planted patches of corn, cotton, garden vegetables, and, in some sections, sugar cane. But soon they learned the value of beef and hides, which in many instances became their chief source of income.

Lack of convenient markets was a drawback to the early Texas cattle industry. Yet, even in Spanish times, small herds were trailed to Louisiana. In the middle 1800's larger herds were pointed east and north and even west to California, where gold-seekers brought a new market for beef. Drives to the north had become a valuable factor in the Texas economy when the Civil War interrupted them.

After the war the resumption of trail driving on a much larger scale enabled Texas to recover from the economic blows of the conflict much faster than did the Old South. The brush country was overflowing with wild Longhorns, mainly of Spanish blood, along with domestic herds that, untended during the war, had wandered off and become half wild.

Capturing these often ferocious beasts, taming them enough for the long drive to railroad towns in Kansas or elsewhere, and protecting them on the trail was the work of the heroic frontier cowboy. He had to fend off Indian thieves, swim the herd across swollen rivers, and gather the animals scattered by frequent stampedes.

From these activities Texas developed a cowboy system that later set the pattern for many a novel, motion picture, and television show. Roundups and branding had been practiced for many generations before Texas was settled, and trailing was known in the day of Abraham. Mexican *vaqueros* were expert ropers before Texans learned their art. Yet Texas cowmen welded many techniques into a method of handling cattle in unfenced ranges, and in time this method spread across the whole West.

The postwar trailing of Texas Longhorns northward, mainly to Kansas, took a spurt with the opening of the Chisholm Trail in the fall of 1867 and reached its peak in the season of 1871. An estimated nine to ten million cattle were taken over this and other trails, in what probably was the greatest migration of domestic animals in world history. This activity and its economic results led Berta Hart Nance to write:

> Other states were carved or born;
> Texas grew from hide and horn.

The decline of trail driving in the 1870's and its gradual fading out in the 1880's, except for short distances, resulted not so much from the building of railroads as from the fencing of the country through which the trails led. Texas had two railroads to St. Louis in 1873, but the trails continued for several years to carry most of the cattle. The pioneer railways were equipped to haul only a small fraction of the cattle, their bumpy tracks caused many injuries to the animals, and their rates were so high that trailing was much more economical.

Trail driving from Texas, in addition to giving rousing adventures to the cowboys who went up with the herds, made noticeable impressions on the nation's economy. Longhorns enlarged the business of cattle feeding in Illinois and elsewhere in the Midwest. They also spurred the starting of cattle ranches on the northern ranges. New spreads in Nebraska, Colorado, Wyoming, Montana, and the Dakotas were stocked largely with cattle that had walked all the way from Texas.

In Wyoming and adjoining states the trails brought not only cattle to stock the plains and the mountain valleys but ponies for use in tending the northern herds. Some of the Texas cow hands who had come up with Longhorns stayed on to work. Mastery of the arts of roping and branding enabled them to command high wages. More than a few set up homesteads and began acquiring herds of their own.

The Texas herds trailed north filled a need for more beef and brought the price down for the housewife. Although some of the early Texas beef was tough and had to be sold at a discount, the feeding of Longhorn steers in the Midwest overcame that handicap. Before the trails were closed, the upgrading of Texas cattle with the use of bulls of British breeds further improved the quality of the beef. On thousands of American dining tables beef replaced pork as the chief meat item, partly as a result of the trail drives.

Even Europe felt the impact of Texas cattle. In the 1870's, Texas beef began to reach Europe in large quantities. Ships carried it on the hoof, in tubs, in tin cans, and in the form of frozen hides.

In the American Midwest the cattle drives spurred the growth of Chicago and Kansas City as centers for beef packing, enabling Chicago to surpass Cincinnati, which until after the Civil War had been the chief meat-packing city.

Texas trail drives also hastened the building of more Western rail lines and affected the routes of some of them. Rival roads raced construction to tap the trails. Others built into the Texas cattle country, foreseeing the day when beeves would be taken all the way to market by rail. The drives, in addition, gave incentive to the development of refrigerator cars and the canning of meat.

For those who went north with the herds, the trails offered not only excitement but broader views and economic gains. Dealings with northern cattlemen helped to heal the animosity that the abolition movement and the Civil War had engendered. And the money brought back to Texas, often in gold, enabled many cowmen to pay their debts, buy and improve new ranches, and bring in better breeding stock.

During the period of the trail drives, important changes were taking place on the Texas cattle ranges. Barbed wire was introduced into Texas in 1875 and, after a slow start, was used by many cattlemen to enclose their pastures. The change from open-range ranching, on land owned by the state, to privately owned and fenced ranches was not made smoothly. A severe drouth in 1883, which dried up many water holes and parched the grass, brought on the Texas fence-cutters' war.

In this conflict many small cowmen who owned no land and wanted to keep the open-range economy, resented the fences that kept their herds from water and grass. They were especially enraged at the action of some big ranchmen in including tracts of public land within their fences. Nightly bands of fence-cutters snipped and destroyed so many fences that a special session of the Texas Legislature had to be called, in January, 1884, to deal with the situation.

Eventually the fencers won, and the days of the open range were gone. Ranchmen improved the productivity of their land by drilling artesian wells, building windmills to pump water, clearing brush, and growing more nutritious grasses. They also gained from the introduction of British breeds of cattle, mainly the Hereford, the Shorthorn, and the Angus. Later came the tough Brahman from India and eventually the new Santa Gertrudis breed, developed on the King Ranch. The broomtail cow pony gave way to a sleek quarter horse. On some of the big ranches part of the work of herding was taken over by cowboys in jeeps or even helicopters.

The late John M. Hendrix lived at a time when many changes were taking place in the cattle industry in the Southwest. Although too late for the open range and the Kansas trails, he knew men who had lived in the old days; and he himself saw important shifts in methods and points of view.

Hendrix was born in Gainesville, Texas, on September 16, 1887. His Ohio-born father had gone west at nineteen and had become a cowboy on a Texas ranch and married his boss's daughter. At the time John was born, his father was trading cattle and running a livery stable in Gainesville, whose Lindsey Hotel was a popular headquarters for cowmen.

With cattle talk coming from their parents much of the time, Gainesville youngsters played less with store-bought toys than with stick horses, corncob cattle, and string corrals. "Our pastures and corrals," Hendrix recalled, "were fenced with twine in which we kept our herds of corncobs, each marked with his father's brand. The brands were placed on the cobs with branding irons made of hay wire by our elders or old cow hands in from the ranches for a layoff."

About 1894 John's father and a partner began operating a cattle ranch in the Arbuckle Mountains, on Honey Creek about twenty-five miles north of Ardmore. This was good country whose clear springs and lush grass enabled cattle to mature quickly. Later it became part of a section known as Hereford Heaven. On this ranch, operated from two camps, the partners grew and fattened fifteen hundred to two thousand yearlings a year bought from dealers in Central Texas.

In 1897 the family moved to Quanah, where the elder Hendrix continued in the cattle business. As a youth of fourteen or fifteen, John worked with outfits near his father's ranch and learned to do all the work of handling cattle. He attended Goodnight Academy and Clarendon College, both at Clarendon. He was associated with his father in the cattle business until he was twenty-one, then struck out for himself. He engaged in ranching near Quanah and, on June 15, 1909, married Ethel Kelly of Whitesboro.

Later John Hendrix entered the automobile business in Quanah. As he prospered there, he set up additional agencies in Galveston, Waco, Tyler, Dallas, and Sweetwater. In 1930 he disposed of his agencies to become manager of the Sweetwater Board of City Development. In 1933 he established the Sweetwater Chuck Wagon, described in a chapter of this volume.

In 1935 Hendrix moved to Abilene to become district administrator of the Works Progress Administration. In the following year he became assistant manager of the West Texas Chamber of Commerce, with

office in Fort Worth. From 1937 to 1940 he was publicity director for
Fort Worth's Southwestern Exposition and Fat Stock Show. He represented the exposition on many occasions and directed special events
at the show. For a decade, beginning in 1940, he was connected with
the Traders Oil Mill in Fort Worth. He died in Sweetwater, April 7,
1952, at sixty-four.

Beginning in the early 1930's, Hendrix wrote articles about the early
cattle industry and frontier cowmen and cow-towns for various periodi-
cals, principally *The Cattleman,* published monthly in Fort Worth by
the Texas and Southwestern Cattle Raisers Association. His firsthand
knowledge of cattle raising and of the Southwestern range country
enabled him to write in the cowmen's language and to capture the
atmosphere of the range and the cow camp.

Hendrix came on the scene too late to ride up the Chisholm Trail
with a herd of Longhorns, but early enough to talk with many of the
rugged men who had done that. "I was born too late to be a real old-
timer," he said, "but soon enough not to be a drugstore cowboy."

In his writings Hendrix describes the West Texas ranges with their
billowing mesquite and their jutting Cap Rock. He tells of the frontier
cowboy at work and at play, and of his horse, his trappings, and his
grub. He includes interesting anecdotes of some of the cattle kings,
such as the Burnetts, the Slaughters, the Snyders, and the Waggoners,
who were among the top men in cattle raising but who have not been
publicized as much as some others. He also gives a proper place to
the range boss and his important work.

Of special interest are his chapters on several of the West Texas
communities. Hendrix traces the development of each, through a few
decades, from a dusty frontier cow-town, whose main street was lined
with saloons and bagnios, to a civilized city with parking meters re-
placing the hitching racks.

While the towns were changing, so was life on the ranches. With
fencing and new breeds of cattle, new methods were coming in and
nesters were settling in dugouts and sod houses until they could build
better homes. John Hendrix, who lived through many of the changes,
writes well of this transitional period. Everyone who enjoys genuine
cowboy lore will find his book rewarding.

Wayne Gard

If I Can Do It Horseback

A Cow-Country Sketchbook

If I Can Do It Horseback

There is a story of an old-time Texas cowboy who packed his bed-roll on his extra horse one spring and pulled out for the Indian Territory in search of a "straight ridin' job." About that time such jobs were becoming scarce in Texas, due to the railroads' putting an end to trail driving, and barbed wire to the need of so many of his kind. He heard that Bill Washington up in the Chickasaw Nation never turned away a hand in search of work.

Arriving at the ranch, he braced old Bill for a job to which the latter replied, "Son, I only have one job open for a man right now; that is digging a well and walling it up. If you want it, throw your bedroll in the bunkhouse and turn your horse loose in the horse pasture."

The cowboy pondered for a time. His last summer's wages had been spent wintering in Gainesville. His horses were poor, and the prospects of "riding the chuck line" until he found a job to his liking were slim, but he was proud. "Tell you what I'll do, Mr. Washington, I'll take that job if I can figure out a way to do it horseback."

The story is typical of the old-time, hard-riding cowboy who never sought, or accepted, other than a "straight ridin' job" if he could help it. As the large outfits broke up and he was forced to seek work under the new order, he approached each prospective job only after closest inquiries as to what kind of an outfit it was and what might be expected of him. Two things he did not want to do—farm or milk. Neither could be done horseback, and to do the first any other way would "gall" him and cause his boots to rub his heels. The latter was entirely beneath his dignity. Hadn't he handled cows by the hundreds of thousands all his life without milking a single one of them? Black coffee was better, and, if you drank milk, your breath would smell like that of a young calf.

He hoped, too, that the outfit was fenced and cross-fenced before he got there, for posthole diggers if used too steadily caused blisters, and then there were the long thirty-foot trips afoot from posthole to posthole with digger and crowbar over his shoulder. He did have one advantage—his long legs, bowed from years in the saddle, precluded the necessity of detouring when he encountered a prickly pear or bear grass en route. Then like as not, if you got with a little outfit working only one or two men, there would be a lot of chores to do, like feeding, cutting stovewood for the kitchen, and carrying slops to the hog pen— all tasks beneath his dignity. None of them could be done horseback.

Come what might, there was one thing he would never sink to—that was herding sheep. It was sure 'nuff a foot job, fit only for greasers, who didn't mind living alone with a couple of dogs and didn't care how many funny stories were told on them. Why, they wouldn't even leave the poor devils a horse, but came out with a team and moved them when their smelly, bleating charges had eaten off all the grass around where they were camped. No, sir! No sheep herding for him! He would have gone on W.P.A. first if there had been one then.

Yes, the old bowlegged boys were hard hit and up against it. The best of them acquired stock farms or small ranches of their own and had a few good saddle horses around all the time. Others drifted into New Mexico and Arizona to work for the mountain outfits which, due to the nature of the country, would always be "straight riding outfits." Some drifted down into Old Mexico to work for the American-owned cattle companies like Cudahy, Hearst, and the Palomas. The majority of these never came out and are buried south of the border.

Quite a few of the best ones became inspectors for the various live-stock associations or for cattle-loan companies. Others settled down in their old communities to run for everything from sheriff to deputy constable. Still others went into the livery stable and saloon business to endure until the automobile and Nineteenth Amendment set them afoot again. A few hardy souls held on firm in the belief that anything on earth worth doing could be done horseback, and proved it—at least to their own satisfaction, if not to that of their employers.

Passing time helped these hardy souls. Net wire fences permitted the sheepmen to turn their flocks loose in their pastures like cattle and train them to be rounded up and handled by men on horseback as well as they had been handled by the unmounted herders. Then, too, most of the cowmen became of the fifty-fifty variety, half cowmen and half sheepmen, for they had learned by observation that the cowman running an equal number of sheep was the first to be seen around the hotel lobbies smoking a ten-cent cigar and having his boots shined after depression or low-price periods. Their cowboys and those seeking ranch employment had, perforce, to learn the half-and-half method if they were going to ride at all. No cowman was inclined to employ a cowboy specialist and sheep specialist to work his outfit, so the men had to like it or else. It wasn't so bad, for most of them had regular chuck wagons like the old outfits. They also had good horses, and there was a chance once in a while to flip a loop over an old ewe's head when she broke back at shearing time. Catching one of them or a goat was harder to do, and more fun, than roping calves.

The tractor came along to relieve farming of its tedium and the old cowboy of any responsibility for operating one as he was past the age when he could hope to learn the intricacies of carburetor, magneto, and manifold, even if he were of a mind to. The few who did take jobs on outfits where there was farming were careful to select those on which the agricultural effort was of the "broadcast" variety, meaning the drilling in of grain sorghums or wheat, which required no cultivating, chopping, or heading, and which for the most part was for the purpose of pasture. One could operate a drill from its seat or a harrow from the back of the "rustlin'" horse.

Do not take too lightly what you may hear or what has been written here of the old cowboys. They were sincere in their efforts to maintain the dignity and prestige of a calling they had invented and perfected in their lifetime and for which, without mass thought or organized effort, they had set certain standards.

Their profession had no precedents, had inherited no standards, but was born of necessity in the years following the Civil War, reached its peak in the middle 80's and waned before the 90's were finished. In the interim, they became the most colorful and picturesque hired men the world has known. They had no formula for their work other than "get the job done"; no working hours other than from the time they could see to catch their mounts in the cool red of the morning until they could not see to read a brand in the falling dusk. Such hours permitted little or no time for menial chores or training in any other line than that of handling cattle on horseback.

The late Eugene Manlove Rhodes who lived with, loved, and wrote of the Arizona and New Mexico cowboy and who, when he died, was buried high in the San Andrew Range of New Mexico overlooking the Socorro Plain and the mesas where still ride the kind of men he loved, left an unfinished manuscript entitled, "Hired Men on Horseback."

J. Frank Dobie, the Texas author, in his charming book *A Vaquero of the Brush Country* has to say of them in this connection:

It was a profession that engendered pride. They were laborers of a kind, it is true, but they regarded themselves as artists, and they were artists. Years of experience, of practice in deftness, and of study in animal psychology were necessary to perfect a top hand. No genuine cowboy ever suffered from an inferiority complex or ranked himself in the "laboring class" along with "clod-hoppers" and ditch diggers. He considered himself a cavalier in the full sense of that word—a gentleman on horse, privileged to come it proud over all nesters, squatters, Kansas Jayhawkers, and other such earth-clinging creatures—He was the aristocrat of all wage earners.

Small wonder then that even with their kingdom gone from them—the open range and with it their profession as they had learned it—they hesitated to climb down from their hand-stamped, concho-bedecked thrones to join the laborers upon whom they had looked down from a fourteen-and-a-half dun, brown, or bay vantage point, or that they preferred to remain until the last, cavaliers—vaqueros—cowhands—men doing their job on horseback.

"When we got to breedin' better cattle 'nd began to be a little proud of 'em, it was harder for the buyer to find his 10 per cent. He usually took out a few short ages 'nd off colors we'd put in for that purpose 'nd quit. Sometimes he'd buy the cut at a couple o' dollars a head less than he'd contracted the herd for if he needed cattle to fill his contract."

The Corn-Belt fellow and the old man's son, their job of cutting and weighing finished, leaned against the scales as they figured weights and deducted "shrinkage."

"What used to be 'cut' in the old days is 'shrinkage' now," said the old cowman, who had been keeping an eye and a couple of ears on the figuring below him. "We don't dare chouse 'em now, for to do that means runnin' pounds off 'em. They're grown to weigh now, not to walk like our old Texas steers did when they had to furnish their own transportation and fatten 'emselves on the way—why, the boy here even trucks his calves to the shippin' pens. That's where the shrink comes in, for the buyer makes you allow a 3 per cent shrinkage of the weights or stand 'em up in a dry lot without feed or water for twelve hours before they are weighed. Guess it's fair though, you can't fool them Corn-Belt feeders much—they figure a lot closer 'n we ever did. They know almost what the cattle they are figuring on 'll weigh when they look at 'em and they know how much corn they have in the crib, what it cost 'em, and what they can make the calves weigh with it. Whether they make any money or not is up to the beef-eaters who make the market."

The old man eased himself over to where he could sit more comfortably with his feet resting on the chute running boards. A faraway look came into his eyes, as though he were backtracking the trails of memory as he mused.

"This weight thing ain't so new, come to think of it. I remember the first herd I ever saw sold by weight. It was about ten years after the Civil War and, as I recall it, the Yankee buyer got the hot end of it on the weight deal that time. If you ain't in a hurry I'll tell you about it.

"Down in Denton County, Texas, where I was raised, the prairies were full o' cattle right after the war, with no market for 'em nearer than one we had heard of way up in Kansas. Now the old folks hadn't forgotten the unpleasantness of a few years before and couldn't see much point to goin' into Yankee territory to sell anything. Old man Medford, over in the Bolivar country, had fifty or seventy-five head o' good cow ponies, half a dozen daughters, and an awful good reputation for honesty, but no money. He propositioned me and a half a dozen

Yankee Market

"They didn't sell 'em by weight when I was a kid," said the old Panhandle cowman as he sat atop the shipping pens and watched his son and the Corn-Belt feeder who had bought them, cut the pen full of chunky bald-faced calves into carlots and weigh them, preparatory to their long ride to the Corn-Belt feed lots.

"In the early days of the business we sold 'em mostly by 'book count,' meanin' that we sold a man all our book showed we ought to have on our range. The brand they wore became his 'nd he could claim any animal he found in that brand thereafter. The cattle weren't thrown together for him 'nd there wasn't anything said about colors, ages, or cut backs. Some called it range delivery. We kind o' liked to sell 'em that way to the Englishmen who were so anxious to get into the cow business.

"Then when we got fenced in 'nd the buyers from the Northwest began to get a little more particular, we had to give 'em a 10 per cent cut, meanin' that after all crippled, blind, and unsaleable cattle had been taken out, the buyer could then cut out 10 percent of the total of the herd to make it uniform as to size, age, and color.

other boys from fifteen to twenty years old that hung around his place
on Sundays, to go up the trail with him if he could get the cattle. Said
he'd pay us when he sold the cattle, just like he was goin' to pay the
neighbors he was gettin' 'em from. The neighbors didn't mind lettin'
the old man have 'em, for they couldn't eat 'em all, but they did figure
that the Yankee traders 'd beat him out of 'em and his cow horses too.
He finally got twelve hundred 'nd fifty head o' big old steers together,
for which he owed his neighbors a promised price o' twelve dollars
per head.

"I rode left point on the herd for three months up through the Nation
and into Kansas. Every mornin', as we pointed the herd out, I'd fall in
alongside a little roan T C steer—he'd belonged to Tom Cross over in
the Pilot Point country. He was a regular little shetland sort of a
steer—low on the ground and 'soggy' as a corn-fed school ma'am. The
best guesser in the world couldn't 'uv hit within two hundred pounds
of his weight. Every mornin' for three months he was in the same place
with the lead cattle, just as if he 'counted off' like the soldiers do when
they're fallin' in line. He kept me from gettin' homesick, for I ran with
the Cross boys—we used to ride milk-pen calves every Sunday. That's
where we learned our bronc bustin'.

"The closer we got to Abilene the more nervous the old man got
about the traders gettin' to him. Few days before we thought we ought
to be close to Abilene, we throwed off the trail to let the cattle rest and
fill, and to see if a buyer wouldn't show up. About the third day we
sighted a two-horse buggy comin' across the flat and us boys kind o'
bunched up to look on when the fellow—he wore a derby hat—drove
up 'nd asked who the cattle belonged to 'nd if they were for sale.
Findin' that they were, he looked 'em over pretty good and propositioned the old man to buy 'em by weight.

" 'Here it comes,' says us boys, 'who ever heard of cattle bein' sold
by the pound.'

" 'Can't sell 'em that way,' says the old man. 'I know what they cost
me, but I don't have any idea what they weigh. I'll make you a price
on 'em by the head if you want me to.'

" 'Nope,' says the fellow. 'I'm from Illinois and used to buyin' by
weight and no other way. I'll give you three cents a pound for 'em
delivered in Abilene.'

"The old man stalled around a while 'nd comes back with, 'Just in
case I did consider sellin' 'em to you by the pound, which I ain't right
now, how could we weigh 'em?'

" 'There's a set o' wagon scales at the new depot in town,' said the derby-hat fellow, 'but no pens with them. We would just have to guess 'em off, I suppose.' The old man went into another deep study, durin' which he knotted 'nd untied the horn-string on his saddle half a dozen times, before he opened up again.

" 'Tell you what I might do if it suits you—I'll pick the heaviest steer and you pick the lightest one in the herd. Then we'll drive the two into Abilene, weigh 'em on the wagon scales, divide the total by two 'nd let the result go for the average weight.'

" 'It's a trade,' says the fellow, 'nd the old man let him have a horse to prowl the herd for his light steer. As he rode into the herd I eased over to where I could locate the roan T C steer, in case he was needed. Old man Medford prowled through the herd awhile 'nd then took a stand near an old cat-hammed brindle steer that looked like he stood fourteen hands high—you could 've seen a windmill under his belly if there'd been one on the other side of him. He didn't look so heavy though, due to the fact that the Nation and Kansas hadn't agreed with him, 'nd he'd been scouring ever since we crossed Red River.

"Pretty soon the fellow with the derby rode over to where I was doin' my best to make it appear that I wasn't lookin' at the little T C steer, 'nd said, 'Son, you look like an honest lad and have been with these cattle a lot; which do you think is the lightest steer in the bunch?'

"I kind of twisted in my three-quarter rigged saddle a little and said, 'There's so dang many o' that kind in the herd I couldn't say; if I was guessin', though, I'd say it was a little roan T C steer that's in here somewhere, or was this morning.'

" 'I've seen him,' says the fellow, 'and I guess you're about right. Let's ease him up to where your boss is holding his steer.'

"When we rode up the derby fellow told the old man he'd picked his steer and added, 'I presume you've picked the brindle.'

"The old man swung his horse away from the brindle steer and said to me, 'Lute, where's Old Sam?'

" 'Down along the creek somewhere asleep, or layin' in close to the wagon,' I answers.

" 'Go get him,' says the old man.

"Now I had forgotten to tell you about Old Sam bein' in the herd. He was an old work steer. Must 've been ten years old if he was a day, and looked like he weighed eighteen hundred pounds if he weighed an ounce. We'd picked him up as we come along off a fellow the old man knew down close to Spanish Fort in Montague County where we crossed Red River. The fellow said he'd got so old and lazy he was no account for a work steer, was eatin' his head off, and we could pay him when we came back if we got through with him. When the herd 'd stop he'd eat a bellyfull of grass and go off away from the herd where he wouldn't have to mill with them or get out of the way if they hooked at him.

"I got him up in the creek bottom and pestled him on the back with the loose end of my rope until I got him up along side the T C steer. Son, I never did get to see Mr. Barnum's Jumbo, but if he looked any bigger than Old Sam did standin' by that shetland-looking roan steer, he must have been a sight."

The old cowman eased himself up a little by crossing his legs opposite to what they had been and continued.

"I thought we was goin' to have to take that derby-hat fellow to a mad stone he was so mad. The old man didn't say anything and the fellow couldn't as it was a fair trade.

"Me and one of the Burnett boys eased 'em into Abilene the third day, with the derby fellow trying to hurry us all he could, which we didn't, havin' been trained not to chouse cattle and horses. We weighed 'em up when we got there. The little T C steer weighed eight fifty and Old Sam knocked the beam down at fifteen fifty, or a grand total, as they say now days, of twenty-four hundred pounds, which made the Denton County cattle bring thirty-six dollars per head. The fellow paid us in gold, 'nd the deal was the start of old man Medford being a cattle king. And what I saved out of my wages was the beginning of the outfit the boy there is running for both of us.

"Well, I guess the boy 'nd that fellow are through weighing up and are about ready to go to the bank, so I'll be gettin' along. Ain't much worried about the boy, though, for it turned out his Ma was a Medford."

Living Water

Springs are no novelty in this land of ours. They abound in practically every section. In the southern mountain country there are countless hundreds of them bubbling, gurgling, and sending their clear waters down the hollows by day and night. These have no claim to fame unless some distiller has built his plant along the banks of one and advertises to the world that he uses only clear, mountain spring water in the manufacture of his product—as witness Dripping Springs, Echo Springs and other brands long known to the consumer. For every one of these so advertising there are a hundred moonshiners turning out a most satisfactory product farther up the hollows, somewhere in the hills where heads a spring branch. These are not advertised except by word of mouth.

There are the springs in the nation which have medicinal properties for which they are famed. These are heavily advertised by both Chambers of Commerce and the medical profession. So it would seem that springs are hardly a subject calculated to yield sufficient material and information to be worthy of a yarn. Be that as it may, there is one section of the United States whose early animal life, civilization, development, tragedy, pathos, humor, and industry have radiated from its springs. I have in mind the great Southwest and particularly the old cow country, where life itself depended wholly on springs and living water.

As civilization through the agency of the cow outfits pulled into the area, the cowmen well knew it to be one of scant rainfall, with no artificial means of watering. Nature has provided the area with an abundance of water, but, in the opinion of the fellows who piloted the first herds in, it has been pretty well "bunched." They came to this opinion as they rode in the dust of gaunt, red-eyed cattle, easing them from one watering place to another.

In these modern ranching days with windmills, pipelines, and government-built tanks which permit man or beast to obtain a good cool drink at intervals of not more than one and one-half miles, springs and spring water do not have the significance they did sixty-five years ago when the South and Central Texas cowmen rode into North and Northwest Texas in the dust of trail herds seeking new ranges or markets in New Mexico, California, or the far Northwest. As the herds had left the southern country, springs had had no particular significance to the cowmen, for water abounded in their home country and meant little; but the farther west they trekked the more they came to follow the creeks with living water.

In the minds and memories of the scattering remnant of those fellows who are still living, there is no landmark that stands out so vividly, no memory so poignant, as those of the springs they located as they scouted ahead of their herds with alkali-parched lips and consuming thirst, in search of suitable camping places, bed grounds, and watering for their herds. Sometimes they were in search of a spring where they might build a dugout to establish headquarters and turn their herds loose. The trail boss, as he rode up the water courses seeking "holes" in the creek that would afford waterings, kept a keen eye open for the spring branches which led into and kept filled the holes he was seeking. (Too, he watched the animal tracks as a means of finding where the buffalo, antelope, and mustang watered.)

Sometimes the spring would be only a few hundred yards away, sometimes a mile or more, but the boss knew that he was sure of a cool draft, sparkling and straight from the bowels of the earth, with no contamination other than the "top water" and the "skimmers" that paddled out of his way as he lay down on his belly to drink, when he did find it. If it was an unusually good spring and he felt that it would be sought by others following him, he would start a "monument" for the benefit of those who would follow. He did this by gathering up loose stones and fashioning a crude round chimneylike affair somewhere on high ground where it could be readily seen. The man who started such a monument rarely if ever completed it, but left his efforts with the assurance that by custom the next man who came along would add a few more stones. Thus, it would not be long until the monument could be seen and read from quite a distance.

Prominent among the large springs of West Texas are the Good Enough Springs near Comstock in Val Verde County, San Felipe Springs at Del Rio, Las Moras near Fort Clark at Brackettville, and the Seven Hundred Springs near the source of the South Llano. As one approaches the Cap Rock that bounds the Great Plains on the east, there are, or were, hundreds upon hundreds of small springs that burst out from the rough hills. Most noteworthy of these are the Comanche Springs at Fort Stockton and the San Solomon Springs near Balmorhea. It is interesting to note here that many of the army and flying fields were made possible by the almost unlimited flow of these springs which provided a water supply for the camps.

San Felipe Springs consist of a group of seven springs, three large and four small. The city of Del Rio uses water from the larger for city water service. A portion of the balance of the flow is used to irrigate many acres of land in the vicinity of Del Rio. The Old Spanish Trail passed along San Felipe Springs and the spot was a watering place for stagecoaches, wagon trains, and military detachments en route to El Paso.

Comanche Springs at Fort Stockton, according to pictographs and other recorded material, has served men and animals for centuries. It is believed that the Indians used it many years before it was discovered by Spanish explorers. Comanche Springs served as a station and depot on the transcontinental trail and served the same purpose for stagecoach lines between San Angelo, San Antonio, El Paso, and the West. It was used by the U. S. Army when Fort Stockton was founded and named in honor of Commodore Stockton, the conqueror of California. The fort was established in 1859, abandoned during the Civil War and reopened in 1867, remaining an active post until 1886. A tunnel running from the old fort to the main spring afforded a sure water supply even in the face of battles or sieges. The spring has a daily flow of

60,000,000 gallons of crystal-clear, sparkling, pure water which irrigates hundreds of acres of farm land without the use of pumps or power.

Probably the most noted historic water holes of the Southwest are the Hueco Tanks, located in the far western corner of Texas, slightly north and east of El Paso, and just south of the Hueco Mountain Range. Archaeologists claim that the Hueco Tanks were inhabited for two thousand or more years by pre-Pueblo Indians and then by the bloodthirsty Apaches until sixty or seventy years ago. During the gold rush of 1849 they were a point of call for the wagon trains of the gold seekers at the end of an extremely dry drive. These, using the methods of the Indians, resorted to pictographs and crude signs to advise those who followed that there was "Watter Hear."

The great water hole or source lies far back in the canyon and is so well hidden that one wonders how even the Indians ever discovered it. It has no lavish flow of water like the springs enumerated above, but it is an oasis with unfailing water in the heart of a desert country.

Springs in the Southwest fell into several classifications that are recognized by those who have ridden the range in the days of old. At the top of the cowman's classifications came the "bold spring" which gushed out from the rocks or bluff to form almost immediately a stream of its own that left no doubt of its being living water. Next in the category and high in the favor of the cowman were the "spring-fed holes" which ranged along a creek for three hundred yards to one-half mile, or sometimes even covered a distance of as much as four or five miles. These were fed by springs coming from the bottom of the creek and were considered among the best of the living water.

Another type of spring high in favor with the cowman who had an artistic sense or a touch of laziness, was the "dripping spring," which was one that broke from the flat rocks forming overhanging bluffs and dripped into small basins hollowed out by age-old drippings. In many instances beautiful and luxuriant growths of fern were to be found suspended from the overhang, through which the spring waters trickled, creating a cooling atmosphere or an area which could well be and was used as a shower bath when the day was long and hot and the cowboy was suffering from too much contact with scrivens and duckins which had resulted in his being severely "galleded." I speak with a certain amount of experience on this type of spring, for there was one just a few hundred yards off our fence line on Canal Creek in Foard County on the ranch where I grew up. I make no claim to being artistic, but in those days I could amply qualify as to general laziness and being "galleded."

Considerably lower in the scale of springs came the "sipe spring," or "seep" as it was commonly called. This type of spring arose almost from a standing start up on the second bluff or valley of a creek. It had no distinct channel and consisted mostly of water accumulated in the cattle tracks about it. It was a cow haven, and a hell on earth to cowboys, during heel-fly season; then the cowboy had to ride bogs and tail-up weak cows who had become mired in it. In many instances, after barbed wire came into general use, this type of spring was fenced off to keep cattle from using it on account of bogging.

As a rule, most of the springs were of pure, clear, soft water equally good for cooking or drinking. Up close to the Cap Rock, however, the springs were heavily impregnated with gypsum or a form of alkali which made the water unfit for cooking, washing, or household use. (It may be interesting to know that navy beans cannot be cooked in gyp water; the more you boil them, the harder they become. On the other hand, the same kind of water makes excellent coffee.) The gyp spring has peculiar, almost medicinal, properties and woe to the cowboy who tanks up on it when he is hot, or drinks it where it runs shallow and hot at any distance from the spring. About the easiest way to explain the action of gyp water is to say that a kildee couldn't fly across a hole of it without contracting diarrhea. The first cowboys to come from the South brought with them a pretty fair amount of malaria, chills, and fever, which the gyp water soon relieved them of. After that they took a second growth; the "yaller" left their complexions, and the sunburn got in its work.

It would be impossible to give an accurate description of the many springs of the Southwest and their connection with the cattle industry. Each section had its full measure of them and their stories and history are about the same. I can, therefore, only speak with authority on the ones in my immediate section: the old Indian Territory and the ranch we owned in Foard County, Texas, for many years. On it and neighboring ranches were to be found practically every type of spring in existence. Probably the best example of a bold spring is the Roaring Springs on the Matador Ranch near the town of Roaring Springs. A fair example of the sipe spring was the Half-Circle Springs on our Foard County ranch. At these springs in the early 80's, Crow Wright, the founder of the ranch, built half a dozen excellent rock dugouts as headquarters for his West Texas operations. A daughter, Mrs. Will

Williams, lives in Denton and recalls visiting the dugout and springs more than half a century ago. The Monument Hole on Good Creek in Leslie McAdams' pasture has long been a landmark and is so named because of a monument of rock erected there by cowboys many years ago as a guidepost to water. The Boiling Springs on the same ranch are a modified version of the sipe spring. They, too, have a history, for near them was located one of the early stage stands or stations for a line that traversed West Texas. Over in the O X pastures was to be found an excellent example of the dripping spring, and until this day that section of the old O X ranch is known as the Dripping Springs Pasture. The Blue Holes in our old pasture was a noted spring and watering place for many years and served to water a great section of that country until we fenced it in 1897. It consisted of a long, deep, blue hole of water fed by one large spring at the upper end and augmented by springs that came up from the bottom and under the overhanging rocks that made up the bluffs on the north bank. Its waters were an excellent example of those herein described as being a cure for chills and fever.

Over in the Nation where springs were not so necessary nor as much a novelty as they were in West Texas, we operated in the Arbuckle Mountains on Honey Creek, which embraced Turner Falls, one of the beauty spots of Oklahoma. Honey Creek, only approximately three miles in length, is fed by a series of bold springs rising about a mile above the present falls. Shortly after the water cascades down to its new level, Honey Creek empties into the Washita River. For its short course, I believe that it has as many bold springs as any stream that I know of.

The breaks part of our Foard County holdings embraced Canal Creek, Half-Circle Creek, Good Creek, and a number of nameless spring creeks, all of which had their rise in our pasture. Canal Creek took its name from the fact that during the many hundreds of years of its existence it had carved a channel thirty or forty feet deep through the soft gyp rock, a channel which resembled nothing so much as a perfect canal hewn and excavated by man and machinery. For their inches, I defy anyone to find any streams containing more pure and unadulterated gyp water than these creeks. It is possible that I may get my hand called on this for farther to the north in the 6 6 6 6 and Pitchfork country there is an area known as Croton Breaks, where the natives just plain break down and call the creeks Croton, after that famous oil no doubt.

As the West Texas ranches were founded, their headquarters were built invariably at, or in the vicinity of, some bold spring. Many of the ranches took their names from the springs on which their head-quarters were located. One of the best examples of this is the Render-brook Ranch, so named after the bold springs on which its head-quarters buildings and corrals are located. During the early 70's Cap-tain Renderbrook of the U.S. Army, stationed at Fort Concho, was killed by the Indians near the springs that were to bear his name. Ultimately J. Taylor Barr set up a ranch headquarters at the spring. He later sold his rights to the Snyders, who eventually sold them to the Ellwoods of De Kalb, Illinois, whose estate is still in possession of the ranch, located in Mitchell County, Texas, south of Colorado City and near the Colorado River.

Another ranch which has been closely connected with a spring for some sixty-five years of its existence is the Spur in Dickens County, Texas. One of the oldest ranches in the Panhandle, its headquarters were laid out around a bold spring which is still in use, flowing into a rock springhouse built to accommodate the milk crocks and jars of the headquarters family when it came to the ranch. The Matador head-quarters in Motley County, Texas were also located at a series of bold springs only a few miles from their famous Roaring Springs. These springs have been beautified by a series of dams which not only add to the beauty of the Matador's famous White House, but afford fishing to guests and others connected with the headquarters setup.

The Double Mountain country, skirting along the Cap Rock, was the locale of many of the early ranch headquarters of that great area. These were invariably built, both headquarters and line camps, near springs and living water. There was no competition in those days be-tween the incoming outfits for control of water holes and springs. Rollie C. Burns, in his excellent book on the Hensley's 2 2 Ranch, described the founding of the ranch and the beginning of the Slaughter outfits in the same country by a single phrase, "Our headquarters were close enough together that we both got water from the same spring."

Rollie also mentions an incident in one of his long rides through the Devils River country to meet a herd. Night came upon him and he sought about for a likely camping place. He came to the head of a draw which contained a fine spring and a plot of grass some forty to fifty feet square which was entirely hemmed in by gigantic rock ex-cept for an opening of sufficient size to ride his horse through. Un-saddling, he turned his horse loose and made his bed down in the

narrow opening. In a few minutes he learned that he had cast his
lot in a rattlesnake den. As the snakes came out from the rocks—as he
described it, all sizes and every one a-rattlin'—his horse took fright
and crowded up to the opening with him. He says the stench and odor
of the snakes was almost unbearable. He lost no time in saddling and
riding out onto the level to make a dry camp.

The daddy of all cow-country springs in West Texas is probably
Buffalo Springs, which stands in the open plains south of the Beaver
and just south of the line that divides the Panhandle from Cimarron
County in Oklahoma. The water apparently rises from a fissure in the
rock. Fabulous stories have been told of its depth. There follows a
chain of deep pools of dark and steely clearness. Chillingly cold, even
in hottest midsummer, they have precipitous banks along which wave
a dense and almost impenetrable growth of reeds and tall wiry grass.
In the days of the buffalo the springs were frequented by these animals
in enormous numbers, crowding and fighting their way to water. Its
steep banks made it a hard place to water a herd, according to those
who know it best.

It was to Buffalo Springs that the first herds of the 150,000 cattle
that were eventually to wear the famous X I T brand were brought.
The springs were selected as a headquarters for the outfit because
they afforded more living water than was to be found at that time on
any other portion of the three million acres controlled by the Capitol
Syndicate Company.

Another area of the Southwest of similar nature is to be found in
the vicinity of Roswell, New Mexico, whose Spring River Valley
abounds in bold springs. It is also the site of the famous Bottomless
Lakes which rise just south of the city. These lakes have long been a
puzzle to geologists who have as yet been unable to determine their
depth or source.

In a sketchy sort of way I have tried to place the springs in their
proper light with regard to the development of a great area. When
the cattleman had had his day on the free range and the nester came
in to squat on, file on, or claim his portions of the land, the spring was
still a most important factor. Squatter dugouts and shacks could not
be built at the larger springs because these had been pretty well
covered by the claims of the cowman, so it came about that the nesters
in an area began to haul water to their claims from the nearest available spring. The spring became a sort of neighborhood gathering place
where men, with barrels in the butcher-knife wagons or on slides, came

to haul their household water. With them came their wives and children to do the family washing and to gossip a bit with others of their kind who were there for a like purpose. Cattle, muddying the springs, eventually were responsible for the nestermen's setting a day to "work" the spring, which resulted in its being boxed off, or a barrel or two set in it, both for cleanliness and for the purpose of getting a head of water.

As the community grew, the long hole below the spring served as a place of baptism after the itinerant preacher had held a meeting in the neighborhood and had persuaded almost everybody to quit stealing beef and rustling dogie calves. I recall such a baptizing at our Blue Hole when a neighboring ranchman and myself sat on a high bluff overlooking the scene. Among those to be baptized was an old fellow who was generally known as a thief and who had preyed upon both our outfits. As the preacher raised him to his feet after immersing him, my neighbor turned to me and said, "John, if one of us had guts enough to shoot that old so and so before he dries off, he might go to heaven free of sin, but if the sun ever hits him and dries him off, he'll still be a cow thief the rest of his life."

Eventually churches and schoolhouses began to appear on the bluffs above the springs and as the population increased, towns began to develop, many bearing the names of the springs which they were near. To attempt to mention all of these would be futile, but Big Spring, a thriving western metropolis, took its name from a bold spring which used to be just south of the city. Rocksprings, sheep and goat headquarters down in the hill country of the Edwards Plateau, is another. Rush Springs in Oklahoma is another, and Hot Springs in New Mexico and Roaring Springs on the Matador Ranch.

Tragedy sometimes sought the spring as its setting, for if a man was on the dodge it was morally certain that thirst sooner or later would bring him to seek water for himself and his horse. Those who sought him knew this and lay in wait for him at the spring he was most likely to head for. An example of this occurred at Sloan Spring on Canal Creek where the highway now crosses it between Paducah and Crowell, Texas. A good many years ago when the R 2's had their headquarters camp on Wanderers Creek a mile or two below where the town of Chillicothe now stands, there came to the camp one night a smart alecky type fellow who was invited to stay all night. During the evening the cowboys, headed by the cook, played an old-time cowboy trick on the fellow who, at the time, showed no resentment. Next morning, boss and boys pulled out with the horses after instructing the cook where to camp the wagon at noon. Coming in at noon, they found that cook and wagon had not arrived. Backtracking to headquarters, they found the cook dead, shot from behind, and the stranger gone. Picking up his tracks, they followed him some fifteen or twenty miles west, finally coming upon him kneeling to drink from the spring which flowed from an overhanging rock. Without hesitation they shot him, dragging his body up into the head of a small hollow nearby, after which they unsaddled his horse and turned it loose, leaving his saddle behind.

A few years later when we acquired our Foard County ranch, we worked out a wagon road from it to Crowell for the purpose of hauling feed and fencing materials. Camped near the spring one night, another fellow and I found the skull, thigh bones, and a portion of one of the old saddle fenders and tree of the fellow who had been killed there. We placed them back in the head of a hollow and kicked some dirt over them. A few years later, while building a telephone line from town to the ranch, I went back up the hollow and found that the dirt had washed away from the bones. Going back to the camp, I got a Clipper Corn box in which I then placed the bones and buried them for the second time. Unless time and erosion have disturbed him, he still sleeps in a Clipper Corn box just to the right of the highway before you come to the bridge. I came to know most of the bunch who had followed the fellow over there, but could never get anyone to assume the responsibility of firing the fatal shot. The best I could ever get out of them was, "We just rode up on the bluff above him and our boss counted off; One! Two! Three!, and we let go."

There is, in the Davis Mountains country, a ranch long known as the Rustler Springs Ranch. Legend has it that in the open-range days Rustler Springs was headquarters for a gang of rustlers who preyed on trail herds and cowmen far to the east in the Buffalo Gap, in the Abilene country. They would gather fifteen to forty head of cattle of different brands, drive them west at night, and finally land at Rustler Springs. The lower country cattlemen, tiring of this form of thievery, trailed them to these springs and hung five of them on a big cottonwood tree near Rustler Springs.

The killings of Morton, Baker, and an old buffalo hunter near the Azul or Blue Springs in the Capitan country of New Mexico are matters of record. Springs in the old days were also the site of many Indian attacks upon wagon trains and cow outfits. Both Indians and pioneers always approached the springs with trepidation and fear, and only after having heavily scouted the vicinity.

Before leaving entirely the subject of old springs, attention must be called to the old Mescalero Spring northwest of Lovington, New Mexico, which for many years was the site of the winter horse camp for the famous L F D, Four Lakes Ranch around which much free range and early-day horse experiences are said to have transpired.

As cow camps were succeeded by the nesters, and towns came to grow at their sites, the springs continued to serve mankind both in an industrial way and as a playground for the ever-increasing population. Del Rio, a thriving border city, has converted San Felipe Springs into an excellent water system for the city and a swimming pool, and has enough water left over to irrigate many acres of land. Fort Stockton, a little farther west, has accomplished the same thing, and the springs as Roswell, New Mexico are nationally famous for their irrigated lands, alfalfa, and apples. Each of these has been the site of one of the nation's flying fields or military encampments. Even proud Dallas, which lays no particular claim to early cattle history, long ago named what is now one of its principal business and residential streets Cedar Springs because its meandering tracks led from the site of the city's log courthouse to the earliest historic site in Dallas County—Cedar Springs, which, in an election in 1848, rivaled Dallas for county seat. Cedar Springs is now a portion of Dallas proper, but the old road has yielded little to the modern in its straggling and wandering through the city.

Time, cultivation, and erosion have taken heavy toll of thousands of springs throughout the Southwest and only the bold ones, located for most part in the higher elevations, have been able to maintain their status as living water. Some are entirely obliterated by over-cultivated and washed-down soils and are fast becoming lost to the memory of man. Jumbles of rock that time has eventually loosened and caused to roll to the bottom of the creeks mark all that remains of others. Regardless of this, I would be willing to bet dollars to doughnuts that if you cared to ask old-time cowboys versed in the way of cow-camp and chuck-wagon horseplay, where Squaw Springs was located—I mean old fellows like Bob Beverley of Lovington, New Mexico, Henry Ferguson of Crowell, Gordon Witherspoon of Fort Worth, or fellows of that day and time—they will tell you definitely where it is.

As I said in the opening paragraph, the most poignant memories of the old-time cowboy is of the springs that he knew in the days of his youth. Years have passed since I rode the ranges and sought living water. I have been many places and seen many things, but in the late afternoons of the present day my mind returns most often and most pleasantly to the old days when the sun was a couple of hours high and I would ride across the flats that led down to the Blue Hole. As I ride in memory, I check the flats for cows that I know have "used" there year in and year out, and note with pleasure that there is a fair sprinkling of calves among them and not a case of worms in the whole bunch. As I ride up to the hole of water with its bluff high to the back of it and a gravelly beach to the front, the kildees chirp and dance along the water's edge. Brown bullbats swirl and dip while a lordly brown-backed bull, paying court to a mellow-eyed heifer, sends clouds of dust skyward over his shoulder as he challenges with a mighty bellow another of his kind coming in to water. Down under the willows at the lower end of the hole where the waters run shallow, matronly cows, keeping an eye on their offspring, stamp and switch their tails in bovine satisfaction. As my horse slakes his thirst, I note the trail made by the water snake wiggling his way back to the shelter of the overhanging rocks, and the turtles up for a sunning as they slide into the water. Up near the boxed-in spring I note three or four immigrant wagons making camp for the night. These are loaded with the tools of a farmer, and each carries a brood of future West Texans, headed for the Long S country on the plains where already their kind are ripping the sod and turning the grass roots to the sun. I pause to pass the time of day with them while my horse fidgets nervously at sights, sounds, and smells which have heretofore been unknown to him. I sometimes wonder if I realized then, as my horse picked his way up the path that led out along the bluff, that all of us—cows, calves, snakes, turtles, and immigrants—were there for one reason and one only—"living water."

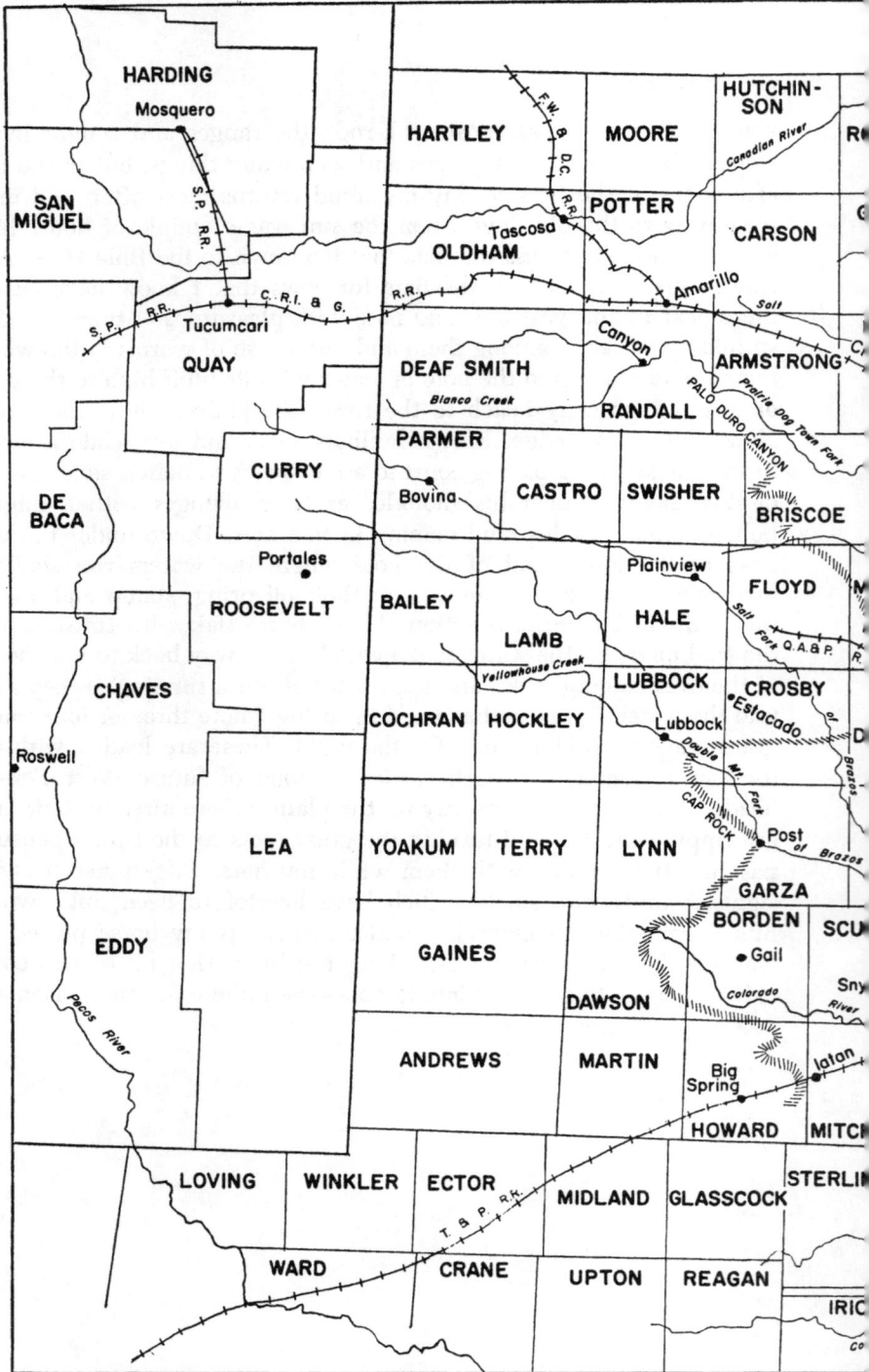

North Texas, Eastern New Mexico, and Southern Oklahoma.

GREER

Mangum

HARMON

JACKSON

HARDEMAN

Quanah

Chillicothe

Vernon

Oklaunion

Harrold

Crowell

Beaver Cr.

FOARD

WILBARGER

Red River

River

of Red River

Washita River

COMANCHE

Ft. Sill

Frederick

TILLMAN

COTTON

Red River

Burkburnett

Electra

Iowa Park

WICHITA

Wichita Falls

LAKE KEMP

Wichita River

KNOX

Seymour

BAYLOR

HASKELL

ermont

W. V. R. R.

Stamford

JONES

ARBUCKLE MTS.

Davis

Springer

Ardmore

CARTER

LOVE

JEFFERSON

CLAY

Henrietta

MONTAGUE

M. K. & T. R. R.

COOKE

Gainesville

MARSH

Denison

GRAYSON

ARCHER

YOUNG

Brazos

THROCK-
MORTON

JACK

WISE

DENTON

PARKER

Ft.
Worth

Ft.
Griffin

River

Dallas

SHACKEL-
FORD

STEPHENS

PALO
PINTO

TARRANT

DALLAS

Abilene T. & P. R.R.

ater

Buffalo Gap

TAYLOR

CALLAHAN

EASTLAND

ERATH

HOOD

JOHNSON

ELLIS

Clear Fork of Brazos River

NNELS

COLEMAN

G.C. & S.F.

COMANCHE

Ballinger

BROWN

MILLS

Concho R.

Colorado

River

CONCHO

Cap Rock and Brush Country

That escarpment known as the Cap Rock, which marks the breaking off of the Great Staked Plains, or Llano Estacado as the old geographies termed it, is most pronounced between the Prairie Dog Fork of the Red River and the Colorado. The Red has its source in Randall County and uses the Palo Duro Canyon as a vehicle on its way out. The Colorado heads in Borden and Dawson counties.

Just under the Cap Rock, nature seems to have jumbled the earth up and left it in a million draws, canyons, gullies, and creeks that eventually form the Colorado, Brazos, Pease, and Wichita rivers. On their way out they are flanked by half a hundred creeks—Buck, Croton, Catfish, Turtle, Talking John, Deadman, Duck, Beaver, Onion, the Sandies (Big and Little), with half a dozen each of Hackberrys and Cottonwoods to the outfit. Cowboys gave the creeks their names years ago when they rode into the country with the first herds. You may be certain that the reasons for assigning each name were sound—Croton, for instance.

From the base of the Cap Rock until the country comes out into the big flats, are the "breaks." Each outfit has its pet set of them—the "Cuba" in one, the "Croton" in another, and the "Little Arizona" further to the east.

The small wild life that is left in the Cap-Rock country is to be found there: 'coon, 'possum, wildcat, coyote, and an occasional "loafer" or lobo wolf. Sometimes a panther is jumped there yet. Eagles sit on the long points that jut out from the base land and pick up jack rabbits, just as their bald ancestors picked up antelope fawns. In the old days panther and bear abounded in the canyons and on the ledges.

It is a country of color—red buttes striped with varicolored strata of rock—brown, green, and blue—the whole sprinkled with glistening gypsum on which the sunlight plays and sparkles. A sort of grand drape, so to speak, is the dark green of the cedars that abound there. Viewed in the setting sun the country has the appearance of a gigantic stage setting. In the full moonlight it is more beautiful. A night thunderstorm rolling down from the plains with its sheet lightning illuminating the buttes and pinnacles, causes the late riding cowboy to stop whistling or singing so that he may study the beauty before him.

The Cap-Rock country is cow country, has been for half a century, and will be so long as people want good red beef. The order of working cattle has changed but little. Wagons, horses, and men go forth each spring as they always have to brand, deliver, and ship.

The Plains country, once summer range for herds that wintered beneath the "Cap," has changed. Its acres are plowed up and the houses on it are filled with people from every section of America. On a nimble-footed pony you may, by riding a mile of winding trail, pass from the last frontier of the old west into a country as foreign to the cow country as the Fiji Islands. In nature's scheme, however, the two countries are highly essential to each other, for the by-products of the cotton patch on top is necessary to augment the ranges below when winter comes.

There has not been much change in the methods of working cattle under the Cap Rock, but there has been a distinct change in the cattle worked. The area was the first in West Texas to receive the motley-colored Longhorns from the coast country; so was it first to dispose of them when necessity demanded. It was first to begin the production on a large scale of cattle that would meet the demands of beef buyers and yet have the "git up" to be good range cattle.

Each of the pioneer outfits of the Cap Rock who are still there have contributed their part to the building of better range cattle. While the new order was on trial, so to speak, and feeder cattle as a range invest-

ment were in the balance, cattle from the 6 6 6 6 of the Burnetts, the
S M S of the Swensons, and the V of the Matadors were winning prizes
and making feeder history. Smaller herd owners followed the leaders
until a uniformity has been obtained that equals any breeding section
of the Southwest.

Not all red breaks and show setting is the Cap-Rock country. There
are big flats and low-lying hills, heavily grassed with mesquite and
grama grasses. Along the creeks and in the valleys, filaree and rescue
grass spring up when needed most. There are sand hills too, covered
with shinnery, diminutive oaks, and evergreen, with succulent leaves
that help out wonderfully during a dry year. Hills predominate, but the
old-timer, boss, or owner, does not mind that, for hills denote running
water and are a safeguard against the plow. Nature has provided well for
the cattle of the Cap-Rock country—grass, water, protection, and salt.

In a leisurely couple of days driving you may visit the headquarters
of half dozen of the old outfits, old in years, but modern in cattle and
equipment. Among these are the Matador, 6 6 6 6, Pitchfork, and S M S,
the latter having two divisions in the Cap-Rock country—the Spur and
Tongue River. Deep in the pastures you will forget, perhaps, that
fences bound you, for they are large pastures, and the men who ride
them are of the type that rode before they were fenced.

West Texas cowmen and cowboys who have gone into South Texas
cow country with their cattle during the drouth have found that there
are other ways of handling range cattle besides those so long in use
on the Plains and the Cap-Rock country. The country, cattle, clothing,
and equipment of the South Texas cowboys are in direct contrast to
those of West Texas.

The Plains outfits start a roundup in a pasture or area in which they
can see most of the cattle they expect to work that day. In two hours
they can throw more cattle together than they can brand the calves
from by sundown. Breaks or Cap-Rock outfits can ride to the top of
their pinnacles and see most of the cattle necessary for a day's work.
By the simple expedient of yelling a few times they can start both the
cattle in sight and those unseen, toward the roundup ground at a pace
that will require some tall riding to check them when they reach the
flat. Then it is only a matter of the riders coming down the draws and
canyons with a few stragglers in front of them. In the herd, branding
pen, or at any work connected with the handling of cattle there are no
better cowmen on the face of the earth. They work cattle according
to their country and their training and they do it well.

When the South Texas outfit starts a drive, they are facing an almost impenetrable wall of brush, each species of which seems to be trying to outdo its neighbor in producing the longest, sharpest thorn. Sprinkled generously throughout the brush, as though to mock it in its efforts in producing thorns, is an abundance of prickly pear—not the kind you see in cactus beds or rock gardens—but giants that stand up as tall as a horse. Cattle are in there—cattle that, despite the advances made in breeding during the past few years, still carry a generous trace of their Spanish ancestry or that carry a good share of Brahman blood. They have been brought up to believe that the brush is their refuge and haven, and they retire deeper into it at the first alarm. They are in there and can be brought out if you know your country, its *abras, llanos,* and *senderos,* and are mounted, clothed, and equipped for brush work.

"Clothed" means extra heavy boots with full-length tops, heavy overalls, double-heavy leggings (chaps), and a brush jacket of about the same weight and texture as the heaviest overall "duckins." These are sometimes reinforced at the elbow with leather, are tight fitting, and are buttoned closely when the rider is in the brush. Suede or leather jackets are not used because the brush soon picks them to pieces; neither do they turn water nor dry out quickly when wet. The leggings are of a great deal heavier weight leather than those used elsewhere and they are not of the buzzard-wing type, but fit closely with no buckles, ties, or *conchos* exposed. They are purely utilitarian and the South Texas cow hand becomes so used to them that he rarely takes them off when working in the branding pen. He will discard the brush jackets for more freedom in pen work, but to quote one of the oldest of the brush hands, "I'd feel as naked without my leggin's as I would without my pants."

They explain this contrast to the West Texas cowboy, who if he wears leggings at all sheds them as soon as he gets on the ground, by explaining that if they are called on to pen cattle from trap or holding pasture it means a ride into the brush and a delay while they are getting their leggings on. They are used to them and don't seem to mind their weight and won't budge an inch into the brush without them.

Their saddles are good, but made smooth, with no stamping or carving, for any raised or uneven surface is an invitation to stickers and thorns to begin their work. The saddles are without exception equipped with tapaderos, heavy, bull-nosed coverings over the stirrups. These are not intended, as is the custom in some cattle countries, to prevent the rider's foot from going through the stirrup in case of a fall,

but are used as brush busters. In dashing through the brush the rider
takes the brunt of the whipping brush on his tapaderos and a canvas-
covered elbow thrown up over his face.

Small hats are used because the riders are not exposed so much to
the hot sun and for the very good reason that the ten-gallon variety
requires too much space in the brush. The hats are invariably pinched
or rolled almost to a point in front.

Light-weight horses are used and they show almost as much agility
in weaving their way through the brush at a run as the average cutting
horse does working in a herd. Like the cutting horse, they require very
little reining. They pick their own way and any attempt to rein might
break their stride with serious results to horse and rider. It is a hard
country on horses and requires lots of them. The average cow hand
will have fifteen horses to his mount. He will have five in active use
with wagon and camp and the other ten under herd on good grass and
water. Four or five days' work during the shipping or gathering season
will put his active mount in need of rest and opportunity to let the
thorns work out and the wounds heal. Cow work, in contrast to West
Texas and the Northwest, goes on 365 days in the year and the *remudas*
are used and rested alternately, whereas horses in the west and further
north are used heavily during the summer months and are turned loose
during winter months for rest.

The roundup in South Texas is more of a "drive" or "drag" than
roundup. An outfit spreads out through the brush much as the western
wagon boss places his men on a drive, but their objective is not the
round-up ground several miles away, but the nearest *abra,* or natural
clearing which may be a mile or less from the starting point.

There is no yelling or beating the bushes, for it does not do with
Brahman cattle or those of Brahman extraction. These cattle, while
generally credited with being fighters and hard to handle, are really
very sensible cattle until cornered or excited. Then they usually live up
to their reputation. If handled quietly and in the same manner over a
long period they move out ahead of the rider much like any other
cattle. The first cattle to reach the opening are held until every man
has thrown in and the drive starts to the next opening, with one or two
men moving the accumulated cattle along. In many of the larger
ranches, *senderos,* or artificial right-of-ways, 150 to 200 feet wide, have
been cut through the brush at advantageous places or along fence lines.
Sometimes the drive is made to these clearings and moves down them
with the riders throwing cattle into the herd as it moves along.

The drive invariably leads to a trap or small holding pasture. Traps and corrals play an important part in cow work in South Texas and are indispensable. Good as an outfit, horses, and men may be, and well as they may know their brush, it is almost impossible to get 75 per cent of the cattle on the first drive. Accumulated cattle are thrown into a trap and the pasture worked and reworked until it is clear of cattle. Small traps around windmills or waterings are important and when a pasture is to be driven as many cattle are trapped in on water as possible.

Most driving in the brush country is done as early in the day as possible. Work starts at 4 A.M., and a drive is usually completed by 10:30 to 11 A.M., with branding or corral work being done in the afternoon. Cattle won't work well in the brush in the heat of the day, especially if it has rained and there is water in the brush. A small percentage of the brush cattle outlaw just as they do in Cuba, Croton, or Little Arizona breaks in West Texas. When the men can't get them out any other way, they run the animals into the clearings—with dogs in some cases—where they are roped and necked to gentle lead steers that bring them out into the open country or shipping pens.

The brush cowboy is without peer in roping, unlike the West Texas cowboys, he wastes little time swinging his loop. He uses a very small one and "dabs" it on in a hurry when he gets a chance; the animal he is after is usually headed for the brush. There are no roundup grounds as they use them in West Texas. Some of the trap pastures have cutting grounds on which they trim their herds or do any outside work they care to. More cutting is done in corrals there than in West Texas and a chute and cutting gate play a more important part than in other sections.

Around the herd, the West Texas cow hand works with a great deal better technique than the southern man and with less running and noise. He also works at cutting cattle in a herd much more easily and with less disturbance. Around the West Texas herd, if a man lets an animal get by him, or break from the herd, it is his job alone to bring him back and he resents anyone's butting in. With the southern outfit, when an animal breaks back or out, the nearest man heads him, and if he does not succeed in turning him immediately, two or more hands will join him almost automatically, and the whole bunch will line the runaway back into the herd or cut.

It is characteristic of the southern cowboy to grab his horse with his spurs and break into a run when he starts, even though it be just to cross the corral. In no cow country is more of the work done on horseback than in South Texas. Crowding pens and branding chutes are filled with cattle in a constantly moving stream handled entirely by mounted men. No pen work or cutting is done on foot. They work fast along the branding or dipping chute and it is not unusual to brand a pen of steers at the rate of two hundred head per hour.

The average outfit in the section consists of fourteen to sixteen men against the usual nine to twelve in West Texas. More men are necessary because of the character of the country they are working in.

In deep South Texas cow country—the brush country—a majority of the cowboys are Mexican. They are descended from Mexican *vaqueros* who have handled cattle in the brush for generations and are versed in the ways of brush, cattle, and horses. They are intuitive students of nature, love their work, and do it as years of experience and their fore-fathers have taught them. There are some good American outfits in the section, but they are the exception. The larger outfits employing Mex-icans, use white bosses who delegate authority to Mexican *caporals*— "straw bosses."

North or South, on the Plains or in the breaks, cowboys or *vaqueros*, they get their cattle out and to the shipping pen. "Hi! Yi! Git on out, you lousy so and so," says the Panhandle puncher as the steers go clattering up the runway and into the cars. *"Hilo! Hilo! Afuera! Afuera!"* says the *vaquero*. Both mean the same thing to the steer—it's every man to his own country.

Colorado City

Colorado City, in Mitchell County, Texas, lies some 250 miles west of Fort Worth on the Texas and Pacific Railroad where that line crosses the Colorado River. To the north and west of it lies that geographical subdivision known as the South Plains of Texas. To the northeast lies the Double Mountain country, so denominated because of two giant peaks which rise high above the breaks of the Brazos River. For years these peaks served as a guide for Indians, buffalo hunters, cavalry-men, Texas Rangers, and cowboys—high, bleak, and blue, they have been glorified in song and verse. Larry Chittenden, the cowboy poet, could see them as he sat on the front porch of his Jones County ranch home and he wove them into the poems he wrote of the ranch country. West of them and Colorado City lies the Cap-Rock country. To the south lies the Concho country, so called because the three or four forks of that river head therein.

Each of these, including the town on the banks of the Colorado River, are steeped in the lore of frontier West Texas of sixty years ago.

Through it runs the story of Indian days when Comanches and Kiowas raided to the north and Lipans and Apaches to the south. Blended with this is the story of the millions of buffalo which once roamed the South Plains, and their nemesis, the ruthless hide hunter who hung on the flanks of the Southern herd until the last of them were exterminated in the late 70's in what is now Mitchell County.

Follows the color and romance of the open-range cattle business, the coming into the area of foreign and eastern capital to engage in an industry in most instances as foreign to them as the states and countries they came from were to West Texas. Interspersed with these are the stories of the coming of barbed wire, wagon freighters, "die-up," drouths, rustlers, fence cutters, hired gunmen, cowboys, cowmen, Texas Rangers, and "badger pullings."

As a final, or up-to-date phase, is the story of the transition of the area into one of the nation's richest agricultural and oil-producing sections, which in itself contains the story of mile-long ricks of cattle and buffalo bones, of the arrival of the nester and his battle with nature until he had gotten his plowshare sunk deep in the turf of the old ranch country. It tells, too, of the building of railroads into trackless country, the forming of a hundred or more thriving towns and at least two fair-sized cities.

Fortunately for posterity, there are living yet in these areas a goodly number of people who have seen and had a part in bringing these things about. They are empire builders to whom has been given the privilege of living for an added time to enjoy the empire they helped to create. It is from the records that these have kept, and what they have told me, that this chapter is made up. The majority of them have lived beyond their allotted three score and ten years. In some places their memories have failed them in the matter of names and dates, but they have been patient and careful in answering questions and generous in the loan of written data. Their desire to give information correctly, and modestly where they themselves were concerned, more than compensates for any small errors.

Central to the events and developments outlined here, was the town of Colorado City. Over it hangs a haze of romance and color almost as heavy as the blue haze which rises from the burning cotton bolls every fall at the half-dozen gins which lie along the banks of the river in the outskirts of the town. Ironically enough, these are on ground which gave to Colorado City a great part of its color—ground occupied more than a half century ago by a red-light district dependent upon cowboys and frontiersmen for its patronage, and said by many to have been second only to those in Dodge City and Abilene in Kansas.

Back through the years Colorado City has had a number of euphonious titles fastened upon it. One group has called it the "Dodge City of the Southwest"; another referred to it as the "Queen City of the West." Still another group, with more thought as to what really transpired, likes to refer to it as the "Mother City of West Texas." So, gentle reader, when the story is told and you have what purports to be facts, you too, may vote according to your lights. I am warning you, however, that there will be stiff competition from the proponents of the last mentioned name, for they argue—and soundly, too—that lumber for the first buildings in many of what are now good solid South Plains towns, with all conveniences, paving, towering water tanks, and tax rates equally high, was hauled from Colorado City by freight wagons. They will tell you also that material for the scattered ranch headquarters and homes which replaced the early dugouts of the area came from the same place, as did the first store-bought furniture and cook stoves which went into them.

These will be augmented by the votes of a number of fine old gray-haired mothers, grandmothers, and great-grandmothers, who made up the brides and young mothers who followed their men folks out onto the Plains and into the Double Mountain country when they moved their herds in. These will be influenced by memory of the fact that when the stork hovered over far-flung ranches or dugouts, or their husbands moaned with pain from broken leg or ribs smashed by a prairie-dog hole fall, it was down the long road towards Colorado City that they watched eagerly for first sight of the doctor's buggy. They will recall, too, that it was there they went on infrequent trips to shop and see how their sisters in town dressed or to take the train for a long-delayed visit back home. They really had something, that bunch.

Mitchell County, of which Colorado City is county seat, was created August 21, 1876, along with fifty-three others carved out of the last remaining slice of Bexar Territory. Prior to its organization in January 1881, it had been attached to Shackelford County for judicial purposes.

In the first election held April 10, 1881, J. R. Dobbins was named county judge; Branch Isbell, county clerk; A. W. Dunn, county treasurer; L. A. Henley, county attorney; W. W. Marshall, county surveyor; Ira Butler, inspector of brands and hides; and R. C. (Dick) Ware, sheriff. The latter was a former Texas Ranger who a few years before had participated in the famous battle at Round Rock in Williamson

County in which the bandit, Sam Bass, was killed and his gang broken up. Ware is popularly credited with firing the shot responsible for Bass's death. He was elected in the first election by the thin majority of one vote and, after serving fourteen years, lost the office by one vote. His services as sheriff had an important bearing on Colorado City which will be discussed later. After his defeat for sheriff, he was made U.S. Marshal for the Western District.

Dobbins, the judge-elect, left the country before he could qualify and the court appointed Judge R. H. Looney to fill his place. Not only did the newly appointed judge serve the county well from a legal standpoint, but, being a cowman in his own right, owning ranches in Scurry and Jeff Davis counties, he was able to see the cowman's point of view and was valuable to both town and county in their formative years. Branch Isbell, the newly elected county clerk, was an old-time cow hand and trail driver who had seen much service on the Kansas trails.

Next in importance to judge and sheriff, more especially in the matter of compensation, was the brand and hide inspector. It was his duty to inspect each herd leaving the county either by trail or rail, for brands other than those of the owner and to issue certificates of his inspection. In the case of rail shipments, the railroad did not accept cattle for shipment until the owner presented his inspector's certificate. Trail bosses were required to furnish these on request to brand inspectors of the counties through which their herds moved. For his services the inspector was allowed to collect from the owners ten cents per head for the first fifty head in a herd and three cents per head for the balance. Each herd belonging to one brand constituted a separate inspection. In a day when anything less than twenty-five hundred head was referred to as "a small bunch of stuff," the inspector's job had splendid financial possibilities. As the Cattle Raisers Association of Texas grew and widened the scope of its operations, it gradually took over the work of these inspectors.

Prior to the organization of the county and the selection of its officers, order was maintained by a company of Texas Rangers comprising about thirty men encamped on Lone Wolf Creek east of the business section of Colorado City. The Rangers were under command of Captain Sam McMurray. These not only looked out for the new town, but kept an eye on an extensive territory from that base as well.

The Texas and Pacific rails reached Colorado City in 1881. Prior to this time, A. W. Dunn, who had operated a store at Coleman, had decided that there were fair possibilities of a town being established at the crossing of the Colorado River. With lumber for a store building, he had moved onto the site by 1880, arriving there in time to be elected county treasurer and have the honor of opening the first store in the town. The store building was approximately twenty-five by sixty feet in size and was constructed of lumber which had been freighted from Weatherford.

The honor of opening the first saloon went to Joe Birdwell, who raced a man from Fort Griffin to see who could open his tent saloon first; Birdwell won by about one hour. The drouth period did not last long, for within a few weeks fourteen more drink emporiums were established.

It might be well to pause here to discuss A. W. Dunn. His name will occur in this chapter a number of times and in a number of capacities. It will be recalled that he was elected first treasurer of Mitchell County. He was Colorado City's first merchant, and, when the postal authorities in Washington recognized the existence of the new town, he was appointed its first postmaster. Then when a bank became a necessity, he took the lead in organizing it and was elected an officer in the town's First National Bank. In later years he organized the Colorado Cattle Company in Fisher County, known to most old-timers as the 1 8 Ranch. He may well be said to have been the father of Colorado City.

To him, or some well-wishing friend, may also go credit for the first billboard advertising to be done in West Texas. An old-timer, name unknown, reminiscing in the *Colorado Clipper* in 1884, tells how in 1880 she with her parents were en route to Colorado City, then known as Dunn's store, in a covered wagon. With team almost worn out and despairing of ever reaching their objective, they came to a fork in the roads where they found an enormous bleached buffalo skull propped between the two roads and facing to the north, on which had been inscribed in pencil or charcoal "4 miles to Dunn's Store by G—D."

When the Texas and Pacific Railroad pushed out of Fort Worth through to El Paso, it was to engage in a race with the Southern Pacific Railroad then building from San Antonio toward the same destination. It was a race between the two for certain benefits and bonuses for prior arrival in El Paso. For this reason, construction was not halted at any point along the line where any town might have railhead advantages, as was the case when the Fort Worth and Denver Railway held up for more than two years in Quanah and Harrold to the distinct benefit of both towns. Through Weatherford, Baird, Abilene, and Sweetwater swept the construction crew until they came to the east bank of the Colorado River in September, 1881, to find the county organized and an embryo town built of materials freighted from towns to the east.

It was but natural that the founders of the town should build it on the bank of the river with an eye toward a water supply—the only sort they and their prospective customers knew—that provided by nature. It was natural also, for the same reason, for it to be called "Colorado." The suffix "City" was added by merchants already on the ground visioning business to come which would justify the addition in name. In this they were aided and abetted by certain influential cowmen who had in mind the creation of a cow-town which might rival in importance Dodge City, Kansas, at that time at its peak and known as the cattle capital of the West. According to postal records the town was never officially known as Colorado City.

So with the railroad safely in town, stock pens being built, and track-laying crews disappearing over the hills to the west, let's pause for a survey of the town's possibilities before we plunge into details of its development.

Three years prior to the coming of the railroad, there had been fewer than a dozen inhabitants in Mitchell County. Waddell and Byler had a cow camp at China Grove on the head of Champion Creek in the southeastern corner of the county. Just above it on the creek was the frontier store of R. S. McClintic built of willow poles and covered with buffalo hides with the hair to the outside. This was operated principally for the benefit of buffalo hunters who were "mopping up" the last of the southern herd which had sought refuge there. Brown and Kelly had a cow camp at the mouth of Cottonwood Creek south of town and Choctaw Kelly had a dugout on Lone Wolf Creek on the site of Colorado City, that creek running diagonally across the eastern portion of the town. Taylor Barr, credited by many as founder of Renderbrook Ranch, had a dugout at Renderbrook Springs. A Captain Bell, who had built the first water-works system for the city of Waco, is said to have founded the T U F Ranch in the southeast corner of the county in 1876.

Principal cattle in the county in 1878 were four hundred head owned jointly by S. McClintock and Ed Forsythe, thirty-five hundred head owned by Waddell and Byler and some fifteen hundred head owned by Brown and Kelly. By 1883 there were on the tax rolls of the county more than a hundred thousand head of cattle. Carey, Adair, and Solomon's outfit, south of town, alone accounted for more than thirty thousand head, and their calf branding in that year totaled more than there were cattle in the county five years earlier.

Waddell and Byler had increased their herd on Champion Creek to more than five thousand head. Winfield Scott, Sug Robertson, and Clay Mann were also increasing their herds in number, as rapidly as possible. Ben Van Tuyl had established an outfit on eighty sections south of town, in what is now the Spade country, and Bush and Tillar were operating in the northwest part of the county along the Howard County line. Kelly and Hudson, the Peacock brothers, and half a dozen other outfits of like size had also taken up ranges in and adjoining Mitchell County. Other outfits operating adjacent to the town whose ownerships cannot be clearly established were the Deep Creek Cattle Company, the Cross Tie, and the Horse Shoe.

In the fall of 1882, the Snyder brothers, D. H. and J. W., of Georgetown, began the operation of what for many years has been known as the Renderbrook Spade Ranch. The Snyders had been important factors in handling South and Central Texas cattle over the Northwest trail to Wyoming, Montana, Colorado, and Idaho. Their first Northwest drive was made in 1868 with Llano and Mason counties cattle which they had purchased at the rate $1.50 per head for yearlings, $2.50 for two-year-old steers, and $4.00 for cows. The herd went to Fort Union, New Mexico, where the beeves from it were sold for government use at $35.00 per head. In 1870 they drove a herd of five thousand head, the first to cross the Union Pacific Railroad, to a point seventy-six miles west of Omaha on the Platte River. To them goes credit of driving the first herd to Cheyenne, Wyoming, in 1871. Each year thereafter until 1885 saw their herds en route to the Northwest. Probably the largest single delivery made by them was to J. W. Iliff of Denver, Colorado, consisting of seventeen thousand two- and three-year-old steers which they delivered to Iliff in Julesburg, Colorado, in June and July, 1878. Shortly after delivery was made, Mr. Iliff died and at his widow's request, they took charge of the Iliff cattle interests, one of the largest in America. After three years of this partnership, they purchased the entire outfit, operating it until 1887. In the annals of Texas cattle history there were no finer men than the Snyder brothers.

In 1882 they had come to the conclusion that if they were to remain cowmen in Texas it would be necessary that they own and fence ranches there as other old-timers like Goodnight were doing. A few years earlier, J. Taylor Barr, who died recently in Big Spring, had set up a ranch headquarters at Renderbrook Springs. This consisted of a two-room house built of chittim poles, with no floor, a thatched roof of tules, with a windbreak of buffalo and cowhides to the north of it.

The Snyders purchased Barr's rights and soon acquired a range of some 125,000 acres. They greatly improved the original headquarters and brought the late Frank Yearwood from Williamson County to serve as ranch boss. Yearwood will be recalled by Texas Hereford breeders as one of the organizers and first presidents of the Texas Hereford Association. His death occurred about a year ago on his Hereford stock farm near Georgetown.

The ranch was stocked with an unusually good type of cattle of the Shorthorn breed, most of which were purchased from Andy Long of Sweetwater. The ranch was fenced and under the Snyders' management was soon an excellent self-sustaining project. In 1883, realizing the necessity for expanding, they purchased a 128,000-acre ranch on the South Plains, which they stocked with the same type of cattle as were on the Mitchell County ranch. Steers from both ranches went northwest each year to buyers with whom the Snyders had become acquainted in their trail days. They continued to operate these ranches until 1889, when they were sold to Colonel Isaac Ellwood of De Kalb, Illinois. The Ellwoods at their home in Illinois, were breeders of fine horses, and the Snyders were lovers of fine horseflesh—this common love of a good horse figured in the purchase of the ranches for, according to Hiram Snyder, son of D. H. Snyder, his father and uncle received from the Ellwoods for the ranches a stud horse and $1,000,000. Ellwood heirs still operate a greatly enlarged and improved ranch in Mitchell County. Full details of its operation under the Ellwoods will occur later in this chapter.

To the north and west of Colorado City the Slaughters were gradually spreading out into what was in a few years to become the famous Long S Ranch, one of the best known cattle properties in North America.

To the north of the town was 150 to 200 miles of virgin cow country lying partially on the Plains and partially under the Cap Rock—ideal for both summer and winter range and well-watered by half a dozen rivers and innumerable creeks which, in those days, "ran" the year round. There was no competing town to the north nearer than Dodge City, Kansas, and to the northwest nearer than Springer, New Mexico, or Trinidad, Colorado. In that area lay what are now the counties of Mitchell, Scurry, Fisher, Stonewall, Kent, Dickens, Motley, Crosby, Garza, Lubbock, Lynn, Cochran, Yoakum, Lamb, Hockley, Bailey, Floyd, Terry, Andrews, Gaines, Dawson, Borden, and Martin. Added to this was the scattered territory in eastern New Mexico into which a few cowmen had come with their herds. Directly south, the Colorado City territory extended well below San Angelo through Sterling, Coke, Glasscock, and Reagan counties. There was a scattering of trade and shipping which, prior to the building of the Southern Pacific Railroad, at times reached the Rio Grande, Devils River, and Pecos country.

If you are of an analytical turn of mind and care to reduce this territory to square miles, remember that each of the counties listed is approximately thirty miles square, some of the southern ones being larger. You will find an area far in excess of many European nations. Throughout the area, the average distance to the nearest railway prior to 1880 was approximately 250 miles.

The area to the north and northeast had not been made safe from the Indians before 1875, and the whirlwind campaign of General R. S. Mackenzie to dislodge the South Plains Indians from their stronghold in Palo Duro Canyon, and place them back on their reservations in the Indian Territory. The campaign, highly successful, was climaxed by a battle in Palo Duro Canyon in which the Indians were put to rout and some fifteen hundred head of their horses were destroyed, after which the Indians were driven on foot to Fort Sill. With the exception of occasional raids by small bands of Indians seeking principally to steal horses, there was little more Indian trouble.

The cowmen of Palo Pinto, Young, Shackelford, Callahan, and Colemen counties had heard from the buffalo hunters of the ready-made cattle paradise in the Double Mountain and Cap-Rock country. Already in their home counties they were being crowded by incoming settlers, and development of large cattle operations was becoming restricted. In 1878 there moved into the Double Mountain area John Hensley of Palo Pinto County to found his 2 2 outfit, with headquarters on the Salt Fork of the Brazos. With him came Fate Wilson to found the Paddle Ranch, establishing headquarters with Hensley. In the same year came Clay Mann from Coleman County to found his outfit and 8 0 brand near the Double Mountains in Kent County. At about the same time, the Elkins and others came into the area.

Then, in rapid order, came the Slaughter brothers—four of them, all from Palo Pinto County, Will, John, Lum, and Mace—to establish ranches that were to make them leaders in the industry. Their achievements were talked of wherever cowmen gathered in the Southwest for years to come. Followed the Daltons from Palo Pinto County, the Hittsons from Callahan to establish their H I T outfit near Double Mountain, and dozens of others, among them Bud Browning, Pete Campbell, and Lon Barkley who was afterwards to become postmaster in Fort Worth. A majority of these outfits settled in Stonewall, Dickens, and Crosby counties, in a large part of the territory which was later to become the Spur Ranch. Prior to the founding of Colorado City their contacts and bases of supplies were Fort Griffin on the Clear Fork of the Brazos, and Fort Worth. Supplies for the stores of Fort Griffin were hauled by wagon freight from Fort Worth and Weatherford. Lumber for early ranch houses was hauled from Fort Worth mostly by ox team. One or two small stores in Dickens County left over from buffalo-killing days served the immediate needs of the area.

By 1885, the Matador Ranch, lying principally in Motley County, had been founded and was being operated by the Scotch syndicate which owned it and were beginning to build it into the fine property that it is today and has been for more than half a century. In 1884 the Espuela Land and Cattle Company Ltd. of London, England, generally known as the Spurs, had begun the operation of a ranch lying principally in Dickens County with considerable acreage in Kent, Crosby, and Garza counties. When the ranch began operating in 1885, it had a tally of 42,777 head of cattle; in peak years it is said to have owned nearly 70,000 head of cattle. None of these outfits were under fence, and it is almost impossible to estimate the acreage they used prior to fencing.

To the south about the same things had occurred. Under the protection of Fort Concho at San Angelo, Fort Chadbourne in Coke County and Fort Lancaster on the Pecos and due to the fact that Goodnight and Loving and their New Mexico-bound herds had made a trail up to the head of the Conchos on their way to the Horsehead Crossing, that country was pretty well filled with cattle whose ranges were tributary to these forts and their settlements. These, prior to the establishment of Colorado City, received their supplies by freight wagon from San Antonio.

With the county well established in cowmen and cattle and the town under way, let us turn to the development of the great range area lying to the north of Colorado City whose operation by large cattle companies was to bring an unprecedented boom to the town and make it for a five-year period the largest cattle-shipping point in the nation. These lands lying to the north and only recently cleared of Indians by hard-riding cavalrymen and of buffalo by the hide hunters, fell into three classifications—public domain, school lands, and railroad lands— and could be purchased or leased very cheaply.

Word of profits made by the promoters of the Matador and Spur ranches in the immediate south and the Prairie Land and Cattle Company and the Goodnight-Adair J A ranches farther to the north, had become known in Eastern financial circles with the result that there was a stampede of Eastern capital to get into the cow business in West Texas where range could be had almost for the asking and cattle sold at tremendous profits. It didn't matter whether or not the investor had any knowledge whatsoever of the cow business and its ramifications— in most instances, they did not. They seemed to feel that their capital freely spent would buy them the necessary experience.

As a result, over a five-year period, capital from two foreign countries and fifteen states ranging from the Midwest to the deep South was invested in generous quantities in the territory tributary to Colorado City. Among the companies thus established were the Magnolia Cattle and Land Company, owned by the Kentucky Cattle Raising Company; the Square and Compass, owned by the Nave-McCord Cattle Company of St. Joseph, Missouri; the Curry Comb owned by the Llano Cattle Company made up of Texas and Illinois capital; the I O A of the Western Land and Livestock Company made up for the most part of officers of the Moline Plow Company, the Moline Wagon Company and the Moline Paper Company; the Three H, owned by the St. Louis Cattle Company; the Triangle H Triangle Ranch, owned by the Alabama and Texas Cattle Company; the Two Buckles, owned by the Kentucky Cattle Company; the Two Circle Bar owned by Charles Weirn of Scotland; Sawyer, McCoy and Rumery of Oshkosh, Wisconsin; the Yellow House division of the Syndicate Company. In addition to these corporations, German B. Stout of Kentucky had a heavy investment in land and cattle, as did an Englishman, F. Theodore Cookson. Wishart and Bilby of Whitman, Missouri also had heavy investments in Stonewall County. The foreign-owned companies consisted of the Matador Land and Cattle Company and the Espuela Land and Cattle Company.

What this influx of capital meant to Colorado City and the development of the area can be appreciated from the fact that these companies were organized with capital stock ranging from $300,000 to $800,000.

In most instances, under their method of operation, they found their original capital insufficient and increased it a number of times.

Almost without exception these company-owned ranches not only failed to pay dividends, but when finally closed out fell far short of returning any appreciable portion of the original investment to the stockholders. The notable exception is the Matador Land and Cattle Company which, since its incorporation some fifty-five years ago, has passed dividends only four times.

A number of things contributed to this condition—looseness in original purchasing, mismanagement, excessive overhead, overstocking, ignorance of the industry, drouths, blizzards, and cow thieves. Some few of the ranches held their lands after they had disposed of their cattle and were able to cut down losses somewhat by sale of lands to actual settlers, but these were in the minority.

It will be impossible to give details of original location and operation of all the companies, but one or two will be highly typical of the balance. The Western Land and Livestock Company was organized at Davenport, Iowa, under Iowa laws in 1884 with a capital of $800,000. Its representatives sent to Texas to acquire land and cattle seemed to feel that their company had been tardy in getting started. They began to purchase lands right and left along the Yellow House Canyon in Lubbock County. Within two years they had leased or purchased the south half of Lubbock County, not calling a halt until they had acquired a block of land fourteen by thirty miles, in area totalling 420 sections. The range was partially watered by Yellow House Creek, but ten wells and windmills were necessary before the outlying portions could be used for cattle. The company began almost immediately to fence its holdings. Posts for fencing were cut and hauled from the Cap Rock, a distance of fifty miles, the wire coming from Colorado City by wagon freight. Including cross fencing, an even one hundred miles of fence was built at a cost of approximately $15,000.

If the representatives had been lavish in the purchase of lands, they were even more of an "angel" to the Texas cowmen who really knew how to sell cattle. As a result they bought stock cattle already at peak prices—twenty thousand head of them at prices never again reached until the Spanish-American War in 1898.

Another $8,000 went for cow horses. Because a majority of the stockholders were from Iowa and because it seemed like a good idea at the time, the letters I O A were burned deep into the hides of the twenty thousand high-priced cattle. No sooner had these been turned loose on

the range than rustlers began lying awake at nights figuring out how
many ways the I O A could be burned into unrecorded brands which
they might record as their own. According to Rollie Burns who ran
the outfit the last seven years of its existence, there were some twenty
variations which could be made from their original brand. In 1886
after severe losses from rustlers and upon recommendation of their
foreman, J. K. Milwee, a veteran of the Chisum's ranches in New
Mexico, the brand was changed to Cross C, and the I O A brand closed
out as fast as cattle could be disposed of. The I O A ranch was closed
out in about 1893, the remnant of the cattle being sold as cheap as
$7.50 a head.

Another ranch highly typical was the Two Buckles in and on both
sides of Blanco Canyon. It comprised some two hundred sections of
land and was owned by the Kentucky Cattle Company, with headquarters in Louisville, Kentucky. Principal officers of the organization
were H. J. Tilford, president; C. M. Tilford, resident manager, J. Tilford, secretary, and John T. Viley, resident secretary and weather observer. Just what part the weather observer played in operating the
ranch, or how successful he was in predicting rains and sand storms, is
not shown in the old ranch records.

The Tilfords were distillers manufacturing the "Belle of Nelson, Old
Fashioned Hand Made Sour Mash Whiskey." They are still well known
in the trade and are marketing their liquor today under the name of
Park and Tilford. By 1884 they were rendering taxes on 13,500 head
of cattle and 130 head of saddle horses. They continued to increase
their stock until 1890, when the price of beef slumped and the company, facing bankruptcy, began to reduce its stock. In 1893, they were
ready to go out of business and contracted to sell the remainder of
their herd to White and Swearingen, owners of the O X Ranch in
Cottle County. The contract called for approximately 10,000 head to
be delivered, but because of rustlers, who were extremely active
around 1890, the number fell short of this.

There have been legions of stories told of "range delivery," "book
count," and "counting cattle around the mountain" to eastern purchasers. There have been other stories of downright chicanery. In few,
if any, instances did the bona fide old cowmen of the area have any
part in these transactions. They may be charged almost wholly to promoters seeking to fatten on the gullibility of moneyed men from their
own states or sections. The old-time cowman would sell his cattle
"book count" to the promoter for he had been doing business with his

fellow pioneer on the same basis. He had sold his brands from time to time "range delivery." In each of these instances he was dealing with men as able to calculate the value of book appraisal and range losses as he. He wanted no part in "skinning" anyone, no matter where he might come from.

There was a custom at the time of organizing cattle companies and taking out a charter of incorporation. The owner having a herd of cattle that he valued at $150,000 would incorporate with a capital stock of $300,000, sell his cattle to the corporation for 51 per cent of the stock and sell those desiring to engage in the enterprise the remaining stock for cash. The Main Concho Land and Cattle Company was organized on this basis. Major W. F. Johnson organized the Kentucky Cattle Raising Company. He had bought a brand of cattle, receiving them "range delivery" running on Deep and Beall creeks in Scurry County. He conveyed this brand of cattle to the Kentucky Cattle Raising Company, retained the profit for himself and disposed of the rest of the stock to friends in Louisville, Kentucky.

Another promoter had come into possession of a ranch in the Double Mountain country which he valued at $100,000. An Englishman, F. Theodore Cookson, bought a half interest in this ranch, paying the owner $50,000 in cash for the same. The owner retained a half interest in the ranch and the management of it. Cookson returned to England and came back a year later expecting to get some profits on his investment. The owner told him he had not marketed any cattle other than enough to meet operating expenses, telling him at the same time that the herd had increased in numbers, took him out over the ranch and convinced him that it was in good condition and sold him half of his remaining one-half interest for $25,000 in cash. The owner retained a one-fourth interest and the right to manage it. The Englishman returned a year later and still there had been no cattle marketed according to the information received from the general manager who then sold him one-half interest in the remaining one-fourth interest for $12,500 in cash. In the meantime the original owner had gone to El Paso and began operations in Old Mexico. An elder brother of Cookson gathered up and sold all the cattle he could find in the brands, realizing less than $5,000 on the original investment.

Lord Aylesford, from England, came into the area and bought a brand of cattle "range delivery," paying $40,000 for them. He was a heavy drinker and neglected the management of his cattle. After his death his administrator sold his cattle, realizing less than $750 for the entire brand.

Other eastern capital came into Colorado City to be loaned to cattle-men for the development of ranches. In most instances the loan of capital was made by fairly shrewd businessmen who looked to their security better than did the incorporators of the cattle companies.

In addition to the foreign-owned ranches and others not heretofore mentioned, there were in the area the Lanc Ranch owned by W. R. Moore; the Jumbo in Scurry County, owned by Gulf and Will Beal; the O S Ranch owned by Frank and Andy Long; the T Bar of the Tahoka Land and Cattle Company, of which C. O. Edwards, now living in Fort Worth at the ripe old age of ninety years, was principal stockholder. Edwards still owns the original ranch. Boley Brown and Pete Scroggins were also considerable operators in the country north of Snyder. John Nunn ran some fifteen to twenty thousand head of cattle in Scurry County during the late seventies, moving them to Terry County in 1885.

The Brigham brothers also ranged for a year or two on Yellow House Creek just east of the present site of Lubbock. To the south and along the Concho, the Tankersleys ranged for a number of years, finally sell-ing their cattle and ranch to Sawyer, McCoy, and Rumery of Oshkosh, Wisconsin. The Tankersleys, however, remained in the cattle business in their old country and have been factors in the development of the country west of San Angelo. Fayette Tankersley, one of the original Tankersleys, died only a year or two ago at Mertzon.

No more had the occupation by the corporation-owned ranches been completed than it became obvious that if they were to hold their ranges and leases, it would be necessary to purchase and fence them. The tide of emigration was moving further west each year. The "little men," with smaller herds, were eyeing the leases and "range rights" of the larger outfits with a jealous eye.

Fencing meant ton upon ton of barbed wire which had to be bought and freighted from the nearest source of supply. It meant also that a water supply would have to be developed where there was no natural supply. This called for miles of pipe, well casing, and windmills, all to be bought at the source from which the wire came. Add to this the necessary material for headquarters buildings, corrals, and camps, and the supplies for the army of cowboys working on the ranches, as well as horse feed for the winter horses—and there was business, plenty of it, in sight for a town properly located on a railroad and with facili-ties for handling business on a large scale. Then, too, there was the matter of the shipping in and out the hundreds of thousands of cattle which populated the new country.

Colorado City was situated exactly right from any direction. It was a straight shot south from the Plains and Cap-Rock country to town, with fairly level country, watering, and camping places. The same was true of the country to the west and south. There was no immediate source of competition, for the Fort Worth and Denver Railroad was not to reach Amarillo until 1889, nor was the Santa Fe to extend its lines from Temple to Ballinger and San Angelo until 1887. Had there been such a thing at the time as the economic maps now appearing in newspapers and trade journals, Colorado City most certainly would have occupied a space in the "white."

Let us drift down off the Plains and see what the town had done to meet the new situation and get the business. Due to lack of records and limited space in which to discuss them, the writer will make no special effort to deal with events in chronological order, but will deal with the town and its developments in a general way during what is referred to by old-timers as the "boom days."

Since we left it, shortly after the arrival of the railroads, the tents, shacks, and dugouts had given way to more permanent buildings and the town had strung out towards the north and east. Dunn's hurriedly built store had been replaced by brick buildings and warehouses occupied by the Dunn-Coleman Company who did a general business in merchandise and ranch supplies. Uncle Pete Snyder, who during buffalo-killing days operated a store for hide hunters on the site of what is now Snyder, Texas, known then as Hide Town, had moved to the railroad, erected a brick building and was getting his share of the ranch trade from the new order as he did from the old. J. M. Cupps also was a veteran in the mercantile business, as were Lawson Smith and a number of others of smaller caliber.

In 1881, a survey had shown twelve merchants, five saloons, two livery stables, two wagon yards, two lawyers, three hotels, and one restaurant. By 1884, occupation taxes were being collected from seventy-five merchants, twenty-eight saloons and beer parlors, seven pool halls, four theaters, two livery stables, three land agents, twelve lawyers, one photographer, four hotels, one broker, seven general peddlers, and two lightning rod agents. The latter did business, too, for you may still see the results of their efforts on the old Two Circle Bar headquarters still standing north of Rotan. It is interesting to note by way of comparison that Newton and Honeywell in Kansas, both famous trail towns in their peak days, never rated more than twenty-seven saloons and dance halls each.

The long railroad sidings were filled with material-laden cars. So great was the demand for this material that most of it was loaded directly into freight wagons, never seeing warehouses or material yards. The stock pens east of town had accumulated hair on every nail head and splinter from the thousands of crowding cattle which had passed through them.

News of the town and its unusual prosperity had spread abroad and merchants from all sections of the state and some from east of the Mississippi River opened stores, most of them with an excellent stock of merchandise. Many of these merchants were of Jewish origin and came from Cincinnati. Others with capital came to invest in buildings and lots, among them M. Lasker of Galveston, who erected a block of brick buildings. Joseph Frenkel of Cincinnati came, saw, and built a block of three-story buildings which included an opera house with an auditorium of larger seating capacity than was to be found in either Fort Worth or Dallas. Traveling troupes playing the state included the town each year on their itineraries. Particularly do old-timers recall the annual visits of Stutz Opera Company which "made" Texas for many years.

The Lapowskis and Sig Simons operated dry-goods stores, catering to the wealthy cattle trade. Mrs. Robert Terrell, who has spent her entire life in Colorado City, recalls the quality of merchandise handled by these merchants and says that in those days it was the custom for Colorado City ladies to come into Fort Worth or Dallas to show what was being worn in Colorado City rather than come back home to show their friends what was being worn in Forth Worth or Dallas. A few advertisements taken at random from old papers show that a French style in dressmaking was effected by Madame DeFontaine's dressmaking establishment on the corner of Elm and Second Street. A plain and simple dressmaking service was also offered by Mrs. E. Gilbert on the south side of the square. Versatility of its merchants was indicated in the ad of Joe Good—who labeled himself as "well known to the Texas frontier"—featuring a saloon, livery stable, and hotel on Oak Street. Another queer combination was shown in the ad of Nichols & Son on the "Public Square" who heralded to the world that they were "carpenters and undertakers—sheep-dipping vats and boilers made on short notice."

The C A Bar Ranch, about the same time, advertised a warning against people penning or keeping up cattle in their brand for milking purposes. It was a queer mixture of frontier and cosmopolitan, this town which in a few years, from a standing start, had obtained a population of nearly ten thousand people.

Prominent among the mercantile firms were Coman and Shear, who were listed as grain dealers but were, in fact, purchasing agents and handled the business necessary for the fencing and equipping of the larger ranches, particularly the Spur and X I T. They purchased, received, and assumed responsibility for the delivery by freight wagon of this material to the place where it was wanted in the ranch country. Sometimes they also became international factors when the Spur or Matador sent a hard-riding cowboy 125 miles from the ranch with a message to be cabled by Coman and Shear to the home offices in London or Edinburgh, the cowboys often enjoying the flesh pots of the town while message and reply made their way across the Atlantic.

The Western Windmill Company dealt in well-drilling supplies and equipment and is still operating under the same name in a number of West Texas towns. Jake McCall was also a prominent merchant and in later years became owner of the Keystone Ranch in Fisher County, which is still the property of and operated by his heirs.

During an attempt to secure a deep well to serve the railroad stockyards, a flow of salt water was discovered, that eventually led to the forming of a company financed by Michigan capital to manufacture salt. The plants were built and flourished for a number of years. Most of their business came from crude stock salt sold to Plains ranchmen, but they made refined salt in the later years of their existence. An enterprising citizen, one Frank Lester, laid out a town-site addition to the east of the business section and developed a park known as Phoenix Park. In this he had a zoo of Texas wild animals—coyotes, badgers, rattlesnakes, antelope, and deer. Just why natives who were accustomed to kicking these out of the way from the ranch to town would want to pay to see them in captivity is not understandable. To further attendance at the park, which was near the stockyards, Lester built a streetcar line from Oak Street to the park. The cars, which like the Gainesville system depended on small mules for motive power, were patronized largely by cowboys who staked or hobbled their horses on the prairie south of the stockyards and came into town in grand style for an evening along the river.

By this time three banks, each with unusual capital, had been organized to handle cattle paper and business on a large scale. The town had the usual number of good saddlers and bootmakers and old-timers like to recall the excellent boots made by Fred Myers and the saddles by Sam Gustine.

Mail lines served by white canvas-topped hacks fanned out from Colorado City, serving an area that reached in one instance as far north as Amarillo. A line to Dockum's served the Spur and Matador country with an extension running on to Estacado in Crosby County, where young Paris Cox had come from his Indiana home in 1878 to found a colony of North Carolina Quakers. In the period just prior to the arrival of the Fort Worth and Denver Railway in Amarillo, that town was served with mail by a stage line operated from Amarillo to Estacado. Other lines served Snyder, Gail, and outlying stores towards the New Mexico line. It is interesting to note that the city of Lubbock received its first mail under that name from Colorado City as late as 1891, when a tri-weekly service from Colorado to Lubbock was established. A post office at Sangers' Store, founded on the site of Lubbock in 1884, had been receiving mail from Colorado City weekly for a number of years before Lubbock was established.

Cowmen with ranges and interest in the Colorado City area moved into it during these years and erected elegant homes, many of which are still in use. Prominent among cattlemen in the state and rated as "cattle barons" of their day were Winfield Scott, Wilson Lewis, A. W. Dunn, J. B. Slaughter, John A. Peacock, Alfred Peacock, M. Z. Zeisen, John T. Beal, Gulf Beal, W. O. Oxsheer, W. T. Scott, Franke Byler, Joe Adair, W. V. Johnson, H. M. Catlett, Sam Malin, Willis Holloway, A. P. Bush, O. J. Wiran, A. B. (Sug) Robertson, Dick Robertson, Will Robertson, John McWilliams, George Y. McWilliams, John W. Nunn, Sam Wiles, I. Stevens, Tom Stevens, H. A. Holmes, T. J. Martin, John Haines, Bill Peck, John Murchinson, and dozens of others whose names are not obtainable.

To any list of Colorado City cattlemen must necessarily be added the name of "80 John" Wallace, an estimable Negro cow hand who came into the area with the pioneer cowmen, worked with them and did as they did—acquired land while it could be obtained by filing or purchased at a very low price. Wallace never became a cattle baron, but at the time of his death he was rated as one of the most substantial cattlemen and stock farmers in Mitchell County.

Others living in Fort Worth and from the East having cattle interests in the area made Colorado City their headquarters for weeks at a time on their annual visits to their properties. Old-timers still recall the visits of Messrs. Nave and McCord, en route to their Square and Compass Ranch. On these visits they were accompanied by colored body servants who attended their wants en route and at the ranch. On one occasion they brought with them by express a specially made

hack and a spanking team of Missouri bays for their personal use.
Scotch and English stockholders en route to the Matador and Spur
ranches detrained in Colorado City to await the arrival of ranch equipment with which to continue their trip to the ranches.

There were several good livery stables to furnish teams for long-
distance ranch driving as well as to care for ranch-owned teams and
equipment in town. One of these was owned by Malin and Colvin. In
later years Colvin moved to Fort Worth to engage in the banking business. Another was operated by the Mooar brothers, John and Wright,
who had been buffalo hunters on the South Plains several years prior
to the founding of Colorado City. Wright Mooar, who acquired fame
from the number of buffalo, some four thousand, killed by him personally, lived until two years ago in Snyder, where he died one of the
last famous hide hunters.

Visitors were often victims of local pranksters and fortunate indeed
was the visitor who escaped the "honor position" at a hastily arranged
"badger pulling" in the rear of one of the town's saloons. They were
no respecters of persons, these pranksters, the more important the
victim, the harder they worked to make the "pull" a success. On one
occasion Senator Brown, later Governor of Georgia, who owned a
considerable part of the section on which the town was built, came
to Colorado City to look after his interests and to donate a site for
a new courthouse. After the business had been transacted, a badger
fight was arranged at which he, because of the fact that he owned no
interest in either dog or "badger," was selected to "pull" the latter,
which he did with good grace, buying many rounds of drinks in high
good humor. An old issue of a Colorado City paper carries an item to
the effect that "it was reported that there was a genuine badger in
Colorado City."

Another form of diversion practiced was the "Kangaroo Court," before which visitors were hailed on trumped up charges which were
presented by a pseudo-prosecuting attorney while some local wag or
attorney defended the victim. Whether the verdict rendered was
"guilty" or "not guilty" made little difference to the victim as he had
to buy drinks all around in either event.

Half a dozen physicians living in Colorado City served the entire
area—driving hundreds of miles each year to reach outlying ranches
and settlements. These maintained several good teams each and drove
night and day when on calls. Often they were piloted the nearest way
by the cowboy who had been sent for them. Ranches responded readily
with fresh teams and cared for the tired ones until they were picked

up on the return trip. Swollen rivers were crossed and operations performed in dugouts and one-room shacks by the light of smoky kerosene
lamps. Prominent among these doctors were A. R. Smith, P. C. Coleman, J. W. Pierson, and E. T. Terrell. Dr. Coleman, in his memoirs,
tells of many one-hundred-mile trips to relieve suffering. He estimated
that in the years he practiced he officiated at the birth of more than a
thousand children in the Colorado City area, and prided himself on
the fact that he lived to bring the children of many of these into the
world. Not only was he a good physician, but he had much to do with
the development of Colorado City and West Texas.

The town had a strong bar, evenly divided between civil and crimi-
nal attorneys. Corporation work, due to the ranch organizations, gave
rise to much legal work, as did land matters of the day. The late I. H.
Burney, who died recently in Fort Worth, after a long and useful life
as attorney and civic leader, was a struggling young attorney during
the boom days in Colorado City. Others were Judges Looney, Earnest,
and Adams—these practiced over a wide area in West Texas and
New Mexico.

The first hotel to be established in Colorado City was the Grand
Central, owned and operated by M. Deyer. Like Lou Gore's famous
hostelry in Dodge City, it served as headquarters for the early cowmen and cowboys coming to Colorado City on business. Lang Aycock
of Sweetwater, however, states that hotels were never a problem in
the town's early days, as most people carried their "hot rolls" with
them, ate canned goods and crackers, and unrolled and went to bed
whenever they happened to get sleepy. The Grand Central was followed in a short time by the Pacific and Renderbrook hotels, both
popular with cowmen.

As the town grew and prospered, its citizens felt the necessity of a
newer, more modern hotel, and with Winfield Scott as leader, a corporation was formed to build the St. James Hotel, a three-story brick
structure as modern as the times would permit, with barber shop, bar,
and indoor plumbing. It immediately became the social and business
center of the town and country and, like the old Lindsay House in
Gainesville, was the scene of many transactions involving hundreds
of thousands of acres of land and thousands of cattle. Managers and
owners of many of the foreign-owned ranches made it their headquarters, some living in it or keeping permanent quarters there. In its
lobby or bar, or on its veranda could always be found some of those
prominent in the West Texas cattle industry.

At the peak of the boom and shortly after the completion of the St.

James Hotel, which was signaled by a grand opening and ball with music from Fort Worth, Colorado City cowmen in their affluence felt it incumbent on themselves to "throw a party" for their cowmen friends from other sections of the state. This took the form of a "Stockmen's Ball" held in 1885, to which cowmen from over the entire state, New Mexico, and, in fact, from any section where men rode horseback and branded cattle—their own or anyone else's—were invited. Old-timers recall that R. J. Kleberg of South Texas, Al McFaddin of Victoria, Burk Burnett, Colonel Parramore, and Clabe Merchant were among those in attendance.

According to Dick Pierson, still living in Colorado City, and a young sprout at the time, they "put the big pot in the little one" and really went to town. A fifty-piece orchestra was brought from St. Louis to play for the dancing. Cowmen's wives and daughters wore beautiful gowns and flashing jewels. The festivities extended from the hotel to the Frenkel Opera House a block below, and to prevent soiling of the afore-mentioned gowns, a solid walk of red brussels carpet was laid between the two buildings. Beside the wives and daughters walked more than one young cowman whose boot heels, adorned with spurs inlaid with gold and silver and with rowels made of twenty-dollar gold pieces, tinkled in perfect time to the silken swish of his companion's skirts.

It must have been a real party for, according to Pierson, eighteen hundred pints of champagne were iced and served gratis to guests. Add to these the necessary drinks, friendly drinks, throat-clearing ones, those pledging undying friendship, and those necessary to clear up various and sundry misunderstandings of brands, fence lines, and water rights—all taken straight—and the affair must have been a howling success with far, very far reaching effects. Several old-timers, Hiram Snyder among them, recall clearly when the ball started—few, if any, are clear as to just when it was over and the last of the cowmen headed for home. In importance, only the meeting under the tree at Graham takes precedence in cattle history over the "Stockmen's Ball." The "Cowboys' Christmas Ball" at Anson and "Colonel Ben's Soiree" of song and poem just couldn't hold a candle to it.

Society in Colorado City to a certain extent revolved around the Colorado Light Guards, a state militia company made up of prominent young men of business and cattle families. Young Ben Van Tuyl was a member and in his memoirs recalls a trip the "Guards" made to Austin on the occasion of the dedication of the new State Capitol for which the state had swapped three million acres of its West Texas lands. Dick Pierson, also a member—one of the few left living—has a photograph of himself in full dress uniform—a sort of cross between the present-day college drum major's outfit and a lion tamer's uniform, but well in keeping with the times.

Several good newspapers flourished in Colorado City at various times. These devoted most of their space to ranch news, cattle transactions, and discussions of fence cutting and homestead laws, all highly important at the time to the cattle industry. Serving on one of these for a number of years was George M. Bailey, who in later years served with distinction as Washington correspondent for Texas newspapers. For a number of years and until his death he was editor of the Houston *Post*. Don H. Biggers, whose word sketches of cowboys and cowmen of fifty years ago were gems of perfection and whose book *From Cowboy to Cotton Patch* (now out of print) has become a valuable collector's item, also served on Colorado City papers and drew much of his color from what he saw and heard.

As new brick business buildings, residences, churches, and public buildings were erected and the town grew in size, so grew the red light district along the east bank of the river, until it had attained the reputation second in the southwest only to the famous "Hell's Half Acre" in Fort Worth. Principal attractions of the district were four or five prominent dance halls, which had combined with them saloons and theaters of approved frontier type. Principal among these was the Gayety, the People's, and one or two others whose names have been forgotten. Their theatrical performances consisted of buxom chorines, weepy soubrettes, vaudeville acts, and a piano-pounding "professor."

Across the river, Frankie Lee operated a theater and dance hall in what was then and is still known as Mexican Town. It was of much lower order than those on the east side of the river and catered largely to the Mexican sheepherder trade and outcasts from across the river. While there may be some question as to it, stories told of Frankie and the goings-on over there, gave one reason to believe that she was a member of that partnership made famous by the old song "Frankie and Johnnie."

The balance of the district was made up of saloons, dives, and gambling houses, with about the usual number of "big houses" and cubicles. The better of these catered only to the best cattlemen trade, were elegantly furnished, and in some well defined instances were "town headquarters" for bookkeepers, stockholders, managers, and representatives sent from the East and North by the directors of the company-owned ranches in the area.

To the district came derelicts from every section of the nation, and many were the stories told as to why Miss So-and-So was in the district. To it came those from the booming mining camps of the Northwest, from Tascosa, Dodge City, Abilene, and Fort Griffin, all seeming to sense that it was the last stand of the free and easy people of the roaring mining camps and wide-open cow towns.

Acting as sort of overlord of the district and having his finger in most of its businesses was Archie Johnson, "Uncle Archie" as he was known to most of Colorado City. He was in direct contradiction to the moving picture or story dance-hall owner, usually depicted in long-tailed Prince Albert coat and fancy vest, and with a two-pound watch chain, black mustache, and roaring voice. Johnson was small in stature, meek in appearance, with a high falsetto voice that hardly carried across his own bar when he inquired "what will it be, gentlemen" as he took a turn back of the bar during the rush hours.

It is said that he was an ex-Confederate soldier who never signed the oath of allegiance, but after the close of the war, drifted into the mining camps of the Northwest and was back in Abilene and Dodge City dealing monte when he heard of the Colorado City boom. He brought with him to Colorado City plans for a saloon and dance hall patterned after the best in Dodge City—horseshoe bar, booths, rooms upstairs, with a plentiful supply of keys, a bevy of dance-hall girls and a "professor." When the plant was finished, according to Bob Weatherby, who was working for the 18's at that time, "it was a thing of beauty and a joy as long as it lasted."

When the town had been organized its promoters felt that they wanted it to be a wide-open town, but they did not care to have a recurrence of the bloody duels and feuds that had occurred in Dodge City, Abilene, and Tombstone. They passed this word along to Sheriff Ware and he, in some manner, and working through Archie Johnson, was able to get it over to those operating in the district. They knew just how far they could go without bringing the wrath of the town and its law down upon them. Also contributing to the avoidance of undue bloodshed and the failure of Colorado City to develop a number of officers with notched guns was the fact that the hide hunters were gone and there was no military post close by. In the history of Western cow-towns the trio of cowboys, hide hunters, and soldiers accounted for much of the rough stuff which occurred. Then, too, the

order was changing and the best of the cowboys, who figured on staying with their companies, did not want to be classed as "hell raisers."
They were working almost under the eyes of the men who signed their
pay checks and wanted to be accounted for when their final "time
checks" were written.

Colorado City and its red light district never acquired a reputation
for robbery, hi-jacking, or "rolling," which was again possibly due to
the close alliance between Dick Ware and Archie Johnson. The district
got the cowboy's money all right, but without resorting to crude
methods. One old-timer who has lived in domestic bliss for more than
half a century and hesitates to risk rocking his matrimonial bark at
this late date by having his name published, says,

"I remember in the spring of '86 we were coming back from the
Pecos with a 'pool' outfit of some twenty wagons and 150 or more men
who were throwing cattle back that had drifted during the winter. We
pulled into Iatan with a herd one afternoon that, as I recall, had almost a five-mile front. We boys had been collecting a few long-eared
calves and 'sleepers' as we went. We sold these to our outfits and with
the proceeds and our time checks, pulled out for Colorado City to see
the sights. We were all pretty well heeled with cash but by the next
morning there was not enough left in the whole outfit to buy a feed
of oats for one of our horses. Old Archie and his gals had gotten it all,
but nobody kicked."

Due to Archie Johnson's domination of the district, it never incurred
the enmity of the town's best people, as was the case in a great many
cow-towns. He had a manner of ingratiating himself with the better
element until they did not oppose him very much. One of his philoso-
phies of life is brought out in a story told by Harvey Means, an estimable colored barber now living in Fort Worth who was a bootblack in
Colorado City during the boom days. It seems that Johnson's chief
colored porter had drifted down into Big Spring on a visit and was
shot and killed there by a white man. Johnson was summoned to appear as a witness in the case. En route to the depot he stopped in
Mean's shop for a shine. "They got me going down to Big Spring on
that killing," he told Means.

"Which side are you going to testify for, Uncle Archie?" inquired
Means.

"Well, guess I will be for the living man," he replied, "I can't help
the dead one any and I might get a little business out of the living
one and his friends."

The district enjoyed its greatest business during the spring and fall shipping periods when there were hundreds of cowboys in town or lying out back from town with their herds awaiting cars. During these periods the lights burned a little brighter, the pianos jangled a little louder, and the bells on the tills rang merrily. There was a steady business, however, throughout the year from the freighters, who almost equaled the cowboys in number and worked steadily between ranch and town.

There were a great many independent freighter outfits that sought business where they could get it, and about an equal number of outfits owned by ranchmen, who kept them on the road continually, hauling barbed wire, lumber, windmills, and well supplies. These carried with them their bedrolls and camp boxes which they used on the road and in the wagon yards when they were in town. Long strings of them headed in the same general direction would move together and camp at the same place for several days at a time. The dust from their clucking wheels mingled with that of incoming herds, and often the "point" men of the herds would have to "throw around" a string of these wagons to avoid splitting their herds. Prices for freight varied according to distance, but averaged approximately sixty cents per hundred to points north of Colorado City.

There has been a good deal of argument as to how far north freighting was done from Colorado City. The X I T records show that they freighted from Colorado City for their ranches to a point where it was nearer to freight from Trinidad, Colorado, and there are to be found records of freight shipments by wagon to the L I T ranch just east of Tascosa, which was about even distance from Dodge City, Kansas, and there are also other records of freighting to the J A Ranch in the Palo Duro Canyon and the T Anchor where Canyon is now located. The majority of the outfits were equipped with six- or eight-mule teams, but a great deal of freighting was done with oxen because it was not necessary to carry a supply of feed for them as was the case with mules.

Down in the district, the freighter rated a little lower in the scale than the swashbuckling cowboy, but he was there oftener and his money was equally good. If you should be in Colorado City, get Frank Smith, the cattle commission man, to tell you the story of the young freighter who took his old uncle around to see the sights on the occasion of his first visit to the town. It cannot be written here, but it is a darn good story.

The town's better saloons were up in the business district and drew their patronage largely from the better type of cowmen and business-men. Prominent among these were the Red Light, the Lone Wolf, Page and Charlie's, and Tom Powers'. The latter, when the boom broke in Colorado City, moved to El Paso to open the Coney Island, one of El Paso's most famous saloons, which was patronized largely by border peace officers, gun men, and "killers." From these Powers accumulated a collection of famous guns that has never been equaled. Among these was the gun with which Pat Garrett killed Billie the Kid and the gun used by Dick Ware in the battle with Sam Bass at Round Rock.

Monte games were operated in all the saloons in Colorado City, the tables being placed much as the domino tables in the saloons of later days. Monte, faro, and black-jack predominated among the gamesters. Crap shooting was an unknown quantity to be introduced many years later with the advent of the cotton-picker. There are tales of cowmen's poker games in the old St. James Hotel where as much as $4,000 was wagered on the turn of a card. There were sporadic attempts from time to time to do away with open gambling. A search of the early court records shows that at one time there had been filed on the records 168 charges for "operating a monte game," but further search of the records fails to show that any of the indictments resulted in a verdict of guilty.

About the same time an effort was made to stop cowboys from carrying six-shooters openly when in town. In this, the same method prevailed as in other cow-towns—that of checking the six-shooters on arrival. They tell a story on Van Sanders, a popular cowboy of the 2 2 outfit who failed to check his gun the first time he was warned, nor would he check it the second time he came to town. Upon the occasion of his third visit, officers laid for him, saw him dismount from his horse and noted the customary bulge in the neighborhood of his right hip pocket. Sensing that they were following him, he made a complete round of the saloons to enter the one which had the largest number of patrons lined up along its bar. While he awaited his drink, two officers closed in on him from each side and proceeded to disarm him—not of his "hogleg," which he, recalling that discretion was the better part of valor, had left safely in his bedroll at the ranch, but of a rusty old buffalo horn which he had stuck into his hip pocket en route to town. Needless to say, the saloon, which he had selected be-cause of its crowd, enjoyed a rushing business for a time at the discomfited officers' expense.

Despite the frontier nature of the town and the fact that they were dealing with men who had not as yet become used to the restrictions of law and order, there were only five major clashes between officers of the law and citizens during the boom period. Because some who were involved in these clashes are yet living, and children and grand-children of others, we shall not attempt to analyze them. There are two instances, however, which prove the type of men enforcing the law and their ability to act and shoot under fire and which were so unusual that we believe they should be related here. Wayne Parks, a deputy sheriff under Dick Ware, was called to Page and Windom's saloon one night to handle a couple of bad men, who were taking the place in. He entered the saloon and edged up to the bar to order a drink and size up the situation. As the bartender pushed glass and bottle toward him, he looked into the bar mirror in time to see both men preparing to draw down on him, whereupon, using their reflec-tion in the mirror as a guide he shot over his shoulder, killing one and wounding the other. Sam Lancaster was called into the saloon from the sidewalk one day by a party with whom he had had some trouble a few nights before. The fellow suggested that they let bygones be bygones and have a drink together. Lancaster, mistrusting him, never removed his eyes from him, but as he reached for his drink the fellow drew his gun and stuck it in Sam's stomach. The latter managed to get the web separating thumb and forefinger between hammer and chamber of his adversary's gun, thereby preventing him from shooting. He took the full brunt of the heavy 45 hammer five times before he could draw his own gun and fire the three shots necessary to kill his opponent.

There was a certain amount of promiscuous shooting, sidewalk rid-ing, and bluster, of course, that usually ended with the sheriff or his deputies disarming the wild man and sending him on his way. Here again, the good judgment and knowledge of men of Sheriff Ware saved the town from gaining too much of a reputation as a bad town.

After fourteen years of service, Sheriff Ware was defeated by one vote. Will and Gulf Beal always felt that they were responsible for his defeat even though they were his closest friends. They were riding in from the Jumbo Ranch on election day for the express purpose of supporting Ware. The way was long and the day warm, so they un-saddled on Deep Creek for a short nap and to let their horses rest. They awakened several hours later and they were unable to reach Colorado City before the polls closed and always felt that one of their votes would have tied the race and the other won it. Ware was after-wards made United States Marshal for the Western District and died as he had lived his entire life, a peace officer of the West Texas frontier.

There has been much written about Colorado City being the largest cattle-shipping point in America for a number of years. Similar claims have been made for Amarillo and Giles in West Texas, as well as for a number of South Texas towns and others in the far Northwest. Probably there is no way of determining just exactly what town might lay claim to the honor. Just who made the first shipment of cattle from Colorado City has unfortunately been lost to posterity and the Texas and Pacific Railroad, due to the fact that their first agent, after a few months of service, destroyed all records and absconded with such cash as there was in till and safe. The *Colorado Clipper* of June 15, 1884, states that in the two previous months, 16,122 head of cattle had been shipped and that the Texas and Pacific expected to move another 70,-000 head that season. It also stated that the shipping pens had been enlarged and that the company hoped to be in position to provide cars as needed.

W. A. Crowder, who still lives in Colorado City and who served the Texas and Pacific Railroad as its agent for thirty-five years, handled the majority of the cattle shipments during the boom days, as well as thousands of tons of incoming freight for the ranches. According to his statement, he wore out two depots for the company before they retired him a few years ago. He states that it was not unusual during the spring and fall to have orders for from five to six hundred cars at a time and that he was always behind on cars, most particularly for herds coming in that did not have cars on order. He recalls at times that there have been as many as a dozen herds being held to the north and south of town, awaiting cars. During the heavy shipping period, it was his custom to accumulate as many cars as possible on the sidings at Sweetwater, Roscoe, Colorado City, Westbrook, and Iatan. When needed, he would requisition an engine and crew who would pick up the empties as they came in.

"Cars were only twenty-eight feet long in those days and we loaded yearlings about forty-five to the car and grown cattle about twenty-five. Fourteen to eighteen cars of these made a load for one of our little old engines. I remember when the company put Engine 40 into service, which could pull twenty or twenty-five cars. About all my business in those days was billing cattle out and lumber and barbed wire in. Twenty-five or thirty cars of barbed wire was no trick at all in those days. I loaded out the first wire that went to fence the X I T Yellow House division.

"After the big blizzards and 'die-up' of 1885 and 1886, we began to ship cattle and buffalo bones out by the trainload. I recall that at one time we had a rick of bones nearly half a mile long, thirty feet wide and sixteen feet high. I could not begin to estimate how many tons there were. I do recall that buffalo bones brought about $2.00 more than cattle bones because the thigh bones were larger and of a good deal better quality than the cattle bones. They used both in making buttons and in refining sugar. As I recall, buffalo bones brought about $9.00 a ton and cattle bones around $7.50. In the later days when the country was settling up and we were trying to attract settlers, the Colorado City papers used to refer to buffalo bones as 'country produce.'

"Speaking of shipments, if anything our heaviest shipments came about the end of the boom, when the cattle from our country were being sold and shipped to the four corners of the earth it seemed. I recall that the C A Bar outfit, the Adairs, shipped thirty-five thousand the year that they were cleaning up. Almost that many I O A cattle went out about the same time. I will have to say this about the old cowmen, they were fine to get along with and did not belly-ache as much about the delay in getting out a train of cattle as the nesters who came in later would about getting one immigrant car spotted. I have many pleasant memories of the old-time cowman, and many of them were my closest friends."

During the boom days, Colorado City was truly the cowboy capital of West Texas. The men liked Colorado City because it liked them and appreciated that it owed its existence to them and to the men who signed their pay checks. Merchants, restaurant keepers, saloon keepers, saddlers, and bootmakers, courted them and sought their patronage and insisted that they make their places headquarters when in town. When Christmas rolled around Colorado City merchants, particularly those supplying the larger ranches, always saw to it that a case of Scotch or Bourbon was sent out to the ranch manager with their compliments. In the event there was one who did not care for either Scotch or Bourbon, which was rare, he was usually the recipient of a Stetson hat, a saddle, or a suit. It became an accepted custom of Colorado City merchants to extend credit to, or advance money to any cowboy who was known to be on the payroll of one of the major ranches. This custom was much appreciated after a session at monte or draw poker. While there is no way of checking it at this late day, you may be sure that such debts were liquidated in due time. As a result, when a cowboy in the area received his "time" by request or otherwise, he hied himself immediately to town to look 'em over and dispose of aforesaid "time" as quickly as possible.

Upon his arrival there, after his horse had been placed in a livery stable or wagon yard, he would go to his favorite "man's" store where he would purchase a pair of scrivens drawers, with elastic in the side and tie strings in the ankles, undershirts and socks, and a new shirt. With these he would make his way to his favorite barber shop to enjoy a good hot bath, in one of the four or five cell-like bathrooms to be found in the rear of barber shops in those days. His ablutions completed, he would come back up front and instruct the barber to give him "everything." This meant a haircut, shave, and shampoo, and the blacking and waxing of his mustache. While this was going on the shop's bootblack was removing sand and other extraneous matter from his boots and giving them an extra high polish. Upon this being completed, he emerged from the shop clean and with his sun-scorched face as red as the proverbial spanked baby, and as liberally powdered. He headed then for his favorite bar to lift a few drinks and "augur" with kindred spirits until time to drift down into the district for the evening.

Jake Maurer operated a restaurant and was known as the cowboy's friend. It is said of him that he never refused a cowboy credit, food, or the loan of a few dollars during his lifetime. They do say, however, that in the later days when things were breaking up, he would require a man to bring a horse bearing the brand of the ranch he claimed to work for around where he could see it, just to keep the record straight. They tell also that he could serve forty or fifty orders of brains and eggs per day notwithstanding the fact that the hide and brand inspector's records could show only five or six beeves per week being slaughtered by local butchers. In giving information on Colorado City, more old-timers speak a kindly word for Jake Maurer than for any other person in business there during the boom days.

By 1887, over-stocking, blizzards, and drouths had wrought havoc with the company-owned ranches. Late in the fall of 1884 and before much fencing had been done, a blizzard sent cattle cascading over the Cap Rock like a living Niagara to drift before it far into New Mexico. Many landed on the Pecos River and some few drifted to the Devils River and to the Rio Grande before they halted. From the northeast, cattle from the Spur and Matador drifted onto the Plains and Cap-Rock ranges until no man knew where his cattle were. Thousands died, and the Plains ranches were nearly two years getting remnants of their herds back from the south and onto their own ranges. More than thirty thousand head, the result of a pool roundup along the Pecos, were drawn back east of the Colorado River in the spring of 1885. Practically the entire calf crop of two years was lost in the drifts. These pool roundups were comprised of some fifteen to twenty wagons from the upper country, who went as far south as they could hear of the drifted cattle, to work them back toward their own country.

The year 1886 was "dry" and cattle suffered severely from shortage of range and water. The fall of that year saw blizzards equaling in intensity those of 1884. The story this time was even more pitiful than in 1884, for after the drifts of that year, many of the outfits completed fencing, and the fences prevented Plains cattle from seeking shelter under the Cap Rock. As a result, thousands upon thousands of them, weakened by a summer's drouth, huddled along fence lines and froze to death. Many that survived the blizzards had their feet frozen until their hoofs dropped off and then they died.

Rollie Burns, who was running the Square and Compass outfit at that time, estimated that the company lost fifteen hundred head or 15 per cent of its entire herd in one blizzard in January, 1886. Weakened by the storm, other hundreds failed to survive until spring.

What was true of the Square and Compass was true of the other corporation-owned ranches: with the possible exception of the Matador, they all fared alike. The Spur incurred losses in these years, which they were never able to overcome. Inventories of cattle were shrunken and could never be reconciled to the book count on which most of them were purchased. Indebtedness piled up and the Eastern stockholders were disgusted and refused to put any more money into the Southwestern ventures. Practically all of them at the next stockholders meetings voted to sell their cattle and close out, thereby stopping losses.

Many of the old-timers and pioneers were wiped out at the same time. John Nunn had moved to Scurry County with a small herd in 1880. He kept his increase and by 1885 had between fifteen and twenty thousand cattle. When prices went down in 1885, '86, and '87, he held his cattle and started borrowing money on them. By 1889 he was broke, and his creditors took over his land and cattle. I mention him only because his case was typical of many cowmen who over-expanded because of too much credit and easy money.

People like the Slaughters, who knew the country and the cattle business, and who had men of the type of Gus O'Keefe in charge of their range affairs, fared better. They were able to get their cattle back on their ranges. They knew also how to get range and hold it, and were able to hold on profitably until the nesters finally claimed the last of the big ranges on the Plains in the late 90's.

Colorado City had seen its hey-day. The boom days were over. It was to enjoy an additional spurt of cow business from the outfits shipping out the last of the big herds, sold at ruination prices and scattered to every section of the Southwest. The C A Bar outfit is reported to have shipped out more than thirty-five thousand head in their final clean-up. Another fifteen thousand head of the high priced I O A cattle helped write "finis" to the Colorado City stockyards, as they were shipped out for Kansas in 1893.

But the town was not to enjoy this final business without competition, for the Fort Worth and Denver Railroad had reached Amarillo in 1889, and since that time the Plains herds from Lubbock and north had been going there. The Spur, the Matador, and the Double Mountain herds were going to Giles, Estelline, and Childress, lower down on the Denver, and their freight wagons were hauling supplies from the same towns. The Santa Fe had built into San Angelo, cutting off cattle trade and freight from the south.

Colorado City banks were loaded to their limits with cattle paper and loans made on brick business buildings and on merchandise stocks. The seventy-eight merchants began going bankrupt or moved their stocks out, where they were able to. Buildings, once the pride of owners and the town, sold for twenty cents on the dollar, and cobwebs gathered on the pianos and windowpanes down in the district. Bob Weatherby says, "It was plumb pitiful to see the gamblers sittin' around playing 'sol.'" These and the better of the saloons moved on west to Pecos, Toyah, and El Paso. The streetcars ran no more, because the population had dropped to less than fifteen hundred persons, who held on to see what the new order might bring, and to salvage what they might from the boom days.

Winfield Scott, who had not suffered so keenly as the other old-timers, moved to Fort Worth to establish ranches west of town and invest heavily in Fort Worth property. Sig Simons moved his store lock, stock, and barrel to Ardmore, Oklahoma, then in its ascendancy as an Indian Territory border town. Nathan Lapowski moved to Gainesville to enjoy a few years of cattle trade, and eventually became well known in Texas military circles. The exodus was pretty well completed by 1890, and the town lay dormant with only a fraction of its former glory and business until the beginning of the new order, which was marked by the coming of the nester. The cow business was not entirely gone, but the day of the big company-owned ranches was. These, for most part, had been cut into smaller units of from twenty to seventy-five sections, all of which were either owned or owed for by those holding them. The day of the "little man," as far as the cow business was concerned, had arrived.

Overcrowded Central, East, and North Texas were seeking outlet for their surplus farmers, and the natural trend was toward West Texas, with its plentiful lands, which could be bought cheaply. In many counties, there was yet state land which could be filed on by bona fide settlers. The few remaining big-time cowmen, and the largest of the "little men" did not look with favor on this invasion, and did little or nothing to encourage it. In this they were assisted by nature which showed no more favors to the nesters in the matter of drouths than she had the cowman in past years.

While there was never outright war in the Colorado City country between the cowman and the nester, there were flare-ups and outbursts from time to time, which caused both cowmen and nesters to sleep on their arms. Most notable of these was the conflict between the two over possession of Block 96, northwest of Colorado City, which was well watered and had been occupied by settlers. According to the best evidence obtainable, there was considerable night-raiding, some fence cutting, and at least two deaths before the matter was settled.

The first wave of farmers to occupy West Texas made no effort to raise cotton but confined their agricultural efforts to planting patches of feed on sod land, which yielded little or no revenue. For the most part they existed by freighting, gathering and selling cattle and buffalo bones, cutting fence posts, and doing odd jobs for the ranches.

In 1890, A. M. K. Sowell, living just to the northeast of the town section of Colorado City, planted a few rows of cotton experimentally. These yielded enough seed cotton for a bale, but it was necessary to ship it to Abilene for ginning, there being no gin farther west than Abilene at the time. So much interest did this create that it was returned to Colorado City, where it was purchased by citizens and businessmen to be placed on exhibition for six months in the lobby of the First National Bank.

In the years which followed, cotton crowded the remaining cattle back into the rough country of the Cap Rock and the breaks of the Brazos as every acre that might by any stretch of the imagination be termed tillable went under the plow. Land colonization companies, with a vigor almost equaling that of the ranch promoters of a decade earlier, brought in farmers by the hundreds to settle them on the fertile acres of the Plains country. Counties wherein a few short years before had been only ranches, were soon taking the lead in the state for the production of cotton. Truly a once great cattle empire had in less than ten years come from "cows to cotton patches."

Colorado City saw the new opportunity and began catering to the farmer as she had the cowman in the past. This time she had competition, however, for settlements and towns were springing up at fifteen or twenty mile intervals throughout her old trade territory. Snyder to the north became a central trading point and soon enjoyed a business almost equal to that of Colorado City. However, order came out of chaos and in a few years Colorado City was prospering again and on her way to being one of West Texas' leading agricultural cities.

Let's take a final "prowl" over the old trade territory as we found it in 1881 and see the changes which have been wrought. In it have been developed a couple of thriving cities: Amarillo on the northern extremity, which got her first mail from Colorado City in 1888, and Lubbock, with its splendid agricultural section and ever-growing Texas Technological College—she received her first regular mail service from Colorado City in 1891, along with lumber for some of her earlier buildings. The country around Lubbock has now been developed into a cattle-feeding area, which, due to its ability to produce grain sorghums cheaply, promises to take rank with any other feeding section in America. Less than five years ago Lubbock County, one-half of which at one time was the old I O A ranch, led the state in the production of cotton and ranked fifth in its production in the United States. To the north of it lies Plainview, center of one of the Southwest's largest dairy developments. To the south of Lubbock and within a few miles of the old Square and Compass headquarters is Post, with its whirring cotton mills. To the northwest, in Gaines and Yoakum counties, oil has been found in unusual quantities.

To the northeast, the Double Mountain, Spur, and Matador country, due to its rough terrain, remains practically unchanged. Each spring, as they have for nearly sixty years, Matador chuck wagons go out with good men and good horses to brand the calves, which have become so highly bred that they rate among the top with the Northern feeders. The Spur ranch was purchased by the S. M. Swenson interests a good many years ago. Its tillable lands have been sold to farmers and the Swensons operate the balance as a unit of their S M S ranches.

The Double Mountain country, ever an excellent breeding and developing section, is today a cattle country of small ownerships, made up in many instances of the sons of pioneers and in others of men who have lived in the section over a long period. These have brought their cattle up through the years by careful breeding to a standard equal to any in the Southwest. Among them are the Wallaces, Bert and Eck; the Dennises, the Smiths, and So Relles. The Beggs brothers and Price Stell operate the old Paddle Ranch, and the Jackson brothers of San Angelo the old Magnolia. Prominent in the Aspermont and Peacock sections are J. D. Patterson and Will Flowers. The O S Ranch of the Connell Estate in Kent and Garza counties, is almost intact, as is the T Bar of C. O. Edwards. The Slaughter Estate near Post owns a remnant of the Square and Compass and have their headquarters where the original ones were located. Mrs. J. B. Slaughter, wife of one of the original brothers, makes her home on the ranch. Lands of the Llano ranch along with others were purchased by C. W. Post, who colonized them and established the town of Post. K. Stoker has a nice thirty-thousand-acre ranch in the south portion of Garza County. Under the Cap Rock in Borden County, Clayton and Johnson operate an extensive ranch.

Highways, highlines, and railroads criss-cross the old range country, and there is little left except the towering Double Mountains to remind old fellows like Jake Raines, Prinkle Moore, and Bob Weatherby of the days when all trails led to Colorado City, with its hot baths, haircuts, and high-jinks.

Mitchell County is still rated as one of the cattle counties of West Texas. In its southern portion and lapping over into Coke and Sterling counties in places, lies the 250 sections of the Renderbrook Spade Ranch, owned by the Ellwood heirs, of De Kalb, Illinois. It is rated as one of the best big ranch properties in West Texas. It is watered by the Colorado River and numerous creeks and springs. It was one of the first large ranches in West Texas to utilize pipelines as a means of providing a uniform water supply for its cattle. Headquarters, modern in every respect, are located at Renderbrook Springs, about thirty miles south of Colorado City. The Ellwoods were among the earliest manufacturers of barbed wire and much of their earlier product is to be seen in the fences on the ranch.

Until his retirement a few years ago, D. W. Arnett, who came to the ranch from Williamson County with the Snyders, was in charge of operations. Upon his retirement, Otto F. Jones became manager.

The ranch uses a wagon in its work and maintains five camps strategically located. In recent years, a good portion of it has been fenced for sheep. At this time, sheep and cattle are on it in about equal numbers.

To the east of the Spades, Price Maddox and Son operate the old R U F Ranch, running both sheep and cattle. They also operate the Combination Ranch in Nolan County. Maddox Senior is president of the Texas Sheep and Goat Raisers Association. Hiram Snyder, son of D. H., runs cattle west of Colorado City in the Westbrook country. Eudie Wulfjen and Lay Powell operate ranches to the south of town adjoining the Spades.

Until recent years, for a few hours each fall, herds milled and a cloud of dust reminiscent of the old days hung over the pens east of town, when the Spades would be loading their yearlings for shipment to the Plains ranch or Price and Jimmie Maddox would be delivering their calves to feeder buyers, but in recent years, these too have fallen into modern ways and truck their cattle from ranch to railroad.

As the years went on, old-timers passed away and the younger generation gradually dropped the suffix "City" from the name of Colorado. Three years ago, the few remaining old-timers, recalling the glory of the day when Colorado City merited the suffix, promoted an election to have the town officially renamed Colorado City—so Colorado City it is today—a Colorado City sans seventy-eight merchants, twenty-eight saloons and dance halls, innumerable cowboys and freighters, the streetcar lines, and the salt works, but withal a sturdy, modern little West Texas city, happy in the new order and pardonably proud of the part it has played in the development of West Texas.

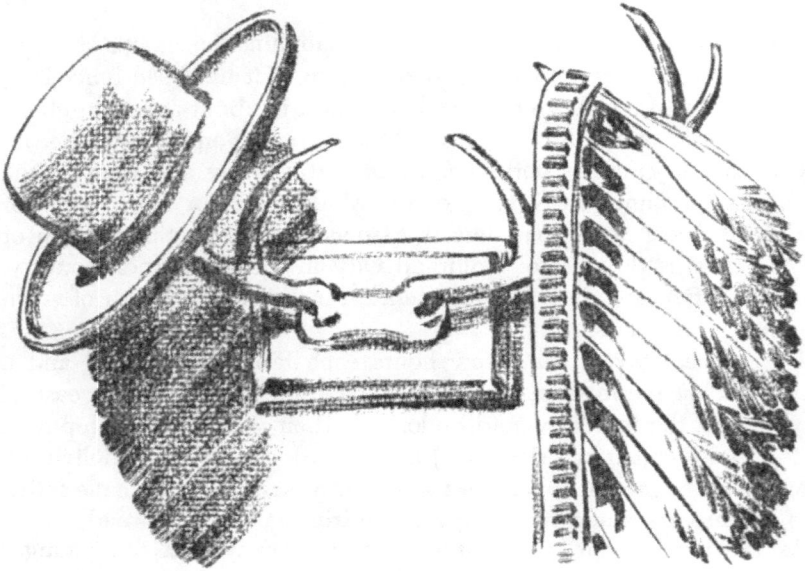

Tom Burnett

The ranch house of the late Tom L. Burnett is perched high on a hill a few hundred yards to the north of U.S. Highway 82 about six miles west of the town of Iowa Park in Wichita County. There is a neat cream-colored brick ranch house with an excellent stand of smaller dwellings, corrals, and barns surrounding it. Its own railroad loading pens lie just across the highway at Tom Burnett Switch.

Modern America scurries by the headquarters by the thousands each day in automobiles, trucks, or crack Burlington trains headed for Colorado and the Northwest. Scarcely an hour of the day passes but what the drone of an aeroplane can be heard high overhead at headquarters or by those riding the pastures. To the uninitiated who pass by, the buildings represent only the modernization of West Texas. Unless they happen to know, or, someone tells them that the red triangle worked into the chimney on the south end of the house is the Tom Burnett brand and symbol of ownership, they will pass it by as another country home or stock farm. An occasional horse lover will ease up on his accelerator to study and admire with a horse lover's interest, the stallions and harems of mares which graze with their foals in the smaller pastures near the home place. Further up the highway the cow buyer scurrying westward in search of cattle to fill his orders slows up to gaze with appraising eye at the sleek, well-bred Herefords grazing in contentment and deep fat in what he in his vernacular terms "belly deep" grass. The Cap-Rock ranchman homeward bound and perplexed by the infestation of the pestilent mesquite on his own acres, pauses to view the thousands of acres of pasture that have been cleared of it and to estimate the value of the cords of wood neatly ricked as far as the eye can see.

The ranch house atop the hill is a living monument to the settlement of West Texas and the advancement of the cattle industry. Its entire modernity is a tribute to the ability of a cowman to reverse the old order of the open range and replace it with the elements of the new. Past the site of the present ranch house has flowed four generations of Texans, on horseback, in livery rigs, "private conveyances," prairie schooner, "link and pin" Fort Worth and Denver Railroad emigrant cars, and the sleek, long-hooded autos of this day. It was such as this cowman who made West Texas ranching, railroads, cow-towns, agriculture, oil, and thriving cities possible. There had to be one who came ahead. He was Captain S. B. Burnett of Denton County.

A dugout and houses on the site of the present one have housed or provided headquarters for four generations of a family which has been for nearly seventy years engaged continuously in the ranching business on a large scale. They were of the "big fellows" of the industry throughout the entire time. In Texas, particularly West Texas, seventy years is a long, long time. The range-cattle history of the state, based on the driving of cattle to the Kansas markets, dates back to the first years after the Civil War. If this reckoning is accepted, the industry founded on that basis in South Texas five to seven hundred miles away, antedates the founding of the Burnett ranches and the building of first dugout headquarters and corrals near the site of the present buildings by less than ten years. The lives of the Burnetts have been interesting, colorful, and successful. They embrace the period of pioneer ranching in Denton County, open range ranching in West Texas and the Indian Nations, and modern ranching.

The achievements of Captain S. B. Burnett, one of America's leading cattlemen, have been thoroughly recorded. The story has been told of his early experiences as a trail driver and how with a small holding on Red River on the Texas side he negotiated with the chieftains of the Kiowa and Comanche tribes for grazing rights on more than a million acres of their lands for himself and other Texas cowmen who were losing their grazing acres to the men of the plow. How he came back into Texas when the Indian lands were to be thrown open to settlement, to place his herds on the newly acquired 6 6 6 6 ranch in King County and on this property to develop his cattle by careful culling of cows and importation of highly bred bulls until their offspring were early consistent winners as feeder cattle in the Nation's leading livestock shows, is cattle history. Epic are the stories of how he maintained sovereignty of his acres and the sanctity of his brand. He died June 27, 1922, honored and respected by all who knew him.

Because he was active in the conduct and improvement of his ranches until his death in December of 1938, not so much has been recorded of the son of the cattle king, who rode at his side from his sixteenth year and learned the industry from him so that he might, by his own effort, acquire ranches and carve a name and place for himself in the cattle annals of the nation. Probably no cattlemen in America crowded as much of living into sixty-eight years, or saw so much of the color and romance of the Southwest, as did Tom L. Burnett, son of Burk Burnett. Certainly no one of them lived so evenly divided, one-half of the old order, the other of the new, achieving equal merit in the conduct of his affairs under both.

Necessarily, to complete a biography of Tom Burnett and sketch of the Triangle Ranch, we must drop back to the founding of the Burnett Ranch between the Red River and the Big Wichita, just west of the Dan Waggoner holdings. The story begins there and ends there. Headquarters were established sometime during the middle 70's. Luther Clark of Quanah says he visited them on a cow work in 1877 and that there was a ranch house and commissary there at that time. Dick Sparks, an old Negro cow hand, who came to the section with Burnett Senior from Denton County is authority for the statement that they operated from a dugout along the creek to the south of the present site for a couple of years prior to the building of the first ranch house, lumber for which was freighted by ox team from Fort Worth.

The lands used as a basis for open-range operations were owned by Burnett and his father-in-law, M. B. Loyd. The latter was purely a financier, having been persuaded by Burnett on a trip to Missouri to move to Texas to engage in the financing of Texas cattle loans. In later years he came to Fort Worth to establish the First National Bank and see it grow into one of the Southwest's leading cattle banks.

Tom Burnett was born in Denton County in 1871 and spent the first years of his life in that county. Shortly after the Burnett operations were transferred to the Wichita country, the family moved to Fort Worth. He attended schools there and a private school in St. Louis, with vacation periods spent on the ranch where he rapidly developed into a cow hand at an early age, as did most youth of half a century ago. His father was anxious to give him educational advantages and persuaded him to attend the Virginia Military Institute, which he did for three years. This was not accomplished, however, without several false starts. Already love of the cow business and the color and romance of the Indian country had gotten into his blood. As a special inducement to attend V.M.I., his father agreed to go there with him and spend a few days seeing that he was comfortably settled. Leaving Virginia for home, the elder Burnett came back leisurely by Washington, D.C., and into the ranch ten days later where he reported young Tom happily settled in school. "Like hell he is!" quoth the ranch boss. "He came by here last week, cut a mount of horses and pulled out for the Fort Sill country hunting the wagon." He did return to Virginia, however, to complete a course in that ancient institution.

By the time he had completed his schooling, the Burnett herds had spread over the big pasture country of the Comanche Nation. Headquarters had been moved from Iowa Park to the Red River ranch on the present site of the town of Burkburnett. The old headquarters became a sort of south camp and basis for the ranch's shipping. The Denver road had been built and had established a station and shipping pens at Burk Station, now Tom Burnett Switch. So long as they had cattle in the Nation they shipped from this station, many of the herds being trailed from within six miles of Fort Sill, Oklahoma. Queerly enough, the old headquarters had been established as far south as possible to offer safety from the Indians, for in 1875 there were still sporadic Indian raids from across the river into Wise, Montague, and Wichita counties during the light of the moon. Then when the Indian lands were leased, the base was moved as near the river as possible that they might be in closer contact with the Indians and their country. During the entire time the Burnetts were in the Nation, operations were carried on from the Texas side. The Big Pasture was worked by chuck wagons operating from that side.

In the years that followed, Tom Burnett worked as a hand with the wagons in the Fort Sill country, drawing the same wages as the cowboys riding with them. These crews were made up of hard-bitten adventurous fellows from every section of the cattle countries of the

Southwest. Among them were no few Comanche Indians employed for their skill as cow hands and as a means of maintaining friendly relations with the tribe. Among the names appearing on an old-time book are George Blackstar, Crazy Man, Nohanna, Indian John, Sapoak, Tom Greenpersimmon, and a half dozen others equally weird. The old book shows that more than three hundred men worked with or under Tom Burnett during the period they were in the Comanche Nation. It lists the names of men who later became cattlemen in their own rights. It also lists the names of some who died by gunfire and at least one who went out kicking at the end of a vigilante's rope after a bank robbery in Wichita Falls in the early 90's. It was a big country where men who could handle cattle, ride afar, and hold their own, were in demand with no questions asked, as long as they were loyal to their own outfit. More than one of the pages show that a newly hired hand gave one name to be entered when employed, worked through the summer, was laid off in the fall and returned in the spring as the wagons were starting out, to give his real name to be entered on his old page with last year's name scratched out. Bob Beverley, a long-time wagon boss in the Pecos country, maintains consistently that a cowboy who couldn't wear his name out and take on a new one in six months was not to be depended upon. What was true of the Burnett outfit was true of the other big fellows operating in the Nation. It was an era of the Southwest and in no way reflects on the integrity of the cowman.

Negotiations for the Comanche grass lease had been conducted by Burk Burnett with Chief Quanah Parker. A warm friendship had developed between the cattle baron and the old chieftain. This friendship was extended to young Burnett when he came to the outfit. He soon became a warm favorite with the chief and the other men of the tribe. In a short time he had mastered the Comanche language and the universal sign language by which all Indian tribes are able to discourse with each other. From the older Indians and in working with the younger ones at the wagons, he learned much of Indian lore and the art of trailing and reading signs. From the beginning he had the confidence of the Indians and in a short time was sitting in their councils when the matter of dealing with the white men would come up. Later he was to carry on the fine relations between the Texas cowmen and the Indians which resulted in mutual good to both. Probably no white man was permitted to learn so much of the early history and relations of the Southwestern Indians and the white settlers as Tom Burnett. Most certainly no white man enjoyed their confidence more than he.

This feeling and relation between him and the Comanches existed long after the herds had left the Nation and the Indian leases were but memories. So long as he lived old Indians and their descendants visited him at his ranches. Shortly before his death and evidently sensing the end, he visited the old Indian country to "hob nob" again with the few of the older ones still living. With an almost uncanny sense of direction he had his chauffeur drive through field, pasture, and even small towns on what forty years before had been open range, to find spots where his wagon had camped or certain herds had been held or worked. Then he shook the hands of his Indian friends and told them in their own language that the Indian country would see him no more. His home at Iowa Park and his ranch houses contained many garments of buckskin, bead work, and feathered war bonnets given him by Indian friends.

Around Fort Sill he made the acquaintance of post commanders, cavalry captains, and troopers, veterans of the Indian wars, Indian agents, and officials from the Department of Indian Affairs. He came in contact with Indian police, scouts, pack masters, and post traders. There was no phase of reservation or agency life that did not come under his observation.

These years of contact with cowboys, good and bad, along with knowledge gained from military and civil employees of the Army Post and Indian Agency had given him a keen understanding of men and how to handle them. His contacts with governmental agencies were to be valuable to him in handling such affairs where they affected the grass leases. This knowledge was to be put to test, for somewhere near his twenty-first birthday he was made boss of the Nation wagon and ran it until the last of the Burnett cattle were sold or had been crossed back into Texas just after the turn of the century. During these years they were handling an average of ten thousand cattle per year, scattered afar in the unfenced Nation. Few of these were stock cattle, the majority being steers purchased in South and Central Texas, brought to the ranch where they were fattened and trailed to the railroad for shipping. It was a task calculated to develop a cowman.

In these years he became known as one of the outstanding ranchmen of America. He was noted for the ease with which he handled men, cattle, and horses in large units. Authorities like Luther Clark of Quanah, his brother Si of Wellington, Farmer Jennings of San Antonio, the late Horace Wilson of Fort Worth, Tom East of the King Ranch, and Price Maddox of Colorado City, all of whom worked with him or had opportunity to observe him at work, rate him among the best wagon bosses of their long careers as cowmen. It is told of him that he once received orders from his father to gather and divide a herd of six thousand steers into two equal herds. When the cattle were thrown together, instead of taking the time to divide the herd by cutting individual cattle or small bunches, he, with two cowboys following him, rode through the herd throwing cattle to the right and left forming herds of each. When the herds were completed and counted it was found necessary to cut less than seventy-five head from one herd into the other to make them of equal number.

Young Burnett and his father were close friends and ardent admirers of President Theodore Roosevelt. In 1902 the virile, "All-American Teddy" was guest of the Burnetts in the Big Pasture. Tom Burnett brought his Nation wagon, horses, and cowboys to a point in the Big Pasture near Frederick, Oklahoma, where a camp was established that the President might hunt coyotes, see the Southwestern cowman at his work, and visit his Texas and Oklahoma friends. To the camp came Quanah Parker with his three pet wives, Too-Nicey, Topay, and Nama, with their papooses. From Texas came Captain Bill McDonald, of Texas Ranger fame and representatives from the other cow outfits. During the 10-day visit the President had opportunity to study the young cowman and the efficient manner in which he conducted his wagon with its men and horses. It was not the President's first knowledge of him, however, for when the latter was forming his celebrated Rough Rider contingent during the Spanish-American War he had tendered Tom Burnett a captaincy in that famous organization of Western fighting men.

Back in the seclusion of his Oyster Bay home around the fireside, he recounted the thrills of the ten-day trip to his own manly sons and described young Tom Burnett as the typical young American. Later, in his book, *Intimate Letters to My Sons,* he dwelled at length on the accomplishment of the young Texas cowman. An oil painting of Roosevelt hung on the walls of Burnett's Iowa Park home.

About the time he assumed charge of the Nation wagon, Tom Burnett married Miss Ollie Lake of Fort Worth. They lived for a number of years at the old Red River ranch. To them was born a daughter, Ann Valliant, who spent her childhood at the ranch. She too became a favorite of the Comanches who, with their squaws and papooses, would journey down by horseback from Fort Sill, Cache, and Medicine Bluff from time to time to see that all was well with parents and daughter. Particularly was she a favorite of Too-Nicey, one of the wives of Quanah Parker, who spent long periods at the ranch. This friendship endured until the aged Indian woman died near Lawton a few years ago. Of Quanah Parker's wives, only the aged Topay still lives near Fort Sill.

Shortly after the turn of the century the Indian lands were allotted and thrown open to settlement. The days of the Big Pasture and "big fellows" were over. By 1903 all of the cattle were out of the Nation. Waggoner had acquired new country on Beaver Creek in Wilbarger County, and Sugg, a ranch in the San Angelo country. Burk Burnett had purchased 286,000 acres and the cattle on them from the Louisville Land and Cattle Company in King County. Tom Burnett received and branded the cattle for his father, placing them in the famous 6 6 6 6 brand. The veteran Bud Arnett, who had been with the properties since their founding, was retained as ranch manager.

The 6 6 6 6 Ranch is still operated as a Burnett property. There have been additions to the original King County property in acreage and another unit of 107,000 acres has been acquired in Carson County. On the latter has been developed extensive gas and oil fields.

In his last years in the Nation young Burnett had acquired some few cattle and horses in his own name and had been in a few small ventures with his father. But it was the earnest desire of both his father and grandfather that he make his own way in the world as they had. So he set about getting into business for himself. According to his own statement, he had cared very little heretofore for anything other than the privilege of handling men, cattle, and horses on a large scale. His father, whose principal interest was by now the 6 6 6 6 ranch and other investments, leased him the old Texas ranch between the Red and Wichita rivers on which he engaged in trading and handling cattle on a much smaller scale than he was used to.

Upon the death of his grandfather, Captain Loyd, in 1912, he came into possession of one-fourth of the ranch and some monies. He continued the lease on his father's portion, stocking it with the best cattle the times afforded. His portion of the land took in the old Iowa Park headquarters. He transferred his activities to the old headquarters house emblazoning a huge red triangle on the old chimney at the south end of the house, long a landmark to those traveling the dusty wagon road.

About this time he, with several associates, went back to Fort Sill to purchase and dispose of four thousand head of cattle owned by the Apache prisoners of war held at Fort Sill. These were the property of

264 of the followers of the Apache chieftain, Geronimo. They were branded U S on the left side, and in addition, each was branded with the number by which the Indian was known on the Government records (thus, U S–15). Each of the tribesmen owned a number of cattle and it became a long tedious job having each Indian identify and pass on the number brand. Only one with a knowledge of Indian nature and infinite patience could have accomplished the job. Delivery was made by Major Goode of the U.S. Army and marked the passing of the last big herd on the Indian Reservation.

Oil came to Wichita County. Generous quantities of it were found on the Tom Burnett land and from its income he bought more land surrounding him until he had acquired upwards of thirty thousand acres in Wichita County. He continued to improve the quality of his cattle by culling and use of the best bulls available. Never a dweller in cities, he established a home in Iowa Park from which he ran his ranch and oil wells. He accepted the new order and the sedentary life with much more ease than was to have been expected of one who had lived so generously and long in one of America's most colorful periods. As an outlet for his surplus energy, he financed and promoted several of the Southwest's outstanding rodeos, at his ranch. Into these he brought Indians, cowboys, and buffalo from the old Nation, along with the best rodeo talent available in each line. These shows were also staged in Wichita Falls, Houston, and Fort Worth.

His income from oil had increased steadily by extension of his original field and he began casting about for a new and larger ranch. In 1923 he purchased the Pope Ranch in western Foard County. To it the next year he added approximately fifty sections of the old Jim McAdams Ranch. To the west of it and in Cottle County lay the remnant of the old Moon Ranch, belonging to the estate of W. Q. Richards, of 3 D fame. This was added to his other holdings in 1925. In 1929 the Y L, a thirty-two-thousand-acre tract, originally a part of the O X Ranch, was added to the ever-growing Foard County outfit. His last addition was in 1938 when he purchased another twenty thousand acres of the old O X outfit which had been operated for several years as the 7 L outfit. To old-timers, this last tract will be recalled as the old O X Dripping Springs Pasture.

His final purchase and some little leased land, gave him a total acreage in Foard, Cottle, and Hardeman counties, of approximately a hundred thousand acres. In the purchase of the ranch he gave no consideration to its future value from an agricultural standpoint, as the majority of the Foard County ranch is rough grazing land, well grassed, with some wide tillable valleys. In discussing the purchase with friends, he remarked that it was his desire to own a ranch which could never be plowed up. Sometimes when vexed by the ramifications of the oil business, he also expressed the wish that he might die owning a cow ranch without an oil well on it. So far no oil has been developed on it.

The ranch is watered by some fifty windmills, nearly one hundred earthen tanks, two rivers, and a number of spring-fed creeks. The Wichita River passes through the southern edge of the ranch and Pease River is its northern boundary. Good, Cottonwood, Catfish, Cactus, Childs, Talking John, Hackberry, and a number of other never failing creeks augment tanks and windmills. Tanks have been built steadily under the Government program until cattle do not have to go farther than one mile for water. The entire ranch is well fenced and sub-divided. Old-timers in the area consider it one of the best ranches of its size in West Texas because of the fact that it embodies several of the best old ranches of the early days. The pastures carry approximately five thousand well-bred Hereford stock cattle. Offspring are sold ordinarily as yearlings to Corn-Belt feeder buyers. Range bulls from the best herds of Texas and the Middle West are used. Cattle from the ranch are shipped from Swearingen on the Quanah, Acme and Pacific Railway.

A headquarters central to the ranch is located about half way between Crowell and Paducah, in Cottle County, approximately six and one-half miles south of the highway. These are on the site of the Jim McAdams headquarters and consist of a modern ten-room brick house with all conveniences, quarters for cowboys, manager's house, barns, and corrals. Branding is done by chuck wagon and crew, much of it in the open. Camps are maintained on the Moon, Y L and 7 L divisions. Approximately nine hundred acres are planted each year to oats and barley. Of this a sufficient amount is bound and threshed to provide winter feed for *remudas* and the balance is cut and baled for feeding to weak cows and for wintering bulls. The *remuda* consists of some eighty head of the best West Texas cow horses.

Operation of the ranch and the wagon is under Charlie Hart, veteran Burnett employee. His employment runs back over a forty-seven–year period to a time when Tom Burnett and his father found him a fifteen-year-old white boy living in the home of Quanah Parker at Cache, near Fort Sill. He had been taken into the chief's home at the age of nine years to live with his own sons. During that period he developed into an expert bronc buster. The Burnetts, in need of such a man, employed

him to work with the Nation wagon. With only three years difference
in their ages, a close friendship developed between Charlie Hart and
Tom Burnett which continued until the latter's death. Charlie Hart has
had but two employers during the sixty-six years of his life, Quanah
Parker and the Burnetts. In handling a ranch and cattle he uses much
of his early training in trailing and reading signs. Little happens on the
ranch that does not come under his eye or knowledge. He has a vivid
recollection of the Indian country which includes many stories told by
the older Comanches of their achievements and exploits as young
warriors. To know him intimately is a rare privilege.

Down at "The Park," as the Wichita County ranch is known, while
the Foard County ranch was developing, Burnett was gratifying his
desire to raise good horses—not race horses, jumpers, or high school
horses, but cow horses to his liking. Always he had the best *remudas*
available with his wagon in the Nation. From this he naturally topped
a personal string that was his pride and joy, as well as the envy of
neighboring cow outfits and steer buyers. Always he favored the
staunch, well-muscled horse, "soggy" he and his kind would call them,
and a little larger and heavier than the average native cow pony. He
based this liking on his early experience in countries where distances
were great and a horse had to have bottom. As he expressed it, he
wanted one that could carry a man as large as him thirty or forty miles
out and back if necessity demanded and come in with his head up.

The Morgan horse offered more along these lines than any other and
he adopted that breed as a basis for his breeding, varying it occasionally with lighter mares. A few years ago in Oklahoma he came across
a peculiarly bred and built stallion in which was combined both speed
and size. By many he is considered a freak horse in that he has the
legs of a running horse and the body of a light draft horse. He had
raced successfully in Oklahoma and was seeking new fields to conquer
when Burnett purchased him. By judicious selecting of mares for mating to him Burnett developed many excellent horses of the style he
liked for his *remudas* with a surplus each year of young stallions.
These, known as "Joe Hancock colts," he sold or gave to friends who
held the same ideas in the matter of cow horses. They are to be found
on the Richard King Ranch near Corpus Christi; on the McGill brothers' ranch at Alice; on the Bell Ranch in New Mexico, and on ranches
along the border near Laredo.

During the last years of his life he became interested in the breeding
of Palomino cow horses, seeing in them the possibility of a smooth

horse of his kind if the stallions were mated to mares of the proper size, type and color. Heading his stud of Palominos was the California stallion, "Gold Rush," presented to him by his daughter and son-in-law. For him he purchased a harem of twelve sorrel and dun fillies from his old country up in the Nation. Unfortunately he did not live to see the result of the mating. Colts being born on the ranch are justifying his selection of mares and fulfilling every promise shown by their sire.

Good horses were an obsession with Tom Burnett; no man ever saw him or one of his men mounted on an inferior animal. He could not resist a good type cow horse and never failed to stop to admire and attempt to purchase one when he saw it.

Horses were not all that claimed his attention at "The Park," however. The country between the Wichita and the Red rivers is flat and fertile. As the years passed by it assumed a thick growth of mesquite which threatened its productivity as grazing land. Long before the Government had recognized mesquite as a menace and included it in range programs, Burnett was clearing his lands at his own expense. To date more than one-half of the ranch has been cleared and grubbed. The program goes on for he demonstrated that one acre of cleared land has the grazing value of four covered with mesquite. Grubbing goes on also by the section on the Foard County ranch.

Good bulls were almost as much of an obsession with him as good horses. Each year new drafts of the best of these were to be found in the traps and grazing on the grain pastures around the home place. As a result of these and careful selection of replacement heifers, he, whose early training had been with Longhorns and "Coasters," saw steers of his own breeding and feeding win coveted honors at the Southwestern Exposition and Fat Stock Show at Fort Worth, several years ago. Cattle now on the Iowa Park Ranch consist of carefully selected two-year-old heifers awaiting their first calves before they are sent to the breeding herds of the upper ranch. The choice bands of brood mares are there also. The ranch is in charge of Lige Reed, native to the section and well trained in the ways of the West Texas ranch.

As he grew older, Burnett interested himself in banking and civic affairs. He maintained an office in and was a heavy stockholder in the Iowa Park State Bank. Not only was he interested in the affairs of his home town, but in those of the neighboring city of Wichita Falls as well. A few years ago he was voted the most useful citizen of Wichita County and the City of Wichita Falls. His charities were many but never publicized. When the depression hit the oil fields, he, at his own expense, provided one hot meal per day for such school children in Iowa Park as could not afford them. He extended this to some sixty needy children in Wichita Falls public schools. When eight more sewing machines would provide work for an additional crew of women in a local sewing room, he purchased and presented them to the officials in charge. It is estimated that he provided business education for twenty-five or more young people. His books will never reflect his charities nor show the amounts given to old cowboys in hard luck who had worked with and for him.

Earlier in this chapter we have referred to four generations of Burnetts, having in mind S. B., Tom L., and Ann Valliant. Six weeks before Tom Burnett's death, a granddaughter, Ann Valliant Hall, was born to make the fourth generation.

He died December 28, 1938, much as those who knew him feel that he would have preferred to—between suns and without pain or the long lingering illness that is the dread of cowman or plainsman. He died after sixty-eight years into which had been crowded the glory of plains, mountains, cattle, horses, and men, and the ways of the great outdoors. He left these in their glory before they were trampled and torn by the plows of men. That he had faults, his closest friends cannot dispute. They loved him no less for them. Without them he would not have been Tom Burnett.

When they came to say the final rites for him there were gathered together men from every walk of life: bankers, cattle barons, capitalists, and business associates. From the ranches came gaunt, bowlegged cowboys and bosses, some old and some young in the service of Tom Burnett and his father. There were Negro cow hands, grey and saddle-stiffened, who had spent a lifetime in the service of the family. From villages and towns in Oklahoma, where was once the Big Pasture, came old men in old cars who in their prime had ridden with young Tom's wagon. From Cache, in the Indian country, came Laura Birdsong, daughter of Quanah Parker, last chief of the Comanches, with her husband, daughter, and granddaughter, to represent her people. When the last word had been said she approached the flowers heaped high on the bier and in the sibilant tongue of the Comanche requested of Charlie Hart that she be permitted to carry a red rose home to her people in memory of the stout young fellow who had counseled in the long ago with her father and his head men when they were sorely perplexed and trying to follow the ways of the white man.

Men gathered in small groups, as they do on such occasions, to discuss the merits and achievements of the friend who had gone. As they discussed these they agreed, one and all, that never again would they see another like him because the thing which had made him what he was no longer existed to make more like him.

The mantle of the Burnett's has fallen on fair shoulders for by the terms of his will his daughter is sole owner and executrix of that which was his. The property will be conducted henceforth as the Tom L. Burnett Estate. It has fallen on shoulders strong with the traditions and convictions of the Burnetts—that there is no finer industry in America than the grazing on Texas acres of good cattle tended by loyal men on good horses.

Waggoner's Outfit

Dan Waggoner began his West Texas ranching career and the founding of the properties in Wise County in the 50's, 60's, and 70's, gradually moving westward until he and his son, W. T., centered their holdings in Wichita County and were the largest landholders in that county when the Fort Worth and Denver Railroad reached it in 1883. Then came the years when Waggoner, Burnett, and Sugg used the Indian's lands—more than a million acres of it—of the Kiowa and Comanche tribes. By 1896–1897 it was evident that these lands were to be thrown open to settlement and their cattle would have to come back into Texas. Burnett hedged by acquiring the 6 6 6 6 Ranch in King County; the Sugg brothers about the same time acquired tremendous acreage in the San Angelo section.

The Waggoners had retained their Wise County–Wichita interests when they went into the Nations. Faced with the necessity of acquiring more acres if they were to remain in the cow business on a big scale—and they had no other idea—they continued their onward march to the upper regions of the Wichitas and the headwaters of the Beaver, a country they had long had their eyes on. Agents were commissioned to buy lands in big blocks consisting of ranches, large and small, from the section claim holders, and the struggling nesters who farmed, or attempted to, in the then unsettled country.

By 1897 enough land had been acquired to form the nucleus of the present ranch, but Tom Waggoner, on whose shoulders the development had fallen as the years came upon his father, continued to extend the borders of the ranch until it reached its present size.

The ranch consists of 504,000 acres lying partly in six Texas counties: Wilbarger, Baylor, Archer, Knox, Foard, and Wichita. In area it embraces 789 square miles. Large as Texas is, it could accommodate only 333 such ranches within its boundaries.

In 1931 the ranch acquired from the Bell Ranch, for steer development purposes, a pasture in Harding and San Miguel counties, New Mexico. Roughly it consists of a strip thirty-five miles long with an average width of eight miles. Its excellent strong grasses and high altitude make it an ideal adjunct to the Texas breeding ranch. Its shipping point is Mosquero, New Mexico.

The property is owned by the W. T. Waggoner Estate, which consists of E. P. and Guy Waggoner and A. B. Wharton, Jr. The latter is a son of Electra Waggoner Wharton, deceased, who was an only sister of the Waggoner brothers. Mrs. W. T. Waggoner, mother and grandmother of the three, and widow of the late W. T. Waggoner, is trustee, but owns no interest in the estate. Each of the owners lives on the ranch and maintains a beautiful and modern estate. Paul Waggoner occupies a home on the banks of Santa Rosa Lake; "Buster" Wharton lives in the ranch home built by his mother prior to her death, sixteen miles south of Vernon; Guy Waggoner makes his home at Fort Worth, but spends a substantial part of his time supervising the Mosquero Ranch in New Mexico.

Headquarter operations are carried on from Zacaweista Ranch, sixteen miles south of Vernon in Wilbarger County. In twenty-three camps established at strategic points throughout the ranch are located line riders who keep up fences, doctor for worms, and look after the ranch's interest in general. Called camps, these are in fact comfortable cottage homes, some of rock construction with excellent outbuildings, horse pastures, and waterings. It is the policy of the ranch in building, to do the job so that when completed it will be permanent with a minimum of repairs and upkeep. Principal among the camps are Santa Rosa, Four Corners, Old Mitch, Pony Creek, Sierreta La Cruz, Casa

Blanca, Red Pasture, Alamosa, La Paloma, Flippen Creek, Cedar Bluff, and the Self Place.

There is an average of sixteen thousand breeding cattle on the Texas ranch. The New Mexico property has at this time approximately three thousand head, but is capable of caring for the yearling crop of the Texas ranch. Like most highly developed West Texas herds, the cattle have come up from native Texas cattle, through Shorthorns, with forty years of Hereford breeding. They are the equal of any cattle in the Southwest in breed.

Bulls, one to every twenty-five cows, are purchased from the leading Hereford breeders of the North and Northwest—about four hundred each three to four years. There is being developed a purebred herd to provide a portion of the bulls needed. Foundation cattle came from the herd of Harris and Sons, of Harris, Missouri, and consisted of forty-nine choice heifers. Recently the first draft of bulls from these cows— fourteen yearlings—were sent to the New Mexico ranch.

Offsprings of the commercial herd are sold as yearlings each June. From the yearling heifers are selected a sufficient number to replace aged cows. As a rule the cattle go to Midwest feeders. They have gone to the same buyers for a number of years—a tribute to their breeding and feeder value. The familiar Waggoner brand, three reversed D's, goes on each animal born on the ranch. Cattle shipments are made at the ranch's two shipping points, Oklaunion on the Fort Worth and Denver for the east side, and Fulda on the Wichita Valley for the west end. Cattle work is in charge of Tony Hazelwood, who has spent practically his entire life with the Waggoners. Operation of the chuck wagon and branding crews is in charge of Fred Albright, another long-time employee of the ranch. Cattle are worked entirely with the wagon, with much of the branding being done in the open. The *remuda* is of the best, made up of horses of thoroughbred breeding, for which the Waggoners are noted.

The ranch, one of the best watered in the state, depends entirely upon surface tanks and impounded water in the two streams that traverse it—the Wichita River and Beaver Creek. There is but one windmill on the property, it being for convenience in providing water for household use at one of the camps.

The Lake Kemp irrigation project, covering some thirty thousand acres, is on the ranch land. While the lake is the property of an irrigation district, all shore rights, hunting, camping, and fishing privileges are under control of the ranch. A diversion dam on the Wichita River, some fifteen miles below the main structure, permits an even flow of water through the pasture at all times. A dam has been constructed on Beaver Creek by the ranch, creating a lake of some six thousand acres for irrigation purposes. It, too, maintains an even supply of stock water for miles below the dam.

These sources are augmented by some 250 earthen tanks scattered over the pasture. The construction of these tanks and the ultimate goal of the management as to more tanks will be discussed later. In the nearly forty-year history of the present ranch, it never has experienced a water shortage nor had to move herds for grass or water. Curly mesquite grass intermingled with needle grass predominates throughout the pastures.

Some five to seven thousand acres are in cultivation. It is the intention of the ranch to increase this to approximately ten thousand acres, much of which will be under irrigation as ditches from the Santa Rosa dam on Beaver Creek are extended. There are now about ten miles of ditches. This acreage is planted to wheat, oats, sudan grass, and a minimum of grain sorghums. No effort is made to raise products for the market and none are sold except when wheat planted for pasture develops heavily after winter grazing. Oat straw is baled by automatic pick-up balers which follow the combines. This is used as winter feed for late calves and weak cows. According to Manager Robert More, "It beats throwing them a snowball."

Modern machinery and labor-saving devices are used in the work wherever possible. Two 60-horsepower caterpillars handle the breaking. These are augmented by seven lighter tractors, half a dozen trucks, and three large combines. Most of the farming lands lie in the fertile Wichita and Beaver valleys. The lands are killifered each three years to guarantee turnover of soil and deep season.

Oil came to the ranch in 1908, when a deep-water test developed petroleum. Since that time thirty-three hundred wells, ranging in size from small pumpers to gushers, have been developed on the property and are producing oil. These are confined to less than 15,000 acres of the ranch. Only 5 per cent of the 504,000 acres are under oil lease at present, leaving 95 per cent of the great potential oil area undeveloped. Most of the wells have been developed by the leading major and independent companies, who deal with the ranch on a royalty basis. Eighty wells have been drilled by the ranch in its own right.

To care for royalties paid in oil and production from their own wells, the ranch owns and operates a modern four-thousand-barrel refinery at Electra. A casing-head plant, located in the pasture near Rock Crossing, cares for a portion of the production. Underlying the ranch are several hundred miles of pipe and gathering lines.

Mesquite brush thrives on the big flats of the ranch, and is fast becoming a menace. According to Mr. More, when he came to the ranch nearly forty years ago a wagon and ten men could work the pasture and account for 100 per cent of the cattle. Due to brush encroachment, it now requires eighteen to twenty men to the wagon and these are able only to account for 80 to 85 per cent of the cattle. Dense brush hampers branding and dehorning if screw worms are prevalent. Worm-infested animals retreat into the brush and can neither be "prowled" nor worked to advantage. Heavily mesquited land requires almost five times as much moisture for grass as open land.

The ranch subscribes to the Government's range program. It is centering its efforts on mesquite and prickly-pear eradication and the building of surface tanks. To date mesquite eradication has been successfully effected on approximately fifty thousand acres. As many more acres will be treated during the coming year. The fight against mesquite will be carried on continuously regardless of the Government program.

In this work they have resorted almost wholly to the kerosene and roller process. During July and August kerosene is applied to the trees a few inches above the surface of the ground in a band approximately six inches in width. Results are apparent in from ten to fifteen days. Trees are allowed to dry and decay until the winter months. A ten-ton roller towed behind a 60-horsepower caterpillar equipped with a heavy bumper bar is driven over the treated area, breaking off and mashing down the dead trees. Largest of the wood is piled for fuel or branding wood. Light wood and brush are used for burning prickly pear. As a precaution against reseeding, horses being used in the uncleared areas are kept in dry lots until they have evacuated all mesquite beans before they are taken into the cleared area.

Eradication of the pear is accomplished by a ranch-evolved device resembling the familiar buzzard-wing sweep, only more exaggerated. This is operated by a lighter farm-type tractor much as the ordinary cultivator or sweep is used. The pear is sheared off level with the ground. One machine will cut as much pear per day as a crew of fifteen men can pile in that length of time. The piles are interlaced with brush and burned when dry. Under the eradication program, as many as 750 local workmen have been employed at one time. In excess of $38,000 was expended for kerosene alone in one year's program. A study of the cleaned area will readily show the results accomplished both in increased grasses and ease in handling cattle.

In the matter of tank building, the ranch has set a goal of eight hundred tanks—one to each section of land on the ranch. When this program is completed no animal in the pastures will have to travel over one and a half miles for water. All tanks are built by drag line. Two of these tremendous dirt-moving machines are in operation almost continuously for ditching and tank building. Experience with this type of tank has been of the best. The machine-made tanks may be dug to unusual depths, giving a maximum of deep cool water, and a minimum of evaporation. Locations for the tanks are carefully selected and in no instance are the dams built across either small running streams or dry-weather creeks. It is the theory of the ranch that the small creeks and washes are silt carriers, and that a dam thrown across them must necessarily be on a silt base. Sites are selected which have as their drainage long or gentle slopes, heavily grassed. A drag-line tank may be completed in from four to six days. Of the nearly three hundred machine-built tanks on the ranch, there has not been a dam broken by high water, nor has there been an animal lost from bogging in one of them. Narrow circumference and depth do not permit the cattle to wade or stand in the water. They use the tank much as they would use the concrete drinking tubs of the windmill-watered country.

In the matter of water conservation, the ranch does not favor the usual furrow-contour method. To attain the same result, they have evolved a ten-ton roller heavily studded with objects about the size of and resembling inverted bean pots. To the apex of these is attached a long narrow spike which punctures far into the depression made by the pot-like spikes on the rollers. The rollers, in tow of caterpillar tractors, are dragged across flat and hillside. The resulting depressions absorb run-off while the long projections enable the water to penetrate far into the ground. By this method the turf is not disturbed nor is additional weed growth encouraged as in the case of furrow terracing. Experience has proven that enough water can be retained by this method to dry up small creeks and waterways in an area so treated.

Continual improvements in watering and trails are being made on the New Mexico property. Since its acquisition twenty-five additional windmills have been erected. Five rock and twenty-one dirt dams have been built. These augment the four running streams on the property.

Improvement other than that of range conservation is constant on the big property. Crews are engaged at all times in the maintenance and improvement of the twelve hundred miles of fence which surround and subdivide the ranch. A few years ago they fell upon the idea of utilizing the vast amount of discarded pipe from the oil-field operations for fence posts and stays. It makes an excellent and everlasting fence and all was well until the junk-buying wave hit West Texas. Then line riders reported that three miles of fence on the west side had been stolen—posts, stays, wire, and all—by the junkers.

More corrals are being built at advantageous points with the idea of eventually abandoning entirely the branding of calves in the open. Comfortable quarters for the working crews at headquarters and for cowboys when the wagon is in, are also a part of the improvement program. A stone bunkhouse, light and airy, with showers, tubs, and lockers, has recently been completed. Refrigeration, natural gas, electric lights, and modern kitchen equipment are standard at the headquarters.

Wide, well-graded roads cross and criss-cross the ranch, giving easy access to camps or operations. Recently a motorized chuck wagon, the first one in use, according to Ripley of "Believe It or Not" fame, has been added to the ranch equipment. Its mobility enables it to render unusual service to both cattle and agricultural operations. It augments the conventional four-horse chuck wagon, still in use. The Waggoners believe in good wages, pay their cow hands well, and have a minimum wage for laborers of two dollars per day.

The Waggoners believe in game conservation. There are several thousand wild turkeys on the Texas ranch and some few deer. It is estimated that there are from fifteen hundred to two thousand antelope in the New Mexico lands. Black tail deer are also to be found there and trout have been placed in the mountain streams. A trapper and assistant work continuously on predatory animals and watch for game violations. Each tank on the ranch is stocked with fish. Paul Waggoner, at his home, has pens and breeding runs for the propagation of quail, pheasants, and other small game.

When the lands were being purchased back in 1897–1898, agents and attorneys were instructed not to quibble over minor defects in title. In many instances quit-claim deeds only were taken. There was renewed interest in agriculture throughout the lower Panhandle and the Waggoners wanted to acquire a block of land before prices soared. Titles could be cleared at leisure.

Young Robert L. More, an abstractor who was well known to the Waggoners and who was from their home town, Decatur, was employed to move to Vernon to clear titles and prepare abstracts to their many acres. Comments More, who has served as manager of the Waggoner Estate for many years, "I hired to them to do that, but it's about the only thing I haven't done in the thirty-eight years I've been here." Do not infer, however, that it has not been attended to, for no holding of its size is more complete in blocking and perfect title than that of the Waggoners. At no time in the history of the oil business have they been troubled by vacancy hunters. "Claim jumpers used to give us a fit, though," says More. "Back in 1902 I remember we had thirty-eight move in on us one summer afternoon. We were in the right so we had them enjoined and they moved on."

Other branches of endeavor were being added to the Waggoner cow business: a string of gins in Oklahoma and West Texas and an oil mill here and there. Incoming settlers were offering to pay well for certain sandy lands the ranch owned along Red River. These were subdivided and sold into what came to be known as the Waggoner Colony. Someone with more than cow experience had to see to these things. Then came oil to add to the burden and vexation of a man who wanted only to be a cowman and a good one. With it came duties new to all, for the Electra Field on Waggoner lands was the first oil field west of Fort Worth and followed closely Texas' initial fields at Corsicana and Beaumont. So Bob More learned the oil industry as the industry itself learned it. That's why he knows how to deal with it on equal footing when it contacts the ranch.

Dan Waggoner was dead and his son had reached the age when if he was ever to enjoy the fruits of his labor he must be about it. So he slacked up, to direct his ranch in a general way and to gratify his longing to breed and race thoroughbred horses. Until the day of his death he never learned to love oil and its ramifications nor ceased to love the ranch and its ever-improving herds. He and his sons realized that their business had long since outgrown a mere cattle ranch. So vast and varied had become their interests that an organization with an executive head was necessary.

So the burden of handling cattle, oil, lands, and properties gradually slid onto More's narrow, but capable, shoulders. He is a queer combination of lawyer without sheepskin, cowman who does not ride a horse—because he doesn't have time—a mechanic without tools, a diplomat without portfolio. He has more capabilities in that line than a college president, and enough Scotch in his makeup to guarantee the economic operation of the vast properties under his charge. He has surrounded himself with the best executives possible, who, along with him, counsel with the Waggoners as to operation. He will give any cowpuncher or laborer as much time as he wants to explain an idea that might benefit the ranch. The business is not a one-man operation.

His loyalty to his job and the Waggoners is a thing that has long been the talk of the cattle country. Illustrative of this is a story they tell about his appearance as a witness in a minor lawsuit against the ranch, filed in a neighboring county seat. When More, replying to routine questions, stated that he was in the employ of the Waggoners, the plaintiff's attorney, young and new to the country, squared away with, "So you're Waggoners' Good Man Friday, eh?"

"Yes, sir," came the reply, "I'm their Good Man Friday, Saturday, Sunday, Monday, Tuesday, Wednesday, Thursday, day and night."

Conduct of the ranch is along conservative lines. There are apparently none of the leakage and loss which contributed to the breaking up of the old-time company-owned ranching operations of the middle 80's.

The late Will Rogers was a close personal friend of the Waggoners. On a visit to the ranch a couple of years before his death, he date-lined his daily squib from it, saying in part, "I'm down here in Texas on a little old ranch where every cow has forty acres of grass and an oil well." When a plan, now being inaugurated, is complete the humorist-philosopher's statement will not have been a misnomer. On the contrary, it will fall far short of the actual condition.

Plans have been made and are partially under way to reduce the breeding herd to a maximum of five thousand hand-picked young mother cows and hold it to that level. To compensate for the reduction in cattle, it is planned to bring oil production from fee-owned wells and royalties to four thousand barrels per day, the exact capacity of the Waggoners' refinery.

Anticipating completion of this program, let us analyze the position of a Waggoner cow. She and five of her sisters will have for their private use one full section—640 acres—of the best range and agricultural country in the Southwest. On it there will be a deep cool tank of water. Too, she will have the privilege of going to creek or river if she feels that a change of water might benefit her. As a safeguard against short grass and hard winters, she will have her proportionate interest in ten thousand acres—in other words, an undivided interest in two full acres—of growing feed under irrigation each year. In addition to this, she will have the added security of a one-half interest in a producing oil well. Any well-brought-up heifer with these surroundings and securities should go ahead and do her full duty as a mother, safe in the feeling that her offspring will thrive and do well until selling time. If she doesn't, it is a cinch that she will "go to town."

As the Waggoners see it, nature put the oil there and if, through its use, they can create an ideal cattle condition and restore their country to the virgin state in which their forefathers found it, they should do so.

We titled this chapter somewhat affectionately "Waggoner's Outfit." For three-quarters of a century it has been known as such from the headwaters of the Trinity to the upper reaches of the Red, Pease, and Wichita. Thirty-three hundred more oil wells and a few gold mines may come to the ranch in the future, but so long as there is a Waggoner left living, it will be just that—"Waggoner's Outfit"—a cow outfit. The boys feel that if "Grandpappy" and "Pappy," as they affectionately refer to their grandfather and father, could have stayed on, they would have wanted it that way.

John Molesworth

It was on a typical midsummer Panhandle evening that I called at John Molesworth's home in Clarendon to ask his permission to record for publication the highlights of his sixty-three years as a Southwestern cattleman. The story I had in mind was to have its origin in England in the year 1858, and its finale there on the Molesworth front porch. It was to touch America in the year 1879, and thereafter wend its way into the principal cattle countries of the Southwest with a brief excursion into South America to look over cattle possibilities in the neighboring continent.

To one whose sole acquaintance with English home life of half a century ago was by reading rather than by actual experience, the setting that evening with a few allowances, could be regarded as typically English. The evening was cool, as Panhandle evenings are when the sun is set. Mr. Molesworth and his daughter sat on the spacious front porch, the former enjoying the English pipe which has characterized him for so many years. Both were enjoying the peace and quiet that seems to come with the evening. The rector had dropped in for a periodic call, and they discussed the church, the parish house, and the welfare of the rector's good wife. The illusion of England was heightened and modernized by the drone of a score of planes high overhead bound for points west. When proper felicitations had been passed, and the rector had said his good-byes and departed, I turned to the business at hand.

First mention of personal publicity insofar as he was concerned, was cut short by a negative nod. I had expected this, as it is characteristic of the successful old-time cowman who insists that any success he has had as a businessman and the friends he has made in the years gone by are sufficient records of his acumen and fair dealings. Invariably they add, as did my host this evening, "I have not done anything." I had "heerd different" about John Molesworth in the years I had been associated with cowmen, and I wanted the story as only he could tell it. I argued that it would be a word picture of Texas and the Southwest in days when its civilization was in the making. I argued also that it would be a record of how that civilization received and helped a raw English youth whose principal assets were health, sincerity, and willingness to work. I was aided and abetted in these arguments by my friend Harold Bugbee, who shares my respect and admiration for Mr. Molesworth, and by Mr. Molesworth's daughter who, while having no desire to see her father extolled, did feel that a permanent record of his life in the cattle history of the Southwest should be left for the coming generation.

It was on this basis that he grudingly consented to give me the story, and so it shall be recorded, except for brief interpolations to bring out certain details more clearly. There will be a distinct loss in its writing, for space limitations and lack of ability on my part cannot put into the writing the fine philosophy, good horse sense, and sparkling wit he put into the telling, nor will the fine blending of English accent and cow-camp jargon be present. Though the setting in 1879, the heyday of trail driving, was conducive of such, there will be no reek of six-shooter smoke, tales of saloon encounters or bawdy-house brawls. John Molesworth was no paragon of virtue, but he had a job to do, and had no time for such except as he saw it in passing. Fortunately, his ability to record in his memory past occurrences is such that he is able to give true color and background to anything that has come under his observation. Here is the story as he told it to me.

"I was born in Little Borough, sixteen miles outside the city of Manchester, England, in 1858, and was of a family of thirteen chil-

dren. My father was a lawyer and was of a family that for several
generations had been professional people—physicians, lawyers, artists,
and the like. At an early age I was sent to boarding school—Winde-
mere College. In those days and at that school you worked from the
time you entered it until you had finished. We had a ten-day Christmas
holiday and a short mid-summer vacation, both of which were spent
at home. It was apparent from my grade cards that I was not going
to follow in the footsteps of my professional forebears. As a matter of
fact, it was so evident that my father informed me that unless there
was marked improvement, he would take me from school and put me
to work. The grades did not improve, and my father kept his word,
and bound me out at the age of thirteen, as was the custom in England.
I was apprenticed to N. A. & W. Laws, a manufacturer of flannels and
woolens, and who were first in England to learn the art of successfully
blending cotton and wool. They were large operators and received
shipments of wool from America, Australia, New Zealand, Africa, and
anywhere else where wool was produced in quantities. The particular
portion of their business which the Laws taught me was the sorting
and classifying of wool. Through this work I learned much of wool,
its qualities, where certain wools came from and the use for which
they were best suited.

"I served the customary eight years' apprenticeship and then set out
to get work, only to find that there were many men older and more
experienced than myself seeking work in the same line. They were, of
course, given preference. In England at that time, it was impossible
to secure work other than in the profession in which you had been
trained. You could not swap professions overnight to accommodate
your own needs. I could not see any possibility of obtaining work in
my line in England for some time. In my rounds, and in discussing
the wool industry, I got the impression that San Antonio, Texas, in
North America was the sheep and wool center of that nation. With
visions of ready work in the wool factories of San Antonio, and with
$500 in cash given me by my father, I set sail for San Antonio.

"You can imagine my dismay when I arrived there with less than
$300 left of my $500, to learn that while San Antonio was about central
to the sheep growing country of the Southwest, the real wool market
of the nation was, and still is, in Boston, Massachusetts, hundreds of
miles to the north. At the time I landed in San Antonio, it was in its
heyday as a cow-town and headquarters for some of the big Texas
cowmen who were making cattle history by driving cattle over the

Kansas and Northwest trails. It had a population of approximately twenty-five thousand, of which it was estimated fifteen thousand were Mexicans.

"I came to know by sight and casual acquaintance such fellows as John Blocker, Captain Lytle, Coleman, and Mathis, and Fulton, and others who were to go down in history as cattle barons and pioneers in seeking outlets and markets for Texas cattle. Through hearing tales of their exploits and profits they were making, I became somewhat interested in getting into the cow business via the route of working on trail or ranch.

"My first speaking acquaintance in San Antonio was with one Tom Muldoon, an Irishman who operated three hacks there much as the present taxicabs are operated. I discussed with him the possibility of getting ranch work as a means of getting into the cattle business. I shall always be deeply grateful for the fine advice and help he gave me after we had discussed the matter. He explained that if I took work on ranch or trail it would be at a small wage and, due to my inexperience, only at odd jobs where I could learn but little. He knew from our conversation that I had experience with and a deep love of horses. He suggested that I purchase a good freight outfit and engage in hauling ranch supplies to the towns and ranches to the west, most of which were in the heart of the sheep country. He argued that in doing this, I could learn the country, its people, habits, and much about the livestock industry. I would also be earning my livelihood with a chance of making some money for myself toward a start in the ranching business.

"He not only argued these things, but justified his faith in me by helping me select my teams and wagon and loaning me the balance necessary to purchase them. It was not a partnership; merely my promise to repay when I had earned the money. I thought at the time that Tom Muldoon was the finest, kindest man I had ever met, and I still think so. I was to learn that his attitude was characteristic of that of the Southwest toward the newcomer who was trying to make his way in the new country. I felt then, and have always felt that no country on earth offered more opportunity and no people were more willing to help a young fellow along than the people of the Southwest a half century ago. I freighted for two years into the Llano and Junction countries, my outbound load being groceries, lumber, and ranch supplies, and my inbound, wool.

"In these years, San Antonio was headquarters for a host of young

Englishmen who had come to America seeking adventure and the opportunity of doing something for themselves. They were generally
known as 'remittance men.' The term was sometimes used in derision,
but as a matter of fact, these young fellows were of the finest of families and had been highly educated, but due to the English custom
that the eldest son inherited the family's estates, funds, and business,
they were left without funds of their own except those necessary for
maintenance. Ranching at that time was much under discussion in
England, being looked upon as a gentleman's business offering a great
deal in the way of sport and horsemanship. There was also a sprinkling
of former British Army officers who for some reason or other had left
the Army to come to America and had drifted into San Antonio. These
and the younger Englishmen were excellent horsemen and hard riders,
and were more or less attracted to the San Antonio section because it
offered plenty of good horses and a freedom they could find nowhere
else in the country. San Antonio was not the best place in the world
in those days for a young fellow in their state of mind to land. There
was lots of drinking, with gambling wide open. As a result many of
them used to the restraint of home life, became dissipated, went into
debt, and finally dropped out of sight, but on the whole, they were an
excellent group of fellows.

"Social life among the English centered around the ranch of Captain
Turquand down on the Balcones near Boerne. Turquand, a former
captain in H.M.S. Coldstream Guards, was a hail, well-met sort of
fellow, a genial host, an excellent horseman, and one who enjoyed
having kindred spirits about him. A clearing was made on his ranch
as a sort of riding field in which the younger fellows broke and trained
horses and on special occasions indulged in pig-sticking contests, a
sport prevalent at that time among British Army officers in India. As
I have stated before, I had ridden considerably as I grew up and had
a love of horses and horsemanship that has remained with me all of
my life. In my freighting business there came times when it was necessary to rest my teams. On these occasions, I stayed at the Turquand
Ranch, the attraction being the fellowship of my countrymen and the
opportunity of riding and handling good horses with them.

"Among those who foregathered at the Turquand Ranch was one
Captain Sherburne who had been a British cavalry officer in India. He
was a colorful, romantic sort of fellow and I recall that he used to
be referred to as 'the most extravagant officer in the British Army.' He
was a top horseman and a devotee of any sports that could be played

on horseback. He was particularly interested in polo which he had played in India, and which was just then coming to be known in America. He sensed the polo possibilities in the group of hard young riders who were at the ranch and in the availability of ponies in and around San Antonio. Under his direction and tutelage a couple of teams were organized and trained at the ranch. They became excellent players and were well mounted, for ponies were cheap and plentiful.

"San Antonio in these years, in addition to being a cattle center, was the leading horse market of the Southwest. Great herds of these were brought in and held on the prairies in every direction; brought there in the hope of selling them to Northern buyers who took them to Nebraska to sell to farmers who were settling that country and wanted cheap teams. I asked one buyer how they made any money. He said, 'I bring a carload of pudding-footed studs down and trade a stud for a carload of mares. Then I go back and trade a mare for a carload of studs.' From the looks of the studs he brought in, you could easily believe he was not stretching it much.

"Before Sherburne had his teams mounted to his satisfaction, we had bought and tried out a good many ponies. This process was not as expensive as it sounds. We would go to a horse herd, pick out a few likely candidates and buy them. After a few workouts on the polo field, we kept such of them as had polo possibilities and sold or traded back the balance for about what we had paid for them, and repeated the purchase and trial plan. As I recall now, we finally accumulated a very fine bunch of ponies.

"Interest in polo in this section developed rapidly and we were soon playing matches with teams from Austin and from the Army post in San Antonio. To play these matches, we selected one team from our teams at the ranch. We won most of the time. I have always had some pride in the fact that I was a member of the first polo team organized in Texas. There will be more about this team in its proper sequence.

"Despite the thrill of playing polo and the good fellowship around the Turquand Ranch and in San Antonio, I had not neglected my freighting business nor changed my plans about thoroughly learning every angle of the ranching business. I continued my freighting for nearly two years, and then sold my outfit for what I had paid for it. I paid Tom Muldoon back and had $1,200 in cash above my original investment.

"Just prior to this, I had suffered a severe accident through being thrown from a young horse I was breaking. The nature of the accident made it imperative that I undergo a very serious operation. I went back to England for this, and to await its final outcome. I had no intention of remaining in England but was anxious to get back to San Antonio to resume my apprenticeship in the ranching industry. This was the second of thirteen crossings of the Atlantic that I have made.

"On my return, Ashville Mitchell, a young Englishman who was eventually to become my brother-in-law, and I took a scouting trip into the head of the Devils River country in search of land where we might establish ourselves a small ranch. In these years, the Devils River section was real back country, and we felt we could locate to better advantage closer in. We eventually secured a section of land in Nueces Canyon in Uvalde County. Getting located and settled there had about exhausted our capital. I made a second trip to England to visit my people and get money with which to stock my ranch. My relation with the Laws under whom I had served my apprenticeship had always been of the best sort, and I was able to borrow one thousand pounds from them to be repaid on easy terms. [Author's note: In those times a pound was the equivalent of about $4.86 in American money.] I might add here that before the obligation fell due, the elder Laws died, and in his will there was a provision that my indebtedness be cancelled out. I might also add that in my whole business career it was the only beneficence ever given me other than the $500 given me by my father when I left England originally. The balance, like my experience, came the hard way.

"Back in Texas again, we invested our capital in cattle and settled down to ranching in earnest. It was while I was on the Uvalde ranch in 1886 that an invitation came to me to rejoin my old polo team who were going to challenge the only other organized team in America, the Westchester team in New York. Things were moving along nicely at the ranch. I wanted to go and have the honor of playing on the first polo team to go from Texas. In view of the many fine players and horses that have gone from Texas to the East and abroad in the years since, I think my desire to be on the first team to organize in Texas, and interest the South in polo was justified.

"It developed that the trip was to have more or less the aspect of a promotion proposition. We were to take our horses to New Orleans and play a series of games there, the proceeds of which were to finance our trip by boat to New York. In New Orleans our mounts and ourselves were quartered in stables and buildings at the New Orleans race track. Polo did not appeal to New Orleans folks, but the social life of the Crescent City did appeal to the majority of the team members. As a result the venture went cold, stony broke.

"We lay around the New Orleans race track figuring on ways and means to get our bills paid and ourselves and mounts back home. The upshot of the matter was that we sold our carefully selected and trained polo ponies to an outfit operating a pony express line in Florida and made our way, sadder and wiser, back to San Antonio. I have never regretted being a member of the team, but I have been a little shy ever since of anything that savors of promotion.

"In these years I met and was married to Miss Emma Maude Mitchell, an English lady who had come to the States a year before I did, in 1878 I believe it was. She was a cousin of Captain Turquand, and it was on visits to his ranch that I became acquainted with her. In all that I shall record hereafter she was my constant companion, loving wife, and helpmate, going with me into new sections and ventures to endure the hardships of ranch life as our needs dictated until her death in December, 1941.

"The ranch in Uvalde County continued to grow. The days of free range were drawing to a close and I sold my half interest to my brother in 1886. I enjoyed the years I lived in the Uvalde country; I made friendships that were to endure and be of value to me in later years. I had opportunity, however, about this time to get employment which was remunerative and would at the same time prepare me for bigger things in the cattle industry. I went to work for Francis Smith and Corkle of San Antonio, a firm engaged in the general loan business, specializing in cattle, and ranch land. Certain of their loans came under the classification of 'guaranteed loans,' meaning that their financiers were guaranteed against loss and collection troubles should one of these loans default. As a result, when one of them went bad, the firm immediately made good the loan and took over the assets to protect themselves. My work took me into the cattle sections south of San Antonio. It was interesting, instructive, and colorful work, which I enjoyed and profited by.

"The country was beginning to come under barbed wire and occasionally we had trouble with the wire-cutting fraternity. At one time the resourcefulness of a member of the firm kept us out of serious trouble and broke up one of the largest organized gangs of wire cutters in the Uvalde section. Through the presence of these fellows in the country, I made the acquaintance of a number of Texas Rangers and peace officers who have been famous in Texas history.

"I continued with Smith and Corkle until 1897, at which time I was offered a position with the R O Ranch in the Panhandle with head-quarters at Clarendon. The ranch was owned by the Rowe brothers of England: Alfred, Vincent, and Bernard. It was one of the big ranches that lay in Donley and Wheeler counties. By the time I got there it was under fence and with the exception of a small herd of stock cattle, was handling steers principally. The Rowes would buy them as yearlings and hold them, range conditions permitting, until they were three- or four-year-olds, or until the market was suitable. It was their boast that they bought only the best steers obtainable. By doing this they built a reputation for their steers similar to that enjoyed at this time by certain sections for their feeder calves. I have a picture back there in my office of a choice lot of R O steers in the Clarendon shipping pens in 1908. You will notice they are pretty well spotted up, but they offer a good comparison with modern-day cattle, and show conclusively the improvement in cattle over a thirty-five-year period. They also indicate the change that has come about in the ages at which cattle are marketed now. Their steers were either sold to Kansas buy-ers, or sent by the ranch to Kansas pastures on their own account. In the last years I was with them, quite a few went to the Corn Belt.

"Vincent and Bernard Rowe disposed of their interests, one going to Kansas City, and the other returning to England to make his home. Alfred continued to operate the ranch until his untimely death on the Titanic.

"I left the R O in 1901. My work there for various reasons had not been what I had hoped for. I shall always be thankful, however, that it brought me to the Clarendon country, right in the heart of the last of the 'big-time' cattle business, and that it brought me contacts with fellows who in years to come were to become my partners and good friends as long as we shall live. Clarendon had been founded in 1878 as headquarters for certain ranching interests that were being de-veloped there by a Mr. Carhart. It soon became one of the Panhandle's important cow-towns and was headquarters for practically all of the big cowmen operating in that section of the country.

"About the time I got there, many of these were living in and operat-ing out of the town. Among the big ranches tributary to it were the English-owned J A Ranch, the Cresswell and Day Ranch near Giles, the Goodnight Ranch, the Bugbee interests, Mill Irons, Shoe Bars,

Shoe Nails, and others. Estelline to the southeast of Clarendon was headquarters for the Mill Irons and shipping point for many of the ranches southwest of it. Giles, a few miles to the east of Clarendon, was also a heavy shipping point for the outlying ranches. As a matter of fact, you could generally find plenty of cowmen and shipping going on along the Fort Worth and Denver from Childress to Texline in those days. Among the Scotch and English cattlemen I became acquainted with in the Clarendon and Amarillo sections were Murdo Mackenzie of the Matadors and his son John, Dick Walsh, manager of the J A Ranch and his assistant, another Englishman named Clark, Fred Horsbrugh, manager of the Spurs, Frank Hastings of the S M S, John Hollicott of the L X, and Arthur Lighterwood who for a time managed the Matador. There were also in and around Amarillo at the time quite a few of the various executives of the Prairie Land and Cattle Company. All of these were fine fellows and made excellent cowmen. Like San Antonio in the old days, Clarendon and Amarillo were meccas for the English cattlemen. Clarendon was shipping point for many of them and Amarillo the meeting point for the ranchmen and Northwestern steer buyers in the spring. It has often been said that more cattle were bought and sold in the lobbies of the Amarillo hotels than in any other city in the United States.

"Of the English cowmen who foregathered in Amarillo twenty-five years ago, there are few living today. Dick Walsh left the J A to manage the ranch properties of the Brazil Land and Cattle Company in South America, and later he was manager of the Cecil Rhodes ranches in South Africa, where he died. His range boss, Clark, who was a colorful sort of a fellow, had learned his ranching originally on the big foreign-owned ranches in the Northwest, in Montana and Wyoming. He became involved on the side of law and order in one of the big cattle and range wars prevalent in the Northwest about that time. After a narrow escape from being killed, he was placed in jail and narrowly escaped being lynched by the citizens who, for a time, had the upper hand. He was turned loose but had to leave and came to the Panhandle to run the L X Ranch, later coming to the J A. After a few years there he left and eventually met his death by being burned in a prairie fire in Old Mexico. He had a good story of his adventures in the cattle wars and it should have been recorded and published as significant of the era.

"Fred Horsbrugh left the Spurs and moved to Amarillo to enter the commission business. He died there a few years ago. John Hollicott moved to Douglas, Arizona, to be near his old friend of Tascosa days, Jim East, who had become police judge in the Arizona town. While East was away on a short visit a good many years ago, Hollicott drew his funds from the bank, disappeared, and was never heard of again. It is thought by many that he drifted across the border down into Mexico where he might have been killed. He was a rare sort of fellow with a keen sense of humor. In his work of getting around over the ranch he used a buckboard to which he worked teams of four light, fast mules. These were kept in excellent condition and were always ready to go. A steer buyer came to Amarillo one day requested that John drive him over the ranch and show him the cattle. For some reason John did not like the fellow and did everything possible to keep from taking him out, but as he insisted, John ordered buckboard and mules brought around from the livery stable. They came prancing and 'rarin' to go. They were held in until the pasture was reached, at which time Hollicott, with a little urging, permitted them apparently to run away. This sent the rig careening over the rough Canadian country at breakneck speed. He would pull them up occasionally to permit them to blow, but when a bunch of cattle were sighted, he permitted them to run again—always away from the cattle. This was kept up for some hours, the buyer never being able to see any of the cattle at close range, but he didn't weaken. Finally they drove up to a windmill and Hollicott got out of the buckboard with a bucket which he filled and offered to the mules. When they refused to drink, Hollicott knowing they were jaded and not likely to keep up their running unless severe measures were resorted to, dashed the bucket of water into the off mule's face and exclaimed, 'Well, if it insults you to drink out of a bucket, maybe you will take it this way.' The mules broke away as he had expected, but he caught the buckboard as it went by and let them run until the buyer called it a day and asked to be taken back to town.

"Murdo Mackenzie passed away a few years ago. His son, John, manager of the Matador, received his training on the ranch under his father. Almost the oldest of the Englishmen who came to America in the early eighties and who is still living in this section is John Arnot of Amarillo, who came over in about 1882 to work on the L X, then English owned. I also knew Major de Maud, an English Army officer who at one time leased the Moon Ranch in Cottle County. The ranch passed on to the hands of another Englishman, James Gray, who eventually sold it to W. Q. Richards, whose 3 D Ranch adjoined it.

"During my years with the R O they shipped their cattle and did their commission business exclusively with the John Clay Commission Company of Chicago. Through this I made the acquaintance of and formed a friendship with John Clay that was to continue until his death in March, 1934. It was a friendship that was to be of inestimable value to me in my future operations, and one from which I was to learn much of the cattle industry that I had not heretofore known. Probably the influence of no individual has been so keenly felt in the American livestock industry as that of Mr. Clay. It is also doubtful that any individual had so much to do with foreign investments in American ranching as he. Born in Scotland in 1851, he came to America to stay in 1879. For three years he was an employee of the British Government, making a study of livestock conditions in America and Canada. A genuine lover of livestock, he owned a small share in the Bow Park stock farms in Ontario, and eventually became its manager, attending many of the early livestock shows both in Canada and America for the purpose of exhibiting Bow Park animals. In this way he met many Western ranchmen and interested them in breeding better livestock, and became interested in the range cattle industry for himself. Because of this interest, he gave up his work at Bow Park farm to become agent for several Scotch and English investment companies. He traveled extensively through the ranch country examining ranch properties, reporting on prospective loans and purchases, and learning the industry. He was instrumental in forming the Swan Land and Cattle Company, one of the largest ranching ventures ever to be financed in America with Scottish capital. The company at one time had a capital stock of $3,750,000 and a book count of eighty-nine thousand head of cattle. In later years, when hard times fell upon the Swan outfit, Clay was called upon by the Scottish interests to assume management of it, which he did and succeeded in placing it upon a paying basis in the eight years he was there.

"He was also instrumental in founding the Wyoming Cattle Ranch Company, the Cattle Ranch and Land Company, Western Ranchers, Ltd., and many others. By the time I had come to know Mr. Clay he had retired from active range work to form the John Clay Livestock Commission Company with offices in the principal livestock centers of America. It was a wonderful organization and through its founder's knowledge of cattle and range conditions, as well as of finance, was an important factor in the adjustment of the livestock industry from free ranges and large ranches to its present state. I believe I share the opinion of many other cowmen that, if the weight of his years had not been upon John Clay, he would have been able, with his business acumen, financing ability, and knowledge of the cattle industry, to forestall many of the evils which beset the industry after the First World War.

"About the time I left the R O, the John Clay Company, through its order-buying service, was sending thousands of cattle each year to its customers on the Northwestern ranges. The cattle were bought and received by the company at the shipping points in the range country and were loaded and billed to the customers. It was the custom of the commission company to have a shipper or custodian accompany the train to its destination. I applied for one of these positions and it was given me. I felt that I could give good service to the company and at the same time make contacts which would be of value to me later on. For this service I received $5.00 per day. I stayed on this work nearly a year.

"The Boer War came along and with it the demand for horses for the British Army. Billy Anson, an English cattleman and horse breeder in the San Angelo country, had a contract to buy horses for the British and I took a direct-buying contract under him. It was necessary to ship all horses to Fort Worth where agents passed on them finally before they were accepted and paid for. In the latter days of the buying, it had become a practice of these agents to turn down horses heretofore acceptable to the Army, at the price they had set on them. They would then offer to buy the turned-down horses from the contractor at a much lower price, apparently for speculation. As a matter of fact, they were held a short time and then sold to the Army at full price. The quality of horses I had been sending them were so near specification and the demand so good that they had not had opportunity to turn any down on me. I was doing too well, I guess, for they caught me in this manner on a shipment of six carloads and caused me a great deal of difficulty. The war was drawing to a close, so I was ready to turn to something else.

"In 1902 I formed a partnership with Will J. Lewis, a cattleman of Clarendon, who had come into the section from Maryland as a youth and who by his energy, ability, and willingness to do hard work, was making a success of the cattle business. The partnership was formed at a time when the larger cowmen and outfits were coming to realize that their lands had to yield to the incoming settlers. Land prices were good and they were liquidating their cattle, and subdividing and selling off their lands. We watched these pretty closely and were always on hand to buy their cattle if we could make a dollar on them. In the years that followed we bought and disposed of the V V N herds from their ranches along the Texas-New Mexico border. There were, I think, some fifteen hundred head of these. We also bought fifteen hundred to two thousand F D W cattle from F. D. White of Denver. From the Bar V Ranch in New Mexico we bought seventeen thousand at $14.00 per head, which we sold in a short time at $17.00. We also bought eleven thousand head from the Prairie Land and Cattle Company. At about the same time we handled out the excellent purebred J J herd of the J A Ranch. There were many other smaller transactions that I do not recall just now. It became generally known throughout the Panhandle that we were buyers of cattle in large quantities and business came to us largely without our having to seek it.

"Along with this, we did a general order-buying business both on our own account and acting for the John Clay Company. Many of these cattle went back into the country and to people whose acquaintance I had made in the Northwest in my shipper days, and during the Boer War time.

"One of our major deals was the purchase and delivery of fifteen thousand two-year-old heifers for the United States Government for distribution to Indians on Northwestern reservations. Through the John Clay Company, Webster and Knorpp had been given the original contract and they commissioned us to handle the cattle for them. We filled the order with little difficulty with the exception of the time we received a wire order calling for immediate delivery of one thousand fresh milk cows. That had us stumped for, at that time, I do not believe that there were a thousand milk cows, wet or dry, in the entire Panhandle.

"During this partnership, we operated two ranches; one of 113,000 acres in the Canyon country, and the old Diamond Tail Ranch of 15,000 acres in Donley and Hall counties. We used these as holding ranches and to handle remnants of cattle we accumulated in handling the various herds we bought. In the peak years of our partnership we handled a good many cattle. [Author's note: T. M. Pyle, a member of the firm, and Alan Wilson of the John Clay Company, estimate that in its peak year the firm handled in excess of seventy-five thousand cattle.]

"We took into partnership with us T. M. Pyle, a cowman originally from Blanco County in South Texas. He had served a number of years as inspector for the Cattle Raisers Association in the Panhandle section, but through his ability and wide acquaintance gained in Association work was becoming a successful cowman in his own right. He had a nice little ranch in Hall County near Newlin. In the years we were together, we handled thousands of cattle over a wide area. Each man did his part and more to see that we kept our word in the matter of delivery dates and the quality of cattle delivered to our customers. Those were happy years and the hard work did not hurt us. Our partnership was dissolved in 1911 after eight years of association that were profitable and pleasant at all times.

"My family was growing up and I wanted to rest awhile and be with them more than I had in recent years. This rest took the form of a trip home to England for all of us, at which time I had the pleasure of showing to my children my early home and seeing with them some of the things I had loved as a boy—horse races, cricket, and tennis matches. While I was in England I received a cable from my old partner, Lewis, stating that the Spur Ranch, the Espuela Land and Cattle Company, had been sold to the Swensons and was for lease with its cattle, and asking if I cared to join him in the venture. I was still enjoying my rest and was not quite ready to get back to work so I declined the offer.

"When I returned to Texas I found that Lewis had leased the Spur Ranch and purchased their cattle. I leased 100,000 acres of the Spur range, placing upon it two thousand head of cows which had been a part of the divisible assets coming to me when Lewis and I dissolved partnership. I operated in the Spur country with these and other cattle for two years, at which time I sold cattle and lease to Swearingen and White who operated the O X Ranch in Cottle and Foard counties. The Spur had been a great ranch and had a colorful history. The brand had its origin in 1879 when J. M. Hall trailed eight hundred heifers into the headwaters of the Middle Pease River country. These were followed by other herds, both of Hall's and of other cowmen who were coming into the country.

"In 1883 Hall sold his brand and cattle to Stevens and Harris who eventually sold them to the Espuela Cattle Company, a corporation composed of Eastern financiers with A. M. Britton of Denver as president and S. W. Lomax of Missouri as secretary. Two years earlier, Lomax and Britton had sold the Matador to a syndicate of Scotch financiers. They proposed to and did sell the Spur to another Scottish syndicate, the Espuela Land and Cattle Company of London. It was operated for a time as a free-range outfit with an almost unlimited territory, and had a range count of upward of seventy-five thousand cattle. When it eventually came under wire its fences enclosed 569,120 acres, and by book count some sixty-nine thousand cattle. The ranch had started under an ill-fated star, and its entire course was beset with difficulties and losses. Some very able men managed it at various times, but these were seriously handicapped by the restrictions placed upon them by the Scottish board of directors. The principal error was in not allowing funds for the drilling of wells, erecting of windmills, and building of tanks after the ranch was fenced.

"The Spur brand was used for twenty-five years. When I took over my Spur lease there were in the country many fellows who had worked on the ranch through the years it had been in existence as cowboys and wagon bosses. One of these, Jake Raines, came into the country with the original eight hundred Spur heifers and at this writing I think is still on the ranch now being operated by the Swensons. Others were Luther Jones, Handy Cole, Bob Wilkinson, and Doc Ellis. All of these were excellent cowmen and knew the Spur Ranch thoroughly.

"During the years the ranch operated they employed close to four hundred cowboys as shown in the Spur Ranch book written by W. C. Holden. They were all good hands, most of them having a keen sense of humor. It is from these and other hands of the area that many of the quaint sayings attributed to the cowboys of the 80's had their origin. It was the Spur cowboys who, when a new manager was sent to the ranch and they heard his wife refer to him by first name as Spottiswoode, immediately dubbed him 'Spot' and changed it as the years went on to 'Old Spot.'

"The story I like best of them is the one told of the trick played on a new hand by the Spur boys. It seems that the ranch had an estimable old lady keeping headquarters and cooking for the outfit when the wagon was in. When the work became too much for her a boy was hired and brought out from town to assist her by milking, wiping dishes, peeling potatoes, carrying in wood, and the like. Now if there is one type the old-time cowboy had no use for, it was a man who would do menial labor or anything savoring of femininity. As a result, the Spur cowboys were soon referring to the new employee as 'Miss Sally.' Tiring of it, the boy quit and asked to be taken into town, giving the nicknaming as his principal reason for quitting.

"Another boy was brought on and this time the cowboys were warned that a repetition of the 'Miss Sally' episode would result in the immediate dismissal of him, or those, responsible. Apparently all was going well until one day the second boy asked for his time and that he be taken to town. Before giving him his check the manager asked if by any chance the boys had been calling him 'Miss Sally.' 'No, Sir,' he replied, 'but they won't have anything to do with me, and every time I pass the bunk house on the way to the milk pen with the buckets in my hand they all raise up and tip their hats to me.'

"Shortly after selling out I made a trip to South America at the request of Murdo Mackenzie to make a report for the Brazil railroads and while there had an opportunity to make a trip over a good deal of Uruguay and the Argentine which was most enjoyable and instructive.

"I was looking for a pretty good big outfit this time. Out in West Texas the Laniers had taken a long-time lease of three hundred sections of Texas State University lands and spent in excess of $100,000 for fencing, watering, and improvements. The lease had a long time to go and I needed country, so I bought them out and moved to my new headquarters forty miles north of Sierra Blanca, in Hudspeth County, on the Southern Pacific and Texas and Pacific railroads.

"It was a new sort of country to me, but I liked it as a steer country. In the twenty-five years I was out there I handled steers almost exclusively. In these years I handled the steer output or a portion of it for the Palomas Land and Cattle Company, whose ranches were in Old Mexico, and the Cananea Cattle Company, another Mexico outfit. Years when these were not available I went on buying trips into Sonora, Mexico, to get cattle I needed, buying them from smaller outfits and individuals. I also bought steers from my neighbors in the immediate section—the Gages and others.

"I did business with and sold many steers to Dick and Lee Russell in the years they were handling so many big steers. I was thrown in contact again out there with my old friend and partner, Theodore Pyle, who was then operating a ranch south of me in the Marathon country. Our relations were neighborly and pleasant, just as they had always been in the Clarendon days.

"Another good cowman I came to know and formed a warm friendship with was the late Alfred Gage. In several instances Mr. Gage and I were partners in unusually large steer deals. Sometimes these made money; again they did not, but you could never tell from Mr. Gage's attitude any difference when settlement time came. If the deal had been profitable he slapped me on the back and said, 'Good.' If it were unprofitable he said, 'Better luck next time; this won't ruin us.' His encouragement was equal in value to his financial assistance. His ranch was well managed and I had a wholesome respect for his executive ability and knack of surrounding himself with able men. His ranch foreman, Jim Roberts, was one of the best I have ever known (his ability is evidenced by the fact that he now owns and operates an excellent ranch of his own in the Marathon country). The ranch is being conducted now with the same general efficiency by Jim Roberts and Warren Henderson, who is business manager of the Gage Estate.

"Most of the time we had the Hudspeth County ranch my family lived in San Antonio, so the children could be in school. Eight years of the time, however, they lived with me out there. It was a lonely sort of a country with neighbors few and far between and we welcomed the few visitors who came to the ranch and the fine friendship of the neighbors like Joe O'Keefe and others with whom we visited and who visited us. Our principal points for relaxation and shopping were El Paso and San Antonio.

"Speaking of visitors to the ranch, I recall with a great deal of amusement yet the first visit of a young Scotchman to the ranch. He was comparatively new to the States then. Because he tells the story on himself and will, I am sure, have no objection to its being told here, I am going to say that the visitor was John B. Kennedy, now of Fort Worth. He lives on a model stock farm in the northern outskirts of the city and is a successful importer and exhibitor of English and Scottish hackney ponies.

"At the time, he was connected with the John Clay Company and was in El Paso on business for the firm. It was a cold, blustery afternoon with a trace of snow in the air when he telephoned the ranch to say he was leaving in a car from El Paso and to ask directions to the ranch. I did my best to dissuade him from starting so late, telling him it was snowing, that the roads were mere trails, and that he might hang up en route. Being a hard-headed Scotchman, he thanked me and came on—with the result that his car did stick in a snowdrift, causing him to trudge the last eight miles to the ranch on foot. He arrived about three o'clock in the morning, tired, cold, hungry, and lugging a huge canteen of water. While he was warming up I told him I would prepare him something to eat. 'Don't trouble too much,' he said, 'a piece of toast, a bit of jam, and a pot of tea will do nicely.'

"Now he had called for three items that to my certain knowledge had never been in our larder on the ranch, and I doubt if they could have been found on any ranch in the Big Bend country. It stumped me for a moment, then I thought, 'Young fellow, your education had just as well begin right here.' So I informed him politely but firmly that he was not in Scotland and that all the refreshments he would get at that hour and in that temperature would be cold biscuit, cold beans, and colder sow belly. He is one of my closest friends and we often laugh about his first visit to the ranch.

"In 1936 the American-owned cow outfits began coming out of Mexico seeking range on the American side. I felt that I had been in the country long enough, perhaps a little too long, for the trend in cattle was changing. The demand for big steers had been supplanted by the feeder calves, so I sold my range and rights to the Palomas Land and Cattle Company. The deal came up quickly, and my acceptance was based on my ability to give almost immediate possession. I had on hand, which they would not purchase, some two thousand cows for which I must find pasture. I succeeded in disposing of a thousand of these, and wired my old partner, Lewis, in Clarendon asking if he knew of pasture or lease available in that section. He wired back almost immediately in his characteristic cooperative way. 'Mill Irons have eighty-four thousand acres for lease. If you can use half, I will take balance.' I accepted immediately.

"After twenty-five years absence I was glad to get back into the Clarendon country. I thought when I first landed there in 1897 that it was the finest cattle-breeding country I had ever seen, and I still think so. It is fairly well watered by nature. There might be a better cow country, but I have not found it yet. It was good, too, to be back with my old friends, and where I could see more people than I had been used to for the past twenty-five years.

"I used the Mill Iron country for five years, during which time I worked off my cows. Then Will Lewis took over my portion of the lease, and I was again out of the cow business.

"Recently, I have bought the Oak Creek Ranch, a portion of the old T. S. Bugbee ranches in Hall and Donley counties. This has been leased for a twenty-year period to my son, Jack. He has it stocked with well-bred modern cattle. Henceforth, any connection with the cattle industry insofar as the Molesworth name is concerned will be carried on by him. It is in good hands, for Jack has learned the business much as I did, in the hard way. He began his cow work wrangling horses for the Molesworth-Lewis outfit, and has worked his way up until he is a cowman in his own right. For the first time since I bought the six mules in San Antonio sixty-three years ago, I do not own any livestock, unless you count the three ducks you saw in the back yard as livestock."

Mr. John tamped his pipe, lighted it, and when it was going good, said with just a trace of sadness, "That's about all," and then added, "Unless we sort of throw my old partners on the round-up ground and see what they are doing. Will Lewis now owns and operates the R O Ranch, having purchased it in 1917. It was on this ranch that as a boy he did his first cow work, and it is most fitting that he should own it now, and a fine tribute to his ability.

"Theodore Pyle came out of the Marathon country shortly after I did, and now owns an excellent ranch in Quay County, New Mexico, just across the line and adjoining the Matador Plains ranch. He is a successful cowman, prominent in the livestock industry, and has for many years been a member of the Board of Directors of the Texas and Southwestern Cattle Raisers Association, the organization he originally worked for as a young man.

"What I am going to say here now, might sound a bit egotistical, but it is not intended that way. In the years that have passed, because of drouth, high prices, low prices, and the general vicissitudes which beset the cow business, each of us have been 'pretty badly bent' at times, but not one of us was ever 'plum broke'."

The hour was late, very late, when we had finished, Mr. John walked with me to my car. As we shook hands he said, "If this stuff is really going to be published, I wish you would say to my friends that if it was all to do over again I would ask nothing better than to come to the same country and to do business with and know the same fine fellows I did this time."

A grand old cowman, and a rare gentleman is Mr. John Molesworth.

Gonzales Cowmen

There is a story behind the almost life-sized, metal, Longhorn steer mounted atop the city hall in the center of the square in the little South Texas city of Gonzales. It is a story reminiscent of the days when Gonzales was a cow-town and trail-driving center for the South Texas herds seeking markets to the North. It is reminiscent of the days when the men of Gonzales counted their wealth in mossy-horned steers, either on the range or grazing their way up trail to the railheads of Kansas; of a day when men paid homage to the source of their wealth—the Texas steer.

Gonzales is steeped in Texas colonial history, but that is not her sole claim to honor and position in the development of the state, for from her environs have come some of the leaders of the industry in which Texas leads the world—cattle. Shortly after the Civil War, Gonzales took the lead as a financing center for the trail herders and for cattlemen seeking new ranges to the Northwest. Bankers took their customers' notes and counted out the money in gold rather than handing them checkbooks as is done today. In the settlement the banks were paid in gold, and it was not unusual for the president or cashier to be awakened in the middle of the night to receive the gold from some cattleman who had just returned from a trip up the trail.

From Gonzales came Major George W. Littlefield, whose L F D cattle eventually covered far-flung ranges in Texas and New Mexico, and who was in a large measure responsible for the development of the South-Plains country of West Texas by opening to settlement his 300,000-acre Yellow House Ranch, and for the introduction and development of irrigation in the Roswell section of New Mexico. When he had amassed a fortune from the handling of cattle, and the years had come upon him, he retired to Austin and became a benefactor of the great Texas State University. He paid homage to the Texas steer in metal by having the great bronze doors of the office and bank building in Austin, which bears his name, cast with a panorama of his ranch holdings, prominent among which is a panel depicting an L F D steer herd on the trail. His nephews, Tom, Phelps, and Will White, each prominent in Southwestern cattle history, were Gonzales born.

Colonel J. H. (Jim) Parramore left Gonzales in 1879 to establish a ranch in the then West Texas frontier county of Runnels. In 1883 when farmers began crowding him, he, with his kinsmen the Lewises of Gonzales and with C. W. Merchant, pushed their herds across Texas and New Mexico to claim the Apache- and renegade-infested San Simone Valley of Arizona as their range. The San Simone Land and Cattle Company founded by them grew until its average calf branding each year was in excess of fifteen thousand head. It was on their range that Geronimo, last and most bloodthirsty of the Apache raider chieftains, surrendered to U.S. cavalrymen.

To the Big Bend country went the Kokernots, Herbert and John, to claim a range that they still own in the Highland country. To far Montana went Tom Matthews to establish a range and stock it with South Texas cattle. Jim Bailey Wells, Doc Burnett, Gus Jones, Milam Fitzgerald, and a score more equally as well known to the cattle industry, called Gonzales their home and headquarters. The student of Texana will find that the books covering the trail-driving era are filled with the achievements of trail bosses and cow hands from the Gonzales country.

Steer business was good in '85. The coast fellows below Gonzales, with their millions of acres of range and their mild climate, were producers. The men of Gonzales were traders and of hardy pioneer stock. They had found markets to the North, and had heard of new and virgin ranges to the far Northwest—a good combination.

Among the cowmen whom steers had made prosperous were R. A. (Bob) Houston, who, with his brothers, Dunn and Will, had been sending herds up the trail each year since 1880. On a trip to the lower coast country in quest of steers, R. A. dealt with a cowman friend who was just completing a new ranch house, almost baronial in size. Houston wanted one as good—maybe better. Back with him to Gonzales, he brought the carpenter who had superintended the building of his friend's home. He instructed him to hire such help as he needed and advise him when he was ready to begin work. On the day set by the carpenter, Houston accompanied him and his men to the site he had selected, and with the toe of his boot, traced out in the sandy ground the plan of the house he had in mind.

While the house was under construction, Houston had occasion to be in Kansas City on cattle business. In the Missouri Valley as he traveled en route, he noted the white houses and red barns of the farmers, and was particularly intrigued by an occasional weather vane in the form of a gilded, crowing cock mounted high on the gable of a barn, or a flashing stallion with flying mane and tail on another, or perhaps a lordly bull with tail and head held high, each in miniature.

"Every man should be proud of his calling," thought Houston. "If these little fellows are proud of their chickens, work horses, and Jersey bulls, I surely ought to be proud of my Longhorn steers." And as an afterthought, "If I do put something of that sort on my house, it will be a real one."

The idea grew, and in Kansas City, Houston asked the aid of a commission man in having a steer made. They called in a designer, whom Houston took down into the yards that he might show him a typical Texas Longhorn steer as a model. When the drawing was completed, it was found that Kansas City did not, as yet, afford a metal shop or workmen capable of fashioning a life-sized steer from sheet brass, or anyone who would assume the task of covering the steer when completed with gold leaf. A New York firm was commissioned by letter to create the steer, and ship him knocked down, or in pieces, to Gonzales.

The steer arrived in due time, and W. C. Franks, who was a tinner of Gonzales at that time and who still lives there, was commissioned to braze the sections together and mount the steer on the roof of the new house, a great Southern rambling home of many rooms and porches, which was by now nearing completion, and which was eventually elegantly furnished.

When they were ready to hoist the figure to the roof, it was discovered that, through some error—possibly from lack of experience in such matters—the New York firm had failed to place the Houston brand on the animal's side. In the sands of Gonzales, amid the debris of the new building, there took place what was probably the most unusual branding in the annals of cattle history: the brass steer was laid on his right side while Franks, the tinner, with maul and punch, pounded the owner's brand, T 4 1, into the metal of the left side, then flopped him over to repeat the branding process on the right side.

According to Mr. Franks, when the steer was finally mounted, marking the completion of the new home, the entire day was spent by Mr. Houston and his cowmen friends in celebrating the event—barbecue was eaten, games were played, and things like that, no doubt. Among those whom Franks recalls as having been present were J. S. McHenry, the carpenter who had been in charge of the building, Milt Fly, Gus Jones, Milam Fitzgerald, Captain Bill Jones, Arthur Johnson, and Mr. Franks, the tinner.

For forty-five years, the gilded T 4 1 steer swung with the winds and flashed in the sunlight above the old Houston home. Men prophesied the weather by the way his nose pointed; housewives, leaving home for the afternoon, glanced toward him to determine whether or not they had better pull down the windows before leaving.

A few years ago, the Houston home was torn down, and a son of the elder Houston gave the steer to Mr. John D. DuBose, Sr., an old friend of the family, who, in turn, gave him to City Marshal H. D. Cone to be placed on top of the city hall, where he is now.

He faces into the winds, even the north winds, contrary to the habit of the range steer who always turns his tail to the northers. Sometimes in a vagrant breeze or whirlwind, he swings a complete circle as though he might be looking to see whose saddled horses stand at hitching rack or with dropped reins around the square. Soft breezes from the Gulf keep his head mostly to the north. [Editor's note: There seems to be a contradiction here.] Perhaps if he was a reincarnation of the last of the Longhorns, he would choose to face that way that he might look out over the trail which millions of his kind made on their way to market and to establish the cattle industry. Children on their way to school pause to look up at him in wonder, and their elders answer their queries by telling them of the glory of the day of the Longhorn steer.

The Bosses

Trail, range, and wagon boss—each had his place and did his job well in the development of the cattle industry. Without them it could not have progressed as it did, so fast moving and vast was the industry with its far-flung fronts.

Many of the cattle fortunes were made for the successful cowmen by the bosses who worked for them. Had men like Ike Pryor, Major Littlefield, Dillard Fant, the Snyders, Blockers, and half a hundred more who could be named, with all of their personal knowledge of the cow business, genius of the trail, and unlimited finance, not been able to surround themselves with efficient wagon and trail bosses to whom they could turn over thousands of cattle with the assurance that the animals would be delivered eight to fifteen hundred miles from the starting point at a given date, and in better condition than when they started out, their activities and profits would have been limited.

The fine thing about it is that the owners of the fortunes admit that fact. It is not unusual when you inquire of an old cowman as to the merits of some former boss who worked for him, to have him reply, "He was all wool and a yard wide, and made me many a dollar in his day."

Now it would be fine, if space permitted, to go back and review and at the same time pay tribute to the early trail bosses who pointed the first cattle out of the state toward a market, and who used the trails they made until steel came to their own ranges, after which they pointed their owner's lead cattle toward West Texas, New Mexico, and Arizona in search of new ranges. Fortunately, this story has been told far better than it can ever be told again in that volume, *The Trail Drivers of Texas*, compiled by the late George W. Saunders.

This book was a labor of love by Mr. Saunders, who gave little thought to profit. Had there been profits, however, they would have gone toward another ambition of his—the erection of a monument to trail bosses and drivers, somewhere in San Antonio.

The glory of the trail drivers cannot be better told than it has. Their outfits' names and brands are graven in the granite of the monument the survivors have erected at Doan's Crossing on Red River, where the bosses used to ride back to meet the herds and say they would cross because they had seen the turbulent stream, at flood most of the time in those days, "wasn't over the willers" which at best meant two or three hundred yards of swimming water.

The range boss was almost purely a West Texas product and was in the picture from the time cattle came to West Texas until the land was surrendered to the nester, cotton patch, and wheat farmer. He functioned mostly with the company-owned outfits. His work was largely that of securing and holding the outfit's range, administering over it, and keeping the wagons, both trail and range, at work. His work was not so picturesque as that of the trail boss, but he was as essential to the industry in his time as was the other. He came from the higher type cow hands and was usually a man of education and ability. When the work of the range bosses was over, many of them went into the cow business for themselves and as a rule were highly successful.

Outstanding among the range bosses of West Texas was the late Gus O'Keefe who for years reigned over the vast Long S domain of the Slaughters on the South Plains. At one time he had in his charge more than forty thousand cattle with a small army of cowboys under him, and a dozen or more wagons and crews on range and trail. He is said by old-timers who worked under him to have been the best range executive the industry has produced. It was the ambition of every cowboy to grow into a leader of men and to know ranges, cattle, and horses as he did. With the break up of the range he went into business for himself and accumulated a fortune before his death. His sons are still engaged in the cattle business.

Other West Texas range bosses who were well known in their day were Givens Lane of the Day Land and Cattle Company, Joe Johnson of the R 2, Campbell of the Matadors, Joe Erricson of the S M S, S. W. Lomax of the Spur, Richard Walsh of the J A, Bud Arnett of the 6 6 6 6, D. B. Gardner of the Pitchfork, and Rollie Burns, now of Lubbock, who guided the destinies of several of the company-owned ranches of the South Plains.

It was given the trail bosses to write the opening chapters of the range days, and to the range bosses to carry the story of the range while in its hey-day, but to the wagon bosses was given the unhappy task of writing finis to the most glamorous story the nation has known— the open range and the break up of the big outfits that tried to operate under fence, windmill, high overhead, taxes, and the steady inflow of an immigration that came into their range towing breaking plows and cultivators behind its wagons.

No books, movies, nor songs have been written of the wagon boss, but it was he who acted as liaison between the cowman and nester in the final days of the big cow business. It was he who helped wind up the outfit's affairs, bring the last of the cattle to the shipping pen, sell the saddle horses, and store the chuck box. Then he tucked his final check in his watch pocket, and faced a world he knew little or nothing about.

By the time the range country had come completely under fence, and the cowmen had title to their lands or had cowboys "filed" on that they did not own, the cowmen had begun to show their years. Hard rides, cold nights, and loneliness had placed their stamp on them. If they were ever to enjoy hard-earned fortunes and their families, it was time to begin. Times had changed too, central markets and commission men in the cow-towns had made marketing easier. So the cowmen moved to the cow-towns of their choice and turned over the active management of their outfits to their wagon bosses, sometimes a combination ranch and wagon boss.

These took charge of outfits ranging in size from forty sections to half a million acres. Their work went on for a good many years much as it had in the past, except for the fact that their activities were limited by fences and there were no more pool wagons nor trail outfits. They branded calves as soon as it was time each spring, delivered yearlings to the railroad for shipment to the northwestern steer ranches, shipped dry cows in the fall, and placed the winter men in camps. They kept peace with the nesters, looked after tanking crews and windmills, and acted as the local head of the outfit. Some owners lived in Kansas

City and eastern points, and the country and its people seldom knew or looked to any but the wagon boss for their contact in ranch matters.

These wagon bosses were "naturals" and, though chosen from the cow hands, stood out from the rank and file. One who knew the cow country could ride up on an outfit at the chuck wagon or in the branding pen, for the first time, and go straight to the boss, though he be hard at work and his dress no better nor worse than that of the twelve or fifteen men with the outfit. His appearance and attitude denoted leadership.

They were selected by the owners who had watched them from the time they came to the outfits as horse wranglers or kid cow punchers; sometimes they were sons of old bosses. The owners had seen them develop in cow sense and show evidence of having the qualities necessary for a good boss when called on in emergency.

They were given their opportunity by being made "straw bosses" during the busy times when the outfit had to be split to work range and make railroad deliveries at the same time. When an old boss quit they took his place. The wagon boss was the product of the hard school of the range, a school without textbook, slide rule, or lecture room.

For the most part they lived apart in a small world of their own, a world with fifteen or twenty people in it. Theirs was a more or less Dr. Jekyll and Mr. Hyde existence. From the time the cook gave them breakfast, at early dawn, until after supper in the twilight, they were constituted authority and had to maintain their positions as such. Between supper and breakfast, or when not at work, they were friend, neighbor, and one of the boys. It required a fine sense of distinction to draw this line and not let the dual personalities overlap, or display traits that would weaken their position with the men during working time.

They were usually quiet with a certain measure of reserve, for the old time cow hand had little use for a man—boss or puncher—who was given to "shooting off his mouth." The wide silences and space of the Plains did not breed chatterboxes. This was one of the reasons the young nester hands never did fit in with the older men; they talked too much.

Yet the boss could not be sour or sulky, either on or off duty, for the old cowboy was sensitive almost to a fault and mistook mood for anger a little quicker than the average. For this reason the boss had to have better than average intelligence in order to understand the nature of the old-time punchers. They were a race apart, and mighty independent. As a rule, each man had a high sense of what was expected of him and liked to leave it at that. To arrange for each man's work and place, day and night, without the appearance of giving orders or being "bossy" called for tact and understanding.

The boss selected his men because he thought they knew their business and his orders to them were more or less in the nature of suggestions. Let the occasion arise though, and he could call a hand's attention to derelictions with a withering sarcasm that was far more scathing and effective than the average "bawling out." A hand caught spurring his horse unmercifully would be told "that it might be a good idea to borrow the cook's butcher knife if you really want to cut that horse up fine," or to one covering his own lack of cow sense by "jerking" his horse's mouth with the bits until it was covered with blood, the boss would suggest. "If you want to split him why don't you use an axe." The hand spurring his horse in the shoulder would be advised that the part of the horse between the cinches was his to spur, the balance belonged to the company. These rebukes were never administered before the rest of the outfit. The hand did not have to be told not to let it occur again. He knew.

The boss could ease out of a tough spot a good hand who was having an off day and would not admit it, without drawing his ill will, as easily as he set the erring right. Perhaps the fellow would be cutting yearlings from the herd or roping calves for branding, and was tearing up the herd pretty badly. The boss would move into the herd gradually lining himself up alongside the worried cowboy, to say, "Think you'd better ease out and roll yourself a cigaret and let your horse blow a little; I'll take 'em a while." That hand knew, too, that he was being told in a nice way.

Sounds a little sissy, don't it, for a boss to handle grown men that way, but not if you know the kind of men we are talking about. Then, too, the boss, if he is the right kind, had an ace in the hole if these tactics did not work—he was not afraid of the devil or high water, or you might say, man or high water, for he had to face the sheepman once in a while, or the man with the ticky cattle who was going through the pasture whether or not. Then, too, he had a few brushes with cow thieves who would not believe rustling days were over.

He did not have to be a bronc buster nor top roper, but it helped lots with the men if he was or had been. They liked capability in their bosses. He rode the top horses in the *remuda*, as was his right. It was not much encouragement to a hand to develop a good cutting or roping horse for the boss took him as soon as he noticed him.

Bob Beverley, an old-time cowboy living now in Lovington, New

Mexico, holds wagon bosses, as a whole, in the highest esteem. Bob should know, for he has worked under many wagon bosses and has himself been one.

He has this to say of them. "I met a lot of these old fellows in my time, and the good sound judgment that they used in many ways was a mystery to me. One of them would light his pipe after supper on roundups, lean back against a roll of bedding, smoke a few puffs, and call every guard, both the cattle guards and horse guards, without calling a single man's name, something like this: 'Cross L man and Scribe M man, L Bar man, take the cattle on first guard and wake up 6 9, J F, and U L A man on the second guard. They can call W Cross, L I L and Call man on third, and they will call the cook at three o'clock.' Horse guards would be named the same way, and I would stand back somewhere in the dark to one side and think to myself what a great governor of some state that fellow would make."

It may interest Bob and other old-timers to know that more than one wagon boss did become governor of his state. John Sparks, a Williamson County cowman, took his trail herds to Kansas and ran his own wagon until farmers began to crowd him. Then he pointed his lead cattle toward Nevada, and founded a ranch in that state. In later years, he became the foremost Hereford breeder of that state, and one of the leading breeders of America, and was eventually elected governor of Nevada. John Kendrick, well known to cattle circles of America, originated as a wagon boss in Texas "so close to the Gulf of Mexico that the roar of the surf could be heard plainly as the boys rode 'round the herd at night." He served as governor of the state of Wyoming and died as United States senator from the same state.

It would be impossible to list even a small number of the outstanding wagon bosses that the industry has known. Fortunately so uniform was their work and ability that it is possible to select any half dozen in a given area and through a description of them pay tribute to all. Cow sense has no geographical bounds and it matters not that in one section of the range country men ride saddles with a center-fire girth, use a sixty-foot rope, take turns or dally, while in another they use flank rigging and a thirty-two-foot rope, and tie fast. Nor does it matter if in one section a depression in the earth is called a "coulee," in another an "arroyo," or that the Texan calls the same thing a "draw." They are the same to the cattle and it is the cattle that the cattleman has to outguess if he is to get them out of breaks, bad lands, or brush to shipping pen or new range with their calves at their heels.

Some of the best wagon bosses that the cow country has known were to be found in the country that lies from the Cap Rock east to the Wilbarger County line, with Motley, Childress, Cottle, and Hardeman counties as the north boundary and south to include Dickens, Stonewall, King, and Foard counties. Here were many of the large ranches of the West Texas area in the early 80's. Within the area were the O X, Moon, 3 D, R 2, S M S, Matador, Pitchfork, 6 6 6 6, and Spurs. Jim McAdams' Hat, Tom Richards' Stripe, the Witherspoons' U L A and 9 outfits comprised the medium-sized layouts.

The R 2, owned by Dick Worsham of Henrietta, and later by the Worsham-Stevens Cattle Company, claimed a range from the west line of Wilbarger County to the east line of Childress, with the Red River on the north. Their range headquarters were at the R 2 dugout on Wanderers Creek, a mile south of the present town of Chillicothe.

Joe Johnson was range boss and general manager. Their principal wagon bosses were Jim Olds, now living in Crowell, Lou Hollenbeck, Newt Gibson, and Julian Moody. The latter was put in charge of wagon and outfit, doing both range and trail work, by the time he was twenty-one years old.

The R 2 attracted a middle-aged following of cow hands; seasoned fellows who had worked on the Kansas trail and in the Indian Territory. They were top hands and good fellows to let alone unless you were spoiling for a scrap. Their outfit resented the coming of the nesters and did all in their power to discourage them. They broke up in the late 80's, Joe Johnson taking the remnant of the cattle to Foard County to form the S T V outfit which is still operated by his son, W. B. Johnson of Crowell. There is some distinction accorded in the old country, at this late day, to the fellows who can lay claim to having been R 2 men.

That a wagon boss must, above all things, know his country, and not be dependent on his men for this knowledge is proven by the methods used by Julian Moody, who, when the R 2's broke up was recommended to and hired by a Southwest Texas outfit as a wagon boss. They had been experiencing quite a bit of difficulty due to the fact that former bosses had permitted the men to run them. If they could not they ran them off.

Moody reached the outfit's headquarters at a time when work was slack and men and wagon were in. He had the *remuda* thrown together and had the top cutting and roping horses pointed out to him. These he tried, claiming for his own string such as he liked, regardless of whose mounts they came from. He then selected an easy-riding saddle horse and a pack horse on which he tied his bedroll, frying pan, and coffee pot. Leaving instructions with the men to repair corrals and fences until he returned, he spent a week prowling the outfit's pastures alone, studying the cattle, locating roundup grounds, water holes, and trails to the railroad. When he knew that he could start the outfit to work without having to ask the advice of his men as to the various pastures and locations, he began work and ran the outfit successfully for a number of years. Moody lives near Sweetwater now on his own stock farm. He is seventy-two years old and retains all the characteristics of the old-time cowman. A mention of his name brings a smile and chuckle to old-time cowmen who knew him and admired his technique in handling men and cattle.

Over between the Wichitas in Foard County, Ed Bomar ran the 9 outfit of the Witherspoons. He knew his country and men, and had begun his trade in the old Indian Territory when twelve years of age. It was said by his men that he could deliver an "eating out" to an erring cowhand and smile all the time he was doing it. He had a faculty for picking good men and demanded that they know their business. Of the owners he demanded good food and horses, it being his theory that no boss could attract and hold good men without these essentials. When the ranch was sold to settlers and stock farmers, in 1903, Bomar attended to the details of closing it out as a ranch. He served Foard County as sheriff for a number of years, and is now sheriff of Clay County. Old-timers recall the ease with which he handled his herds on roundup ground and on the move. He was also noted for his skill with the rope.

In 1882 the Swensons began fencing the thousands of acres they owned in West Texas for the purpose of stocking them to get some revenue from their holdings which had lain as open range since the Civil War. A. E. Dyer, a kinsman of the Swensons, came out from Williamson County to superintend the fencing and found the ranch. With him he brought Joe Erricson, a Swedish boy nineteen years of age and only a few years from the old country. During the fencing period Erricson had charge of four ox teams used in hauling fence posts and stringing them along the boundary lines. By the time the fences were built he knew the country they enclosed perfectly and, when Dyer came in with the herds, was able to make a hand locating the cattle on the new range, and in establishing headquarters and camps for the outfit. He worked under Dyer for several years and when the latter died was made range boss for the Swenson ranches, which consisted at that time of the Jones County ranch, now known as the Flat Top, the Throckmorton in the county of the same name, and the Tongue River in Cottle County. At the peak of his activities he had twenty to twenty-five thousand cattle under his charge, with an average of seventy-five cowboys and five hundred saddle horses.

For a number of years he had complete charge of the details of the ranches. Then A. J. Swenson, the present manager, who came to the ranch in 1883, assumed charge of tax matters, land office affairs, and the general business details of the vast holdings. Erricson, eager to devote his entire time to the cattle, gladly relinquished these duties, and a life-long friendship grew into being between the two.

Erricson employed the very best men he could find and put them on the payroll only after assuring himself of their ability and disposition, for according to those who knew him, he had a horror of discharging a man and would often do a lagging hand's work for him until he could ease him out at lay-off time. He had the respect of the more than five hundred cowboys who worked under him at various times. Outside men and their bosses respected him and enjoyed working with his out-fits, or having S M S men work with their own. He had a peculiar tact in handling the nesters as they settled around the ranches and experi-enced little or no trouble from thieving as other Cap-Rock outfits did.

According to the Swensons, his judgment as to cattle was almost uncanny, an attribute highly necessary to a first-class wagon boss. He had to know cattle and he had to know how to trim a herd for delivery so that the buyer would be hard put to find his 10 per cent cut when he rode into the herd. If the buyer quit cutting at 5 to 7 per cent and offered to take the cut at a slightly lower figure than the herd had been contracted, it was a distinct compliment to the wagon boss. It was said of Erricson that he could size up a pasture, estimate its grass and water for a given period of time, cut a steer herd to go on it, and estimate almost to a pound what they would weigh when ready to ship. This was true of him in the day of the Longhorn and just as true when those cattle were replaced with the modern beef animals. During his tenure many changes came to the cattle on the range, experts and specialists in their lines came to effect the changes, but none of them questioned Erricson's judgment in the selection of cattle. On the contrary, they relied almost wholly on his judgment in cutting a shipment—carload or trainload.

During the years he rode for the Swensons, artists, poets, and writers visited the ranch, for it was colorful and one of the few that remained after the breakup. Each of these carried away an impression of Joe Erricson as they saw him going about his work. An artist of international fame painted a life-sized portrait of him in typical pose and titled it the "Range Boss." It hangs in the Adirondack home of E. P. Swenson of New York, a tribute by an owner to a boss who had helped him along with his fortune. A poet termed his riding "the poetry of motion."

Fifty-four years Joe rode S M S horses with only a six-month break in his employment. The story of this break is characteristic of the cowboy. The price he paid to get back into the saddle seems high unless you know the love of a cowman for the feel of a good horse between his legs, the dust of the roundup grounds, and the sight of the blue haze that hangs perpetually over the Cap Rock. The intermission came shortly after he was married to a lady who could see no romance in ranch life and insisted that they move to town. After six months of pavement and attempts to make his living at trades he knew nothing of, he drifted into the S M S office at Stamford and sought his old friend, Swenson. "Andrew," he said, "I'm so lonesome."

"Lonesome for what, Joe?" said his friend.

"The ranch," he replied. "If you have a place for me I am going back. I've made the decision."

Swenson had just purchased the Spur Ranch of nearly half a million acres and needed him to operate it. So he went back to the ranch where he spent the remainder of his life. He died in August 1931, at the age of seventy-three. He died as those who knew him best felt that he would have preferred to have died. For two years he had been in poor health, riding only occasionally. Two weeks prior to his death he had been confined to his home. Knowing that a herd was being worked a few miles from his home, he called a man to get the old ranch buggy and drive him to the roundup grounds. After they had driven onto the flat and up to the herd he signaled the driver to stop and rose to his feet. His eyes swept the herd and the men working in it, dwelt on it a moment and then turned to gaze at the hazy Cap Rock in the distance. Without a word, he sank to the seat of the buggy and a few moments later was dead. A fitting end for a fine cowman who had exceeded his allotted three score and ten years, all but a fraction of which had been spent in the saddle and with men, cattle, and horses of one ranch.

His work goes on with the S M S. Of the four wagon bosses there now, John Selman of the Flat Top, Bob Crisswell of the Throckmorton, and Dip Holmberg of the Tongue River divisions received their training as cowboys and wagon bosses under him. Doc Ellis of the Spur division came to them from that ranch when they acquired it. He worked under Erricson and succeeded him at his death. They carry on as Joe would, hoping to do as well, not expecting to do better.

The Moon cattle, belonging to Charlie Cannon, came into Cottle County in the spring of 1878. In its lead rode young Ike Pickering, an elongated Denton County boy who had been sent in charge of the herd and to locate a range. He threw them off the trail at the Hackberry Mott, fifteen miles southeast of the present site of the town of Paducah. Other Moon cattle came until there were upward to ten thousand head, summering on the big flats and wintering in the breaks of the Wichitas. For forty-six years Ike Pickering stayed with the outfit. He stayed until the last Moon brand was run and the cattle and ranch sold to W. Q. Richards of the 3 D. Four times in these years the ranch, cattle, and horses were sold, Pickering staying with the new owner each time. In 1882 ownership passed to Lindsay, Bedford, and Hinton. In 1889 it was sold to Major William S. de Maud, a British Army officer who sold it to a fellow Englishman, James Gray in 1894. Maud returned to the British Army and was decorated for valor in the Boer War.

Pickering, trained on the prairies of Denton and Cooke counties, worked men and cattle quietly. He prided himself in this and often told his men that a spring's work could not be done in one day. He did not work cattle in the heat of the day, with the result that his men and horses and herds were always in excellent condition. He could do anything that could be done with range cattle. His men knew it, and knew that when he sent them on an apparently impossible task it was with the knowledge that he could do it himself.

As a boss he figured that his outfit was no better than its cook. He was correct. Nothing can tear up an outfit so completely as a poor cook or having a good one leave on short notice. Pickering knew this and kept the same cook with his wagon over a period of twenty years. He awakened cook and men each morning about time the morning star came up by singing a little song to them (not suitable for print, but old Moon men will recall it). Not only did he have a cook of twenty years service, but many of his men worked even longer periods with him. Many left his outfit to become bosses in their own right, for training under him was recognized in the cow country. He did not permit drinking on his outfit, but when they were in town shipping, and the loading was done, they were free to "whoop it up" all they pleased. He would give them all the time necessary to get over their celebrating, often holding the wagon in town until the last of them were in shape to ride. His men took their troubles to him, he advised them, and they believed in him. If he made an enemy in the forty-six years he worked in the section no one knew it. If there was a "Dean of Wagon Bosses" in the Cap-Rock country he merited the appellation.

When Gray came to the ranch he looked upon it as a sporting proposition and soon had the headquarters equipped with a pool room, hot and cold showers, and anything else conducive to the English idea of comfort. He accompanied the wagon during branding season, and it is said by old-timers that each camp of the wagon could be traced by the beef hides and empty beer barrels that had been left behind. Pickering formed an attachment for Gray and carried the cattle work on efficiently, while Gray enjoyed himself. So well did he like Gray and so great was his confidence in him that he turned over the greater part of his wages to him for a long period of years.

When the ranch was sold to Richards, Gray moved to Long Island to found a duck farm. Before leaving he attempted to return Pickering's money, but Pickering insisted that Gray invest it in whatever he might go into, telling him that he would call on him for it when he could no longer ride.

Gray sold the Moons to Richards, and Pickering stayed with him until the latter colonized the greater part of his ranch lands and disposed of his cattle. He was suffering from an old wound inflicted where a bull had hooked him in the groin. His years were upon him and he decided to retire. A short time later he showed up in Clarendon to look up John Molesworth, whom he told that he had written Gray for his accumulated savings and expected to spend the balance of his life somewhere in Colorado. A few days later he saw Molesworth on the street and inquired if he could get a job from him, or if he would help him get on the English-owned R O outfit near Memphis.

"What's the trouble," inquired Molesworth. "Haven't you got your money from Jimmie Gray yet?"

"No, and I never will," replied Pickering. "I don't mind losing the money so much, but it sure does hurt me for Jimmie Gray to lie to me."

"What is all this?" inquired Molesworth.

"Well, here's a letter I got from Jimmie in answer to one I wrote him about my money. You can see for yourself how it is," said Pickering.

Molesworth read the letter which, in effect, said that Gray would market his ducks within a few weeks, after which he would remit $1,500 of Pickering's money to him.

Molesworth passed the letter back to Pickering, telling him that everything would be all right and that Gray would send him the money when he sold his ducks.

"Like hell he will," said Pickering. "Why, Mr. Molesworth, don't you know there ain't $1,500 worth of ducks in the whole world?"

Pickering's money came in due time, and he spent his last years in Denver, Colorado, dying about ten years ago.

On the upper reaches of the Wichitas and on the north corner of King, Cottle, and Foard counties, G. Backus ran the 3 D wagon for W. Q. Richards. The ranch was founded originally by a Mr. Adams, who sold it to Richards in the late 90's.

It was Adams who taught his wagon bosses to pull out from head-quarters a mile or two and make their first camp on the afternoon before they started spring work. He figured that a lot of time could be saved if the cook only had to come back two miles for something he had forgotten rather than the fifteen or twenty miles the outfit would be from the ranch at the end of the first day's work. This also gave the boys a chance to get the smoking tobacco, calomel, and Black Draught they had forgotten to put in the roundup drawer of the chuck box.

Backus grew up on the edge of the pasture, his parents operating a stage stand in a dugout on Good Creek, a mile north of where Les McAdams' ranch house now stands. He was a born leader and cowman who attracted good men to his outfit. Cow work was sacred to him and he brooked no interference from outsiders when working a herd. Once in Quanah, when he was shipping a herd of skittish two-year-old heifers, a town boy afoot insisted on walking between the herd and cut to visit with a friend working for the outfit and on herd duty. Backus requested him to get further away and offered to take him up behind him. When the fellow refused he dropped a neat loop over his shoulders and took him on the run toward the shipping pens where a number of cowmen, including the sheriff, sat perched on the fence. He flipped his loop off and galloped back to his work. The fellow insisted that the sheriff arrest Backus, but being a cowman in his own account and having witnessed the occurrence, the sheriff quelled the belligerent by telling him that if he didn't shut up he would put his rope on him and tow him into town.

Backus worked until the 3 D began breaking up and was succeeded by Tuck Sheets, who ran the wagon until the last 3 D calf was branded. Sheets lives now at the Hackberry Mott of Moon Ranch fame.

Backus moved to California and was on the Los Angeles police force for many years and is in the employ of the city of Los Angeles at this time.

Bud Arnett spent his entire working life managing one ranch in King County. He assisted in founding it for the Louisville Land and Cattle Company in the early 80's. Later it was sold by them to Sam J. Lazarus, Arnett remaining in charge. S. B. Burnett purchased it about thirty-five years ago and established it as the 6 6 6 6. Arnett again stayed with the new owner and remained in charge until about eight years ago when he retired to his home in Amarillo. His knowledge of his country, men, and cattle won him the respect of all cattlemen in West Texas. The late Billy McClaren served him as wagon boss for many years and later Horace Bryant, son of Hawley Bryant, a former Pitchfork wagon boss, handled the wagon.

Since Mr. Burnett's death the ranch has been operated by an executive board. John C. Burns, of Fort Worth, has active management of the ranch's affairs. The wagon is in charge of George Humphreys, an aggressive young wagon boss who is also sheriff of King County. The ranch is wholly intact, none of it having been sold to settlers or stock farmers.

In Dickens County the Pitchforks, founded in 1883, was in the charge of D. B. Gardner, who served as manager and range boss combined from the time the range was founded until his death about ten years ago. Their principal wagon boss was Hawley Bryant, who worked for them until he retired to go into business for himself. His son, Horace Bryant, ran the 6 6 6 6 wagon for the Burnetts for a number of years and married the daughter of Bud Arnett, manager of that ranch. The ranch, practically intact, is now in charge of Virgil Parr.

The Scotch-owned Spur outfit, lying just under the Cap Rock, was in charge of managers until it was sold to the Swensons. These attended to the business end and marketing for the ranch. The active work with wagons was handled by J. P. (Handy) Cole, who had as his lieutenants, Joe Stokes, W. A. Wilkinson, Van Leonard, N. R. Pierce, the latter a nephew of the famous Shanghai, B. G. Davis, Pink Hayes, J. D. Martin, and Luther Jones. Cole seemed possessed of a personal magnetism which attracted good cowboys to him. He said little around the wagon and at work, smoked incessantly, and stayed largely to himself. No one of his own outfit, however, mistook this timidity for fear. They knew he was afraid of no man. That was proven in the days when the Spur was beset with cattle thieves and land jumpers. Cole handled these situations well and when he left the Spur he went to the O Bar O in Kent County to straighten out difficulties that a former boss had gotten them into with the nesters and small ranchmen. When the job was finished he moved to Dickens City and became interested in a bank there. Later he was elected sheriff of Dickens County, a job he held until his death.

Sometimes a certain type of boss was required for a specific purpose. So it was when Pat Leonard came to the O X. The ranch had been founded in 1876 by Major Forsyth and the young cowman, Doss Swearingen of Gainesville. During the open range era of the ranch the latter was in active charge of the range and its cattle.

About the time fencing began Sam White of Weatherford became a partner, taking over the Forsyth interest. Swearingen had developed into a good trader and his time was worth more at that than running the wagon, so Pat Leonard was hired for the job. He was dark, swarthy, and a little on the swashbuckling order and was not afraid of the devil.

As the ranch came into wire bounds and was gathering its cattle from the range, the outside men were continually running into cattle at roundups which they knew belonged to them beyond a doubt, but which they could not cut without a fight. The O X brand was carried on the left ribs of their cattle. Over the range and at roundups, cattle began to show up in the C O X, S O X, L O X, D O X, B O X brands, and many other combinations that the O X would lend itself to.

So prevalent did this custom become that the ranch instructed the wagon boss and men to cut any animal that had in its brand the O X as central figures. Now it took a boss and men with guts to ride into a herd and do this. The fellows who had burned the brands had a liberal supply of "innards" too. For a time O X men rode about their work and into the roundups with Winchesters under their right legs. Only once did gunfire flame out. On that occasion Leonard was not the one to fall.

When this thieving was well in hand the ranch found itself possessed of a number of "claim jumpers" who had filed on lands in the pastures—lands which the ranch was holding in some instances in the names of cowboys who worked for it and "lived" out their claims after which they sold them to the ranch. This custom was prevalent throughout West Texas and was entirely legitimate.

These jumpers had no idea of becoming actual settlers. Either they wanted to sell their claims to the ranch at a bonus or wanted to turn a few cattle or horses loose in the pasture and use them as a nucleus for a growing herd via the long rope and hot-iron method. They seldom fenced their claims but built a shack or dugout from which they operated. The bonus seekers, the ranch usually got out of the way by trading them equal acreage on the outside or on the outskirts of the outfit. The other kind of jumper could not be handled so easily. It was necessary for the boss or some of his men to be constantly on the intruder's heels to watch every move in the hope of catching him red handed. Sometimes these methods did not work, and it was up to the boss to figure out something that would.

John Molesworth delights in telling a humorous story of how Lord Alfred Rowe, English owner of the R O ranch in the Clarendon country succeeded in moving an old-time land jumper who had filed on a choice spot in that ranch. It happened at a time when Rowe was at the ranch on one of his visits. Informed of the situation he asked that he be allowed to handle the jumper. He spent several days preparing an appeal to be made to the intruder. When it was completed he drove to the latter's camp and delivered the oration with apparently no effect until he summed the matter up, stating that the land was his through an inalienable right, due to the fact that his forefathers had fought for it. The claim jumper studied for a few moments and said, "If you feel that way about it; your 'grandad fit' for it; I'll move on." Which he did without stopping to inquire which side Lord Alfred's grandad had "fit" on.

Leonard left the ranch in the middle 90's, lived around Childress a number of years and eventually committed suicide in a Quanah hotel. He probably came nearer fulfilling the pulp writer's idea of a Texas cowboy than any who rode in the old days.

Sherman Swearingen, brother of Doss, ran the wagon a few years and was succeeded by Rufe Bedford, who had learned his trade of breaks riding and handling wild cattle on the Wichitas in Knox County.

The O X by this time was crowded down into the breaks of three prongs of Pease River, each of which had dozens of high-walled creeks, canyons, and gullies on its flanks. It was rough country filled with wild cattle. It required wild riders and tough horses—lots of them, and a wilder boss to lead them if the cattle were to come out. During a portion of Pat Leonard's regime and that of Swearingen and Bedford, a wild riding kid, Johnnie Jones, a nephew of Julie Moody of R 2 fame, had been wrangling horses for the outfit. His riding, skill with the rope, and knowledge of the breaks had come under the notice of the owners. They noticed also that the men liked to fall in behind him and keep up if they could when they were thrown off on the drive.

When Bedford went back to the outfits of the Wichitas, Jones, who had graduated from horse wrangler into cow hand, was placed in charge of wagon and men. Young himself, he attracted young riders to his outfit, recruited mostly from the families of the old O X hands who, when they had gotten too old to ride steadily, had settled down along the open spots on the rivers, working part-time for the ranch and farming after a fashion the balance of the time. Boys from these homes knew the traditions of the O X and developed rapidly under Jones' guidance. He encouraged them to be rough, permitted them to rope all they wanted to, and set a pattern for them in roughness and horse-play. It was his delight when an unusually mean steer or bull had been roped and thrown to leave his own rope on the animal's feet and tell the other fellow to get his horse. Usually when the fellow had gotten about half way to his horse, Jones would slacken his rope, allow the animal to rise and chase the cowboy. The fellow was not in much danger, however, for Jones' ready loop usually picked up the animal's forefeet before it could do any damage.

Ninety per cent of their horses were affected with "ring tail," caused by heavy spurring. Ring tailed they might have been, but an equal number of them were roping horses of the very best caliber. Probably on no West Texas outfit was the art of "fore-footing" so highly developed as among the men of the O X. Leslie McAdams, who worked with them as a kid estimates that they had more cattle killed from fore-footing on the ranch than it had when closed out. Jones was a great roper of heavy stock and of calves in the herd. He could throw a rope from any angle, sideways, backward, or ahead as necessity demanded. He won a great many roping contests in old Greer County, Quanah, Haskell, and Seymour.

Outside men of the neighboring ranches detailed to work with the ranch under Jones' regime always topped their outfit's *remuda* for roping horses and overhauled their gear carefully before leaving home. They knew they were going into fast company. Sometimes in the news reel, one sees pictures of crack Italian or French cavalrymen performing almost unbelievable feats of horsemanship in riding off of embankments, crossing streams, and the like, but the old-timers who knew Jones and his riders would not give an inch to any rough-riding organization of men anywhere on earth.

Jones kept his outfit on the run from sun up to sun down, and let nothing interfere with his work. Once when the wagon was working deep in the breaks and far from town, he developed a bad tooth. Rather than lose the time a long ride to the dentist would necessitate, he insisted that burly Sebe Nichols pull the offending molar with a pair of wire pliers. Nichols not only extracted the tooth, but a good deal of the jawbone with it. Infection set in and Jones spent months in a Fort Worth hospital and carried scars of the operation to his grave.

In 1910 the O X began selling off the lands in small ranches. Jones wound up the last of the cattle. He was inordinately fond of rough country and went to a mountain outfit in Arizona to run, not a wagon, but a pack outfit, as the most of the ranch was too rough for a wagon. His children were old enough for school by this time and after a couple of years, he came back to settle down on a stock farm that he owned overlooking the breaks where the old Paducah wagon road dropped into them and the old O X pasture at Catfish Crossing. He died there two years ago.

A wagon boss and his men usually partook of the nature of the country and cattle they were working. If it was open country of big flats and better-bred cattle, you would find a quiet, easy-riding bunch of men. If the country was rough and the cattle wild it took rough riders to get the cattle out. So it was with Johnnie.

It was through a story told by Johnnie Jones that the phrase "would bog a saddle blanket" originated. One spring as he was riding out the mouths of the boggy creeks, he unsaddled his horse and spread his saddle blankets to dry on a limb that projected over a sand bar from which he had just pulled a weak cow. While he lay back in the shade, a whirlwind lifted his Navajo blanket from the limb to blow it down on to the sand bar where, according to Jones, it bogged from sight before he could scramble down the bank to save it.

This story stood as the best until another O X hand came in and reported that he had found a raccoon bogged in the mouth of Catfish.

Much has been written in recent years on the founding of the great Matador Land and Cattle Company by Mr. Campbell and its acquisition by the present company. The ranch is divided into three divisions: the steer ranch in South Dakota, the Plains ranch near Channing, and the Matador proper, under the Cap Rock. A list of its trail, range, and wagon bosses constitutes a sort of "Who's Who" in bosses: R. D. Stelzer, J. L. Harrison, John Beasley, J. D. (Jeff) Harkey, John Smith, J. D. Starks, G. I. Walker, S. L. Pepper, J. D. Boone, Jesse L. Baker, R. A. Haley, John M. Jackson, C. W. (Charley) Morris, Jack Luckett, W. J. (Will) Drace, John Wheeler, J. M. (Matt) Walker, John Southworth, Henry Cook, R. T. Alley, E. H. (Rang) Thorton, Claude Jeffers, Bernice Harkey, Gilbert Keith, Walker Williams, and G. S. (Red) Payne.

Due to the number of bosses and their transfers from one company outfit to another the Matador bosses, with a few exceptions, were not so generally known to the present generation as those of the outfits having only one or two bosses. That each of them was of the best is evidenced by their employment by the company.

Best known in recent years are Jeff Harkey, the genial John Jackson, and the veteran bronc buster, Claude Jeffers, who with his sons is still on the ranch. They operate three wagons each year under G. S. (Red) Payne, Walker Williams, and Gilbert Keith. Local management of the vast holdings is in charge of W. J. Riley, who came to Texas from the Dakota steer ranch several years ago.

There is no ranch in the Southwest so typical of the old days nor one which is better managed than the Matador.

As has been said, the remaining old ranches in the area operate as to men and method about as they did in the 80's. The cattle, of course, are improved and there are many conveniences and means of communication now that the old fellows did not have.

The smaller outfits have passed into many ownerships. Leslie McAdams owns a neat ranch in Foard County made up of part of his father's old Hat outfit. Furd Halsell of Fort Worth has the old Witherspoon ranch and with it is B. J. Glover, who has been wagon and ranch boss for the Halsells for many years. Tom Richard's Stripe outfit passed into the possession of his children and was divided when he died a good many years ago. The original 3 D outfit, a good-sized ranch yet, belongs to Johnson and Herring. It and its one wagon are in the charge of Jim Roark who learned his trade under Ed Bomar of the Nines, having gone there as a horse wrangler in the late 90's.

Scattered to the four corners are the old wagon bosses who are still living. Wherever they may be, they are and have been getting by, for a good cow hand will be doing his best wherever he is and regardless of what he is doing. Any of them in the free and easy days could have stolen a start from their employers. Few, if any, did, and those who did never prospered with their ill-gotten herds, but went broke and were soon forgotten.

A majority of the bosses have long since died. If square dealing, clean living, and a deep sense of loyalty to their employers has been properly accredited to them, they are in "a plumb good country." It is not hard to visualize them, sitting around in groups or leaning against their celestial bedrolls with the sort of satisfied look they always wore in the evening when the yearling herd was turned loose in a tight holding pasture for the night. They won't be telling each other how tough they were in the old days or boasting of their skill with rope or bronc. They didn't do that down here.

The Cowboys

No curfew tolls the knell nor fixed rule measures the hours of the day for the cow hand, who works from "see to see"—from the time he can see to catch his horse in the early dawn until it is too late in the evening for him to see what he is doing, whether it be with the wagon or branding crew, or in lone camp far from the companionship of the outfit's other hands. He is a man trained by environment to work, and work hard. In his opinion "throwin' off" on the boss or outfit is an unpardonable sin.

If he is working with the wagon he will arise to the cook's call to find the east not yet red. While he awaits his turn for the wash pan he may wonder (to himself), "How in the hell can anyone see to work cattle this time of the night?" He snorts a couple of times in the wash pan and hunts for the cleanest place on the towel which has been used, and well, by the other men of the outfit. Hot coffee, bacon, biscuits and "lick" (molasses), and he is ready to face the day, which is just making its appearance along with the *remuda* that the horse wrangler has driven up near the wagon.

If he is in a "batchin' camp," he arises to the call of the dollar alarm clock that the boss so thoughtfully included in the initial bill of groceries sent him. He arises to no cheerful light of an early morning campfire, or savory odors of frying meat or hot coffee; he faces the cold gray ashes left in the No. 8 stove the night before, and eyes the grounds-streaked graniteware coffeepot while he debates whether to throw the grounds out and start over, or just add more water. He compromises on a 50–50 basis, and adds a little more coffee and a little more water. While the cold, white grease of the meal before is warming up in the frying pan, he hacks half a dozen slices of sow belly from the side hanging on the wall, and while it sizzles and pops, he inventories the seven cold baking powder biscuits with the Mt. Shasta covering by hefting them in his palm and testing their density with his thumb. Deciding on three of them, he bounces the other four out the door.

After eating and promising himself to wash the dishes when he gets in that night, he catches and saddles the horse, turned loose in the "starve out" the night before, and is ready to ride by the time the sun peeps over the long ridge east of the camp. He will prowl the ridges all morning, and watch the points where the old loafer bitch denned last year. Maybe he can dig her out after she whelps. He will ride by tank and water hole, whether it be bogging time or not, for occasionally strong animals will slip on the rip-rap and spraddle out so that they cannot arise. Too, around the water holes he may find a calf or two whose mother has died and which he can take in for the headquarters lady to raise on a bottle. He will check the trails to and from water holes to note horse tracks that might not be those of his own outfit. He will read the story of his charges and their range as he rides. In this he can be assisted by his horse, for it will often note a strange rider, woodcutters in the pasture, or things unusual, even quicker than the rider.

When the sun and his stomach tell him it is high noon, he will eat a snack of cold biscuits and bacon taken from his saddle strings. His afternoon's work may take him along the fence line, by bog hole or to the gates on the east string which the woodcutters have been leaving open. When he starts across a range or pasture, whether it be to prowl or with some destination in mind, the cowboy operates much as did the lookout on the old-time whaling ship, high in the crow's nest above the deck.

His eyes search each flat, hollow, and ridge as he moves along, alert for the unusual. He makes rapid inventory of the grazing cattle without counting or closely examining each bunch. He knows fairly well where the different bunches "use" and water. If they are spread out grazing he knows all is well with them. A cow bawling or showing nervousness indicates that her calf is dead or in trouble, and he veers by to ascertain the cause. If it is dead and she is an unusually good milker, he may have to catch and milk her to prevent her bag from spoiling.

An animal gaunt of flanks, with swollen jaw and low swung head means a rattlesnake bite. There is little he can do in that case, except possibly open the wound with his pocket knife.

Two- or three-year-old steers sometimes form the habit of chewing the bones of old carcasses, mostly because of lack of salt. Occasionally one will swallow a section of vertebrae which will lodge in his throat, leaving scant room for the animal to breathe. If not attended to immediately, the animal usually dies, either from starvation or the laceration attendant on the bone's removal.

A calf with hide twitching, hoofs stamping, and tail switching means screw worms, and in a short quick dash to rope him for doctoring, the horse may plant both feet in a blind "pup's nest," (a prairie dog hole), and go down to send the rider popping like a whip out over head to land with a knee twisted or ankle bent under him. The resulting fall would send a varsity football player off the field on a stretcher, while sports writers clicked a story to the nation that So-and-So would probably be out of the game the balance of the season on account of a badly wrenched knee. The cow hand spits the needle grass and dirt from his mouth, and rubs the injured member before limping over to catch and mount his horse which the dragging and never-tied bridle reins had stopped within a few yards.

By this time it is "a couple of hours o' the sun," or to be exact, 5:15, and if he moves out pretty "peart" he will just about have time to cover the six miles and grease the High Lonesome windmill by sundown, and get into camp by good dark. The short cut to the mill leads down off the ridge and across the big flat where the cows are moving out from water for a final hour or two of grazing before they bed down for the night. Calves butt and play with each other, stopping in their frisking to gaze at the rider in wide-eyed interest. A lordly bull, moving with deep rumblings from one grazing bunch to another, pauses to throw his muzzle high in the air and bellow notice of his coming, and, while waiting for an answering challenge from some other lord of the herd, sends clouds of brown dust over his shoulder with his strong right leg. Circling bullbats swoop and dive, almost under the horse's nose. Kildees ground hop and shrill as the brown horse swings in to the water for a hurried drink.

Headed toward the mill, the little brown horse pulls pretty hard to the right, the direction in which the camp lies, and requires a little "gigging" and an occasional whack with the loose end of the lariat to keep his mind on his business. When the mill is greased and the rider climbs back into the saddle, he swings toward the camp and begins to "pick 'em up and lay 'em down" in a long, easy, running walk that will soon bring them into the camp.

This "batchin' camp" of the isolated cowboy is a very necessary part of life in the cattle country. Most big Texas ranches have a head-quarters outfit from which ranch activities are directed. It is usually near some small town or shipping point and may or may not be any-where near the center of their holdings. To facilitate work and afford protection to fences and cattle, one or two "camps" are located at strategic points on the ranch. While these are called camps, to dis-tinguish them from headquarters, they are usually pretty fair outfits consisting of a three- or four-room house, corrals, chutes, horse pasture, and sheds for feed storage. They are usually occupied by some married cow hand whose wife cooks for the two or three men that work with her husband.

The headquarters camps ordinarily take care of a good-sized outfit if its holdings lie in a body and there are no detached pastures, and not too many creek mouths that become death traps to cattle during heel-fly time. If the latter be the case, it is necessary to have smaller, "batchin'" camps in the detached pastures or the bog area that may be occupied when the outlying pasture is stocked or the bogs are bad.

These are usually one- or two-roomed affairs with small corrals and storage for saddle horse feed. In the cow country they are called "Boar's Nests" because of the fact that they are occupied for the most part by one man who is more interested in his duties as a cow hand than in culinary or housekeeping arts. They are equipped with as little stuff as possible so that they may be left at any time without much loss if prowlers should visit them. Men placed in these camps are usually middle aged, have no families, and do not mind loneliness or eating their own cooking. Their duties consist of riding fence and bog, doctor-ing screw worms, and letting the neighbors know that the outfit has a man on the job in case they should get beef hungry and not choose to eat their own.

The kitchen equipment generally consists of one very small cook stove, one very black coffeepot, one frying pan (same color), one biscuit pan, a bean pot, stew pan, combination dough and dishpan, platter, and half a dozen each tin cups, plates, knives, and forks. Most "batchers" like to have at least one complete change of tableware so that two meals may be eaten with only one dishwashing. A square pine table, with or without red-and-yellow checked oilcloth, and a couple of cane-bottomed chairs complete the kitchen furniture. In case of company, staple kegs or corn boxes provide extra seating.

The commissary department—made up of several wooden boxes nailed to the wall, shelf fashion—contains, soda, baking powder, salt, pepper, navy beans, dried fruit, syrup, a bottle of pepper sauce, coffee, flour, lard, and canned tomatoes, corn, and hominy. A slab of white salt-covered "sow belly"—not breakfast bacon—hangs suspended from a nail. The batching camp doesn't get much beef as there is too much waste in killing a beef for one man.

The bed chamber furnishings consist of one cheap iron bed and springs on which the cowboy's "hot roll" is spread. If another man drops in for the night and doesn't have his roll with him, what bedding they have is split and another bed is made on the floor. A small center table contains three saddle catalogues, one boot catalogue with measurement blanks, an almanac, writing tablet, alarm clock, and coal-oil lamp. A couple of chairs complete the equipment with the exception of a small shelf that holds, among other things, a Wade & Butcher razor, a teacup with shaving soap and brush in it, a small round box containing quinine capsules, and same size and kind of box containing calomel tablets. Add one gall cure, one vaccine calendar on the wall, a pair of run-down half worn-out boots, and an old suit case, and you have a complete "Boar's Nest."

Sometimes, when work demands, two men are placed in the camp, and the duty of cooking is a matter to be settled between themselves. If both are equally good cooks, are clean, and make bread about alike, the rule is—first one in starts the meal. If one is a better cook than the other, he soon assumes the cooking job in self-defense and the other is perfectly willing to let him.

The wagons of the southern cowboy ordinarily do not start out until late April or mid-May, and the work is finished by mid-September or early October. Occasionally, however, in the old days an outfit moving a beef herd from the Cap-Rock country to the railroad in Amarillo in the fall would be overtaken by an early storm. These were felt very keenly by the cowboys with their "hen skin" bedrolls, consisting of a couple of soogans and one pair of blankets. The only redeeming feature was their heavy tarpaulin, which, when properly snapped up, was almost weatherproof, especially if a few inches of snow or ice encrusted it.

Ordinarily the southern cowboy depended almost wholly upon his tarp and slicker to turn any weather he might encounter. When the storm hit, the herd immediately turned tail to it and began to drift south. With the stinging sleet cutting into their eyes and noses, they could not be stopped. There was no hysteria nor madness such as accompanied a stampede. Most wagon bosses, upon encountering such a storm, would attempt to hold their cattle, but would finally wind up by telling the boys to get to the wagon while they could still find it. The boss knew that the cattle would hold together and would be pretty well bunched against a drift fence when the storm broke.

Then, too, there was danger of losing both the horses being ridden and the *remuda* if the horses were choused too much and got hot and sweaty before being unsaddled or turned loose. Back around the wagon the boys would huddle about the fire or climb into the wagon for relief from the icy blasts. I recall one occasion when an outfit, overtaken by a storm, attempted to make themselves as comfortable as possible within the sheeted wagon. One cowboy, reaching it first, preempted the water barrel in front of the wagon and held it as a sort of seat and bed until the storm had broken. The water barrel was one from which the top had been saved, cleated together and fitted loosely into the barrel. After he had occupied his seat for two days and nights, as he dismounted from it the third morning, when the storm had broken, the lid became loosened and plunged him into the barrel. After that he had to crawl from the cover of the wagon into the icy wind with the riding part of him thoroughly soaked, much to his discomfort and to the amusement of the rest of the outfit.

Occasionally a trail herd, bound for the Northwest, would encounter snow, sleet, or blizzard en route, and again the lack of proper clothing and wagon facilities resulted in much discomfort to the outfit. In the middle 80's the X I T outfit had four trail herds en route to Montana. In the midst of these was an X herd of the Reynolds brothers. A sudden storm forced them to abandon the five herds. When the storm had blown by, the Reynolds outfit had lost twenty-eight saddle horses and a good many cattle. The five herds of more than fifteen thousand cattle were found solidly bunched against a railroad fence.

In the Southwest when a light snow or cool spell blew up, it was not unusual to come upon a wagon with the men sound asleep in their "hot rolls" with chain harness, saddles, and other impedimenta pulled up on their beds to give them additional weight and to prevent the cold winds from blowing the covers off their feet.

The Northwestern cow outfits who had to prepare for cold weather fared better than their Southern brothers. Most of them were equipped with sleeping tents. In some instances a tent, as one Texan expressed it, "biggern old Molly Bailey's show tent" covered the entire wagon, affording protection for the cook as he went about his labors and a bedding down place for the cowboys. The first of this type of outfit to make its appearance in Texas was introduced a few years ago by Mr. Riley, late manager of the Matador Motley County outfit and former manager of their Northwestern outfit. It soon found favor with the southern cowboys and has been adopted by several of the outfits.

In the days between trail driving and trucking, almost all cattle traveled to market by railroad. When a stock train was loaded and ready to pull out, it was customary for the boss or owner to designate some cowboy of his outfit to accompany the train and look out for the welfare of the cattle. He was usually given very short notice accompanied by a ten-dollar bill and the suggestion that he purchase a prod pole at the town's hardware store. The ten-dollar bill was for eating money and the prod pole to be used when the train stopped for water in getting "downers" back on their feet. It was about the length and size of a pitchfork handle with a blunt spike in the smaller end. Sometimes a screw was placed about one-half its length in the prod pole about two inches back from the barb. When continued prodding with the spike end had cleared a space around the downer sufficient for it to rise, the cowboy aided it in its efforts to get on its feet by entangling the bush of its tail in the screw head which permitted him to twist the animal's tail in about the same manner he would in the branding chute or crowding pen.

When the cowboy entered the caboose, especially if it was his first trip, he was transferred into a world wholly foreign to him and with a jargon of which he had no knowledge. After the train had gotten two division points from the cow country, the trainmen looked upon him, in his queer garb, as a hayseed or rube wholly ignorant of their world and its usages, and they made no effort to hide their feelings from him. He rated much lower in their estimation than sheepherder or cotton picker did with him. The cowboy had no fixed opinion of the railroad men, nor understanding of a language which called for "being laid out for Number Eight," "going in the hole for Number Seven," "sawing by Number Three," "having to double Newburg Hill," and "big holing the air."

By nature he liked everybody and was in a notion of "throwin' in with them" and asking a lot of questions about their work and the country they were passing through as soon as the train was under way. His friendly overtures usually met with a gruff "yes" or "no" which left little or no opportunity for continued conversation.

When the conductor had made his wheel report and the rear brakeman finished filling and cleaning his lamps and lanterns, both climbed in the cupola of the caboose to ride comfortably with outstretched legs mile after mile without speaking to each other. The cowboy from his bench seat downstairs noting this was of the opinion that they were so danged "honery" and sorry that they wouldn't even talk to each other.

When the train made stops for water or lay on the siding to meet another train, the cowboy, mindful of his duty, got out with his prod pole and began an inspection of each car as he walked towards the engine. Invariably the train began to get under way before he had gone two-thirds its length. Before its wheels had completed a revolution he was skinning up the ladder of the nearest car. His six-foot prod pole hampered him some but he was taking no chances of letting the train get a start on him.

It mattered not how hot the sun nor cold the winds, he stayed with that car until the train came to a complete stop again, be it minutes or hours afterwards. He never learned to brace himself against the wind and motion of the train and step from car to car along the swaying tops. Each gap between two cars was a grand canyon to him. Some of the old boys caught out on top in Kansas in the late fall learned to pry the hay hatches off and climb down into the hay racks above the cattle to be warmed by the heat from them—an old hobo trick.

With no knowledge of railroading or train orders, the cowboy always had a sneaking idea that the trainmen deliberately started the train up when it would cause him most inconvenience. This feeling was furthered by the fact that he could never get them to tell him how long the train would stop, so he could get something to eat. Their usual reply to such questions was "just a little while" or "a long time." If he took them at their word on the "long-time" answer, he would usually have to leave a plate full of fine food and scald himself gulping hot coffee in considerable less than a "little while." If he considered it from the "little-while" angle and grabbed a sandwich and a cup of coffee, he usually had time to have ordered roast beef and boiled potatoes and had these prepared from scratch before his train moved out.

Another sore spot with him was the fact that he had to change cabooses at each division point. The moving of his prod pole and valise did not entail much work if he could just find the new caboose. Inquiry of the switchman usually brought the reply "your caboose is number six on the west house track." He could have found Mushaway Peak or Squaw Spring in the Cap-Rock country in the dark much easier than he could the west house track, for three or four days and nights of riding and jolting had temporarily cost him his sense of direction and besides he didn't want to risk dodging switch engines and cuts of cars being pushed in on the tracks he had to cross, so he just planted himself with grip and prod pole at the rear of his train far down in the yards away from lights, coffee, and much-needed smoking tobacco, and let them bring the caboose to him.

He never ceased to be fascinated by the way the trainmen waited until the train had gotten in motion to catch step with it and swing gracefully onto the rear platform. He couldn't help wondering how graceful they would look cheeking and mounting a half-broken bronc on a cold morning. He felt pretty sure he could do a better job than they.

He was sincerely glad when he had signed the last conductor's condition report and the trip was over.

This record so far might appear to be an indictment of the old-time freight trainmen, which is not the case. Their world and that of the cowboy lay far apart and they had little or nothing in common. But I will bet you a plug nickel that 80 per cent of the old-timers who rode stock trains will tell you that it expresses their sentiments. The other 20 per cent were fortunate in finding congenial fellows, who recognized their inexperience. These made a trip pleasant and permitted the lonesome cowboy to view the country and its checkerboard farms, red barns, and big plow teams from the honor seat in the caboose cupola. Incidentally the cowboy always managed to out-fumble the trainmen for the meal check in the eating house.

Conditions have changed in recent years. Cabooses have been modernized. Steel bunks take the place of the old hard benches and there are toilet facilities and ice water. In the Corn Belt the better railroads attach a tourist pullman to their stock trains. These not only are equipped with comfortable berths, but have cooking facilities as well.

Had there been such a thing in the cow country as the modern health unit with its visiting nurse, no doubt its personnel would have thrown up their hands in despair, when she turned in her first report on sanitary conditions in the cow camps and around the chuck wagons of her district. If they could have pulled themselves together, however, and waited until their annual report was compiled, they would have found that the sanitation and health of these fellows had been well taken care of by the men themselves, in their own way.

They would have found that the death rate from sickness was practically nil, as were contagious diseases and days lost from work due to illness. Broken collar bones, sprained ankles, and boils would have made up the list of disabilities, unless they cared to include several severe cases of "gypping" that had occurred during the hot months of the year.

Like the Indian, the cowboy depended on nature to remedy many of his ills: soaking a sprained ankle in cold water would make the swelling go down until the boot would go on; a few shots of tepid water from Croton Creek would rid a fellow of that bilious feeling and bad taste in the mouth right away. An outfit working down the Wichitas, in King and Foard counties, found that a skin eruption had broken out among them—itch, if you want to be plain about it—and cured it by bathing several nights in succession in the saline water of the Big Wichita.

"Cooties," or their ancestors, were seldom found in a cow outfit, and hard was the lot of the extra hand picked up in town to help during the rush, who was suspected of having them. Usually the boss, wise in the way of cow hands, would take the newcomer out on the morning circle and tell him kindly, but firmly, that hot water and blue ointment would fix him up, and that he had better tend to it right away or he would have to send him to town by the next passing.

Medicine was practically unknown around the cow outfits. Boys coming from East Texas filled with the desire to become cow hands, and just as full of malaria, brought their calomel and quinine with them, but a few months on native water cured them of the chills and fever and cleared their complexion up. When a cow hand was sick enough to lay around the bunkhouse or under the wagon while the rest of the outfit was working, you could figure that he was pretty sick, for he would work with a high fever rather than have the outfit think he was "soakin'," or just belly-aching.

In an earlier paragraph, mention was made of cowboys getting "gypped." Lest some reader think that grafters, stock salesmen, or confidence men were preying on the poor cowboys and taking their hard-earned pay from them by various forms of chicanery, it might be well to explain the term as it applies to the cow country of the Southwest. We mentioned in the chapter on "Living Water" that many of the creeks and rivers in the Cap-Rock area are heavily impregnated with gypsum, or other alkaline salts, picked up as they make their way through dozens of formations. So like in effect are these waters to the famed croton oil that many of the creeks have been given that name.

If fairly cool and if taken in moderate quantities, the water causes no ill effects, but if drunk in large quantities during the summer months when it is tepid, and the drinker is hot from the branding pen or dusty roundup, the effect is similar to that suffered by the small boy who has eaten too freely of green apples, only worse—much worse. No matter how old the old-timer, or how much of it he has drunk in the past, he is never immune to gypping. He knows it, but if thirsty enough, will drink water wherever it is found, regardless of mineral or other content.

No health unit or dietician need ever worry about the physical condition of a bunch of hard-riding cowboys who eat a balanced ration of beef, beans, stewed fruits, black coffee, and sour-dough bread, washed down by nature's own liver regulator, cowboys whose bodies are bathed and dried by the cool, clean air of the cow country. Most of the fellows who worked and lived under these conditions have outlived their allotted three-score-and-ten by from five to fifteen years.

The cowboy was as clean as his working conditions would permit, and expected the same of the fellows he ate, worked, and bunked with. More especially did he demand cleanliness of the outfit's cook. When a new one came to wagon or camp, he was appraised by the outfit before he cooked a meal. If his clothes were clean, his hands white, nails short, and no black showing—good; if he heated a pot of water and scrubbed out the chuck box and utensils before he used them, regardless of how clean the last cook left them—better! It proved that he was clean, and if he could only make fair bread, the boys would go a long way with him.

There were certain articles always to be found around wagon or camp house. Among them were a ten-cent writing tablet, a package of stamped envelopes, and a Wade & Butcher razor with an unusually heavy blade. The razor was usually the property of the cook or one of the boys who had had ideas about his personal appearance when he left home. It could be used by anyone who had nerve enough to try it. There was sometimes a wonderfully and fearfully decorated shaving mug, which bore the picture of a cowboy dressed in fringed buckskin trousers and a flat-topped hat with the brim a yard wide, the like of which was never seen in the cow country. He was mounted on a dun horse with long black mane and tail, and had just thrown his loop over the horns of a steer that seemed to realize that it was conquered and was showing its submission by kneeling gracefully on one knee as the dun horse faced him, reared on his hind feet, and the cowboy waved triumphantly to all present. More often, though, there was a cake of dried barber soap in a tea cup.

If the cowboy's whiskers got to the point where they gave him too much trouble, or he was going over into the nester settlement, he might take this razor and try to shave himself or get someone else to, but it had to be a serious case if he took that risk, for he usually came up scarred and marred almost beyond recognition. Haircuts didn't bother him much, as he usually let his hair grow until he got to town. If it got so long that it interfered with his hearing or started down his back, he might get some friend to trim it up a little for him.

As has been said, the cowboy was as clean as his limitations would permit, but if hard work, or long drives prevented him from doing the things the town man did after a hard day's work, he was not squeamish, and made up for it when he got to town. He couldn't go to the showers and come out with fresh linen after each session in the branding pen, but he did the next best thing, even though it might be several days later, by going to tank or water hole to take a cold bath without soap or towel, and letting freshly rinsed underclothes dry out while he bathed. It is conservative to say that 75 per cent of cowboy bathing was done in cold tank water without benefit of soap.

Let him get to town, however, and after buying new clothes throughout, he would make a bee-line to the barber shop and enjoy a long, hot bath, with plenty of soap and big woolly towels, after which he would tell the barber to "give him everything he had," which in those days meant hair-cut, shave, shampoo, hair oil, and the blacking and waxing of the mustache—if he had one, and providing that hirsute adornment was inclined to be downy, or run to red.

Most hands started out in the spring with a pair or two of extra socks, a couple of red bandanna or black silk handkerchiefs, a couple of black sateen shirts, two pairs of drawers with separate undershirts, and a spare pair of overalls, called "duckins" in the cow country. Shorts were unknown, and would not have been used if they had been known, because a party by the name of Scrivens was turning out drawers with elastic seams down the side of the leg, which reached from waist to ankle, and were heavily reinforced at the points of stress. A fellow could take a turn of the knitted anklet of these drawers around his ankle, pull his socks up over the wrap, and be sure that they would not work up into a knot and chafe him when he got down to real hard work. They were good drawers, and barring getting messed up in brush or barbed wire, two pairs would last a man a season.

The sateen shirts wore well and didn't show dirt, but sometimes when the afternoon had been hot and the calves big, a rim of salty white would show up across the back of one in the cool of the evening after the day's branding was over, as the cowboy sat on his bed roll and let the breezes dry the perspiration from his clothing. Along toward the last of the season the shirts might turn green or look as if they were beginning to mortify. Socks were good as long as there was a "chin-strap" left to keep them from climbing up the leg. These were washed carefully and often, for tight boots and cotton socks made feet sweat and scald. The cowboy was careful of his feet and never let an opportunity pass to soak them in some shaded water hole while he let his horse blow.

When work would slow up, the boys would take advantage of the lull to "boil out" their extra underwear, shirts, and socks. If the boiling-out periods were too far apart, they would rinse their clothing out in cold tank water and hang them out over night to dry.

Reams of paper have been consumed by writers, more particularly the lady ones, in discussion of the cowboy's boots. The writers go into great detail about the high heels, length of top, and the red-and-yellow stitching thereon, winding up with a snappy paragraph or two on the vanity of the cowboy, insofar as his feet and boots are concerned.

As a matter of fact, one word—utility—would cover the matter adequately. Some men have punched cows a lifetime without owning a pair of boots, but 98 per cent of the bona fide hands use, and have used, them because they need them.

The heels are made high for the same reason that cleats are put on a baseball player's shoes—to keep the wearer from slipping. The tops are made long or short, according to the country they are to be used in. If it be South Texas, they will be long so as to take the popping of the brush and provide protection against thorns. There is a distinct tendency though, in recent years, toward lower tops as a means of saving weight, for the modern cow hand or cowman is afoot in his business now, almost as much as he is on horseback.

The fancy stitching is also highly utilitarian, for the tops are made of lightweight, high-quality leather. The stitching serves to stiffen them, keeping them from wrinkling too much at the ankles, where they contact the stirrup. This contact between ankle and stirrup is the principal reason boots are used. Shoes with eyelets are too uncomfortable and the cowboy cannot "lean against" the stirrup in shoes with any degree of safety or without pain.

As to the vanity of the cowboy, it is very doubtful if many of them gave the appearance of their feet much thought. If they did, there is much to be said in their behalf. The majority of them, the old ones more especially, began riding at tender ages and for this reason had very small, neat feet. They were descendants of riding ancestors and, in a manner of speaking, inherited small feet. Their elders began having boots made for them as soon as they reached the age when they could wear a pair out before they outgrew them. The bootmaker, who in many instances had made boots for years for the father, was careful in selecting a last for the youngster and as he grew up, expanded it to cover the growth since the last pair. As a result of this careful attention, the feet were never permitted to spread.

Now, those who knew the old, hard-riding hands will have to admit that small feet were about all the break nature gave them as to looks. They were tall and angular when they reached their maturity. A diet of beef, beans, and sour-dough biscuit had given them strength but no surplus flesh. Riding in their formative years had bowed their legs until the crease in their trousers would not stay put, had there been a crease.

The winds, both hot and cold and the heat of the sun and branding fire did things to their complexion. What the elements didn't do, the occasional shaves, often far between, with a dull razor, cold water, and laundry soap, finished. Usually when the cowboy cleaned up, his face, at best, resembled a freshly boiled beet.

Years in the saddle and sitting cross-legged in the shade of a chuck wagon to eat, did not give him any parlor graces, nor an even break with the spoons and forks at the dining table.

When he got a pay day and a few days in town, he usually "fixed himself up" with a new California suit. Don't be fooled when you see

California suits advertised now. There are not any more of the old clay-colored kind with the white outlined checks, unless they are hanging in closets or packed in mothballs, alongside a Confederate uniform. The California suit of the late 90's may well be said to have been the dress uniform of the old-time cowboy.

With a new suit, checked shirt, and red tie, he was neat, clean, and highly representative of his outdoor calling, but he felt awkward, looked awkward, and was thoroughly aware of it. Not until he sat down in hotel lobby, smoking car, or parlor, and crossed his legs did his only claim to daintiness become apparent—his feet.

Neatly encased in shopmade boots they gave the impression of having been poured in and allowed to harden. So, if his calling and the vagaries of nature had robbed him of other claims as a Beau Brummel, why begrudge him this one, or make so much todo over his feet and footwear? Besides, the California suit covered a square-shooting frame and a heart as large as his feet were small.

Mention was made of a bootmaker making boots for father and son. Each of the cattle sections had its favorite bootmaker, who served his area for years. Mostly, these fellows came from foreign shores, having served their apprenticeship in their native countries. They came to America and the new West to ply their trades. In a short time they found what the cowmen wanted and began turning out boots, each putting his own characteristic stamp into his product. One who knew the cattle country could tell, almost at a glance, where the wearer of a pair of boots was from and who made them.

The cowboy had no use for "hand-me-down" boots, meaning the cheap, heavy, flat-heeled cowhide boots made in the New England shoe factories, with no particular design, and used largely in the North and Middle West, by farm boys as protection against snow and cold. He didn't have much respect for the character or ability of a cow hand who wore them, either. Such men rated little, if any, better with him than the "two buckle" hand who came from East Texas or down South, with his furrow-flattened feet encased in the old-style, heavy-leather brogan shoe, which had for its fastenings a buckle of the type used on galoshes.

In recent years and with the passing of the old-time bootmaker, the industry has become highly specialized. Factories that turn out boots equaling those of the old-time bootmakers have overcome the prejudice against quantity-made boots. The cowboy still is particular about where his boots come from, however, and wants to know that the makers have some boot background, which the best of them have.

Sometimes the cowboy pays for his vanity in close-fitting boots. When the rains come and he works in muddy corrals or fixing water gaps for several days they contract and are hard to put on. He skins his heels, cusses, tugs, and swears he will never own another pair of boots. On the contrary, he will get himself a pair, yes, a couple of pairs of "two buckles" the next time he is in town. He greases the inside of the spur pieces with laundry soap, rubs flour on the instep and sometimes runs a broom handle through the ears and suspends himself between two chairs before his feet slip down into them. He never cusses the man who made them, however, for he would not have paid him a dime for them if they hadn't fit "close." They soon expand when he walks a few steps or the sun dries them out and he continues to look askance at the nester boy wearing "hand-me-downs" or "two-buckles."

There was an era some years ago when cowboy equipment was undergoing drastic change. It was in that period that the severely plain saddle with straight fork, high cantle, and square skirts gave way to the artistically carved, concho-bedecked creation with swelled forks, low cantle, round skirts, and leather-covered stirrups.

At the same time the OK spur, long standard, together with its younger brother the Underwood, made way for the "gal-leg" type shop-made spur highly ornamented with silver and copper. Occasionally the pattern varied from the girl's leg to the gooseneck type, in which case, the simulated goose carried in its silver-plated bill the saw-like rowel. Both of these types often had ten-cent pieces covering the buttons to which were attached the broad, curved spur leathers with their nickel-plated buckles. Concurrent with these changes, the old-time white pot-metal bridle bits, made either with long shanks or in the form of the popular "grazing bit" gave way to hand-forged numbers, also highly decorated with valuable metals.

This same era marked the passing of the $1.75 hen-skin saddle blanket and yellow sweat pad. The Navajo blanket was in the store window. No longer was the old-time checked jumper and red badanna handkerchief considered "class." The black sateen shirt, even though it showed dirt and signs of mortification quicker, and the black silk handkerchief or square of sateen replaced them.

This change in accouterment brought about a mild economic hiatus among the sons of the range. More especially did it affect those who had not been saving of their wages. The new saddle cost around $65, whereas the bulk of the cow hand's life had been spent in one costing from $35 to $40. The old spurs had cost from $.75 per pair for the

OK to $1.25 for the Underwoods. The anatomical numbers ran in cost from $6.50 up, depending on the amount of precious metals used to embellish them and the value of the specie going on the buttons. Bits were in proportion. Then, too, chaps, heretofore considered necessary only in the brush of South Texas or the cold climates of the Northwest, came into general use wherever men rode, adding to the cost of equipment another $20.

Wages had not increased to meet the new high cost of equipment. The cowboy felt that he could not appear at the roundups to represent his outfit unless he had the new equipment, for fear the other hands would call him "nester boy" or "two-buckle hand."

There was a time, back yonder, when the boss gave a hand a check for his time, and most of it went to the saddler for one of his creations to be used for the first time on the hand's "private horse." When the transition was completed, he swung into his saddle to ride down the street with its unset stirrups leathers galling his ankles, making him appear twice as awkward as he was. This was a signal for the bosses along the street to comment, "There he goes, with a $40 saddle on a $20 horse." Those days are gone, however, for the ratio between the presentable horse and a model "roping-type" saddle are about equal.

A discussion of the personnel of the Southwestern cow outfits, old or modern, never passes without mention of one or more of the hundreds of "Shorties" who have worked or are working with the outfits.

Almost invariably in a cow outfit of eight or ten men there is to be found one of diminutive stature who bears the name of "Shorty" and who is the brunt of most of the jokes and rough horseplay of the outfit. Despite this, he is always good-natured and does his part, or a little more, of the hard work around the outfit. There are sound reasons for the diminutive cowboy's sunny disposition and efforts to make a top hand. He is so small that he can't whip anyone and therefore does not get mad easily. Handicapped by his size he has to work a little harder than a big man in order to show that he can do a man's work.

He is invariably a prime favorite with his own outfit and all who know him, even though his boss does cut him the tallest horses in the *remuda* and the boys advise him to "get a box to stand on" or "lead him up to the fence and rake your saddle off on him" when he has roped out an unusually tall mount and is leading him toward his saddle.

Probably the best-known "Shorty" in the Southwest was the late Eugene Clark, known to more cowmen as "Shorty" Clark than by his first name or initial. Of unusually small stature, he was born and learned his cow punching in Denton County when it was cow country. In later years he went to the Midland-New Mexico country, where he worked as a cowboy until he became wagon boss for the Mallett outfit. Eventually he acquired a ranch and cattle of his own in Gaines County, later moving to Scurry County, where he was interested with John Scharbauer and the late W. E. Connell in the O S Ranch. At the time of his death he was an executor of the S. B. Burnett Estate. From an humble start he grew to be prominent in cattle circles and organizations and was well-known throughout the Southwest, numbering his friends by the hundreds.

Of the more recent ones, there is "Shorty" Northcutt, who holds down the Seaman Camp on the 250-section Spade Ranch in Mitchell County and is a top hand and prime favorite wherever he is known. He is an excellent calf roper and since their marriage, has taught his wife, Christine, the art of riding and calf roping until she has become a top winner in ladies' roping contests and cowgirl sponsored events throughout West Texas.

"Shorty" Lucas works for the McElroy Yards in El Paso and is well and favorably known to the scores of cowmen who have been handling Mexican cattle through El Paso during the past two years. He is noted for his courtesy, knowledge of brands, and ability in handling and shipping cattle.

Another is "Shorty" (Carl) Blair. Born in Kent County, "Shorty" has spent his life on ranches and among cattle people in Kent, Stonewall, Fisher, and Mitchell counties. He has been employed by Price Maddox on the T U F Ranch south of Colorado City in Mitchell County for the past fifteen years. He is well liked by the outfits he works with and among the cowmen of the Colorado City and Sweetwater country.

There are several good reasons why the old-time cow hand was not much of a reader. Chief among them was lack of time, early training, and something to practice with. With the wagons there was no time to read as the outfit was catching horses with the first daylight and sleeping as soon after supper as they could turn in. Little or no printed matter came to the wagon if you exclude the Arbuckle coffee packages, Dr. Price's baking powder cans, and Clipper Corn boxes. A quick glance at the provisions each time they came in kept the readers advised as to what was going on in the grocery line. The rest of the news or stories they got by word of mouth.

It was not much better around the headquarters outfits. Occasionally boss or owner, coming back from town would bring a week-old newspaper that was read carefully by those who could read, or cared to. Occasionally some fellow returning by train from Kansas City, or from the outfit's steer ranch, would, after a good deal of haggling with the news butch, buy a copy of Charlie Siringo's *Twenty Years on the Hurricane Deck of a Texas Pony*, or *With the James Boys in Missouri*. If he was a sentimental sort of devil he might also buy a copy of *Lorna, the Shop Girl*. Any one of the volumes constituted a winter's reading for an average outfit.

When the outfits began hiring headquarters men with families it was better, for the wife usually had a book or two and subscribed to a "Home" paper of some kind. When the big mail-order houses began sending out catalogs, reading picked up around the outfits. Many a good cow hand who did not have opportunity to attend any school other than that provided by nature, will tell you frankly that he knew what practically everything on earth was before he had seen any of it, and that he gained his knowledge from a three-pound mail-order catalog. A catalog went a long way in those days.

The boy in the lone batching camp really did not read much, but read what he had well and often. Few of them but could recite to you all of the printed matter of the baking powder cans. An old-timer once stated that the best winter he ever spent in a batching camp was when he was sent to an abandoned nester shack to winter. The people who had built the one-room home had papered and ceiled it with old newspapers and farm journals. According to his story, he read the east, west, north, and south walls during the winter, and was starting on the ceiling when they sent for him to come in.

Star mail routes, country post offices, and more frequent "passing" improved reading conditions and by the late nineties market papers and magazines could be found in most of the "doghouses." Today the boys' room at the ranch is piled high with thirty-seven varieties of western magazines, each a weekly or semi-weekly, not counting the livestock magazines. He doesn't need newspapers for most likely he gets current news quicker than they do in town, radio reception being much better in the wide-open spaces.

Years ago, when Burk Burnett and Dan Waggoner were running big outfits in the Kiowa and Comanche country, in addition to their Texas outfits, it was customary when the wagons came in each fall to lay off all men but enough to fill the various camps and do what was necessary around the headquarter outfits. The result was that Vernon and Wichita Falls caught a lot of these old cow hands who had saved enough of their summer's wages to get them a room for the winter, and by dint of considerable gambling and heavy drinking, managed to while away the winter days until grass came in the spring.

One winter, two old cow hands—we will call them Bill and Ed because those are good old names—took a room together over the old Chain Harness Saloon in Vernon, intrigued, no doubt, by the fact that there would be less loss of time between drinks, and that good company would be plentiful.

As the winter wore on, such close proximity to the bar and steady application of their talents as drinkers, began to do things to them. Bill talked vaguely about a room full of animals and snakes of a color and hue strange to the Kiowa and Comanche country. Finally he got afraid to leave his bed but lay there in wondering contemplation of the works of nature as applied to the animal kingdom. Still able to get to the bar and back, Ed summoned a doctor for his friend and, like a good hand, stood by to see and hear.

The doctor, knowing his country and his men, was not long in sizing up the situation. In his best professional manner he inquired of Bill if he was not seeing such things as red, white, and blue turkeys, pink snakes, and elephants with straw hats on, to which Bill, in a mighty effort to sell himself on the idea that he was not "seeing things," replied in the negative.

Quietly and without a word, Ed took one long look at his friend and, with a sorrowing expression on his face, eased himself out of the room down by the bar, and on down the street to Ben Lutz's undertaking parlors.

"Ben," said Ed mournfully, "guess you got a job."

"Who is it, Ed?" asked Ben.

"It's my old partner, Bill Ellis, that I been a workin' with for many summers, and winterin' with every winter for fifteen years."

"That's too bad, Ed," sympathized Ben.

"Now listen, Ben, I want you to see that old Bill is put away proper," Ed went on. "I would appreciate it a whole lot if you would attend to gettin' Bill a nice, black suit to be buried in, because you know more about them things than I do, and besides, I don't think he ought to be buried in that old California suit he has wintered in for five years."

"When did he die?" asked Lutz.

"Well, he wasn't dead when I left the room just now," replied Ed, "But I left the doctor up there with him and he had just asked Bill if he was not seein' things like pink snakes, red, white and blue turkeys, and elephants with straw hats on."

"Oh, he was seein' things like that, was he?"

"No," answered Ed, "that's what's the trouble. Bill said he wasn't, and, Ben, the damn room was just full of them, so I know old Bill must be nearly gone!"

Life was not dull on the big ranches in the cow country under the Cap Rock in the early 90's. Cowboys worked and worked hard from the time they could see in the morning until they could not see in the evening. If they worked hard it was because they loved their work and were following a boss who set a fast pace. They played as hard as they worked, when they played. To reach a playground in those days meant miles of riding to reach a dance at some neighborhood ranch, to dance a few sets or a waltz with one of the half dozen ladies present.

From the middle 80's to the middle 90's, West Texas was a woman-less country, with the exception of the headquarters men's families and the few ranchmen who brought their wives in when they did their cattle. There were scattered families in the shinnery whose men folks lived by freighting, fencing, or tanking for the company-owned ranches. These, with the ranch women, formed the nucleus of society in the cow country.

Owners and bosses expected hard work and close attention to their duties from their men, but after the wagons were in for the fall, and things settled for the winter around the ranches, they had no objection to an occasional dance at headquarters.

During the winter months, for a good many years, dances were held regularly each two weeks at the Matador, O X, Pitchfork, Moon, and McAdams ranches, with an occasional extra dance, sometimes, over in the shinnery settlement. These dances were usually held on Saturday night so everyone could rest up on Sunday and be ready for work on Monday.

Now, attending one of these affairs did not mean working until supper time, then bathing, shaving, and climbing into an air-flow coupe to drive the twenty-five miles or thirty miles to the dance. The boys did not even ride the outfit's top horses for there were always a few half-broken broncs that needed some miles put on them. They rode these, or "individual" horses, if they had them. No, it meant knocking off as soon after noon as possible, borrowing a washtub from the head-quarters lady and heating several buckets of water on the box heater in the bunk house. After a bath in gyp water with laundry soap, and a shave with a Wade & Butcher razor and the same laundry soap, if no one had been to town recently, the cowboy was clean, red-faced, and ready to drag his old telescope grip out from under the bed. From this he took his Sunday suit, clean, but wrinkled, his shirt with the detachable collar, and his ready-tied cravat with an imitation pearl in the center. From under the bed also came a pair of low-quarter shoes to be tied onto his saddle, or rolled up in his slicker, and put on when he reached the dance. No cowboy would ride twenty miles in shoes; he would stay at home first.

The women folks came to the dance in the ranch buggies or hacks, accompanied by their husbands and children. Music was furnished by a fiddler, of whom there were several in each section. Bud Barron, Cap Bird, and Bill Gowens fiddled for most of the dances and were top cow hands as well. Both square and round dancing were done and there were always two or more callers, alternating, so that each could take his turn dancing. There was an almost endless number of tunes that a fiddler could play for a square dance, but when he dropped into a waltz you could bet your saddle and blanket it would be "Over the Waves."

Sometimes the crowds were augmented by a hack-load or two of young people from nearby towns, and popular was the town boy who brought a few extra girls, for the ratio ran about three boys to one girl.

Probably the dance in West Texas that approached closest to or surpassed the famous "Cowboy's Christmas Ball" of Larry Chittenden fame was the three-day dance tendered by Bill Richards, owner of the 3 D Ranch in Cottle, Foard, and King counties, in honor of the cowmen and cowboys who had come to that section prior to 1879. He timed the dance so that all of the wagons in the country would be through with the spring work and their men could attend. Invitations went out to every ranch in the section and to cowmen and their families living in Childress, Quanah, Matador, and Paducah.

It was held in late July, 1903, in a hackberry grove of thirty-five or forty acres, eighteen miles southeast of Paducah in the old Moon Pasture, which Richards had acquired. From Quanah, fifty-five miles away, the nearest railroad point, wagon freighters hauled material for a dance platform, large enough to accommodate four sets of square dancers at a time. They also hauled out twelve hundred loaves of bread, two barrels of pickles, fifteen bushels of onions, and a baby-grand piano.

3 D hands butchered twenty head of prime two-year-old heifers and turned them over to Ben Johnson, a famous freighter and barbecue artist, known wherever freight was hauled in the cow country.

The dance was scheduled to start Friday at noon and close Saturday at midnight. By noon Friday the grove was filled with ranch buggies, hacks, and wagons with dressing tents scattered in between. Teams and saddle horses were staked outside of the grove and one could inventory who was there by checking the brands on the staked and hobbled horses. From every direction came red-faced cowboys in their Sunday best, with shoes tied on their saddles, and hobble ropes around their horses' necks. After a dinner of barbecue, pickles, onions, coffee and whatever you might have brought with you, the callers announced that they were ready.

The music was in charge of Jimmie Jones, a pianist famous for his hotel dances in Quanah and in Childress. He played for the round dances while Cap Bird and Bill Gowens handled the fiddling. Lee McArthur, Clay Kitchen, and Cliff Rogers, alternated in calling the square dances. From the first music on Friday afternoon until 12 P.M. Saturday night, there was not a moment that dancing was not in progress, except for a short period during Friday night, when by general consent everyone "took out" for about three hours to let the piano cool off. One young lady, now a portly matron, still boasts that she never missed a set nor waltz during the three days. Jones varied the waltz music by playing "A Bird in a Gilded Cage."

While the younger folks danced, the "seventy-niners" sat in circles and talked of days when they had brought their first cattle in on the head of Talking John, Croton, or Dutchman Creek, and Ike Pickering, dean of ranch bosses, then an old man, sat and pointed to where thirty years before, he turned loose the first Moon cattle on their new range. Other old-timers, then in their prime, who sat in the circles were Luther Clark, Jim McAdams, Frank and Ben Easley, Bud Fry, Bob Wilkerson, and a half hundred others. Pausing between dances to listen in were top hands and wagon bosses, like Johnnie Jones of the O X, G. Backus of the 3 D, Bud Arnett of the 6 6 6 6, Dogie Coleman, Pat Leonard, and Lee McGrady. The late R. B. Masterson, with his wife and children, came over from their J Y Ranch in King County. Young folks, now grown into womanhood and manhood who danced and frolicked at this picnic were Leslie McAdams, Tom Masterson, R. B. Masterson, Jr., and dozens of others, now well known in their sections.

About three hundred people attended the affair, all coming in hacks or on horseback, as there were no automobiles in those days. At no time was liquor in any form in evidence, and no sign of a brawl marred the gathering. The writer does not believe that there has ever been a finer gathering of bowlegged men in West Texas than this group. There will be no more such gatherings, for those who prompted it have long been in their graves, and tractor and turning plow have turned over the flats on which Moon and 3 D cows grazed.

Dusky Riders of the Range

Oh, they say there will be a great roundup,
Where cowboys like cattle will stand
To be cut by the Riders of Judgment,
Who are posted and know every brand.
                    —from an old cowboy song.

When the Riders of Judgment have finished with their work on the white cowboys and cowmen and have passed them in, there will still be a job left for them. That will be the judging of the good Negro cow hands who rode with the cow outfits. There will be some craning of necks and looking back on the part of those already in as the dusky riders are being judged. They will be keeping a watchful eye on them, and standing by in case a word or two might help, for they will be thinking of cold mornings when they blew their morning coffee and watched strapping Negro cow hands "top" hard-pitching Spanish branded horses that bore their saddles, or of cold rainy nights when the same Negro hands stood a double guard rather than call the white folk.

The range cattle industry as it is known today had its origin on the Texas Gulf coast whence spread cowmen and cattle to other sections of the state, to West Texas, and to other states which were destined to become range cattle states. As the southern cowman moved his herds west to find new ranges, he invariably brought a good Negro with him, and the Negro had to have faith in his white folk, for he was going into a country that held few, if any, of his race.

After the cattle country settled with farmers and their years came upon them, these Negroes moved into the towns where their white folk lived, and for the most part, lived under their patronage until they died. Some of them, with their accumulated savings, bought small homes or farms, and were respected by their communities.

A peculiar bond of affection existed between the cowman and the Negro cowboy, and as his sons grew, he turned them over to the Negro hand to be taught the rudiments of the cow business—roping, riding, and the lore of the trail, for there was no better cowman on earth than the Negro, nor a more picturesque figure in the Southwest than the dusky rider with his white hat, red neckerchief, yellow overalls, and high-top boots.

Until this good day, throughout the Southwest when old-time cowmen gather to talk of the days that were, you may be sure that before the session has gone far, there will be talk of old Buck, Ebb, Bill, or a dozen other Negro hands, and each of the old fellows will try to outdo the other in extolling the merits and faithfulness of his particular Negro. You will know from what they say why the Riders' last job will be easy, for it is not of record that one of these Negro cow hands ever went far wrong in his conduct or violated the laws of his country.

Every cattle section of the Southwest has and has had its well known Negro cowboys and cowmen. It would be impossible to give even a brief sketch of each of them, but here are sketches of a few typical dusky riders of the range.

The thirty-six years Coaly Owens worked for S. B. Burnett on his Kiowa and Comanche Indian Nation ranches was not forgotten when the owner died, for he provided a pension of $30 a month for Owens and charged one of his nephews, Clyde Burnett, of Benjamin, with the duty of seeing that Coaly was taken care of in his old age.

Heck Bazey learned the cattle trade under Luther Clark, a pioneer of the Texas cattle country, and when the latter retired from active business, went with Tom L. Burnett of Iowa Park, and lived on Burnett's Triangle Ranch until he died. Bazey died in a Wichita Falls hospital fifteen years ago, and his bier was covered with flowers bearing the cards of prominent cowmen of Texas and Oklahoma for whom he had done some favors in the past.

Among the first Negro cow punchers to gain publicity was Bill Pickett, a Williamson County Negro, who, nearly forty years ago, introduced the bulldogging or throwing of steers from a running horse. Bulldogging, or steer wrestling, has become a popular sport in the rodeos and wild west shows throughout the nation. Pickett set a pace that the modern bulldoggers have never been able to equal in that he gripped the steer's nose with his teeth in throwing him. He was a very small Negro, but unusually stout, and had a technique in handling steers that has not been equaled until this day. In his prime, he gave exhibitions of bulldogging in every state in the Union, and made one trip abroad with the Miller Brothers' 101 Wild West Ranch Show. The most spectacular exhibition ever staged by Pickett was in the bull ring in Mexico City, where, amid the hoots and jeers of the Mexican populace, he bulldogged a Spanish fighting bull.

Before Geronimo and Cochise, blood-thirsty Apache raiders, had left the section and while Indian signal smokes might still be seen from the peaks of the Davis Mountains, William Patton came to the Del Rio country to work for R. L. Nevil, T. M. Lease, and other border cattlemen. With money saved from his wages, Bill bought a little bunch of cattle down near the Rosillos Mountains, sixty miles south of Marathon, and later moved his cattle to the lower Terlingua Creek near its confluence with the Rio Grande. His herd grew to around six hundred head, but years of battling with border bandits who raided from across the river to drive back into Old Mexico the cattle belonging to Patton and his white neighbors, caused him to dispose of his land and cattle. He moved to Del Rio, where he lives now, around seventy-five years of age, a little crippled by rheumatism, but in good spirits and with money enough to keep him comfortably for his remaining years. Probably no American Negro knows as much of Mexican border banditry as does Patton.

Tige Avery landed in the Fort Griffin country nearly sixty years ago, a twelve-year-old boy. Fort Griffin at that time was an Indian outpost, outfitting point for buffalo hunters, and one of the most lurid trail towns of all cattle history. He attached himself to the Matthews and Reynolds families, who controlled much of the cattle country, and worked cattle for them nearly sixty years. He experienced every hardship of the trail, and was in many parties trailing Indians who had killed and robbed cowmen of the Fort Griffin area.

In 1881 Tige was on a trip with a herd to the Indian agencies of
Montana, when the outfit was overtaken by a late blizzard in the Platte
River country of Nebraska. After holding the herd as long as possible,
until the temperature had dropped below zero, the boss gave orders
to turn the herd loose and make for the wagon. In order to conserve
fuel and keep from freezing, the cowboys immediately sought their
bedrolls. Tige waited until the boss, a member of the Reynolds family,
was in bed, after which he spread his own bedding over him, saying
that he would keep warm in the wagon. "Like hell you will," said the
young boss, "you crawl in here with me," which he did.

They broke the crust of the ice and sleet on their beds next morning
to find that the last one of their saddle horses had frozen to death
during the night and their herd had drifted far to the south. Another
trail herd, which had been more fortunate in pitching camp in a coulee
where their saddle horses could find shelter, divided their horses with
Tige's outfit and assisted them in gathering their scattered herd.

Tige was a life-long and honored member of the Texas Cowboy
Reunion Association. He died last year at their annual reunion in
Stamford—died in the best hospital the city afforded, with a pair of
new boots, that had been presented to him by friends during the
reunion, under the side of his bed. Members of the Reynolds and
Matthews families were with him when he died, and carried his
remains back to the little cemetery at old Fort Griffin in which are
buried cowmen, scouts, buffalo hunters, army officers, and pioneers.

One of the most interesting stories of the Negro cow hands who
came west, and a story of achievement as well, is that of D. W. (80
John) Wallace, who lives three and one-half miles south of Loraine in
Mitchell County. Not only is it a story of achievement, but an example
of what cows and the cow country can do for one who handles them
as they should be handled. The "80" prefix to Wallace's name comes
from the fact that he came into that section of West Texas riding in
the dust of the drag of a herd of Clay Mann's cattle which had burned
on their sides the numeral 8 0 from backbone to belly.

Born in Victoria County of slave parents in 1860, Wallace knew little
from birth but cow work, and began drawing wages as a cowboy when
fifteen years old. When seventeen years of age, he made the four-
hundred mile ride alone from Victoria through Indian country to the
corners of Runnels and Taylor counties near the present town of
Buffalo Gap, which, in the days of the buffalo and open range, was a
frontier outfitting point. He came to work for the late Sam Gholson,

veteran Indian fighter and cowman. He worked for him one summer, and began working for the N U N outfit, who were claiming a range and running some eight thousand cattle on the headwaters of the Clear Fork of the Brazos River. After sixteen months, he joined Clay Mann's outfit, which was locating South Texas cattle on a range centering where Colorado City is now located. These were the first cattle to come into that section of West Texas.

During the fourteen years that he worked for the Manns, he saw every phase of open-range cow work, saw the last of the buffaloes disappear, and with his outfit, trailed a band of Comanche Indians that had strayed from the reservation and stolen the saddle horses of the Manns, back to their reservation at Fort Sill in the Indian Territory.

With the trail herds, he made long trips to Abilene and Dodge, the railheads and marketing centers in Kansas. He saw the Texas and Pacific Railroad come into the section, and the town of Colorado grow into a thriving railroad city and cattle-shipping point for a vast area of the Great Plains. He worked with and for cattle barons who have made history in the Southwest—Winfield Scott, Gus O'Keefe, the Slaughters, Bush and Tillar, Sug Robertson, the Ellwoods of Spade Ranch fame, and the managers and ranch bosses of the Scotch- and English-owned ranches to the northwest.

In 1885, he began to hear talk around campfire and shipping pen that the days of free grass and open range were nearly over, and that a man who expected to stay in the cow business would have to buy and fence his lands. Acting on this information, he put his accumulated savings into the section of land on which he now lives, and continued to ride with the cow outfits until the country passed from the cowman to the stock farmer. Since the original purchase, he has added twelve and one-half sections of good land to his holdings. Five to six hundred good Hereford cattle are on his grassland, the kind that the 4-H Club boys look to for their feeder calves. Twelve hundred of his acres are planted to cotton and feed each year, and a high percentage of his pasture land is subject to cultivation. His ranch home of eight rooms is modern in every respect, and his barns, lots, and corrals are of the best. When John Wallace tells you that he owns twelve and one-half sections of land and six hundred head of cattle, he means it literally, for no liens, mortgages, or past-due tax bills overshadow his ownership. He did not receive government aid in any form during the depression, nor has he signed waivers on his cotton crop. During the depression, Wallace added two sections of land to his holdings, for which he paid cash.

At seventy-five years of age, Wallace is hale and hearty and attends to his own affairs. He has not forgotten his days in the saddle, and in his seventy-fourth year rode a high-bucking dun pony down the streets of Loraine.

They tell you around Colorado that as the years passed, Wallace has almost uncannily kept track of financial affairs of certain white friends who assisted him in his earlier days, and that when their affairs have fallen in need of ready cash, he has unostentatiously called them aside to proffer financial aid.

He is held in high esteem by the citizens of Mitchell County. At each meeting of an organization of pioneers of the section, he is called on to say a few words, and in manner deferential and in language wholly lacking in Uncle Remus dialect, he tells them of their country as he first saw it more than half a century ago, unsullied by barbed wire and train smoke, a cowman's paradise of running water, grass-covered hills and wide fertile valleys, where antelope played, and the South Texas cows of Mr. Clay Mann grazed among the still fresh carcasses of the slaughtered buffaloes.

Range Language

As the men of the sea have a jargon almost unintelligible to the landlubber, so has the cowboy of West Texas a language of words and phrases to describe his physical condition or the condition of the cattle, horses, grass, and men of the outfit that he works for. To a layman or an Easterner the words would be puzzling, but when two men of the range meet along the fence line, the conversation flows smoothly and freely, and each goes his way with a complete knowledge of the other's affairs and the condition of the outfit—a knowledge that has been arrived at without waste of words.

Ride over to the Block outfit on Talking John Creek for a visit with Lige Hicks, who has been with the outfit nearly forty years, and perhaps by the time you have discussed his condition and inquired about things in general, you will get an idea of the language. Reports have it that he has been "under the weather" for some time. He hobbles out on the front porch in his stocking feet to ask you to "light" and come in. You inquire as to his health and he tells you that he isn't real sick, but was feeling so "unpeart" that he couldn't "make a hand," so he brought his "hot roll" and came in from the wagon to "soak" around the "doghouse" for a few days. Further inquiry develops the fact that he got "gypped" last week when they were branding calves at the corral over on Croton Creek.

Having found that his physical condition is not serious, inquire about the grass on the outfit's 400,000 acres, and, if it be a seasonable year, he will tell you that "the grass is belly deep to a camel" or if it be an unseasonable year, he will tell you that "there is not enough grass to wad a smooth bore single-barrel shotgun." Knowing that the latter condition brings disaster to the cow country in still another form, ask if they are having any trouble this year with cattle bogging, and he will reply, "there ain't a creek in the outfit that don't bog a saddle blanket," and you will know that the high standard of bogging set by Johnnie Jones has been reached.

With range conditions discussed and disposed of, Lige will tell you of an "individual horse" down in the "starveout," that "can turn on a dime and give you six cents change." You will know that the individual horse is his own property, and is running in the fifteen or twenty acres of pasture used to keep the outfit's night horse in or to hold a small herd for a few hours. The name "starveout" comes from the fact that its size, and constant usage permits little or no grass to grow in it. You will also know that the horse in question is a top cutting horse noted for his ability to turn in following an animal being cut from the herd.

Inquire whether or not Sebe Nichols is still breaking horses for the outfit, and you will learn that "this outfit's broncs got to 'pilin' Sebe so regular that he quit bronc bustin', married, and is nesterin' over on Duck Creek." This will mean that Sebe, following the footsteps of all good bronc riders, has got so stiff that he couldn't ride like he used to, has married, and settled down to farming on the creek named.

You might inquire as to whatever became of Pat Leonard, another old-timer that you both knew, and Lige will tell you that Pat "layed 'em down" about five years ago, and was buried at Childress.

Speaking of an outfit on Catfish whose owner, a newly rich oil man, is not experienced in the cow business, you will learn that he works only drug-store cowboys and rodeo hands who "chouse" his cattle and horses something awful. Now this word "chouse" has been handed down from trail-driving days and is in general use wherever cows, cowboys, and horses are to be found. It is used to indicate that a man is hard on his horses and cattle, handles them rough and fast, with no respect for their condition or the damage that might be done them.

To the rank and file of cowmen who work with a technique acquired from long practice, "chousing" is a mark of poor cowmanship. Unlike other words adopted by cowboys to make their descriptions expressive, this word is an orphan unless it traces back to an old English word, "jaust," meaning to cheat or swindle by various underhand means. Its application to the cattle industry is rather vague.

If we had more time, it would be fine to let Lige tell of his "gallin" and "Sunday horses," and of how Talking John, Turtle Hole, Mess Box, and a hundred other creeks on the outfit came by their names. Later, maybe, Lige can be induced to talk about these things.

Before the telephone, radio, and automobile came to the cow country, news of roundups, meetings, and funerals was carried from town to ranch and from ranch to ranch by riders who would bring the news and ask the one given it to "pass the word along" to the next fellow. In this manner, the news soon got out over a good-sized area.

If an outfit was ready to start spring branding and wanted neighboring outfits to send stray men to gather their cattle, a cowboy was sent a few days before to neighboring ranches with instructions to tell the bosses, "We are going to start working Monday week and the old man says tell you to come yourself or send a hand and to tell everybody you see."

Sometimes hands met along trail or fence line and passed the word and then took advantage of the meeting to clear to each other the gossip of the "country" they worked in. Such meetings always eventually found both men squatting on the ground, each armed with the cowboy's fountain pen—a broomweed stalk and plenty of loose dirt to draw in. One may be showing the other a strange brand that has shown up on strays in his outfit, or, he may be showing him how a fence line runs or a short cut to some far camp or ranch. Again, he may be giving explicit directions as to how to reach some nester house where a dance is to be held Saturday night where yellow-haired gals that really know how to "swing partners" will be plentiful.

Then will follow a general discussion of cattle, grass, water, and prices. After the livestock and range situation is covered the talk will drop into a discussion of the merits of various boot- and saddlemakers and their products, and on through the merits of round-skirt saddles, Navajo blankets, and whether thirty-two or thirty-six feet is the proper length for a rope. An hour of this and they go their way, each with a full knowledge of what is going on in the country. It is a "conference" of the range.

There are other "conferences" of the range, whenever a bunch of boys can find a spot to "shade" a bit after a hard job. "Shadin'," if you don't know, means in cowboy language hunting a "black spot," or shade for a few minutes rest or to eat a snack, and does not necessarily mean that the boys are "throwin' off," or "soldiering," on the old man. "Soakin'" in the same language means lying around bunkhouse or wagon all day on your bed. If this is done too much the term is sometimes used in derision.

When the boys drop down for a few minutes rest cinches are loosened and if it be a steady old horse the bit is taken from his mouth for easier grazing, but the head stall and reins are left on. Shadin' affords an opportunity to pull off boots, straighten wrinkled socks, smoke a cigarette or two and do a lot of "augurin'" (talking or yarning). The talk will run from risqué stories, old and mild, to a general discussion of the boss's business and how it should be run. Other outfits, their shortcomings and good qualities, will also come in for general discussion.

There will always be one fellow with the bunch who will take a stick and show you in the soft dirt how the cow thief ran the X I T brand into a Star Cross and tell you to a penny how much the Syndicate outfit paid him to show them how it was done. This brings on more brand drawing and explanations of how they could or couldn't be "run" or changed into some other brand. This winds up by each man tracing the brand he expects to use, when and if, he gets his own little "lay"—meaning a good little ranch—and quits working for wages. This last is usually followed by each of them stretching out full length with his hat over his eyes to silently contemplate the future management of his "if and when outfit." Check back over your cattle history and you will find that most of the big cattle fortunes were founded by cow hands who worked for wages until they got enough for a start of their own.

Cow Horses

On the larger cow outfits which depended upon a chuck wagon as a base of supply for their men during the summer work, so far back as I can recall, each year about "the rise of grass" which in North and Northwest Texas is around the last of April, wagon cooks, with the aid of hands "soaking" around the bunkhouse, rolled the "wagon" out from under the shed at headquarters where it had spent the winter months accumulating dust over the grease in which its equipment had been put down in the fall. Water in generous quantities was put to boil in the headquarters lady's washpot and tubs to which was added lye or lye soap. The cook scrubbed the box to an almost snowy whiteness after which he took an old case knife and dug the dirt and grease from out the cracks and around the nail heads which held the kitchen-cabinetlike chuck box together. With the box clean, he went to work on his pots, pans, skillets, and ovens, supplementing the lye or lye soap with sand to obtain a high ebony polish on the utensils. Cups, plates, knives, and forks received similar treatment after which they went into their respective drawers and cubby holes in the chuck box, along with the working supplies of salt, pepper (both black and cayenne), chili powder, baking powder, a few buttons of garlic, and a can or two of cinnamon and nutmeg. The water barrel which rode in the front end of the wagon also received a good cleaning out and airing.

From a generous supply of flour sacks taken from the ranch kitchen, he unraveled a summer's supply of dish cloths and towels, being careful to save a goodly number of the larger ones for aprons. One week XXXX might adorn his apron, with Pride of the West, Kitchen Queen, Petunia, or Honeysuckle featured the next week. In the use of these he came in closer relation with the domestic life of the ranch owner or headquarters man and his family than at any other time. Full many a cowman who today wears shorts and complains of the shortage and price of them made the change-over from triangular underwear to a more masculine kind which bore the name, front and rear, of some flour favored by the ranch, and which had been run up on the New Home sewing machine (with drop head and full attachments) which his mother boasted as her most cherished possession. No, the use of feed sacks for underwear, house dresses, and such, is nothing new.

When he completed these spring-cleaning duties, the cook's hands, from much recent contact with hot water and strong soap, closely resembled those of the cow-town gambler whom he had always understood washed his hands only in alcohol to keep his fingers nimble and spry in pursuit of his vocation, or those of the town's baker whose contact with flour and shortening made him a close second to the gambler in the matter of white hands. Be that as it may, his next duty was to give his fingernails a very close trimming, carefully removing any signs of winter mourning that may have escaped his pocket knife in the trimming process. Knowing that the boys would help him with sheet, bows, and fly when they were ready to start out, he relaxed against a rear wagon wheel to comment to himself, "Here she is, clean as a whistle. Like to see any of them 'twenty-five-dollar-a-month hands' show me any sign or smell of where rats or mice wintered in this box." He didn't "start" his sour-dough keg or load his supplies of flour, salt, sow belly, beans, dried peaches, canned corn, Arbuckle coffee, and canned tomatoes into the wagon box until the boys got back with the horses and the outfit was almost ready to pull out. His sugar supply was not loaded until last as a safeguard against infestation from a small specie of brown ant, the entomological name of which bore no relation in any form to the one bestowed upon it by the cowboys and cook. Their name must have been eminently correct and in general use throughout the nation for I recall yet that when I was a boy riding a stock train I asked a brakeman who was putting track torpedoes in a rack what they were used for. He replied, in the characteristic tone that railroad men assumed toward cowboys and hog men riding with them who asked too many questions, that they were used to blow the ants off the track, thereby preventing them from eating up the steel rails and wrecking the train. He used the same name for the ant that I'd always heard used.

Meanwhile, even before the cook started his cleaning operations, the bronc buster was at work getting the bunch of young horses ready to join the *remuda* when the spring work started. Changing methods have now done away with the old-time professional bronc buster who used to break horses for the outfits at five dollars per month more wages than was paid the regular hands. Sometimes he did it by the head, or so much per "saddle," meaning each time the horse was saddled and ridden before he was turned into the *remuda* as a "broke" horse.

Bronc busters were born to their trade. Any cow hand could do enough roping to hold his job, and would take his two or three half-broken broncs along with his string of gentle horses and do his best to ride them provided he could not keep them from pitching. A very small per cent acknowledged themselves as bronc riders, and the majority of them dreaded a pitching horse.

When the range-cattle industry was at its height, the majority of the outfits ran a bunch of stock horses from which they raised horses to supply their *remudas*. Others bought one or two carloads of un-broken horses each year as replacements. As a rule, the horses were broken in the spring before they were three years old.

The bronc buster worked to himself at the headquarters place, usually having a hand from the outfit as helper. Work started in the circular or bronc pen, where the first half-dozen horses selected had been penned. The horses knew little or nothing of man and his ways, their only contact having been when they were branded as colts. Bringing them around the corral in a run, the buster stood in the center and picked up the forefeet of the leading horse, and busted him, as he expressed it, "to put the fear of God into him." Sometimes he would let him up and repeat the busting process until the horse had the wind pretty well knocked out of him, after which the helper would sit on his head until the buster fitted a rope, halter, or hackamore to his head. To the shank rope of this would be tied an old lariat rope, twenty-five to thirty feet in length. Allowed to rise to his feet with his wind regained, the horse would start running, only to be jerked down or reversed by the strain on head and nose when he reached the end of the rope.

Some busters caught their horses for the first time over the head, and snubbed or choked them until they fell gasping. This process would be repeated until half a dozen horses were haltered, after which they were taken into the horse pasture by rider and helper mounted on steady old cow horses, with the bronc snubbed close to the saddle horn. They were staked to picket pins, or drags made of large stones or logs, and left to figure out as best they could what was happening to them. They would throw themselves several times before giving up to stand dejectedly with their noses sore and raw from the hackamores.

A day and night on stake found them sore, but still fighting when the buster came to take the first one into the corral for the initial saddling. After hazing him around the pen for a few minutes, the buster and his helper would begin the saddling process by tying up one of the horse's feet. This was done by running a long loop over the horse's head and against his shoulders, tying it so that it would not slip, but would lie on the horse much as an ordinary work collar would. The slack of the rope from which the loop was made was thrown under the fetlock of one rear foot and brought up through the loop and enough slack taken to raise the foot from the ground, after which the rope was tied in the loop. On three feet, the horse could not kick when approached with a saddle.

When the blanket was thrown on, the horse usually threw himself in an effort to run, but a few struggles and the rope began to burn around the fetlock until pain caused the horse to stand while the saddle was thrown on and cinched.

Sometimes, the helper eared the horse down; and sometimes he used a blindfold. When the saddle was cinched tightly, the foot was let down, and loop and rope removed, after which the horse, crazed by the cinching and pain, would do its best to rid itself of the saddle. The buster and helper would leave the corral for a visit to bunkhouse or water trough for half an hour to let the bronc wear himself down before he was ridden.

Back at the corral, the horse was caught and cinches tightened still more. Some riders preferred taking their mounts to the open for the first riding, others made the first ride in the corral, and then turned them out. With the rider ready to climb into the saddle, the helper either snubbed the bronc close to his saddle horn, or eared him from the ground and held him firmly until the rider mounted and got set in the saddle and told him to turn loose.

When the helper turned the bronc loose, he mounted his own horse and became herder for the buster, for when the bronc stopped pitching and began running, the herder had to circle him from wire fence, brush, or creek bank, because the bronc was not bridle-wise and the rider had little or no control of him.

The old-time bronc buster rode "slick," meaning that he would not resort to hobbled stirrups or bucking roll, which was a slicker or coat tied back of the saddle horn to wedge him in the saddle, or take the shock when he was thrown against it. He would sometimes wet his chaps and saddle in riding an unusually "salty" one. Wet leather does not lend itself to slipping, and it enabled him to stay close to the saddle.

He gripped the horse from his spur rowels to his hips, but left the upper part of his body loose up to his chin. A pitching horse has an action similar to the walking beam of an old-fashioned steamboat, the action being magnified and with much shorter stroke. Unless the bronc rider buried his chin into his collar, holding his head and neck rigid, this action would soon have his head popping in such a manner that he could not control the rest of his body. The jolt of the horse landing stiff-legged on all four feet every three seconds sent a jar up the rider's spinal column that shocked every nerve in him. It was this jarring that stiffened bronc riders and made them prematurely old, causing them to lose their nerve before their time. It was not unusual for a bronc buster to dismount from a horse bleeding from nostril and mouth.

This manner of riding is known in rodeo parlance as "tight-legging," and would disqualify a rodeo rider at once, for under rodeo rules, he is supposed to scratch or spur his horse continuously until the whistle blows. The old Spanish horse pitched from three-hundred yards to a quarter mile, and the bronc buster was more interested in staying on than in the performance he was putting up; no whistle blew for him. His calling demanded that he stay on, both as a matter of pride and because outlawed horses were the result of thrown riders.

The best of them would get thrown occasionally, and no professional bronc buster boasted that there was no horse that he could not ride. Freakish as it may appear, if you asked a bronc buster how he was thrown, he would almost always reply, "over the right shoulder."

Probably the greatest of the Southwestern bronc busters was the famous "Booger Red" Privett, of the San Angelo country, who was the idol of Southwestern cowboys as long as he lived. Privett was very small, but had a technique in riding that has not been equaled until this day. Another famous rider of the North Texas cattle country was Bruce Norton, of Quanah, who rode and won first monies at the St. Louis World Fair in 1904, and later in Madison Square Garden, New York, where he was awarded a world's championship belt. Claude Jeffers, of the Matador Land and Cattle Company, has broken and turned into his company's *remudas* more than thirty-five hundred horses during the thirty years that he has worked for them. Jeffers, while an expert rider, always leaned toward the gentler methods of breaking and handling than most of the other riders.

Hazardous as the profession is, there are few, if any, fatalities among the riders.

Now, the buster's job and profits depended on getting the horse worn and broken enough in spirit to turn into the *remuda* as quickly as possible, so he gave him all the pitching and running he could stand the first saddling, after which he took him back to the stake rope or drag to await his turn for the next saddling. A similar process was repeated on each of the six horses until they, too, could be turned into the *remuda*, after which the same process would be gone through with another half-dozen of them. On an average, nine saddlings were considered sufficient before the horse was turned into the *remuda*.

While the spring cleaning of equipment, wagon, and person was in process, and while the bronc buster was doing his job, the winter hands and two or three fellows who had been told to show up around the 20th if they wanted a job of work with the outfit that year had been sent down into the pasture where the outfit's saddle horses ranged and wintered. It was not too far away to be worked without the wagon for there was a camp along the fence of the "Big" pasture where a man or two had been stationed during the winter. This was sort of a favored pasture with good grass and a number of big flats heavily timbered with mesquite brush, which in good years yielded succulent mesquite beans, highly popular with horses and said to have the nutritive value of shelled corn. These flats lay to the south of the hills that afforded protection and were first to have green grass, tallow weeds, and other early growth from which the horses might benefit. An ample supply of water along the creek at the foot of the hills provided practically all-winter green grazing. It was almost a horse heaven where sore backs could hair over and tired muscles relax for six months at a time with no wrangler on their tails in the early morning and no one roping over or at them three or four times a day. If they belonged to the right kind of an outfit the horses had gone into the winter in good working shape with little or no surplus flesh but still full of pep and go that made them good cow horses.

Before they had been turned loose in the fall their owner had given them a pretty thorough going over as to age, condition, and how they had stood the summer's work. Ten or fifteen head had been taken out because of their age, condition, and bad feet, or for various other reasons. By the time the average cow horse is ten to twelve years old he has slowed up considerably from the hard work, jarring stops, and shocks that go with cow work. His knees are not as good as they were nor his feet as sure. The cowboys don't like to ride an old horse in hard work as there is more likelihood of stumbles and falls after a horse has reached or passed the twelve-year mark. From seven to nine he is in his prime and has attained his cow sense if he is ever to have any. Most of the large outfits placed a year brand on the jaw or shoulder of their horses if they were raising their own, to designate the year in which they were born. By this method they could check ages readily without guesswork or the necessity of trying to determine age by the teeth or mouth method. Occasionally an unusually good horse or a fair old cutting horse was held over for "the good he had done," or because there were a couple of years more limited service in him. The older horses were designated as "condemned"; they were left in the home pastures and around headquarters until they had rested up and their backs were sound again. When they were in good flesh once more they were sold "down the river" to horse traders who made a business of selling them in town or taking them to the cotton country for sale to Negroes and tenant farmers to whom they gave a few years of good service if properly cared for.

Ordinarily the condemned horses were replaced with an equal number of young horses just finished with their breaking, at least insofar as saddle and bridle were concerned. There remained the task of teaching them *remuda* etiquette and they had to learn how to take care of themselves under hard work on wholly a grass ration and how to take the fewest steps necessary to get them from place to place, and to graze as they moved. These young horses, scarred and jaded by the breaking process, were issued one or two to each man of the outfit. The man knew that he was getting them with their spirits pretty well broken, and that if he did not keep them that way, but allowed them to recover, he would not be able to handle them. Occasionally some hand would announce proudly that he had drawn a "natural" that would follow a cow to the moon and keep a rope tight on a bull elephant if you tied onto one.

Normally the young horse's first work as an apprentice was that of circle horse, meaning that he was ridden on the circle or roundup which called for no particular skill other than the ability to stand up under three or four hours at a short choppy lope as the cattle were thrown on the roundup ground for the day's work. This was a very satisfactory method of leveling the young horse off and keeping ideas out of his head about remaining a bronc. If the fellow who drew him was sincerely trying to make a cow horse of him, he would get some work on the herd grounds where cutting out and branding was going on and where he might be called on for some close work in assisting between herd and cut. If the animal was a "bright horse" and evidenced it he would soon develop to a point where the pseudonym of bronc was forgotten and he could take his place as a regular horse. If he got too good and came under the boss's eye, the teacher might lose him to the latter's top string. This was one of the boss's prerogatives if he cared to exercise it. There have been cases when a boy had developed a bronc into a pretty fair cow horse, but kept him pitching a little each morning to keep someone else from wanting him.

The learning of *remuda* etiquette didn't require much other than learning to do what the older horses did. The young horse still recalled vividly the burn and sear of the rope that caught and threw him when he was branded or the bite of the hackamore when he was undergoing his initial breaking. When he went into the V-shaped rope corral anchored to tree or wagon wheel, he was highly respectful of the ropes held by half a dozen cowboys as the balance caught out their mounts. A mere twitch of one of the ropes sent him hurrying back into the center of the horse herd. He soon learned to stand still as the loops whirled over his head to encircle the neck of his nearest neighbor. He learned that a rope would not hurt or burn if he didn't run against it, so he stood perfectly still or stopped dead when the loop came around his neck. He was not inclined to break through the corral or head for the open with a queue of first- and second-year broncs following him. He recalled the fine upstanding gray gelding who tried this a number of times with some success until the wagon boss stationed a "slick roper" to pick up his forefeet and "bust him" if he tried it again, and how the roper failed to get both feet but did catch one with the result that the gray crashed to earth to arise with a dangling foreleg and broken shoulder and how the boss rode out from the wagon to end the horse's suffering with the cook's axe, and was met by the apologetic roper whom he soothed with, "Yeah! He was a good horse, but if we couldn't keep him in the *remuda* he'd just as well be dead. He would have had our horses scattered from hell to breakfast every time we tried to change horses." Of course that was when cow ponies were cheap—$20 to $30 per head.

The young horse learned to have respect for the old-timers among the horses who maintained their positions as leaders with nipping teeth and flashing heels that spelled evil to any young upstart who crowded them too much. He learned too that the soft short rope knotted around his neck meant more freedom and fresher grazing in the night and early morning hours when he was hobbled rather than under herd. In time he came to pay little or no attention to the boys or wranglers as they worked among the horses in the dusk, hobbling, or in the cool red morning, unhobbled.

All of this took time, however. Education came the hard way to the young horses of the cow outfits. It was usually the beginning of the third year with the *remuda* before the young horse recovered from the rigors of breaking, and began to be really useful to the outfit. It is not hard to figure that three years of the horse's useful life had been consumed in this breaking process.

These methods are in direct contrast to those employed by most of the ranches today in breaking and training their horses. On the great King Ranch in South Texas, which must have fifteen hundred well-broken and trained cow horses to handle and market its hundred thousand cattle each year, they are using a method that is being adopted by the larger ranches in South Texas and throughout the Southwest.

The breaking process on the ranch begins when the colts are weaned from their mothers. The elementary steps are taken by six- to twelve-year-old Mexican boys, sons of the *vaqueros* working on the ranch— and future *vaqueros* themselves. Colts are issued to these boys, and a handful of oats allotted for them daily. They play with the colts, make and place their own soft rope hackamores on them, and in a few months are riding bareback and reining them with the hackamores alone.

As two-year-olds, the colts go to the *remudas,* not for hard work, but for training under the saddle and in reining. This is done by *vaqueros* under the direction of a *caporal*. He sees that the animals learn not to fear the rope, having been handled only with a soft one that will not burn under the feet and legs as they are ridden around the circular corral.

Until this time, the young horse has not known a bridle, having been taught to rein and handle with only the hackamore. When he is three years old, a limber bit is placed in his mouth, and lessons given in reining and turning before the stiff or curb bit is used. There is no such thing as cold-jawed or dead-headed horses on the King Ranch. So perfect are the horses' mouths and so light the touch of the *vaquero* that they well might be ridden with the reins of silken thread. King Ranch horses fear neither man nor rope, and can be caught from the *remuda* without the use of rope or corral.

It is usually during the third year that the horse is given light work, but watched carefully so that he is not strained nor his spirit broken. In his fourth year, he may take his turn with the other horses during the rush of the shipping season. Not until his fifth year is he allowed to replace an older horse.

The change in method of breaking and training cow horses has been brought about through the fact that fewer and better horses are being used. The advent of the automobile cut into horse breeding severely, and has made real cow-horse material hard to find and worth considerably more than the old-time forty-dollar cow pony. The cowman wants to get the maximum good from his investment in a horse, and insists that the animal be broken so that it may last three to five years longer than the old type did. The evolution of the Texas cow horse into the modern polo pony has also been responsible for more care in selecting and breaking the cow horse. Any good Texas cutting horse is a potential candidate for the polo field, and may bring a fancy price to its owner. Many of the ranches which raise their own horses breed and train them with the polo market in view, for 90 per cent of the polo horses used in America come from Texas.

Another departure from older procedures is the breaking of mares and their use in *remudas* at the King Ranch. These are developed even more carefully than the horses. When a mare gives evidence that she has become an unusual cow horse, she is taken from the *remuda*, and placed in the brood herd. They are reasonably sure her offspring will be a highly sensible cow horse.

King cowboys ride and use the same horses from the day they are broken until they are too old for service. When a mare has been developed by a cowboy and is taken from his mount to the brood herd, she is credited to that cowboy who has first call on her colt when it is born.

But to return to the account of our typical old cow outfit—the 150 horses that the boys turned into the headquarters horse pasture in a cloud of dust late one afternoon were about an average bunch of horses, nearly all of solid color; browns, bays, sorrels, and duns, with no paints for that coloring of horse finds little more favor in the average *remuda* than does a mare. There are no mares in the average *remuda* for the very evident reason that they are a disturbing element. The horses had wintered well, were in good flesh, and represented the motive power of the cattle industry; without them with which to gather snaky cattle from breaks, brush, and plains there could be no cattle industry as the Southwest knows it. The death or entire disappearance of every cow horse in the cow country simultaneously would effect it much as the failure of every engine of the railroad system at one time: everything would come to a standstill.

Some springs the horses did not come in so frisky or looking so good: this was after the winters when they had undergone a siege of distemper, the cow horse's worst enemy except overwork or short grass. It is rarely fatal but leaves them lean, long-haired, watery of eye and nose, coughing, and too weak for hard use. It effects a horse much as a hard cold or influenza does a human being. Almost inevitably it results in a running sore under the lower jaw; the bursting of this sore apparently climaxes the disease and the animal begins showing improvement almost immediately. It usually has a course of three or four months. Some springs when an epidemic was unusually bad it was necessary to postpone horse work and starting the wagon until they had recovered. It yields to no treatment other than rest and time, but may be prevented in many cases by vaccination. Fortunately it did not occur in epidemic proportions each year; cowboys and owners dreaded a distemper epidemic above all things.

Next morning the horses were rounded and brought to the ranch corral for assignment. They were frisky and inclined to break back to seek haunts they knew under the cottonwoods along the creek of the home horse pasture. It required a little pushing to keep them coming ahead. "They'll have all that out of them by the time we get the Cuba breaks worked and some of that grass belly off them," remarked one of the boys riding in the dust of the drag. Once in the corral and after they had ceased milling, the boss gave them the once over. If he happened to own the outfit he viewed them with pride of ownership, noting their sturdy build, solid colors, and smooth backs with no signs of "set fast" or old sores; if he was a hired wagon boss he analyzed them from the standpoint of their capability. They constituted the tools of his trade and he knew his work could be no better than his horses. Too, he knew his ability as a wagon boss would be gauged by the condition of the horses in the fall. Many a good wagon boss based his decision as to whether he would accept the job of running an outfit on the number and kind of horses that it owned.

Our horses were still wearing most of their winter hair but had been rubbing it off against the mesquites and overhanging limbs; their manes and tails carried a knot of cockleburs picked up along the creek bottoms during the fall and winter months. The long hair would cause them a little worry and some overheating for a short time but a few good sweatings would take care of that. There would be plenty of long hair on the sweat pads though for a few weeks. The boys would work the burrs out of mane and tail each time they rode them until they were all gone.

Each of the 150 horses had a name bestowed upon it the first year it was turned into the horses. Ordinarily the names came from some peculiar markings, disposition, or occurrence. This varied, however, for a big rough old horse might carry the name of a movie actress or a dance hall favorite in one of the places in the railroad town. I recall one *remuda* in which there were eight horses named Dick, each with a prefix distinguishing him from the others; for instance, Big Dick, Little Dick, Blue Dick, Red Dick, Dun Dick, Black Dick, Shorty Dick, and Long Dick. In another *remuda* I recall Clara Bow, Big-Nosed Kate, and Cornbread Mat; in still another were to be found Clabber Belly, Dromedary, Milk Shake, Whiskey Pete, Gentle Annie, Dutchman, Stinging Lizard, Vinegarroon, Churn Head, Boot Jack, Seven Up, Red Bird, Little Stud, Sassy Sam, and Gotch Ear. The paper shortage is far too acute to attempt to list all the names one could recall from the various *remudas*, so let it suffice to say that each of them had at least one Brown Jug, one Nigger, one Big Enough, and one Yellow Jacket. Each of the horses in the *remuda* not only bore a name but had an individuality and personality of its own that made it as easy to identify or as easy to miss from the *remuda* as it would be to miss a person whom you are accustomed to seeing in a given place at a given time. Remarkable as it may seem, a cowboy or a ranch boss could identify and rope out any of the horses by name in the early morning hours or in the late dusk so long as he could "sky light" him. I recall one incident where failure to know his horses and men caused a ranch owner to get a severe whipping. It was on an English-owned outfit in the early days in the Panhandle which was managed by a crochety old Englishman far better versed in handling things in the English countryside from whence he came than in handling cattle and cowboys. He fell into the habit of abusing his men and talking roughly to them. One day at a roundup a cowboy came under his wrath and was roundly and profanely reprimanded for his dereliction, whereupon the man climbed down from his horse, yanked the Englishman from his buckboard and proceeded to beat the living hell out of him and informed him that he was not working for his outfit but was representing the Turkey Tracks. As a result, the old Englishman gave orders that the left ear of each horse in their *remuda* be grubbed close to his head so that in the future if he felt called upon to cuss anybody he could be sure that he was cussing one of his own men and not an outsider.

The same men rode the same horses each year insofar as possible. There was no fixed rule as to that but the boss felt that the men liked it better that way, did more efficient work, and were easier on the horses. He sized the hands up according to their ability and what he might use them for during the summer. The outside man who worked with the neighboring outfits must have a good steady string of good-looking well-seasoned horses among which would be a good cutting horse, a couple of roping horses, and a pack horse, with the balance just average cow horses. Boss or owner wanted him mounted well so that he could make a hand and his horses be representative of the kind they had at home. He had to have steady horses that would follow along with the strays when he went to turn in. In the matter of issuing the broncs, the boss looked the hands over pretty carefully and tried to assign them to fellows with fairly good sense for it is a foregone conclusion in the cow country that a man must have more sense than the horse if he is to teach the animal any cow sense.

Bear in mind that the assignment of the horses did not include any of the top string of the boss which was made up largely of the best cutting horses, a good steady roper or two, and one or two with a good long running walk or fox trot for use in going into town to order cars or for "prowling." When the horses had all been assigned there were left over some three or four: old Major, General Grant, General Lee, and Buffalo Bill. On the fence watching the catching and assigning process were an equal number of old hands who had served their usefulness on the ranch but were on the payroll and would be there until they died. One of them was the boss's wife's uncle, and the others came into the country with the first cattle and helped to establish the brand. They stayed around headquarters, riding fence, milking the cows, and helping the headquarters family generally. When there were none left of the *remuda* except the old horses with the military titles, the boss, eyeing the old fellows on the fence, would call out, "You fellows can divide these old-timers up among yourselves." There wasn't much kidding or laughing on the part of the younger fellows at this sally for they could foresee the day when they would stay home and ride old Major and the Generals if they stayed with cow punching.

For a day or two while the rest of the boys were getting in to pitch their bedrolls off and report for duty, the ones already on hand were catching their horses, rubbing the dead hair off them, and getting the burrs from their manes and tails. If there were a few doubtful ones among them or those who had a reputation for having to be broken each spring, they were saddled and used to wrangle horses with, to get the "hell" out of them. Ordinarily these did not buck much but would "goat" a little if the rider jumped them off too quick. Such horses might need to be "cheeked" for a while.

"Cheeking" a horse in cowboy language means "gittin' up in the big middle of him" without giving the horse an opportunity to run or begin pitching before the rider gets set in the saddle. If a man does not know the horse or it does not have saddle marks from withers to hips, you can be sure that it will be cheeked the first time he rides it. He does this because of the inherent dread that all cowmen have of being dragged to death.

To mount a horse in this manner the cowboy grasps the left cheek strap of the bridle just above the bits and pulls the horse's head as far toward the saddle as possible, while he turns his stirrup toward the horse's foreleg so as to place himself as far out of range of the hind feet as possible. The right rein is in normal position along the horse's neck, the left is grasped with the cheek strap. The cowboy places his left foot in the stirrup, moving up and down a time or two without making any effort to get into the saddle. If the horse stands quietly he will ease lightly into the saddle and when his feet are set in the stirrups, will release the cheek hold and be ready for the horse to pitch or pace.

Should the horse have started to run or pitch as he mounted, the cowboy would have been able to pull it directly toward him and in a circle so that he could remove his foot from the stirrup if he did not feel safe in going into the saddle. Having the horse swinging toward him instead of in the opposite direction almost automatically seats the rider. If the horse is a little "salty" and inclined to run or pitch, the cowboy will sometimes press his thumb into the left eye, causing it to lean toward him to relieve the pressure and pain. He dismounts in the same manner by pulling the horse's head toward the saddle and stepping off as far forward as possible.

When a horse has been ridden for a few months, cheeking is not necessary unless it has been spoiled in breaking by cinch sores and sore back. These cause it to swing toward the rider to ease the pain caused in mounting. Some horses spoiled this way have to be cheeked so long as they are used.

Being careful of a strange horse is only one of the traits of the cowboy. He has been taught by experience and tales told around bunk house and chuck wagon that there is nothing so tragic in cow work as to see a man dragged to death by a horse. No man who has picked up the remains of a fellow cowboy who has been dragged around the corral or across a prickly-pear flat with a foot hung to stirrup or rigging and four hoofs cutting him to ribbons, will ever forget the sight or the gloom that it cast over his own and neighboring outfits.

A cowboy's boots are designed with heels that will not permit his feet to go far into, or through the stirrup, and the horn string by which he carries his lariat rope is light so that if a spur catches in the coils of the lariat, the string will break easily.

If he is working in a prairie dog country he will shorten his stirrups a couple of holes and ride with his reins held as short as possible, for he knows if his horse plants both forefeet in a blind dog hole the tight rein and short stirrup will pull him clear of saddle horn and falling horse, much as an arrow is shot from a bow. He does not mind landing on his head, for he figures that cannot be damaged much, but he does want to fall clear. Should he go down with his horse, as is the case when one stumbles, or tries to catch himself and then falls, he will hold his horse down until help comes by the simple expedient of pulling the horn of his saddle down as far as possible and holding on. The horse cannot rise or do more than thresh around with his head. If the man is working alone and does not expect help, he will hold the horse down with one hand while he loosens the cinch with the other.

The horse will scramble to his feet when released, clear of both saddle and rider.

Visitors to the Stamford rodeo one year were given a practical demonstration of holding a fallen horse when Eric Swenson, pick-up man for the bronc-riding event, had his horse knocked down by a charging bronc which he was trying to snub to his saddle horn. Fearing that his foot was hung, Swenson held the horse down on himself until help came, then arose to wonder what the crowd in the stands were cheering about.

Most any cowboy can make a pretty fair ride on a pitching horse if he rides with "hobbled" stirrups, stirrups tied under the horse's belly, which practically tie the rider in his saddle. Woe to him if his horse falls, for so tightly are his feet held in the stirrups that it is impossible to get them clear before the horse is down. Out in the cow country a man who rides with hobbled stirrups is considered "plum crazy."

If you do not believe that cowmen have a horror of being dragged, or seeing anyone dragged, watch the next bunch of them at work and see their lips and faces tighten, their hands fall to their lariat ropes, when they see a horse and rider fall, and relax when they see that the rider has fallen clear.

Don't think that every horse you see cheeked is a bad one. Sometimes the "hoodlum" or handy man around the outfit is sent to the post-office, or over to the nester settlement on an errand. He is usually noted for not being a cow hand, but if there are ladies present he may poke the old pensioned cow pony that he is riding, one which hasn't pitched a jump in fourteen years, in the side with his thumb, grab the cheek of his bridle, and climb up into his "big middle" to impress the nester gals.

Came the day when the outfit pulled out for the breaks, canyons, and big flats to begin the summer's work that would not end until the last of the beef herds had been taken to the railroad and the mornings were snippy and the nights chilly. The horses were now in complete charge of the wranglers and would be for the summer. Much has been written, some of derogatory nature, about the wrangler: his youth and the general laziness connected with his job. For my money he was one of the most capable fellows around an outfit. It was his job to see that the horses were on good grass and water when not in use and that they were brought to wagon, corral, or roundup when needed with the minimum of "chousin'." Right quick, without having to think very hard, I can recall a couple of wranglers in our country who own or operate the outfits on which they once wrangled horses. One of them is Price Maddox of Colorado City, a cattleman and sheepman in his own right, who is high in the councils of both industries, being a past president of the Texas Sheep and Goat Raisers Association, and a director of the Texas and Southwestern Cattle Raisers Association. The other is Otto Jones who manages the destinies of the Ellwood Spade ranches in Mitchell County and on the plains.

In recent years there has been much written about the cowboy and his love for his horse. To judge from the movies a cowboy had only one horse, a sort of combination of cutting, roping, circle, and pack horse, upon which he lavished his affection and to which he sang and played the guitar almost constantly. Economically that would be an ideal situation if all these tasks could be accomplished by one horse. I would like to say here that I have never seen a real cowboy riding a horse and playing a guitar at the same time; the best I could offer would be an old French harp that eventually lost its usefulness from being carried in a jumper pocket with loose specimens of Bull Durham. I have never heard a real cowboy yodel unless it happened to be some kid with the outfit whose voice was changing and he yodeled without intending to. Times change, however, and it is possible that some of the *remuda* boys can do good work provided they have a good supply of extra G- and the strings that precede it in their saddle pocket.

One more thing, being raised in North Texas, I never heard an outfit's saddle horses referred to as a *remuda* nor its cook as a *cocinero*; in North Texas it was "the Horses" and "the feller who cooked for the wagon." Both terms are proper I know and have their origin in Mexico and with the coast outfits, but I can't get used to them. In my mind yet I can hear certain old fellows get up after breakfast and tell the wranglers to "take the horses on over to Shorty tank" and the cook to "camp the wagon under the cottonwood at the mouth of Owl Creek."

Cowboys love their horses as horses and for what they are capable of doing, not as individuals. To turn one loose, slap him with the bridle reins and say, "That's a damn good little horse; wish'd I owned him," was a real compliment. They probably had more sentiment toward a whole *remuda* than any individual horse in it. Andy Adams, in his book, *The Log of a Cowboy*, which deals with a trail trip from Brownsville to the Canadian border covering an eight-month period during which ten or fifteen men used the same horses, swam the Red, Canadian, Platte, and Yellowstone rivers on them and went through numerous stampedes, dismisses the selling of the *remuda* in the North-west by merely saying that there was a feeling of regret when the horses were turned over to their new owners.

An incident typical of the cowboy's feeling toward the horses is vividly described in *Short Grass and Longhorns,* that delightful chronicle of the plains and Cap-Rock ranch country by Laura V. Hammer: A good many years ago the Mill Iron horses suffered a scourge of glanders; a veterinarian was called and as the doom of horse after horse was pronounced, it seemed to the boys that it was always their favorite, their warm friend among all their string, that the sentence of death was pronounced upon. They refused to take part in the wholesale killing, so the veterinarian had to be both judge and executioner. He drove thirty-five horses up into Brewster Canyon and shot them while the boys rode off as far as possible. They shunned the Canyon so long as the ranch was in existence.

Most of this chapter has been based largely on *remudas* and customs of bygone days. The big outfits like the Matadors, the King Ranch, the Spades, the Pitchforks, 6 6 6 6, 3 D's, and others of the larger outfits still use about the same number of horses, raising their own replacements with sometimes a surplus to sell to their neighbors. Their horses are good and are being constantly made better. Their operation and handling of the *remuda* varies little from the old-time outfits. In these modern days with fences, cross fences, trucks, and accessibility to shipping points, the smaller outfits do not require so many horses and can necessarily have better ones.

It is interesting to know that on many of the big South American cow outfits horses are not roped but are trained upon entering the corral to line up along the fence where they may be caught and bridled. They claim this is a time saver. It may work out in theory, but I can't imagine a bunch of Southwestern cow hands handling their horses that way in the interest of time. They could dab a loop on one, have him out and saddled before they could get one hundred and fifty horses lined up in a corral if there happened to be a corral handy.

The preparation of this chapter on the horses has been made both pleasant and easy by access to the wonderful collection of pictures of old-time *remudas* taken by Erwin E. Smith of Bonham nearly half a century ago which shows some of the best of the *remudas* of that day with horses and cowboys in action. [Editor's note: See *Life on the Texas Range* by Erwin E. Smith, with text by J. Evetts Haley. Austin: University of Texas Press, 1952.]

A Roper and a Gentleman

In this day and time when a championship in most anything can be won and lost in the same week, and records in this, that, and the other go tumbling overnight, it must be a satisfactory feeling to know that you are a champion of thirty years standing and that for several good reasons you will never lose your championship honors.

There is a good West Texas citizen—J. Ellison Carroll—of Big Lake who enjoys this distinction and sense of security. Nearly thirty years ago he set a record for roping, throwing and tying a 1000-pound steer in the incredibly short time of 16 seconds, a record that has not been equaled to this day. A few months later he set another record and was awarded the title of World's Champion Roper when he roped and tied twenty-eight steers in an average time of 40-1/5 seconds per steer.

The setting of the 16-second mark came after three or four years of close competition with two other West Texans, Clay McGonigle of Midland and Joe Gardner of San Angelo, both masters of rope and horse. Over this period the three had roped with only a fraction of a second between them, but with McGonigle leading Carroll by less than a full second. Then came a cowboy reunion one day—they called them reunions in the gay 90's—when Carroll, mounted on his pet roping horse, Red Buck, a product of Coleman County, flashed across the dead-line to set an all-time record for heavy roping. Let's reconstruct this event and analyze it for the benefit of the younger West Texans who for the past few years have been watching lithe young cow hands mounted on quarter horses rope and tie 300-pound calves in the good time of from 12 to 20 seconds.

For comparison purposes later on, let's suppose you were a busi-nessman in the town where the reunion was held and that you had a young lady stenographer who was better than the average and could type fifty or sixty words to the minute right along. On this afternoon you have left her plenty of dictation and caught yourself a hack to the reunion ground on the outskirts of the town.

It is a little Southwestern cow-town close enough to the Mexican border that the blue hills of Chihuahua can be seen in the distance. The grandstands of raw yellow lumber, facing the infield of a mile race track, face south and are filled with cowmen and their families as well as cowboys from a hundred-mile area. Down at the lower end of the stands is a plank corral from which a short chute extends and in which there are fifteen or twenty milling, bawling steers. Around the corral are a dozen or more contestants, not the red-shirted rodeo boys of today, but hands fresh from the roundup and branding pen who had come in to compete and to watch each other work. The band strikes up a tune, the mounted judges take their stations, and the reunion is on.

From the chute gate comes a steer. He weighs a thousand pounds or better and is a product of the Terrazzas Ranches down in Mexico. Red and white in color and with black muzzle, he shows plainly his Mexican breeding. He has had very little contact with mankind since the Don's *vaqueros* burned the T R S on his hide as a calf. This didn't increase his respect for mankind and he has not forgotten it during the three years he has spent as a steer on the *ocatillo*-covered flats south of Juarez. Shipping into the reunion has not improved his temper, but now as he steps out of the chute with his face toward his own country things look better. Can he not see the blue hills of his old range? No doubt the silly fellows riding behind him waving and yelling are trying to hurry him back to the flats whence he came. Well, by the horns of the Great Black Bull of Tamaulipas, he will show them some traveling, and woe to the gringo that gets in his way. In one good long breath he is across the deadline, ninety feet from the chute gate. The hazers have dropped back as the timers drop their flags but he does not slacken his pace or lose his resolution to reach the Rancho Terrazzas, pronto.

Back along the chute with his ears forked forward but displaying no signs of nervousness, stands a little red sorrel horse. He is blocky but weighing slightly more than the steer that has just left the chute. As the steer nears the deadline the horse tenses his muscles and waits for the slackening of the reins that will tell him it is time to go. He does not need, nor expect, any touch of spur or quirt, for he and the man on his back understand each other. On his back and sitting as easily and with as little concern as though he were in an easy chair on the double porch of the old ranch house, sits a typical man of the range. Physically perfect in every detail, he is six feet tall and weighs 205 pounds and is in his prime—about twenty-eight years old. Over his right shoulder is draped the loop end of the best twenty-seven feet of 7/8-inch manila rope that man can buy. The other end is fastened to the horn of his saddle by a double half hitch—a knot that once tightened down can be loosened only by picking it out or cutting it with a sharp knife. He holds the bridle reins in his left hand with just enough pressure on them to act as a signal to the red horse when the tension is eased off.

Across the line flashes the red and white steer with head held high and black-tipped horns glinting in the sunlight. Like a flash the little red horse is across the deadline, his four feet, one white, beating a tattoo and his belly apparently only a few inches from the ground. Thirty to fifty feet farther he reaches the steer's tail but does not slacken his pace until he has laid his muzzle squarely across the steer's left hip bone. During the last twenty-five feet the man has slipped the loop from his shoulder and given it a quick flip to widen it. As the horse's muzzle lies over the steer's hip, the man stands in his stirrups, gives the loop a twirl or two over his head, and throws. He throws for a catch over both horns or between the horns and under the lower jaw. If the rope goes over head and horns and settles down over the steer's shoulders it will mean that he cannot be "busted" properly and that he will have a distinct weight advantage over man and horse, for caught in this manner the steer has the pulling power of a yoked ox.

As the loop leaves his hand and settles around horns or under the jaw, the man gives it a quick jerk to settle it in place and assure its not being tossed off if the steer should slacken his pace—which he doesn't. He then drops the slack of the rope down under the steer's right hip bone and leans his weight lightly to the left. As perfectly as if it were an oft-rehearsed football play and the man was calling for a pass, the horse swerves to the left without losing his stride. This places him at right angles to the steer and almost tail to tail with him. In less time than it has taken the writer to pick out the word "time" on his typewriter, the shock comes. When the horse reaches the end of the rope the steer is reversed in midair and pops out almost horizontally, to be slammed down broadside on the hard ground with no wind or fight left in him. The head of the steer is now facing the horse's tail. The man has stayed on the horse until it has taken the shock, so as to give it the benefit of his weight. When he feels that the horse is over the shock and pulling steadily at the steer, he steps off to hit the ground running with his "hoggin'" or tie rope—which has been stuffed in his boot top or wadded into his belt—in his hand.

On reaching the steer the man puts the loop in his tie rope around two of the rear feet, drawing them together. One of the front feet is forced between the rear ones and the three wrapped several times in a half-inch tie that will tighten if the steer recovers and begins struggling before the tie judges have passed on him. When the tie is completed the roper throws his hands high in the air to signify that the tie is complete. Down come the flags of the field judges; click go the stop watches of the timekeepers; and the job is done. The tie judges ride up and roll the steer completely over to test the tie, after which he is released and hazed back into the pen to meditate over his delayed return to the land of *manana*. The roper, coiling his rope in neat overhand coils to keep the kinks out, rides back to the corral to dismount and loosen the cinches on his saddle and bestow a pat on the sweaty, wet neck of the little sorrel. To some readers and a good many writers it may seem strange that I have placed the horse before the man in making this reconstruction, but I have done this because a certain number of old ropers will read this and they would want it that way.

Now let's analyze what has happened since the judges let their flags fall as the steer crossed the line. A thousand pounds of Mexican steer in no playful mood has been chased 150 to 250 feet by a thousand pounds of cowhorse and two hundred pounds of man; in the length of a twenty-seven–foot rope a steer has been caught, the horse has changed direction and pace—as well as the steer—a man has dismounted, run twenty-seven feet and tied three feet of the steer together, and the watches of the timers show that only sixteen seconds have passed. Surely they must be wrong! Why, if a portly woman with a superstition about picking up pins had passed in front of you and, stooping to pick up one, had fumbled it a time or two, by the time she had straightened up the thing would have been over and you would have missed most of it. It does not seem possible that the stenographer you left at work in your office, providing she is dutiful and is writing her sixty words a minute, has only written fifteen words while the record was being made.

What you have just witnessed is a most beautiful example of coordination between man and horse and an exhibition of intuitive timing that could be staged only by a roper of the old school.

You might think that the setting of this mark settled for all time the matter of roping honors. But it did not. Down in the Devils River country cowmen friends of McGonigle made no bones of saying they considered him the best roper and that Carroll's record was a matter of luck. They would bet their last dollar that in a contest where the boys had to rope all day McGonigle would show him up. Up in the Big Pasture country and along Red River there were just as many cowmen willing to bet their saddles and blankets, as well as a few of their neighbors' cattle, that Carroll could hold his own with any man.

It seemed that peace was not to come to the cow camps and chuck wagons until the matter was settled. As an upshot of the argument cowmen in the Southwest financed a roping match in San Antonio in which Carroll and McGonigle were to rope twenty-eight steers each over a period of three days and the holder of the lowest average time on the total number of steers was to receive a purse of $6,000 and a gold medal along with the title of World's Champion Roper. Two carloads of the Terrazzas steers were shipped in from El Paso and the old San Antonio Fair Grounds was secured for the event. Cowboys and range bosses from the King Ranch along the Gulf to the bleak ranges of the X I T outfit in the Panhandle gathered to witness this battle for supremacy with rope and horse between two of the best of their kind. Side bets exceeded the purse many times. Carroll used three horses, his pet Red Buck, Jack Hill, and Necktie. McGonigle had his top horse Rondo and two other good roping horses. Eight steers were roped on the first day and ten on each day thereafter.

That the affair was friendly and of the highest type of sportsmanship was shown on the second day when McGonigle, after breaking two ropes on a steer, was about to ride back and let the steer be counted as lost to him, when Carroll loped out on to the field and handed him his rope. Another highlight of the affair was the throwing of a steer by Jack Hill, one of Carroll's roping horses, after the animal had gotten to its feet and before Carroll could get back onto his horse.

At the end of the third day it was found that Carroll had an average of 40-1/5 seconds on his twenty-eight steers, while McGonigle had a score of 46-1/5 seconds chalked up against him. Carroll had a low individual steer of 17-1/4 seconds and McGonigle one of 22 seconds flat. The $6,000 went to Carroll as well as the title and medal which he holds today and prizes very highly. The records still stand and Carroll has never been called on to defend them.

With his earnings, Carroll went back to his ranch in the Haystack country in Greer County and resumed his ranching operations, roping occasionally at some of the larger reunions. In addition to his other honors, he barely missed becoming the Tom Mix or Bill Hart of the movies, for the Selig Polyscope Company, then about the only makers of moving pictures, came to the Oklahoma ranch and filmed every phase of the cow business with Carroll taking a leading part in the film. The picture was such a success that the film company offered him an attractive contract to make Westerns for them, which he rejected. But he did make a tour of the Eastern states with the film and delivered a lecture on cow work as it was shown. The pavement was not for a fellow of his type, however, and at the close of the tour he returned to the Oklahoma ranch. The film was the first ever to be taken of cattle operations and among other things included a picture of Carroll roping a steer from an early day automobile. Both Hart and Mix were unknown to pictures at the time.

Along about that time—1906—ranchmen were beginning to find out that cowboys practicing for reunions were costing them money, in time and crippled stock and horses; also the humane societies were beginning to sit up and take notice. As a result most of the cattle states passed legislation against "busting" cattle at reunions. This put an end to heavy roping as a sport.

When the nesters began to move into Greer County Carroll pooled his stuff with a brother and they moved their cattle to the Pecos country west of San Angelo where he ran the outfit until it was sold out. He moved to Big Lake and has served two terms as sheriff for his county. He is engaged in the livestock commission business there at this time.

In the early nineties J. Ellison Carroll was the top hand of the cow country along the Indian Territory line. Cowmen hoped their boys would grow up to be the hand he was, and they also hoped they would be square shooters like he was. To those of them that are left he is still the top hand and his name has been handed down almost as a tradition to their grandchildren. Thirty years have passed—Clay McGonigle, Joe Gardner, and Fred Baker have gone to their last resting place. Carroll is the only one living of the four great ropers who set the pace for all time. He still holds the title of World's Champion Roper as well as the super-title of gentleman extraordinary, both of which he will carry as long as he lives.

The Cowboy and the Auto

Shortly after the turn of the century the cowman felt his troubles were over and that he was adjusted to the new order. He had gotten used to opening gates, driving around sections instead of across them, and was even beginning to get on better than speaking terms with the nesters.

Then on the winding, twisting, high-centered roads which wound through the mesquite flats, there sprang at him a red, roaring monster which stank to the high heavens and caused his nigh buggy horse to set a course north by northwest and the off one, south by southwest when he met it in the narrow road. Invariably, he met it at a hidden turn or where the road came around a jutting headland with a sheer drop on one side. The snorting terror had the advantage of him, for he had taken to buggy and buckboard and could no longer ride the ridges and scout the country as he had in the good old days. When he had negotiated a passing with one he would damn it in his own expressive way and covenant with himself to never ride in one, own one, or permit any of his family to do so.

The first automobiles to come into the cow country were driven either by life-insurance salesmen or land agents, neither of which were popular with him just then. Later, he was to learn to love the former when the life-insurance company began making ranch loans. Then, too, he had not forgotten the lightning rod agents and Spaulding buggy men who, with their shiny equipment, spanking teams, and wily tongues, had preceded the autoists.

However, for the same good reason he had permitted his family to move from the ranch to town, he gave in on owning an auto—because the women folks and kids "warted" him into it. Then, too, he saw in it another phase of the progress that had gradually been overtaking him for years. He accepted it as he had railroads, barbed wire, higher taxes, higher interest, standing collars, and olives.

He bought his first one to turn over to the eldest son or daughter to master and drive, and was more than proud but still a little frightened when the youngster, with mother and himself on the back seat, could successfully negotiate Main Street during a Fourth-of-July celebration or county fair, or, when they could show a visiting cowman more country in an hour than he could in a week with his buggy. Few of the cowmen of the vintage of 1904 or 1905 ever learned to drive their own cars.

The first automobiles were not a source of worry to the homeward- or ranch-bound cowman alone. The townsfolk suffered as well. An auto entering the average small West Texas town was signal for a half dozen runaways and a general breaking of bridle reins among the saddle horses hitched along the rails in front of the First National. When it came to a stop the townsfolk gathered around to examine it and question its owner. The modern gangster would have thought the occasion heaven sent for his purpose of holding up the aforesaid First National. It was wholly unguarded until the thing left town.

Down in Burnet one day, District Court was in session. There was a big trial with many witnesses and attorneys, and a good gallery. A visiting attorney perhaps with eyes on the D.A.'s or district judge's job at next election and not inclined to antagonize his potential constituents by flaunting his apparent affluence or by stampeding their buggy, wagon, or riding stock, eased his red and brass two-cylindered Maxwell up to the town limits and proceeded, clothed in full glory of leather cap, gauntlets, goggles, and duster, to the crowded courtroom. When he had transacted his business with the judge and was ready to leave, he was followed by practically the entire court, jurors, witnesses, both under and not under the rule, as well as the complete gallery. The judge left in his glory on his bench pounded for order and called to the departing autoist-attorney, "It will please this court very much, if you will stop that contraption about a mile out of town where there are no horses and permit everyone to look it over so that they may return and the court can resume its regular business."

When the first ones came to town to stay the good ladies who were still enjoying their phaetons and surreys drawn by pet horses brought in from the ranch, arranged their visiting and shopping hours to conform to those during which the auto rested in shop or garage or was out of town. Children ceased driving the family turnout almost entirely. There was a good neighborly custom formed about that time of passing the word along among the women folks to get home quick and unhitch as one of the "damned things" was in town.

The sheriff and city marshal, too, were hard put to chart a course which would keep them in the good graces of the cow families whose children were driving the blamed things. Folks who didn't own one, or never would, were on their bones continually about the damage they were doing and predicting that unless stringent methods were employed the downfall of the county and its duly constituted officers was obvious. For the most part the sheriff and city marshal were broken down cow-punchers or wagon bosses left over from the big ranch days and placed in office by the cowmen. Naturally, their sympathies were with the cowmen, but the railroads were sending out more emigrant cars each day and the roads were choked with white-top wagons loaded with children and towing cultivators and brindle milk cows behind them. There might come a time when these would out-vote the cowmen. So, they took the safe course and administered their rebukes and gave warning to the youngsters, usually saying, "I have knowed your pa and ma a long time and know they don't want you to hurt anybody . . ." These words were usually spoken with serious mien and where they could be heard by the "antis." Their sting was pulled, however, by the sheriff's adding, apparently as an afterthought and in a much lower tone, "Needn't say anything to your pa and ma about me talking to you, it was just for your own good."

Captain S. B. Burnett who made his home in Fort Worth was among the first to realize the time-saving possibilities of the automobile and was among the first of the older ranchmen to purchase one. His first car, a Pierce Arrow, was delivered to him in 1909 or 1910. He employed a chauffeur and in the car entertained his house guests and visiting friends. Among these were his lifelong friends, Clabe Merchant and Colonel J. H. Parramore of Abilene, co-owners of large ranches in Texas and Arizona. Neither of them owned an automobile nor had they ridden in one. The Captain loaded them into the "tonneau" of the car and instructed the driver to take the three of them for a spin out the Handley road. When the city limits had been passed, he told the driver to let out a little, until a speed of thirty-five miles per hour was reached, then forty, and up to forty-five—about the limit of the machine. With each increase in speed the passengers in the rear seat became more and more nervous and took a firmer grip on their over-sized hats which were beginning to blow down into their eyes, merci-fully obscuring the close shaves the driver was giving the buggies and gravel wagons he was passing. Now the old cowmen were not afraid of anything on earth that they knew anything about or could fight on fairly even terms. They had fought the Apache from their San Simone Ranch in Arizona and it was to it that the renegade Geronimo and his band of raiders had been brought after their surrender in Skeleton Canyon. But they did not know anything about cars and to use their own expression, "it was coming up their neck" and they didn't care who knew it.

Between holding his hat on with one hand and wiping the wind-generated tears from his eyes with the other, Merchant finally called to Burnett in the front seat. "Burk, make that dang fellow slow this thing down or you are going to get us all killed."

"Take it easy, Clabe," replied the Captain, "we haven't shown you yet how fast it can go."

At this point Colonel Parramore came to his partner's aid by saying, "Burk, if you just want to show us how fast it will go, why don't you let me and Clabe get out and set on the curb and watch the fellow drive it by us. We can come a dern sight nearer telling how fast it is going that way than we can setting back here with our hat brims blowed back into our eyes and them full of water."

An Indian Territory Ranch in the Early 90's

I think I have mentioned the fact that we once ranched in the Indian Territory in the Arbuckle Mountains near Turner Falls, about twenty-five miles north of Ardmore, Oklahoma. Because the old Hendrix and Royer ranch was distinctive, unique, and had a definite part in the development of cattle feeding in the Southwest, I shall try to chronicle the history of the outfit.

I have hesitated to attempt this for fear of the inaccuracies that must necessarily creep into it from the fact that slightly more than half a century has elapsed since the ranch was in operation. Then, too, there were no section lines or townships by which its boundaries might be described. There were few, if any, ranches near us, or settlers who might be referred to for proper identification of the ranch. I shall make no effort to give the number of acres in the ranch, but will say that it ran from fifteen hundred to two thousand cattle the year around.

The ranch was formed by my father, F. D. Hendrix, and C. E. Royer in 1894, as the result of a meeting in Gainesville, Texas, alongside the old Lindsey Hotel. My father was a 100 per cent cow man, while Royer, a native of Pennsylvania, was more of the student type and a man of business, but was thoroughly intrigued by the cattle business.

Opportunity was great in the Nation in those days. The country, as I recall, was unallotted then and the only settlers in the section were along the fertile valley of the Washita and some of the larger creeks tributary to it, where agriculture was beginning to take hold. Cotton was being grown in these sections, with no market for the cottonseed except at Purcell and Ardmore, both of which had oil mills. Inland gins had no market for their seed because it had to be hauled by wagon to some point on the Santa Fe and shipped to these mills.

My father and Royer were firm in their belief that seed could be purchased and fed on the grass to Plains cattle at a profit. As I recall, their first year in the Nation was on a small pasture known as the Hogg Creek Pasture, a few miles northwest of Ardmore, where they tried their experiment of the grass and cottonseed. Finding it profitable, they moved to larger acreage on what was known as the Eph James Pasture, just below the mountains. Just above it lay the Arbuckles, with high, rock-covered ridges and low, timbered hills. When I first saw them, however, I would have called my knowledge of big mountains complete, had I never seen the Rockies. These hills and ridges were covered with strong grasses high in mineral content—grama and bunch grass, I think we called them. The region was almost unapproachable from the south. Buzzard Hill, a sort of cap rock for the area, was composed of flat rock that looked as though they had been planted there in windrows by the hand of man, rather than by nature. Those who pass along Highway 77 will recall this queer formation between Ardmore, Springer, and Turner Falls. Two distinct mountain ridges dominated the area—they were known as the East Timbered Hills and the West Timbered Hills. The possibilities of the area had been overlooked by cowmen because it was rough country and because they were either going to West Texas or looking farther north for range in the more level country around Ada. The partners scouted it and found it to their liking. From the Eph James Camp they laid out a road over Buzzard Hill to Springer, which was then located about one mile north and a mile or so west of the present Springer. For better description, it was located in what is now known as the Moss Patterson Hereford Ranch. The road was built by knocking off the tops of the slanting flat rock until a four-mule team and wagon could negotiate it. At the top of the hill it bore to the left along the ridge and the east end of the mountain to the first rick yard established by the ranch.

Headquarters were established on Honey Creek about two miles above Turner Falls in a log cabin that, according to my recollection, was there when we took over. The establishment was as primitive as the country, with its log walls chinked with mud, clapboard shingles, and mud chimney. I do not believe there was ten dollars worth of materials, including nails, in the three rooms that was not acquired within a hundred yards of the site. The right hand portion of the cabin was used for cooking. The fireplace was used for this purpose during the first years of our occupancy. The left wing was filled with bunks for sleeping, and the area between the two rooms was used for loafing (if any). The lean-to on the left end was used as a smokehouse and storeroom. Water was carried from a spring about fifty yards from the corner of the kitchen.

We built a huge corral just back and a little to the left of the house, that would handle from five to seven hundred cattle. This was split into two pens by a long branding chute extending almost across it, with a cutting gate at the end, so that branded cattle could be turned into either pen from the chute after branding. These pens were built of rails laid between two uprights and well braced. The log saddle and harness room, with a log corncrib, completed the ranch improvements.

So long as we operated the ranch, the Honey Creek Camp was headquarters. It was strictly a stag camp—I do not recall that a woman ever entered its doors.

When we had got going good, a camp was built at the West Timbered Hills to care for that section of the ranch. Royer was to use this camp, and it was built somewhat according to his ideas, which in a way resembled some ranches of later dates. It consisted of a log cabin about sixteen feet square for his use, and another detached cabin for cooking and eating. This cabin also contained quarters for a Negro man and his wife—the former being a cow hand and his wife attending to the housekeeping. Like the headquarters, this camp was of logs— the only concession to civilization being a corrugated sheet-iron roof. My father always objected to the iron roof, saying that it made so much noise he could not sleep when it rained or hailed. No doubt he preferred the soft patter of rainfall on the sodden and weatherbeaten clapboard roof of the headquarters outfit. We built for this camp a set of corrals and a branding chute—also of rails and logs. Unlike the headquarters pens, this camp's pens had a spring and spring branch running through one corner. Royer at one time rigged up a sort of shower by driving nail holes into an old bucket which could be drawn over a limb with a rope. He had the Negro fill it with ice-cold spring water one cool morning, after which he stripped off and stepped under it. When the cold spring water, mixed with the mountain air, struck him he jumped and let out a yell that could have been heard at the headquarters camp six miles away. He was a confirmed bachelor, and I do not believe that while we were there a woman was ever in his camp.

The ranch was fenced with black-jack or post-oak posts which were sharpened and driven into the ground with mauls. Securing of these posts was generally done by settlers who came in and contracted for a mile or so of them, sharpened and strung along the route of the fence, for from four to six cents each. The fences followed no section lines because there were none to follow. The fence line went where the ground was best suited for it and where a post could be driven most easily. In many instances, extra heavy anchor posts were placed on top of the hills and the four wires weighted down until they could be stapled to the posts. I do not recall that there was ever a pair of post-hole diggers on the ranch, but there was a goodly number of crowbars and post mauls.

When the ranch was finally fenced, it constituted almost a small kingdom in a mountain fastness, with few neighbors, and only such roads and trails as we built and controlled. The whole thing was very primitive, and well might be likened to Longfellow's "Forest Primeval." Does dropped their fawns each spring in the black-jack motts that dotted the pasture. Flocks of wild turkeys, led by stately gobblers, ate and reared their young among the pecan trees along the streams. Squirrels were as thick as cottontail rabbits in a West Texas prairie-dog town. Every hollow contained a spring branch fed by a bold spring at its head. Bobwhites in abundance called to each other in the early morning. Honey Creek gurgled, brawled, and sang its way over the rocks and riffles and into cool, limpid pools, as it made its short way from its spring source down over the falls to its junction with the Washita. The creek was filled with perch of tremendous size, and a mess of trout could be taken with a home-made fly created from a bit of red blanket and a few feathers. After we settled the ranch, our boys caught several otter in the creek.

Huge diamond-back rattlesnakes lived and sunned under the ledges and atop the flat rocks. It was not unusual to kill one of these rusty old fellows who had seventeen rattles and a button. A queer species of lizard from eight inches to two feet long abounded. They were a species of chameleon with colors which varied according to the color of the rock they were upon. We called them "mountain boomers."

Nature supplied most of our needs. With the exception of barbed wire and salt, I doubt very seriously that more than one hundred dollars worth of material was hauled to the ranch in the four years we were there. There were no wells, no tanks, no pipe or well curbing on the entire ranch. A flat stone at the spring served as a steppingstone and footrest when a bucket of water was to be dipped up. Our headquarters outfit did not boast of a single article of furniture that was not home-made, except a small cookstove that finally went into it. Tables were made from goods boxes, and chairs were of hickory and rawhide. There was not a bedstead or set of springs in the camp. Sturdy two-story bunks equipped with shuck mattresses made our beds.

Down the Washita Valley a number of Negro families grew their own tobacco and made their own lye from ashes in a hollow log. With it they made the most excellent corn hominy that I have ever eaten. Our seed haulers got their supply of both tobacco and hominy for the ranch from them.

If we needed a bridge on creek or hollow, we felled our own logs and built it; or if a spring branch spread out in the path between rock ledges creating a bog, we cut logs and built a corduroy road. Even at shipping time the tall hickory saplings along creek and river furnished our prod poles, which we cut and seasoned.

Turner Falls was then a hidden beauty spot having at that time been seen by very few people because of its inaccessibility. Honey Creek rises a mile or so above the Falls from a series of fine springs, and then drops off over the Falls as it seeks its way to the lower level of the Washita. The Falls could be reached more easily by riding down the creek bed from the headquarters than any other way. Otherwise, one had to go around the mountain and down a rough and circuitous canyon trail.

There may be inaccuracies in my description of the ranch; but as to its operation we are on firm ground, for I have the books of the old outfit which reflect its purchases and sales and expenses for the four-year period. The "books" consist of three small leather memorandum books such as the commission companies used to give to their customers in the early 90's. These bear the imprint "C. M. Keys Livestock Commission Company, Kansas City, Missouri." So far as I know, there were no other books kept on the outfit.

It was a fifty-fifty deal, with little or no capital for a start. Its assets consisted of a few saddle horses and half a dozen wagons and teams which had been acquired slowly.

Interesting and humorous was the fact that the first cattle coming to the ranch consisted of twelve head purchased from an old man in the Sivells Bend country. Four of these were branded DAMU, another four UDAD, and the other four UFORK—the fork being depicted by a crudely scrawled pitchfork. Must have been an old-time family way of expressing affection or vice versa.

Several buyers or speculators, as we call them now, who had served the firm at Hogg Creek or the Eph James Pasture, were commissioned to buy steers. The partners evidently set up a standard of what they would pay for their cattle, as practically all of them were bought at $9.00 per head for steer yearlings and $13.50 for two-year-olds.

This method was apparently not getting the cattle needed, so they began branching out into Central Texas for their cattle. Records indicate that a man in Caldwell, Texas, in 1895 assembled a herd of eleven hundred head for them at prices quoted above. Another draft came from the Sulphur Springs area; some from Taylor, Texas; and one bunch from Strawn in West Texas. They were a poor type of cattle, as standards go today, in a multitude of brands, and of a multitude of colors, but the partners took into consideration the average improvement of cattle moved from South and Central Texas north to the mountain country, with its highly nutritious grasses, and the fact that they would be wintered heavily on cottonseed.

There is no record that any cattle of the several thousand the ranch handled were ever shipped onto the ranch. All were trailed in. Early in June each year my father would take a chuck wagon, horses, and five or six good men, and pull out for the South to receive and bring steers back to the ranch. In addition to the men he took with him, he usually hired two or three men where the cattle had been received, to assist in getting them out of the country—these turning back at Fort Worth or Gainesville. The herds came in by Gainesville, crossed the Red River at Rock Crossing into the Bill Washington country, and came on to Caddo Creek just north of Ardmore, and up over the Buzzard Hill to the ranch. Even as early as 1894 or '95, it was not easy to get a herd of cattle out of Central Texas without causing some damage to growing crops. Expense items show where some damages to crops were paid. Sometimes an entire field and crop were purchased and used for a day or two as a holding ground.

At the ranch the steers were allowed a few days' rest after their trail trip; then they went into the long chute to receive the Big 9 on their left side and have the tip of their left horns cut off. This last was a very distinctive type of marking and enabled one to recognize a Hendrix and Royer steer in a roundup instantly. This operation had a tendency to cause the left horns to drop, and as a result, a high percentage of the steers were droop-horn when they grew up. This mark, though, always attracted attention on the Kansas City market. Both ears were under-sloped to make them look as uniform as possible.

By July 15, the steers were luxuriating in the summer pasture on the tall bunch grass and were beginning to pick up after the trip and branding.

While my father had been getting in the cattle, Royer had been busy calling on the gins of the near neighborhood and contracting cotton-seed. All of his visiting was by horseback; there was never a hack nor buggy owned by the ranch. Seed was bought at Berwyn, Davis, Wood-ford, Springer, Hoxbar, Hennepin, and Cornish. The partners had a fixed price they would pay for cottonseed: 10½ cents per bushel. They did not contract seed that could not be hauled from gin to ranch in one day, including the round trip. This was giving a good deal of latitude, for the wagons were usually on their way around 5:30 in the morning. As the seed came into the rick lots it was unloaded onto ricks 350 to 400 feet long and about as high as the top of a wagon box. There were usually four ricks of seed to each lot. The seed was carefully unloaded and the ricks slapped and packed to prevent damage from rainfall. By the time the ginning season was over, the yards held from 350,000 to 500,000 bushels of seed. The seed was never referred to by the ton, and the records indicate that it was bought by the bushel. Seed at the Springer Gin, at the foot of Buzzard Hill, was allowed to accumulate at the gin until other points farther off had been taken care of. Then the entire force of wagons was put on the haul and a camp established (again a log camp and lots) at Buzzard Hill Springs, where a snap team was maintained to help the wagons over the hill. It required a six-mule hitch to get as much seed over the hill as four could haul anywhere else on the route. This camp was in the present Moss Patterson pasture.

Our seed-hauling equipment consisted of half a dozen long, heavy wagons specially built for us by the Peter Schutler Company in their Kansas City branch. They were built long, so as to make it possible for the load to be spread out rather than be stacked high, which lessened the danger of turning over in the rough country. They also had a special type of spring seat which rested upon and was hinged to permanent standards to prevent seat and driver from being jolted off the wagon. Specially built brakes with long foot levers were provided. Motive power was provided by some twenty-five or thirty big, young Missouri mules that we bought on the horse market in Kansas City. The lead teams of these four-mule hitches were almost uncanny in handling themselves among the seed ricks and the gin houses.

Each of our men was adept at horseshoeing. Due to the rough country, all horses had to be shod all around. We often said that our men could do as good a job horseshoeing with a rasp, butcher knife, and hatchet as the average blacksmith. Each man carried horseshoe nails and staples in his saddle pockets. A sprung shoe was soon straightened out and replaced. We bought "turned" horseshoes by the keg, and I expect that a lot of the boys' skill in horseshoeing lay in the fact that they tacked a shoe on and then cut the hoof down to fit it. The mules, due to the peculiar formation of their hoofs, were driven to Springer every so often for shoeing.

We made no effort at farming. Corn could be bought cheaply from farmers along the Washita. A few days' hauling with the big seed wagons would put enough corn in the cribs for the saddle horses, work mules, and hogs for the winter. Early every summer a hay contractor would come in with his outfit to cut and bale what hay would be needed.

Our hired personnel during the years we were there did not vary a great deal. They usually consisted of eight men, and the records give the names of Will Wilson, Will Gray, Will Childs, Scott Locke, Matt Watson, Wes Corless, and Bill Holder—the last two being colored. They were big, strong, middle-aged men, highly temperate and used to hard work. They were of good character, and loyal. Also they were excellent cowmen, but in no sense of the word specialists. They were adept at teaming, fencing, and whatever had to be done at the ranch. We had no regular cook except when the wagon was on the road. The men usually selected one from among themselves, based on his ability and willingness. They were a thrifty bunch, too. None of them drew more than $20.00 per month, and page after page shows where they would draw fifty cents to $2.50 occasionally, and that sundry items were charged to their account from time to time. At settlement time they usually all had most of their wages coming to them. They got along together excellently, as there was little or no time for horseplay among them.

Camp expenses were at a minimum, and I estimate that it cost us approximately $3.00 or $3.50 per month to board our hands. They were well fed, too, on good, strong, coarse food necessary to hard-working men. My father was a firm believer in navy beans, and always saw to it that there was a good pot of them on the stove. Our principal purchases were flour, navy beans, dried peaches and apples, and a small amount of canned tomatoes and corn. Groceries were brought in by the seed wagons. My books show that single purchases hardly ever exceeded $3.00 or $4.00. Quoting from a page of one of the old expense books, I give a sample:

Will Childs, Cash	$.50
Will Wilson, Pants	.85
Soda 2 packages	.35
6 Shooter Cartridges	.75

(Incidentally I still have in my den the old bone-handled, single-action Colt .45 which the cartridges fitted. The gun, however, played no important part in the conduct of the ranch.)

Being a steer outfit, we ate very little beef. We depended mostly on pork for our meat supply. The woods were full of hogs of all ages, kinds, colors, and sexes. Early in the fall of each year we would put forty to sixty barrows up for fattening. At the first sign of cold weather we would have a general hog killing for both camps, which lasted a couple of days. Usually we put down from sixty to seventy-five hams and about the same amount of sidemeat. This, coupled with sausage and the lard we made, usually ran us through the season. The stock hogs ran wild and fed on acorns and mast entirely.

Stealing was never a problem with us. The ranch was well fenced, and the fences were ridden and watched daily. We always cut up the dirt in the gates when one of them was used, thereby obliterating our own tracks. Our men were all loyal and constantly on the lookout for strangers, which were few and far between. I feel sure that 90 per cent of the visitors to the ranch came on business, and on horseback.

Another big day on the ranch was the one in the late summer, set aside for repairing and greasing the twenty-five or thirty sets of heavy leather harness used on the work mules. The harness were completely dissembled at the buckles and given a bath of hot water, followed by a treatment of tallow and neats-foot oil, then hung out on a rail fence to dry. We had no sore-shouldered mules nor sore-backed horses, as my father insisted that the men have good saddles and blankets, and care for them well.

During the winter months the boys hauled seed from the rick lots to the high feeding grounds. Two men worked on a wagon, one driving and one shoveling. My father or Royer were usually on the feed ground to watch how the cattle cleaned up, and to throw in stragglers. It was a nice sight to see five or six hundred fattening steers queued behind a wagon. The cattle were fed all they could clean up each day, and were fed from about November 15 to the rise of grass each year, after which they went into the summer pasture.

Shipping began early in August, or just a little ahead of shipping time in the Osage and Kansas country—the cottonseed having given our cattle a slight advantage over their cattle. At shipping time we handled the cattle as easily as possible. Large wire cutting pens were built in traps containing about a section of land. Cattle were worked in these pens and those selected turned loose in the trap for a few days' rest or pending a favorable telegram from our commission company in Kansas City. Pens and traps were built at the point closest to the railroad—about six or eight miles usually from Berwyn or Davis.

On shipping days—always on Saturday—cattle were started walking as soon in the morning as they could be rounded up and counted, en route to Davis, across the Washita River, which Old Moman Prewitt always described as "crooked as a tubful of hog guts."

We crossed it at a ford near Old Man Russell's place. The banks were of dirt, and very high. In making the crossing we had to dig down the banks until the crossing had the appearance of a long chute on each side. If the river was not on a rise, we walked the steers down the chute and into the water with little or no trouble, and soon had them up on high ground away from the flies and heat. We reached the pens about noon and sent the boys in to Satterwhite's grocery store for a bait of cheese, crackers, sardines, and salmon—with a couple of onions given them gratis by the proprietor, who also furnished dishes and spoons (these showing considerable fly-speck and former usage).

After dinner the cattle were loaded and before five o'clock were en route to Kansas City, which they reached late Sunday night, giving them a chance for rest and fill before coming on Monday's market. A shipment usually consisted of ten to twelve cars, according to the market.

My father and one of the boys usually accompanied the shipment. During the years we were there, all of our cattle were consigned to C. M. Keys Livestock & Commission Company. We did our banking in Kansas City at the Interstate National Bank which is still in business. The Santa Fe Railroad was always highly cooperative about cars and loading. They appreciated our business and for a number of years furnished the partners with annual passes. When they were forced to discontinue this practice it caused almost as much consternation as when my favorite chili stand advanced its price from five cents to ten cents per bowl and hid the catsup bottle under the counter.

Earlier I referred to eleven hundred steers that had been trailed through from Caldwell, Texas. I have traced these cattle through the books, and give details herewith for their marketing the following year:

111 head	Weight	971
121 head	Weight	964
108 head	Weight	951
110 head	Weight	960
50 head	Weight	1,069

These brought an average of $3.45 per hundred pounds. Another draft shows:

100 head	Weight	1,040
108 head	Weight	1,040
108 head	Weight	925
182 head	Weight	1,050
156 head	Weight	1,030
275 head	Weight	1,020

I judge these cattle weighed from five to seven hundred pounds when they came onto the ranch. The lighter-weight cattle were yearlings, and the heavier weight two-year-olds—which would indicate a good gain and a fair profit. These prices are about typical of weights and gains of all cattle so handled by the ranch.

An expense item that partially explains the gain and growth is a series of scale tickets from Suggs Brothers Gin, Berwyn, Oklahoma, which shows that they sold the ranch twelve four-mule loads of cottonseed to weigh approximately five tons each, at an average price per load at $32.40: the total for the twelve loads being $355.56, or an average of 10½ cents per bushel.

Late in 1897, U.S. engineers moved in along Honey Creek, established their camps, and began the work of surveying the Chickasaw Nation into sections and townships, in anticipation of statehood. The handwriting was on the wall for our old outfit—or rather on the tree, for the surveyors cleared a space on top of the highest of the East Timbered Hills, leaving only a tall, bushy-top tree for a backsite. The tree could be seen for miles, and bore a canvas sign on its trunk that it was the property of the U.S. An airline beam now occupies the site of the tree. There was a $500 fine for mutilating or destroying it. We took this sign as emblematic, and began shaping things toward a final settlement.

When it came time to settle, the partners had an excess of $100,000 in money, 660 head of stock cattle, 35 horses, and 32 mules and wagons to divide. There was no outstanding indebtedness. Not big money, as money goes now, but the $100,000 was all their own and was their reward for four years of hard work and hard living. It was the result of following a carefully planned operation and taking advantage of a low operation cost.

I find at no place in the books that we owned a foot of land or paid lease or tribute to anyone for what we used—nor were there any charges for taxes of any kind. Our entire country was under the jurisdiction of the Federal courts at Ardmore. Occasionally, a deputy U.S. marshal would visit the ranch as a sort of routine call. He usually had a pocketful of warrants with him for persons wanted.

During the existence of the partnership there was no dissention, despite the fact that my father was a rock-ribbed Democrat and Royer an equally staunch Republican; nor do I recall any religious discussion. About the biggest argument they ever had was over the roof on Royer's camp. Fortunately, no wars occurred during the time the outfit was operating. However, it wound up during the early part of the Spanish-American War. I recall the consternation when they were forced to place a few cents' worth of documentary stamps on certain papers having to do with final settlement.

From time to time I have used the first person, and have sometimes referred to ownership of the ranch as "we." In explanation, I wish to say that I came to the ranch with the Caldwell Trail herd in 1895, having joined it at Gainesville when my father brought Old Nig in for me to ride. I imagine I was about seven years old. Four or five days I rode in the dusty drag of the herd. Occasionally my father, noticing that I was apparently riding on my entire backbone, rather than on the parts reserved for riding, would put me in the center of the herd between drag and lead, to relieve the monotony and get me out of the dust.

I spent several summers at the ranch after that. Because there were no children to play with, I learned the talk, work, and ways of men. I cherish the memory of those days and the memory of long rides with my father over trails that led up and down and through crystal-clear spring streams.

Final settlement was made in the summer of 1898. Royer held on a couple of years and finally sold out to Hugh Moore, of Fort Worth. The ranch has passed into many hands and owners since then. It occupies what is now the southernmost portion of Hereford Heaven. Some of the best cattle in the world are produced in this section. One or more of these Hereford farms is, I believe, in the environs of the old ranch.

Quanah

From the time the railroads were built through West Texas in the middle 80's until well after 1900 there were a half-hundred communities along the Fort Worth and Denver, Texas and Pacific, Santa Fe and Frisco lines which were classified purely as "cow-towns." They merited this name from the fact that they were contiguous to great ranching areas and were cattle-loading and supply points as well as headquarters and banking towns for the cattlemen operating over wide areas. In later years they became the home towns of these cattlemen when they moved in from their ranches to give their children educational advantages. Here, too, lived independent cattle speculators and commission men who dealt with the cowmen but had few ranches of their own.

To these towns came the steer buyers of the Northwest, the pasture men of Kansas, and ranchmen from other sections of the state to purchase cattle for their ranges. They came to these towns because they were assured of finding what they wanted in the quantities they needed and of finding them in the hands of people who knew how to deal with them in the terms of the industry. These terms consisted principally of buyer and seller having faith in one another and considering one another's word as good as a bond where the matter of quality, price, cut, and delivery date were concerned. There is a story current in one of the West Texas sections of a neighboring ranchman who visited town early in the year to buy stock cattle. Range conditions were bad and he readily found a cowman who wanted to sell, but reports from the buyer's home county indicated that no rain had fallen since he had left. Both wanted to trade so they made a deal with delivery date specified as "after the first general rain had fallen." According to the story the first general rain did not fall for more than two years, but shortly after it did rain the buyer showed up and found the seller still holding the cattle for him and the deal was consummated.

The veteran cowman, Luther Clark of Quanah, in relating his many experiences to the late George W. Saunders for the latter's book, *The Trail Drivers of Texas*, says, "I sold steers to E. H. East of Archer County for four years; he never put up a forfeit and we never counted a herd twice." In those days the handshake agreement was, if anything, more binding than the written one. Cow-towns were jealous of their good names and the reputations of their citizens and woe to him who "pulled a fast one." He immediately lost face in his home and apparently, without much effort, the word of his chicanery preceded him to other towns.

Each of the towns bore a reputation for the type of cattle its cowmen specialized in. Some were "yearling" towns, others "big steer" towns. It was according to the "country" they were in and the ideas of the cowmen.

This knowledge was worth much to the buyer from distant points, as he knew where to come for what he wanted with a minimum of travel, expense, and loss of time. Once he had visited a town and dealt with its cowmen he seldom took time to make the long buggy drive from town to ranch each year to see a seller's current crop of yearlings or two-year-olds. The deal was usually consummated in the town's local "bull pen," a sort of community office usually maintained by the cowmen in the rear of the leading bank of the town. About the only time this procedure didn't apply was when the buyer was dealing with speculator or trader who had "put up" a herd purchased in small bunches. Such a herd might include nester milk-pen calves or small herds purchased from the "little men" of the area and was not likely to be as uniform as those of the larger cowmen. After a deal had been made, the buyer would go his way and not see his purchase until he returned on delivery date to make his cut and route his shipments to wherever he wanted it to go.

The purchaser usually met the herd somewhere en route from ranch to railroad to take his "cut," which he invariably bought at a slightly reduced price. The seller knew this procedure and did not hesitate to bring the whole herd into town before the cut was made. In many instances, after long years of dealing, the purchaser would permit the seller to shape up the cattle himself and attend to their loading.

About every so often a steer buyer, after dealing over a period of years with a Texas cowman and riding his good cutting horse, would proposition the owner to buy the horse to be shipped home with the cattle. The owner had no intention of ever parting with the cutting horse in the way of sale, and the would-be purchaser knew this well. If he got him at all, it would be in the nature of a gift because of the fine friendship that existed between them and in return for favors he had shown the seller over a period of years—the matter of a dollar more per head some years when the market was wobbly or his failure to exact his full 10 per cent cut in the years when cattle were extra good quality. From the seller's standpoint, the gift served to strengthen the friendship between the two, and the presence of "Old Brownie" or "2 Y" on his new owner's range would serve to remind the North-westerner that "Old Man Worsham was a dang good feller and had good cattle ever year, and his word was as good as his bond." Thus, many a good Texas cutting horse went to his new home in the North-west partitioned off in one end of a car of steers that had been loaded a little light to accommodate him.

A majority of the steers were bought by men who made a business of furnishing cattle for the steer men of the Northwest much as feeder calves are handled in the Corn Belt in these days. Prominent among these were John Clay, of the commission company still bearing his name, and A. E. DeRicqles of Denver, each of whom purchased thou-sands of Texas steers for their customers' accounts annually over a long period of years. It was recalled by Mr. DeRicqles shortly before his death, that in one year he purchased from a single ranch in excess of twenty thousand steers, the ranch in question being one owned by Merchant and Parramore in Texas and the San Simone Valley in Arizona.

With the coming of the nesters and the cutting up of the big ranches for crops, these "cow-towns" lost their identity as cattle centers. The spools of barbed wire, kegs of staples, barrels of salt, windmills, wagon sheets and bows in front of and alongside the ranch-supply store gave way to the breaking plow (both walking and riding), one-row planters, horse collars, webbed backbands, singletrees, trace chains, and broad chopping hoes. Where the cattle baron was once wont to stamp in and order a year's supply of necessities for ranch, camps, and chuck wagon, the timid, sunbonneted nester mother with her brood now exchanged eggs and butter for calico, hair ribbons, and a limited amount of stick candy for the children. Her man had already made arrangements to be "carried" for the year on the cotton-country basis for the more staple necessities of life.

They are but memories now—these cow-towns of bygone days. If you know them or visit one of them in search of information you will eventually find a little group of old-timers left over from the cattle days. These will be about equally divided between broken-down cowboys or cowmen who were never quite able to adapt themselves to the new order, and successful elderly gentlemen, who through their ambition, energy, and business acumen, wound up with small ranches or stock farms which their sons operate while they look after their town properties and "keep an eye on the boy." Through a fellowship formed long years ago around chuck wagon and campfire, these consort together now. They like to discuss with an interested visitor in search of real facts rather than "blood and thunder" history the glory of the day when they were cowmen and theirs was a cow-town. Invariably, during the visit you will hear one of them assert that, "It was a danged-sight better town them days than it's ever been since. Why, I remember when freight wagons were thicker right out there in that street than automobiles are now."

Typical of these towns of half a century ago was Quanah, in Hardeman County in Northwest Texas. The county lies just to the east of the one-hundredth meridian, and is bounded by the Red River on the north and Pease River on the south.

In the eastern portion of the county the Belcher brothers of Gainesville had founded the R 2 Ranch in the 70's, with headquarters in a dugout on Wanderers Creek, about three miles south of the present town of Chillicothe. They maintained line camps west of their headquarters, following the rim of the Pease River breaks to keep their cattle thrown back in Wanderers Creek Valley. West of the camps was Indian country, with no neighbors until you reached the Goodnight country in the Palo Duro Canyon. The Belchers had pushed out from Gainesville, and Montague and Clay counties far ahead of the

Waggoners and others in search of new countries. That they were real pioneers is proven by the number of Indian depredation claims allowed them by the United States Government for cattle and horses lost to the Indians, which were then charges of the Government and presumably living on reservations in the Indian Territory.

The Fort Worth and Denver Railroad was building west from Fort Worth toward the Rocky Mountains, and reached Hardeman County in 1887. Prior to its arrival the R 2 had driven its herds to Dodge City until the rails came to Denison. As the Denver came into West Texas they began to meet it with their drives at Decatur, Wichita Falls, and Harrold, in Wilbarger County. The Belchers sold their cattle, headquarters, camps and rights in 1878 to Worsham and Johnson of Henrietta, who soon pushed their range west until they claimed about the area which is now Hardeman County: west to the one-hundredth meridian or the present east line of Childress County, north to Red River and south to Beaver Creek, where it joined the Waggoner range. They soon had twenty-five to thirty thousand cattle in the R 2 brand and were branding fifteen thousand calves per year. They had one or two trail outfits on the road each year taking steers to the Northwest.

During the passing years the ranch had several changes in ownership, Worsham retaining his interest each time. They worked a rough and tumble crew of men, both on ranch and with the trail outfits. Until this good day there is considerable respect accorded the riding and fighting ability of any old-timer who was an R 2 man.

Tipped off by townsite officials of the Denver that a town was to be located in Hardeman County and almost on what section, early birds located a store, saloon, and post office in advance of the coming of the rails. Just who did this seems to have been lost to posterity for the time being, but it is a matter of record that Doc Shaw was the first postmaster and no doubt was responsible for the town's being named for the last great Comanche chieftain, Quanah Parker.

The town's first funeral had been held far in advance of the coming of saloon, store, and post office when Joe Earle, who with the Estes brothers of Henrietta was en route to Leadville, Colorado, in search of work, had been killed by Kiowa and Comanche warriors. They were attacked about fifteen miles northwest of the R 2 headquarters. The Estes brothers escaped the Indians and made their way back to the ranch. Earle was killed, scalped, and otherwise mutilated. Cowboys from the ranch, led by the Estes boys, found the body and buried it where he had fallen. The grave is in about the center of the well-kept

Quanah cemetery. The Indian raid, the last in West Texas of which the writer has any record, took place in a small draw where the feed pens of the Quanah Cotton Oil Company are now located.

So when the rails reached the new townsite in August, 1887, it had some advantage of other railhead towns in that it had saloon, store, post office, and cemetery, and had only to await the building of the stock pens to get away to a fair start as a cow-town. The town profited by the fact that the road did not push on at once, but made Quanah its Western terminus for two years. In this period many South and Southwest Texas herds, either en route to the Northwestern ranges or scheduled for delivery to Panhandle ranches, were loaded into cars— cattle, horses, men, chuck wagon, and all—to be shipped to Quanah, where they were unloaded, outfitted, and resumed the trail. In this way they missed the East and North Texas areas which had been closed to trail driving by fencing and farming.

To the north of the new town and across the Red River in Oklahoma lay the disputed 2,380 square miles of Greer County, a cowman's paradise, deep with grass and very well watered. Cattle had been coming into it, driven from Clay and Archer counties by Cap Ikard, who used the V Bar brand, and the Harrold Brothers, Doc and Ephraim. Their combined herds numbered around thirty thousand head, but while a partnership existed as to range affairs, and they jointly maintained a string of line camps which extended from the mouth of Deep Creek due south to the South Fork of Red River, Ikard and the Harrolds maintained their separate brands. In 1884 they sold their cattle to the Francklyn Land and Cattle Company, an English syndicate, one of the largest operating in this country. A year or so after their purchase the new company moved their cattle out of Greer County to the upper Panhandle, establishing a great ranch northeast of where the city of Amarillo is located.

With the passing of the Francklyn people, numerous small cattlemen came into Greer County. Among them were B. W. Waters, T. J. Peniston, Sam White with the O M brand, Luther Clark, Ledbetter and Tullis with the Z V brand, Pumphrey and Olive, Captain W. J. Good and his sons, Mart Byrd and Ed Hawkins, operating as partners, John Anderson, Elzy Eddleman, A. J. Brown, J. C. Lindsey, Ex and Bill Hughes of Cooke and Grayson counties, Burrel Cox, and others.

These ranches and cowmen were tributary to, and did their shipping from, and shopping in, Quanah. It would be supposed that with the shipping point almost at their door they would have been very happy, but there was a fly in the ointment, so to speak. There was still room for more cattle in Greer County and the Indian country. Heretofore, incoming cattle had been shipped to Harrold in Wilbarger County, unloaded and trailed from there onto the Indian ranges. These herds passed almost wholly around the ranges of the Southwest Greer County cowmen. With the extension of the railroad, however, it was natural for the incoming cowmen to want to ship the additional fifty or sixty miles to Quanah and drive almost directly to their "countries" which would take them across the Greer County ranges.

A representative was sent by the Greer County men to discuss with the railroad executives the matter of stopping the stock trains at Harrold rather than carrying them into Quanah. The railroad officials asserted that if the shipper's order called for Quanah they were obliged to haul them there. Another meeting of the cowmen was held under the cottonwoods somewhere along Turkey Creek or Sandy, and another delegation selected to call on the railroad authorities, this time not to request, but to deliver an ultimatum to the effect that if the railroad did not do something about it and quick, they would individually and collectively drive their herds for shipping Northwest to Woodward, Oklahoma, into which the Southern Kansas Railway from Liberal, Kansas, was just building. The officials saw the light and, not being hampered in those days by too many interstate and Federal commissions, immediately fixed a rate on incoming cattle for Quanah from certain areas at about one-third higher than the one in effect to Harrold. This ended the Greer County men's troubles and threw their entire business into Quanah.

To the south, the Witherspoons, J. G. and P. S., held big ranges between the Wichitas and on the mesquite-burdened flats of what is now portions of Knox and Foard counties. J. G. used the U L A brand and P. S. the 9. The latter, to care for over-production on the West Texas ranch and to provide a finishing ground for his steers, maintained a ranch in the Otoe Indian reservation with headquarters at Red Rock, on the Santa Fe. These cattle, as well as those of J. G. Witherspoon, drove to Quanah for shipping. There were several other smaller outfits in Foard, Knox, and King counties who shipped from there. The O X outfit sprawled among the three forks of Pease River, drove from the east side, or Dripping Springs section of their outfit to Quanah to ship.

Jim McAdams, whose H A T outfit lay in Foard and Cottle counties, along with his kinsmen, Frank and Ben Easley, shipped from Quanah and made it his banking and trading headquarters. Until the railroad pushed on west, the Moon's, the 6 6 6 6, and sometimes the Spurs brought their herds there to ship. The Richards brothers of Cottle County, T. J. with the Stripe brand and W. Q. with the 3 D, also drove to Quanah until the railroad was extended to Childress.

Cowmen to the north and south of it liked the town as a shipping point. The Greer County men could throw their herds across Red River in the early morning and reach Groesbeck Creek, which lay about halfway between the river and the town, for noon and watering. It was open country from the creek into the wings of the shipping pens, which permitted them good country in which to shape up their herds before penning. From the south it was a straight shot from the Wichitas to Quanah, with Wanderers Creek about equal distance on the south as Groesbeck was on the north, with open country again from watering to the pens.

New businesses, principally those catering to the cowmen's needs, came to Quanah. Lumberyards, wholesale and retail stores, a Chinese laundryman, more saloons, and "Cornbread Mat's" resort north of the tracks. Unlike its prototypes in Dodge City, Abilene, and other rail-head and trail towns, it was free of cowboy killings, notwithstanding its patronage came from hundreds of Indian Territory and West Texas cow hands, who visited the town during the shipping season.

About the worst thing that happened was a little promiscuous gun-fire occasionally, or some "sidewalk riding" when there were half a dozen cow outfits camped in and around town waiting for cars. It is of record, however, that a couple of Moon men did make Amos Huckaby, a deputy constable and former cowboy, do a pretty fair job of climbing the smooth, plastered walls of the "Chain Harness" saloon one night by dropping a barrage just under his boot soles. Bob Stone ran a first-class saloon which catered to the best cowman trade, while the hands gave most of their patronage to the "Chain Harness," which was operated by a couple of ex-wagon bosses.

One of the most amusing occurrences happened one night at "Corn-bread Mat's" place when the thermometer hovered near zero and the town was full of hands "wintering" in Quanah, waiting for spring to "break." It seems that one cowboy became irked by the fact that his lady love insisted on dancing continuously with an R 2 hand. Failing to get results with requests and reproofs, and not being inclined to jump the R 2 man, the slighted one took on a few more drinks and, when the dancing stopped to allow the participants to cool off, yanked the recalcitrant lady out the front door and marched her to the corner of the house where stood a rain-water-filled tub, well-frozen. Turning her around, he commanded her to sit down on the ice, which she did. So thick was the ice that it sustained her weight, whereupon the cowboy, with a strangle hold on her blond locks, chugged her up and down until it did break, after which he told her, kindly but firmly, that it was for her own good, to "cool her off."

About this time there came to Quanah a young Englishman, George Rowden, who was to sit in the same twelve by twelve room for thirty-three years and fashion boots which found their way to every section of the nation where boots were worn. He worked out a boot of style and texture which so pleased Western cowmen that he was never able to catch up on orders. During the thirty-three years he never employed a helper but made each pair of boots himself to suit the individuality of the man ordering them. He never accepted mail-order measurements. As a result of this policy, he had a speaking acquaintance with most of the cowmen, cowboys, and peace officers in West Texas. He enjoyed an equally wide acquaintance among the steer buyers and cowmen of the Northwest who came to Quanah every year. It is said that when word reached Quanah of Senator Mark Hanna's death, Hooley Clements, sitting in the local "bull pen," arose and walked to the door. Being queried as to where he was going he replied, "Up to George Rowden's to order me a dozen pair of boots. It looks like all the great men in the world are dying off. Old George might be next, and I don't want to be left barefoot when he is gone." Rowden, however, outlived Clements by a good many years. When he died he had on hand a great number of unfilled orders. Almost equally famous were the saddles manufactured in Quanah by the Sanders brothers, Neil and Ross, who worked half a dozen saddlemakers for years. Ross Sanders is still living and in the saddle and harness business in Portales, New Mexico.

Quanah liked cowmen and they liked her. Men from the Haystack and Navajo Mountain countries would come in for their mail, tobacco, and a change of clothes. In the early days Caldwell's store drew most of the patronage. It was Caldwell who sent their laundry by express to Fort Worth and received it for them on return. Headquarters for transient cowmen was the Quanah Hotel, owned and operated by Mike Kerrigan, a genial Irishman, who had a wide acquaintance among West Texas and Northwestern cowmen. It was not unusual, on a warm summer afternoon, to see a dozen or more cowmen sitting on the long veranda of the hotel being regaled by the Irish wit of their host.

Already the threat of the plow was being sensed. Back down the Denver some good wheat crops were being raised and the head of the long stream of covered wagons, with trailing plow, tools, and milk stock was in Clay, Wichita, and Wilbarger counties.

Worsham's had been steadily losing R 2 range to smaller men who were coming into Hardeman County. By 1887 the country north of town to Red River and following that stream to the line of Childress County was occupied by the Nortons, Clements, the William brothers, W. W. Howard, and T. J. Peniston, all good cowmen and good citizens. In the breaks south of town the Clisbee brothers, Lee and Frank, had established a good little ranch. Southwest of them Tom Haskett and Charley Neeley, both old R 2 men, had established their Swinging H outfit. Bud Summers, veteran Moon man, had acquired a ranch on the north side of Pease River by working for wages, investing them in cattle which he ran on open range until he filed on and bought as much land as he needed. To the southwest, in the Medicine Mound area, Billy Neal was establishing a good little ranch, and to the southwest of him Oscar Dodson, another R 2 man, was building up an outfit from the old range on which he had worked as a hand. Both these outfits were near or encompassed the site of the Indian battle, where Sul Ross whipped the Comanches thoroughly and rescued from them Cynthia Ann Parker, white mother of Chief Quanah Parker.

The long white caravan which was eventually to reach the Quanah country, deposit its farmers, and move on until it had encompassed the Long S, the I O A, Curry Comb, X I T, or any other range where plowing and planting seemed profitable, was drawing nearer. There was to be another ten years of cow-towns, however, before it came.

Over in Greer County the cowmen had prospered, married and had children ready for school. These sought about for a town where they might build homes, school their children, and yet look after their ranches with a minimum of driving or riding. Quanah suited them in these respects. Too, it was a county seat now. After a whirlwind campaign an election was held which—according to the proponents of old Margaret, the original county seat—brought to the town on the railroad Texas Rangers to keep order, and most of the men employed by the Denver road in construction work from Fort Worth to Clarendon to vote. As a result of the election Quanah was made county seat. The county was divided, Foard County being organized from the south half and Crowell made its county seat.

From Greer County to Quanah came John Ledbetter, W. B. Tullis, Captain Good and his sons John and Wallace, and Ed Hawkins, Mart

Byrd, T. J. Peniston and others to plan and build new homes. At about the same time J. G. Witherspoon came to make it his home, as did W. Q. Richards of Cottle County and 3 D fame. Tom Haskett of the Swinging H, Al Yantis from Dickens County, L. B. Watkins from Knox, and H. B. Sparks from the Matador country. D. D. Swearingen of the O X, Jim McAdams of the H A T outfit, A. J. Norton, J. H. Clements, W. W. Howard, and several others had already established homes in the town when these came. Almost immediately they began construction on homes, large and ornate but well in keeping with the architecture of the period. Usually, they bought an entire block of ground, sometimes two. In one corner they built their house and cut off a very small garden tract and orchard. The balance they enclosed with a high picket fence, which except for the pickets—a concession to the fact they were living in town—would have been a plain corral in any man's cow-country. In the far corner they built a substantial two-story barn and along the north side a set of sheds with southern exposures, similar to the old style wagon yard. In these they kept their buggy teams, the wife's driving horses, the ranch buggy, the phaeton, the milk cows, and the old gentle cow-ponies they kept in town for the children to ride.

Sometimes, when it was more convenient to brand a herd of new-bought cattle en route to the ranch than to drive them into head-quarters, these glorified corrals were used for that purpose. It was not unusual in those days to have the minutes of the last meeting of the Ladies Literary Society drowned out by the bellowing of yearlings cut off from their mothers, or the bawling of a calf under the iron. Neither was it unusual for the odor of burning hair to drift into the parlor windows while refreshments were being served. They didn't mind though, these cowmen's wives, and would pass such occurrences off with, "You know, Mrs. Chairman, your husband is delivering his steer yearlings to mine today and helping him brand them."

Quanah was in her heyday. Daily, heavy freight wagons with trailers loaded out barbed wire, Bois d'Arc posts, windmills, lumber, and pipe—some going as far north as Mangum and Elk City and south-west to old Espuela. The Spurs, O X, S M S, 6 6 6 6, Matadors, 3 D, H A T, Moon, and Stripes were fencing, cross fencing, and erecting windmills. Because of the easy crossing on Pease River the town received benefit of this business.

The office of J. L. Elbert, veteran insurance man and lifelong friend of Quanah Parker, back of the First National Bank, became the "bull pen" where cowmen in town on business or to visit their families fore-gathered and discussed prices, range conditions, and things that interested them. To it came Burk Burnett, D. B. Gardner of the Pitchfork, Fred Horsbrugh of the Spurs, Jimmy Gray of the Moon, and Frank Hastings of the S M S to trade with local cowmen and make Quanah their railroad point. Some kept teams and buggies in Quanah regularly. In the Clisbee brothers' livery stable, by checking the horse brands or gold lettered initials on the high, side-spring Haynes ranch buggies, one could keep a fairly accurate check on the whereabouts of the cowmen of the immediate section.

Pat Dooling, genial Irish livestock agent for the Denver road, who had served as scout for General Dodge when he sought the route for the Denver, made his home in Quanah, it being about central of the many shipping points on the Denver's 450 miles of West Texas track-age. Living there also, and under the direction of Dooling, was the crack livestock-loading crew of the road. This crew operated along the full length of the route and were on the move continuously during the shipping season. With camp boxes, prod poles, shovels, and bed-rolls they rode freight and passenger trains day and night, eating and sleeping wherever their work was. It was their boast that when they began sanding a string of empty stock cars the engineer never closed his throttle and the brakeman never ceased signaling until the last car was finished. The cowmen cut their cattle into the crowding pens for them by carloads and they were their cattle until the "bull bar" was up. In big pens, with three and four loading chutes, they kept the cowboys riding hard to keep the crowding pens full. Frank Walker was foreman of the crew until he was made city marshal of Quanah. Arthur Walker, a kinsman, and until his death last year, livestock agent for the Denver with headquarters in Amarillo, succeeded him and managed the crew for many years. Cattle from Quanah for slaughter, prior to the building of the Fort Worth and Oklahoma City packing houses and the building of the Frisco into Quanah, were routed Denver to Wichita Falls, Katy to Denison and thus on over that route to the Missouri River markets.

W. D. Jorden, Federal livestock sanitary inspector, beloved by all West Texas cowmen, headquartered in Quanah for fourteen years. He died recently at Marlin, having gone there from his ranch near Claren-don when he fell ill.

About this time ticks and fever were causing lower Panhandle cow-men considerable worry and financial loss. The quarantine line began on the Oklahoma border on the north line of Childress County, then went down the west line of Childress County, and on down to the southwest corner of Stonewall County, and farther. It was impossible to ship cattle from below the "line" beyond that point without a tick-free certificate. Cattle in any number going into the Panhandle were dipped in Fort Worth and inspected at Electra. "Little men," or nesters with only a few head, or cowmen bringing a load of new bulls in, "ticked" them by hand at Electra and had them inspected for entry into the Panhandle.

Most of the Quanah country was "ticky." This had made little or no difference to its cowmen until the Plains country—which because of its rigorous winters was tick-free—began to quarantine against them and practically refused to look at or handle their cattle. Caught in sort of a "no-man's land," so to speak, with the sales value of their cattle curtailed, they set about, under Government supervision, ridding their section of ticks. They did not do this, however, without a certain amount of grumbling and expressed belief that ticks and Texas fever were the "bunk." Some even went so far as to contest rulings of the board, and the Witherspoons permitted themselves to be arrested for violations in order that a test might be made. The state won its point and the cowmen began their long task of "cleaning up."

As a means of getting their cattle out when sold, they jointly built a vat and a corral capable of holding thousands of cattle on the southwest corner of the town section. Herds were driven to it, dipped, and held on the open sections adjoining it until they were ready for inspection. Many tests of the earlier "dips" were conducted at this community vat. Among the first solutions tried was one originated in Kansas City. It had to be kept at a certain temperature when dipping was in progress. To accomplish this, a set of steampipes were installed in the vat with steam supplied by a traction engine parked nearby. Each herd coming in would fire up the boiler, fill the vat, and start dipping with a cowboy fireman at the engine. The latter would occasionally dip up a small bucket of fluid from the vat to test for temperature by thrusting a thermometer into it. Usually there would be a lapse of several seconds or minutes before the thermometer was put into the fluid, while the fireman rolled a cigarette or discussed with some puncher what the two might do that night on the "north side." As a result of the delay, the liquid lost several degrees of heat, whereupon the fireman would crowd in more fuel and open the steam valve wider to bring it up to what he had been told was the right temperature. The dip was pronounced successful and most of the cattle passed, but it was generally believed by the inspectors that the boiling to which both cattle and ticks were subjected was more responsible than any ingredients contained in the dip.

From the Argentine in South America came two young inventors with a South American dip known as "Sarnol" which met with some success. Eventually each ranch built its own vat and by systematic Government-supervised dipping, in an arsenic dip still in use, the country was cleaned up about the time the cow business played out.

W. B. Tullis, a Quanah cowman, was one of the earlier chairmen of the Texas Livestock Sanitary Commission. In later years, Dr. J. H. Wilson was also a member of the board. Inspectors, working for the Commission in the area were John Cash, Doc Benson, and John Cope, all of Crowell. All had been cowmen or cowboys on ranches in the area. During their tenure of office they traveled thousands of miles by buggy, on horseback, and on train to inspect herds ready for movement. None are living now.

It was not all smooth sailing and prosperity for the town and its cowmen in these years. In the early 90's a bank failure wrought havoc with cowmen and businessmen alike, leaving the town without banking facilities. C. H. Harwell and son, Mason, who operated a grocery business which had for its customers cowmen throughout a wide area in West Texas, filled the need with a private bank that was of inestimable value to the entire section. At one time it was the only bank in operation between Clarendon and Vernon with business running up to points near Mangum in Oklahoma. They discontinued their banking business operations in 1900. Mason Harwell, still in Quanah, is manager of and interested in several West Texas lumber yards. His father died many years ago.

Sometimes tragedy stalked the streets as it does in any cow-town or cow country where men do not settle their differences by fisticuffs. Captain W. J. McDonald of the Texas Rangers, who made the town his home, met and shot out differences with John Matthews, sheriff of Childress County, on the street one day. Matthews went home in a coffin and the Ranger captain, riddled with bullets, lingered between life and death for months. Eventually he recovered and was later to guide President Theodore Roosevelt on his famous wolf hunt in the "Big Pasture" country of Oklahoma, settle the Brownsville Negro-soldier row, and serve as bodyguard for President Woodrow Wilson. He later died a peaceful death while serving as U.S. marshal for the Dallas district.

Tom Latham and Doc Shaw, he who had arrived on the town section in advance of the railroad and was the town's first postmaster, disagreed over some matter. Both were fearless and when they met in front of Fred Rip's saddle shop it was a fight to the finish. Shaw armed, so the evidence showed, with an iron singletree and Latham with a pistol. Shaw was killed and Latham later acquitted.

In 1896 Quanah Parker, his many wives, children, subchiefs, and half-hundred braves, many of them veterans of the Adobe Walls fight, paid his namesake a visit of several days duration, during which they regaled the citizens with Indian war dances, songs, parades, and many speeches, in return for several beeves. In later years he visited the town en route to the Burnett ranch in King County. So well did the Indians draw crowds that the town fell upon the idea of a cowboy reunion in the fall of 1898. Long before the day of rodeos the affair drew heavily from Mangum to Seymour and out to the Cap Rock. O X, 3 D, Moon, and S T V men carried off most of the honors. Ellison Carroll, then in his prime, and on his way to set a world's record as a big steer roper, was on hand. Big Bob Wilson from Knox County bull-dogged a steer, "threw him by hand," they called it then, the first white man to publicly accomplish the feat. Carroll was not in form at the time and roping honors went to Tom Latham and bronc riding to Bruce Norton. In later years Norton and Latham competed in St. Louis, Oklahoma City, Bliss, Oklahoma, and at other reunions. Norton was awarded the title of world's champion bronc rider in St. Louis in 1904. For some reason the Indians did not return for the reunion the next year and the "Order of Redmen" and a local militia company staged a sham battle wherein soldiers drove the pseudo-Indians from a settler's cabin which they were attacking. It is recalled that Billy Bodine of the Noble Order of Redmen, in the heat of battle, had his hip pockets and most of what they covered shot away by an enthusiastic militiaman who drew too fine a bead even though the ammunition was blank.

The white caravan had split down between Wichita and Vernon, for Greer County had been opened for settlers and thousands of land-hungry people were pouring into it. The Greer County cowmen began closing out or seeking new ranges. The Ledbetters, Tullis, Captain Good, Mart Byrd, and Ed Hawkins turned to New Mexico as a last stand, still making Quanah their home, with ranch activities head-quartered along the Pecos Valley and Northwestern Railroad, "Pea-vine" the cowboys called it, at Bovina and Portales. Luther Clark came to Knox County, near Benjamin, to purchase a ranch. He moved to Quanah in 1903 and has lived there since that time.

By the fall of 1900 the white caravan had taken the eastern half of the county and the big flats out from Wanderers Creek were going to wheat and cotton. The cowboy reunion that fall was a combination affair, reunion and county fair, for those who were farming wished to show what the soil would produce.

Horse races—good ones—and a showing of fancy saddle horses, were a feature of the fair. While the races attracted horses from a great distance, most of the winnings went to local horses, some of which were destined to go far on Midwest circuits. Rocky Mountain Tom, a famous quarter horse, was owned by Sam Payne. Neel S, an equally good pacer which made the circuits in Missouri, Nebraska, and Illinois, winning a large portion of his starts, was the property of Dr. McCullough. Equally famous was his colt, Budweiser, who raced successfully over the circuits made by his sire.

There was another feature of the 1900 fair—better cattle. Already the cowmen of the section had seen that if they were to remain in business it would be with less range and better cattle. That year the fair featured one of the first, if not the first, auction sales of registered cattle in West Texas. The Faulkner brothers of Missouri shipped three loads of Shorthorn bulls in for the sale. The auctioning was done by Colonel R. E. Edmondson of Kansas City. They sold readily and as a rule were taken by the cowmen to the home lots in town, where the purchasers wintered them and worked at getting the rings out of their noses. "Papers" mattered but little then. A brass ring in the nose of a bull was sufficient evidence, at least to the cow hands, that an animal was registered.

During the next two years E. J. Wall, who had come into Quanah from the breeding grounds of Missouri, held Shorthorn sales in Quanah, Mangum, and El Paso. The sale in Mangum was held before the Rock Island Railroad was completed at that point, the cattle being unloaded at Granite, the terminus of the road, and driven over to Mangum. B. B. and H. B. Groom, Englishmen and extensive breeders of Shorthorn cattle at Groom Station of the Choctaw Railroad near Panhandle City, sold several hundred cattle at auction in Quanah in 1903. The Faulkners also came back for another sale or two. Colonel Edmondson officiated at each of the sales as auctioneer.

With a foundation based on the Shorthorn, Quanah cowmen suddenly switched to the Hereford. S. T. Howard, a Jersey breeder to the south of town, had developed a Hereford herd that did well both from a show standpoint and on the range. Cowmen, noticing this, began to demand the white faces. L. B. Watkins purchased the bull Regulator for $650 at a Kansas City sale—a stiff price for an old cowman who had been saving his own for so long. He sold the bull on arrival at Quanah to E. J. Wall, who, sensing the trend of the industry, had switched to Herefords. The latter the next year purchased at auction in Kansas City the thirteen-month-old Hereford heifer "Miss Marie" for $224. During the next three years he showed her at livestock shows in Fort Worth, Dallas, San Antonio, and El Paso, winning first in her class and sweepstakes over all classes. Eventually Wall took her to the Kansas City show where she sold in the auction ring for $1,325 to the Studebaker brothers. North of town Aaron Norton was building up a registered Hereford herd to supply himself and kinsmen Clements and Howard with bulls. Possibly to this trio should go honors for being among the first to develop what is now termed the "feeder calf" and for attracting Northern and Corn-Belt buyers to West Texas, for as early as 1904 they had a steady demand for their calf crop from buyers from Letts, Iowa, and Washington Courthouse, Ohio. For many years their calves went to Northern buyers "sight unseen."

The white caravan arrived, seeking the land office or the cowman who wanted to sell off "a quarter" in one of his big flats "on time." The old cowman, stiff, sore, and tired of continually facing the setting sun in search of ranges to which the caravans could not or would not come, accepted the new order. Some had fortunes and knew how to keep them, some were broke and knew it, still others were broke and didn't know it. The passing of the caravans was not the end. Immigrant cars, "zulus" the train crews called them, from eastern Texas, Missouri, Iowa, and Illinois, made up half the freight trains and were set out at every siding along the route. The day of the range cowman was done.

If you should make a listing of the fifty or more cowmen who made Quanah a cow-town and foregathered in the "bull pen" forty years ago and draw a line through those who have passed away, you will find only a few names left open on your list: Tom Latham, now of Oklahoma City, J. M. Williams of Quanah, Wallace Good of Kansas City, and Ed Hawkins, who at last account lived in Carlsbad, New Mexico.

Mart Byrd, who never ceased his efforts to locate a cow country, went into Old Mexico, taking his three boys, wife, and two daughters. Revolutionists imprisoned him and killed his eldest son. The balance of the family barely escaped to the States with their lives. Byrd was later released and died several years ago in Mineral Wells.

Luther Clark, the veteran cowman, who for nearly three-quarters of a century has been actively engaged in the cow business in Texas as cowboy and cowman, with his wife, who before their marriage was Mollie Larrimore of Young County, make their home in Quanah. Mr. Clark is the only man now living who was present at the organization meeting of the Texas and Southwestern Cattle Raisers Association in

Graham, in 1877, and who has been in the cattle business continuously since that time. He will tell you with pride that he has never earned a dollar, eaten a bite of food, owned a suit of clothes, or enjoyed a luxury that was not the direct result of the sale or handling of cattle. He is engaged with his son, L. C. Clark, in the cattle business in the Water Valley section near San Angelo.

Billy Neal has a good little ranch in the Medicine Mound section and Oscar Dodson still ranges along the Pease River. Both use Chillicothe or Mound Station on the Orient if they do not truck their cattle. Walter Williams, foster son of Jim (Hooley) Clements, still ranches and farms in the Hooley Ann section. He has steadily improved the quality of the herds founded by his kinsmen and turns out a few loads of excellent calves each year. Edgar Norton, son of A. J. Norton, trades and handles a good many cattle around Quanah. Glen Ross, son of a pioneer father, operates his business as J. F. Ross & Son and maintains an excellent herd of purebred cattle in the western part of the country, that has been attracting attention in Hereford circles. Con McAdams and Elzy Youngblood, sons-in-law of Bud Summers, operate the ranch founded by the latter on Pease River, south of town. They run some cattle and have a good acreage of wheat each year.

In lush years baled cotton crowds the wings of the Quanah pens. Thousands of other bales are stacked in the old traps and holding pastures near them—cotton that cannot be sold for the cost of production. Perhaps the veteran trail driver, Ab Blocker, was right when he said after planting and harvesting his one and only cotton crop, "If I ever plant any more cotton seed I'll boil every damn one of 'em before I plant 'em." Possibly West Texas farmers should have boiled theirs—at least half of them.

Shortly after the railroad came to Quanah the wife of Joe Earle came to Quanah cemetery, located his grave, and with painstaking effort and only a butcher knife for a tool, carved from a soft, white gypsum rock a beautiful and intricately designed monument to his memory. Time, weather, and curiosity seekers hacking at it deteriorated it until there was scarcely a trace left. A few years ago when the Centennial marker craze was upon the state, a little group of eight or ten cowmen's widows who, notwithstanding their natural frailties and pioneer hardships, have outlived their men, took the lead without waiting for or consulting the Centennial Commission in raising a fund locally for the erection of a granite monument and curb over the grave of Joe Earle, the first cowboy to be buried in the sacred ground where their cowmen husbands sleep.

Not All Were Boot Hills

If you are a seeker of Southwestern color as it applies to the old cow country your quest will lead you to the boot-hill cemeteries of the early towns. Their founding holds stories of the days when the six-shooter smoked and ruled whether to prove that holding more than four aces was not good poker or to defend water hole, brand, or range rights. Sometimes they smoked for the favor of a lady fair—if not so true.

Normally your trail will lead to Dodge City in Kansas, Tascosa on the Canadian, and Tombstone in Arizona, with a side trip if time permits to old Fort Sumner on the Pecos where lies "Billy the Kid" alongside Tom O'Fallard, and Charlie Bowdre, pals of the Kid and all victims of Pat Garrett's and other smoking guns wielded on the side of law and order. These hills have their stories and are emblematic of their day. They are well press-agented by road map and chamber of commerce.

If you slow down a little as you go and look to right and left you will find other small burial plots off the beaten path, usually unmarked, which hold stories of pioneering fortitude, and fearlessness. If you dig into their background you will find that no particular heroism or glory covered the passing of those who sleep under the sandstone markers placed by their kind long, long ago. When you have finished listening to a story from one who tells it from first-hand knowledge you will from some pretext or other take your hat off to pay tribute to those who gave their lives quietly and humbly that the Southwest might be developed for future generations. Then the crude sandstone markers become milestones of progress as well as memorials to those who lie under them.

Pull out of Amarillo early some morning headed for cool Colorado. In a few minutes you will be crossing the Canadian River and pulling up the grade on the other side. In a quarter of a mile if you are a student of Plains' history you may be saying to yourself that straight up the river, fifteen or twenty miles, lies old Tascosa with its boot-hill cemetery, ruins, and Mickie McCormick's girl, who is waiting there yet after more than a half century to join him in the grass-grown burying ground just beyond the old Romero house. Unconsciously your eyes will stray up the river. If the timing is right they will alight on what at first glance appears to be a meter box, valve, or one of the hundred and one gadgets that abound in the gas- and oil-laden Canadian River valley. It is easily identified by a white-painted iron fence surrounding it.

If the grass be short or has been burned off from carelessly left tourist campfires you will see half a dozen sandstone markers and footstones of varying size. That's enough for one who haunts graveyards in search of history. You pull out to one side, set your hand brake and climb the low-cut bank which is topped by a five-wire fence. At the expense of snagged trousers or torn shirt you crawl through to find the graves not only surrounded by the neat pipe fence but with an inner guard of barbed wire of the earliest vintage.

You read from the headstone that the first grave is that of a lady and next to it a tiny grave with "Baby" scratched on the headstone. Three adult graves and another marked "Baby" complete the six.

Back in Amarillo that fall on the way home you may make casual inquiry as to the graves beside the highway. The first dozen people you ask about them will tell you that they don't know who they are or that they have never noticed them. Then someone will suggest that you look up John Arnot as he knows all about such things. Somewhere along the street or around one of the cattle offices you locate him and your well-wishing friend makes the necessary introduction. You find him to be a well-kept gentleman and after a few words you know without being told that he is Scotch. To make conversation you inquire his age and are shocked to learn that he is past seventy-five. Further questioning brings out the fact that he came from the old country fifty-four years ago to enter the employ of the Scotch-owned L X Ranch, one of the oldest in the Canadian River country. Having a little Scotch in your own makeup you do a little fast thinking and decide you have your man and that it will be safe to risk a little coffee on him. Before you have finished the sixth cup you will admit that the investment is a good one, for John Arnot knows more of the early ranch history of West Texas (and how to tell it), particularly the history of the early Scotch- and English-owned ranches than any person we know of. He is presi- dent of the Old Time Panhandle Cowpunchers' Association, quite a historical writer, and hide and brand inspector for Potter County.

It is Arnot who knows best the story of the lone burying ground beside the highway for it was he who selected it—the first burying ground in Potter County—and directed the burial there. Suppose we let him tell how death took its toll from the ranks of the L X, showing no favors, taking a pioneer mother and a new-born babe first, then a cowhand, a freighter, and a lonely camp man. Let's let him tell it in his own language.

"Jimmie Wyness, a young Scotch accountant, came over to work as bookkeeper at the ranch about the same time I did. He was ambitious, too, and wanted to get a foothold in the new country with some range and a few cows that could wear his own brand. He had left a girl behind in London and wanted to work a year or two so that he might go back, marry, and bring her to the States. After a couple of years he did go back and bring her to the ranch. They came to Dodge City on the stage and the ranch freight wagon, I think, brought them on to Tascosa. She was a fine English girl—middle class I would say, and as fine and game as they come. Elizabeth Farris had been her name and she had been raised in London, right in the heart of it.

"First morning the coyotes howled we watched to see if she was scared. Not her. She asked what they were and if they howled each morning at the same time. We told her they did. 'Fine,' said she, 'it'll be like Big Ben back home, I can depend on them.'

"In due time we saw there was to be a baby. It worried us, too, for there was only a more or less hit-or-miss doctor at Tascosa—not much business for one—you were never sure of finding him on the job. There was no Amarillo then. The next nearest doctor was the post physician at Fort Elliott, miles away. She must have heard us talking of this for she called me into her room one day just before her time. I had been pretty close to her and Jimmie. We were both from the same country and then I had worked in his place as bookkeeper while he was away after her. She told me if she died she would like to be buried some- where on the ranch and not taken to a cemetery. I tried to joke her about it but she stood pat that if anything happened I was to select a burial place.

"When we couldn't wait any longer we loaded her in the buckboard and pulled out for Tascosa. As we feared, the doctor was not there.

Time was short, so assisted by a sort of midwife—'granny woman' we called her—the baby was born. It was a bad job. We saw that she was going to die. John Hollicott, a Scotchman, too, was running the ranch then. He sent a cowboy to Fort Elliott for the doctor. Shortly after he left she passed away so we sent another cowboy to cut him off and turn the doctor back.

"With the help of a jackleg carpenter we made the best coffin possible and started back to the ranch with the body. I went ahead to select a burial place. The headquarters was then on Pitcher Creek, a little further up the road and about a mile to the left of where the graves are. I rode out on a point, or headland, that jutted out toward the Canadian River. The river widened out and a little creek ran into it, making a sort of park covered with green grass and shaded by cottonwoods. As near as it is possible to make a comparison it looked a bit like the English countryside. I thought she would like it if she knew. From where I stood you could not see a human habitation and if you will recall when you were there last spring you still, after fifty-two years, can't see a human habitation, the highway and the wire fences are the only differences now.

"L X cowboys dug the grave and had barely finished it when the funeral cortege of half a dozen hacks and buggies pulled in from Tascosa. There were a half dozen ladies in the party, Mrs. Austin, at whose home she had died; Mrs. Lizzie Rhinehart, who was later Mrs. Al Popham, Mrs. C. B. Vivian, Mrs. Charles Ross, and Mrs. Jim East, wife of the pioneer peace officer at Tascosa, who later figured in the capture of 'Billy the Kid.' They sang a couple of hymns and one of the ladies, I don't recall which one, read a chapter from the Bible. Preachers were as scarce as doctors out there then.

"Back in Tascosa the good ladies were doing their best to keep the spark of life going in the Wyness baby, but it was no go. In about a fortnight we laid the poor little tike alongside its mother and carved another sandstone marker for him. Of those who attended the two funerals only Mrs. Austin who now lives in Chicago, Billie Wyness, a brother of Jimmie, and myself are living that I know of.

"The next one to be buried there was the infant of Mr. and Mrs. Charley Mott, employees at the ranch headquarters. Bunch McCrary, killed by having his horse jerked down on him when he roped a yearling, was buried there in 1889. The railroad had gotten to Amarillo by then and Jim Bailey, who drove the ranch freight wagon, stuck in the Canadian River one cold night with a heavy load. In trying to get his wagon out he got thoroughly soaked and then walked to the ranch in his wet clothes. He died of pneumonia a few days later. Jim Bell was the last one. In 1890 he quit the ranch to file on a section of land at the mouth of Plum Creek. During the summer he was putting up hay and a passerby found him lying dead in the corral with a bridle in his hand. We always thought that when he was taking the bridle off one of the mules it whirled and kicked him.

"There are a couple more graves over on Cheyenne Creek where Dud Parnell, who was killed by the accidental discharge of his gun, was buried with Gene Watkins, who was killed by bad Mexicans in Tascosa. They were both L I T boys and we thought they merited better burial than in boot-hill cemetery."

Over the final cup of coffee you reminisce about the early Scotch-English days. "There is blessed few of us left," says Arnot. "John Hollicott was tops among them. He came to the L X as wagon boss, then range boss about '88, and was finally made general manager. He left the ranch in '96 to go to his old friend Jim East in Douglas, Arizona. About twenty years ago while Jim was gone from home, John drew his money out of the bank and disappeared and to this day we have never heard from him. Jim Wyness is gone and, incidentally, he did get into the cattle business for himself and later worked for many years for Swift or Armour, I can't recall which. Yes, they are about all gone. John McBain and Alec Bartley, they came from Aberdeen, Scotland; Scotty Balfour, Charley Lowry, John Hutson, and Tom Carson have all died, John Molesworth is still living and handling cattle out at Clarendon. Dick Walsh, who ran the J A's for a long time, died a few years ago."

Modern Amarillo either forgot or didn't know the graves were there. The Texas Centennial came along with its miles of historical markers and didn't know about the lone graves on the Canadian. But John Arnot through the decades never forgot. For years he tended the lonely graves and was instrumental in getting Potter County to erect the iron fence which surrounds them now. It was he who persuaded Jimmie Wyness' second wife to erect the marble headstone at the head of the first Mrs. Wyness' grave. Again it was John Arnot who through the years tended the L I T graves on Cheyenne Creek and eventually sold the county commissioners of Oldham County on the idea of fencing it as the L X graves were fenced.

It does seem that with so much good marble and granite going into markers in Texas during the past three years that the little English girl who came from peaceful England with its Thames, Piccadilly Circus, and quiet countryside to help her boy carve out an empire in the Southwest should have been entitled to a fair-sized hunk of granite.

The Nester

Gradually West Texas cowmen are being metamorphosed in name by trade publications and fiction writers into ranchers and ranchmen. By the same process its farmers are becoming known as stock-farmers. There is grave danger that a term applied to the earliest of West Texas farmers may be lost to Southwestern literature and posterity. It would be bad indeed should this occur for it would mean the loss of a fine and honorable term that in the late 80's and early 90's formed a connecting link between the cow business and agriculture, both of which, working in conjunction, are responsible for the country's present high development in livestock and agriculture.

I refer to the term "nester," a name given those first few hundred intrepid souls who broke away from the age-old credit farming system of East Texas and the Southeastern states to gain a foothold in the cattle country of West Texas where folks of meager means might hope to acquire a freehold of their own if they were not afraid of hardship and hard work. It would be bad to let the word drop out as it is distinctly of Southwestern coinage and is not to be found as spelled herein in any dictionary, old or new, that I have seen as yet. [Editor's note: The Webster's New International now gives the word.]

It is rather strange too that no one has been able to advance a suitable reason as to why the earlier West Texas farmers were so called, notwithstanding the fact that for more than twenty-five years anyone not connected with the cattle business or anyone who tried to earn a living by farming was known as a nester. Merchants sought their trade as such and candidates that had the nester vote felt safe when election day rolled around. I was raised in the nester country of the lower Panhandle and didn't know that farmers had any other name until I was twenty-one years old. I just supposed they were called that like Baptists were called Baptists, Herefords were called Herefords, and Woodmen of the World were called by that name. It never occurred to me to go to the trouble of finding out why; they were fine honorable people—most of them—who were our outlying neighbors, working for us and giving an honest day's work for their pay. Later when I became interested in sort of an amateurish way in writing of things that I had seen and known of West Texas, I began to seek a definition of the word. As far as I could discover, as might be suspected, the title was bestowed by a couple of hard-bitten old cow hands. It was not until I ran into these and got their version of the title that I had a single clue on which to hang my hat even though I had talked to writers and newspapermen who had used the term hundreds of times. I even talked to a man who had written a book on the subject and admitted in it that he didn't know why they were so called. If, when I have finished, anyone can provide a more suitable definition than I shall attempt, it will be welcomed, I am sure, by everyone interested.

In writing of the nester I am referring particularly to the royalty, those who came first, to stick through drouth, flood, sandstorms, prairie fires, and hard times without going "back home" to visit "their wife's kinfolks" or without letting their claims forfeit when the going got rough; I am not referring to the horde of land seekers, bonus hunters, claim jumpers, and speculators who followed them when they had proven that the land had a future.

The first of them came in the late 80's and early 90's just as the cowman was realizing that the days of the free range were over and that henceforth he must buy and fence such land as he used. Most of those who had made up their minds to stay at the business had selected the lands of their old range that they wanted to acquire and were beginning to fence.

The nester came into the country with his possessions which consisted mostly of a few pots and pans, a bedstead, the old family clock, Bible, breaking plow, and the inevitable water barrel that he was to find so necessary when he got settled down. These were loaded into an old "butcher-knife" wagon which was drawn by, as my two cowboy mentors described it, a "high horse" and a "low mule," neither in very good flesh or strength, and adorned with a set of chain harness with cotton-web back bands and no breeching.

Ordinarily they were of two classes: the young couple, foreseeing the impossibility of ever having anything for themselves at home other than a bare living covered by an almost perpetual mortgage, and the old fellow with a large family of strapping boys and girls for whom he could see no future if they grew up to live under the same conditions he had existed under.

The attraction which brought them to West Texas was the "school lands" which, in that portion of the state, could be purchased at one dollar per acre, payable one-fortieth in cash and the balance on forty-years time at 3 per cent interest. The act under which the lands were sold required three-years' occupancy and involved certain improvements essential to occupancy. (The writer is indebted to Mr. N. J. Roberts of the Roberts, Beverly Abstract Company, Crowell, for certain information contained herein.) Initial steps in purchasing land was known as "filing," meaning a declaration of intent to purchase, accompanied by description of the land and the one-fortieth payment sent to the General Land Office in Austin to be approved by the commissioner of that office. At the end of the three years of occupancy the purchaser could file proof of proper occupancy with the Land Office after which his claim was inviolate and could not be contested so long as he kept his interest paid up. This process was known as "proving up." The last and final procedure came thirty-seven years later should the purchaser elect to exercise his forty-year payment privilege. He could, however, pay the entire amount at any time after he had "proved up." He then received from the state a "patent" or clear title to this land. It was permissible to file upon a section (640 acres) but a majority of the nesters did not possess cash enough for filing fees and down payment, with enough left over to live on until they could get going. A majority of the earlier ones filed on a quarter section (160 acres) which in comparison to the 40 acres and a mule of the eastern section seemed fairly ample for their needs. Occasionally some old fellow would file on a quarter for himself and have three of his children file on the other three-quarters which blocked them a section in a body.

When the nesters came in it was with full knowledge that they were invading the cowman's domain and that they would be more or less dependent on his good will for work enough to keep them going until they got started; so they moved cautiously and tried not to "stick their necks out" in a way that would engender ill will. Usually they came out twenty-five to fifty miles from the railroad and selected a quarter section in the big mesquite flats that abounded in the area and were already a menace to the cowmen who kept both them and cedar to a minimum or had it done for them by nature in the form of prairie fires and drouths. The nester selected the mesquite flats because he had been told that heavy mesquite was indicative of unusual fertility. The ranchers did not pay a lot of attention to where the newcomers filed. There were only a few of them, after all, and probably the first dry years would send them back to where they came from. An occasional farsighted one, who had planned a well-blocked ranch when it was fenced, looked them up and suggested that they file on equally good land on the edge of the pasture, or if they had already filed he would swap them land on the edge and attend to the transfers, filing fees, and so forth. As a result, when the larger ranches were fenced the nesters were pretty well grouped on the outer edges of them. These groupings, in time, became known as "nesterments" rather than "settlements."

First necessity for the nester when he received his papers and pulled into his claim was to provide shelter for his folks and to comply with the requirements of the Land Office as to improvements. He was miles from a source of lumber and wire and without funds to purchase if the source had been within three hundred yards of him. While he and his family camped or lived in their wagon, he set about building a dugout from stone or mesquite poles. Usually he dug back into a hillside until he had his dimensions and then walled up with flat rock until it was roof high. Then he ran his ridge pole, usually of hackberry or cottonwood, laying a covering of poles from wall to wall over the ridge pole. The poles were covered with clay mixed with broomweed for a binder, and carefully packed until a smooth roof was formed that turned water fairly well except during extremely rainy spells. The extra side boards from the wagon went to make a door and the "Clipper Corn boxes," he had brought with him, became window casements. In time to come the structure made an equally good abode for the family and assorted snakes, tarantulas, and centipedes that were attracted to its unchinked walls. He had found out by this time that it was "as near to water overland as it was straight down," so he was hauling all he used from a spring or waterhole somewhere along one of the creeks that missed his place by a couple of miles.

The next job was the clearing of a piece of land for gardening and to provide feed for the high horse and low mule. In building he had taken cognizance of a small clearing in the brush not too far from the dugout. It was only a city block or two in area and not enough for his needs so he set about widening it by cutting the brush and grubbing the stumps until he had a patch from three to five acres in extent. As he cut the brush he piled it on the outer edges of the clearing and mauled it into place until his patch was entirely surrounded by a brush fence that would not only turn range cattle but jack rabbits as well, for the mesquite carries a mighty thorn that, when seasoned, is as hard and sharp as a horseshoe nail. The fence was highly utilitarian when finished and resembled nothing on earth so much as a gigantic bird nest.

Julie Moody, who served for years as ranch, wagon, and trail boss for the R 2's when their headquarters were on Wanderers Creek in Hardeman County about where the town of Chillicothe is located, was prowling the long ridges with one of his men in the late 80's. Their route along the ridge overlooked a verdant mesquite flat.

"What the hell is that down there by that lone tree?" Julie inquired of his man.

"Looks like a damn big bird nest to me," replied his companion.

So they pulled off for a "look see" and to size the fellow up and offer what discouragement they could. Before they pulled into camp that afternoon they had spotted a couple more of the weird-looking layouts. That night Julie reported to Old Man Worsham in Henrietta that there were three or four more of "them nesters" between the ranch and the top of Pease River breaks.

This is my version of how the term originated. Right or wrong, it spread to every section of the nation where cow work was being done. The Texas fellows going up the trail for the last time asked the Northwestern outfits for jobs, giving as their reason the fact that "the nesters were taking our country and I can't go back there." This is borne out by several published letters of the late Charles M. Russell who was in Montana at the time, about 1885. If you have a better or earlier definition, let's have it.

By the time dugout and nest were completed the nester had established himself after a fashion with his cowman neighbor who was more than willing to give him work along at six bits to a dollar a day doing the things he dared not ask his "straight ridin' hands" to do; cutting fence posts and branding wood, digging postholes, building fences and corrals. Some of the younger boys were given regular jobs around the ranch headquarters driving freight wagon and "hoodlum" which carried the bedding and extra equipment of the chuck wagon when it was working.

In the spring "the woman" planted her garden and the man a meager feed crop which required little or no attention except from the Lord in the form of rain. There was no need to plant cotton for there were no gins and no demand for bundle feed from the cowman, so he improved his dugout by plastering it with native gypsum which stayed on until the first big rain, when it fell off.

Money was scarce with them at all times and pleasures few and far between, but their needs were simple. They went to the nearest town once a month and bought such necessities as they could afford: flour, sugar, meal, baking powder, salt, and soda. You could put their average purchases on one of these trips in a "Clipper Corn box," including the meal and flour, and still have room for a half dozen boxes of matches. I doubt if the cash handled by the average nester annually exceeded $150. Within a few years the various "nesterments" had built churches and school houses of a sort with the aid of the ranchers and in the yards of these they had buried their dead, thereby tying themselves more closely to the land. Doctors were few and far between and had to be ridden for when needed; as a result a majority of the children were born without benefit of a physician. By the same token, lives slipped away and bodies were consigned to the earth without scriptural words other than those provided by some grey-haired sage of the country. In times of stress they relied upon each other.

Despite these handicaps, their children grew, thrived, and learned an independence that was to mark them throughout their lives. When hard times fell upon the country cowman and nester alike were affected. The former either went broke or moved his cattle out of the country and could be of little help to the nester in the way of work. Some nesters went temporarily to town to do "public work" until they had accumulated sufficient cash to go back to their claims so that they did not forfeit. Others hauled cattle and buffalo bones, which were beginning to have a market, to the railroad. Some of the weaker ones

gave up and allowed their claims to forfeit, or sold out at a small
bonus to the ranch on which they were located. A majority stayed,
suffered, and starved until conditions changed; they were there to
welcome the second wave of nesters that came in around 1895 to 1900.

At any time after a claim had been "proved up" the owner could
sell it at a profit, the purchaser assuming payment of the balance due
the state. The amount received above the indebtedness was invariably
referred to as "bonus." In the earlier days bonuses varied from a small
flat sum to from seventy-five cents to one dollar per acre. Ordinarily
a ranch making such purchase would immediately pay off the indebtedness and receive a "patent" from the state. Unless the nester
could sell when he couldn't stay any longer or meet his payments, the
land was declared forfeited and was open for filing again. Few of the
earliest nesters ever allowed their lands to forfeit or be sold for bonus.
These and their descendants eventually became the backbone of West
Texas agriculture.

Such old fellows as are still living or some of their oldest descendants
will tell you that had it not been for the abundance of cottontail rabbits inhabiting the flats and prairie-dog towns they would not have
been able to stay and live out the drouth and hard-time periods. There
is nothing so nearly approaches fried chicken as a six-weeks-old
cottontail and flour gravy made with them even excels chicken gravy.
There were plenty of them and when the nester and his family got
too meat hungry they "ran down" a mess of the young cottontails.
They literally ran them down, too, for there was no money for even
.22 rifle ammunition and when the old dog couldn't catch them the
family took after them afoot. Closely pursued, the rabbits would duck
into a prairie-dog hole to stop a few feet down in apparent safety, at
least until the nester could get his "rabbit twister" into action. The
twister consisted of a couple of lengths of barbed wire twisted together and was six to ten feet in length with the two ends of the wire
flared at one end to form a sort of hook. The twister would be run
down into the hole, twisted into the animal's fur and thus the rabbit
would be dragged out. In later years when things were better the
old-timers, many of whom had moved to town, liked to refer to themselves as they visited with each other as members in good standing
of the "Ancient and Honorable Order of Rabbit Twisters." They sort
of looked upon it as a badge of merit and felt that it raised them above
the latter-day folks who had not shared the hardships with them. So
long as I lived in the nester country and it did not rain in the spring

when it should, the old fellows would eye the cloudless skies and say, "If she don't come, I still have my old twister and know how to use it." During these times the number of rabbits to be seen in a community were a sort of indication as to how its folks were faring. One fellow who had been to the railroad for a load of groceries for the ranch was asked on his return how things were over about Quanah. "Must be getting better," he replied, "they had a rain about a couple of months ago and I seen seven rabbits cross the road ahead of me between the top of the breaks and town and there wasn't a soul chasing any of them."

It must be borne in mind that the nesters could expect little or no help from merchants or bankers because they were an unknown quality with little or no security to offer. When things got so bad that the nester could not stay without help and could not leave if he was inclined to because his team was too poor to get him out, the cowman came to his aid with a sack or two of flour and a little work now and then that the rancher could ill afford to pay for.

There has always existed a mistaken idea that the earliest nesters and the cowman were mortal enemies. To a certain extent the cowman resented the nesters' coming, naturally, but his resentment was not violent. His feeling was more of pity that they should think they could make a go of farming in a country destined by nature purely for cattle. He rather welcomed the newcomers because they would work at things that the cowboys would not do. Once the nesters were settled in the pasture the cowman felt a certain responsibility for their well-being and asserted a sort of proprietary interest in them. After he found that they were not stealing beef he began sending a quarter over to the dugouts when he killed one; and as the nester got him a brush milk pen built, he allowed him to milk an old cow or two that had come onto the range with a bunch of gentle stock from the lower country. He and his men particularly felt sorry for the wives and families of the nesters and more or less kept a guardian eye on them as they rode about their work. Towns and doctors were few and far between, and when the stork hovered over a nester dugout or shack, it was not unusual for the nearest ranch to keep a horse up and ready to make the long ride to town for the doctor or to the settlements for the "granny woman." The cowman knew that the trip could not be made in time on the high horse or low mule that made up the team he had watched the nester break sod with. If it became necessary for one of the nesters to be taken to town for medical attention, the cow-

man would like as not send the ranch's buggy or hack over with a
driver to make the trip. Such action on the part of the ranchmen developed a sense of loyalty that was of inestimable value to them in
many ways. One of the managers of the Scotch-owned Spur ranch, in
reporting to the home office on a prairie fire that swept the ranch, said,
"I was pleased that our Red Mud and Dockum nesters turned out to
help us and fed our men as best they could." Pete Scroggins who
ranched up northeast of Snyder had a good many nesters on his outfit
during one of the hard years. He sent them beef and kept an eye on
them until it seemed that they and their families could go no longer
without suffering. He rode over among them one day and told half a
dozen of them to bring their wagons to meet him in Colorado City on
the next Saturday. Meeting them there he arranged for them to get
such necessities as they needed, all of which was to be charged to his
account. When the wagons had been loaded and were ready to pull
out, he rode along the line and inquired if everyone had everything
he needed or wanted, to which one old fellow replied, "Mr. Pete, I
sure would love to have a fiddle, I busted mine all to pieces last fall."

"All right," said Pete, "by God, go in to Coman and Shears and pick
you out one."

In these years the nester had been widening out his original nest
until he had a pretty fair-sized field which he fenced this time with a
two wire fence and chinaberry posts. The rains came and he made a
pretty fair feed crop. With the rains came the second wave of nesters
to file on more quarter sections and build more dugouts. One year,
1890 I think it was, the nesters sowed wheat on top of the sod, plowed
it under, and made twenty-five to thirty bushels of wheat per acre.
Nester towns sprang up with merchants and banks who would, presumably, help them if hard times came again. The rains did not come
again and the nesters trekked back to the East, many of them forfeiting
their claims, others to "visit" until it rained again. The old-timers in
better position now to stand the drouth held on again and grubbed
more land and in some instances added to their holdings by acquiring
additional lands. The ranchers blocked out their holdings, and newcomers came in seeking smaller ranches.

In 1897 my father acquired a fair-sized ranch in Foard County, consisting of railroad lands, claims he bought at a bonus and some twelve
sections filed on by three cowboys we had brought from the Indian
Territory with us. I recall that we hauled enough good building stone
from abandoned dugouts to construct a couple of sets of good corrals

and all the wind breaks and barn walls we needed at our headquarters. Four of the sections we purchased at a bonus of $900. The old fellow we bought it from thought he was rich and moved to town where he soon spent his money and came back along our pasture and filed on four more sections, two of which he eventually sold to us.

Between waves this time the nester had gotten his fields in shape and was selling bundle feed and maize heads to the cowman to winter saddle horses on. The Watkins Remedy man was making the "nester-ments" regularly now, the Star mail route was serving them, and some of the women folks were getting to go "back yonder" for a visit occasionally. Life was no longer so drab for them. As the counties were organized the commissioners courts always included at least two nesters.

The third and last wave of nesters that came in about 1900 nearly cleared up the last of the tillable school lands. They had brought cottonseed with them this time and found that it would grow and produce even better than in "the old country" and that their cowmen neighbors were demanding the seed for feed and even building oil mills to convert it into cottonseed cake.

Feeding

Cowman, nester, and pioneer manufacturer joined hands in West Texas in the early 90's in a common cause—one of necessity—and licked it to a frazzle. Not only did they lick it, but they built an empire, set a new standard for livestock and agriculture, and developed a manufacturing industry which consumed one of their principal raw materials and which, after taking care of domestic needs, has left a vast surplus for export.

It is a colorful, earthy, sound, sort of a story. Colorful because it dips back into the days of the open range; earthy from the fact that it tells of pioneer men breaking prairie sod while pioneer wives made dugouts and shack homes comfortable. Sound in that it deals with smokestacks, whirring wheels, and progress.

Each was drawn to the other by their individual needs, whether they acknowledged it or not. The cowman, just a few years inside barbed wire, needed a stable source of feed to augment his ranges. The nesters, crowded out of the older parts of the state, seeking new homes and fertile acres in the West, needed the encouragement which the cow-

man's need for farm products offered. The manufacturer was finding
that science each year was developing new uses for his products and
he was sorely in need of a stable and increased source for the raw
material he used.

That the combination worked well is evidenced in improved cattle
by the thousands, millions of acres under the plow, the great cotton-oil
industry with its many ramifications. The cities and towns that dot the
empire, and railroads and highways that connect them, and the development in oil manufacturing, and the production of raw material are
the handiwork of the trinity of interests, which, led by a group of
hard-pressed cowmen, laid the foundation for these things.

Nature had been generous with the old-time cowman, providing
grass, water, salt, and shelter over a wide range that rested and
recovered itself automatically, all at no cost to him. When he finally
found himself and his cattle encompassed by barbed wire he was loath
to begin feeding and did not until he awakened to find his "country"
eaten out and his old cows on the "lift."

He did not rush into it then for several reasons. There was no stable
source of feed available. He did not believe as yet that his own country
could produce feed, and he did not care to encourage the nesters,
whom he looked upon as temporary interlopers, by providing a market
which might help to make their tenure permanent. Had he believed in
the productivity of his country he would not have been interested in
producing feed himself. He was no farmer—that's why he pulled up
and left Central Texas and the Denton prairies because they were
beginning to farm there. His boot heels were not built for walking and
the riding plow had not made its appearance.

The men who worked for him felt the same way about their profession of cow punching. They didn't propose to get themselves "galleded"
walking behind a plow. Had he insisted, they would have politely
asked for their "time," packed their bedrolls on "individual horses," and
started riding toward the setting sun. There were still Arizona, New
Mexico, and the steer outfits of the Northwest where a man could be
respectable.

Some of the old fellows had a few hundred acres that required no
grubbing or clearing broken out and started raising sorghum; "cane"
they termed it, "hell" the cowboy called it. They did not ask their cow
hands to do this, but imported farm hands or hired neighboring nesters.
This disrupted the fine spirit and loyalty that had always existed
between the cowman and his employees. The cow hands called the

farm helpers "two-buckle boys," "fodder forkers," made pointed remarks as to which end of the mules they faced at their appointed tasks, and called those who did the milking and chores around headquarters, "Miss Sally," "Lizzie," or "Maggie." They also referred to those who cut fence posts or branding fuel as "wood shellers."

The farm boys, on the other hand, drawing $15 to $20 per month, felt they were being imposed upon when the cow hands in their glory of big hats, silver-mounted spurs, and prancing horses, received $25 to $30 for riding herd, bustin' broncs, riding in the rain, eating when they got to it, and flanking big calves in the branding pen all day. The farmer boys tried to graduate into cow hands to the disadvantage of the growing crops; the resultant feed was negligible.

Nature helped along as she always had, carrying cows and cowmen for a few years, but after a time she became more and more outraged with overstocking and lack of perception.

When the cowman selected his range for fencing it was from his knowledge of the country as he had seen it used under free conditions. He picked some of it from the "Big Flats," where the grass was always good, and a bigger portion of rough land, "cedar brakes" to him, where there had been water "as far back as the Indians could remember." He took a larger portion of the latter because most of the big flats were going to the nesters.

He had given little or no thought in the past as to how many acres were required to run a cow, winter and summer, good or bad, because it had not mattered then. His cattle had followed rainfall and green grass out onto the Plains, leaving the winter range to rest and recover automatically. When the blizzards swooped down in the winter nights, he pulled his "soggans" up closer as he lay in lone line camp or isolated headquarters and knew that his cattle were drifting down under the "Cap" where they would "bow up" in a warm canyon or coulee and that when the storm broke and he again rode forth it would be to find them in the "shinnery" chewing its succulent leaves. If the blizzards came fast and thick he would "bow up" himself all winter and prophesy some "dam big round-ups on the Pecos next summer."

It was another matter now to awaken when the sleet pelted on the roof and know that his undernourished cattle were drifting up against man-made barriers, trying to "bow up" against five strands of nonprotective wire. He knew, too, now that when the storm broke they would trail back onto ranges, ravished by overstocking and lack of rest. It kept him awake, too, for these cattle and this range were his last stand; the stake he had figured on carrying him and his family through their declining years. The grass that had been so deep and lush when he picked his "country" had been eaten out from overstocking and lack of rest. The water that had never failed before was drying up from constant usage, as resultant tramping had muddied-in the sources and springs. He began to get a touch of the ever-mounting overhead that was to come into his business when he built tanks, drilled wells, and erected windmills and storage.

His cattle were not developing as they had in the old days—more dogies now. He had not paid much attention to an occasional dogie in the old days or the fact that its mother, usually a two-year-old heifer, if she survived its birth, did not develop until she was four or five years old. They had plenty of time then to outgrow whatever might ail them. In fact, he didn't look to his cattle for much in these days until they were four or five years old. He wondered sometimes what heritage, if any, he would leave to his sons; the sons he had hoped to train in his own footsteps.

Now the primary cause of the cowman's discomfiture was the influx of farmers from East and Central Texas. The home seeker, who came from the Eastern states to settle the Plains, was to follow years later, but their vanguard had started to Texas now. They were coming into the older settled sections, paying good prices for lands and forever ending the possibility of cheap farm lands and the expansion of the larger and older Texas families in those sections. There was little left for the home seeker but to load his possessions and family into prairie schooner, tie the milk cows on behind and start west to file on, buy, or claim from the state, school, or railroad lands, the acres he so wanted and needed.

The nester invasion of West Texas came in a succession of receding waves during the first hard years when there was scant rainfall, and no market for the things they grew when it did rain. In the hard years they turned their milk cows and extra work stock in on the cowman, loaded their wives and children in the wagons and pulled out, "back home" for "a visit with the wife's kinfolks." They came back, though, each time accompanied by neighbors and relatives, whom, in their patriotism for the new country, they had "sold" by telling them of its possibilities and the markets that eventually awaited them—a land free of boll weevils and the long-established credit "carrying" systems of the old country.

The visits became fewer and fewer. Those who stayed when the going was hard found they could live in the country under any conditions if they so willed, though it might require the "twisting" of a few cottontail rabbits when meat was low in the larder and there were no shotgun shells left on the mantel. The cowman helped out, too, for he was beginning to have a sneaking liking for the nester, as he came to realize that he was just another fellow trying to get along and adjust himself to a new country and conditions. He gave the nesters work: freighting, tanking, fencing, and odd jobs to help tide them over.

Too, the cowman in a hazy sort of way began to realize that somebody was going to have to farm if he stayed in the cow business. He was still of the opinion that he was not going to farm personally, and so perhaps he had better, as he termed it, "throw in" with the nester and encourage him a little. He even bought a little surplus bundle feed from the nester for milk cows and saddle horses.

By this time cotton was getting pretty well started in the cow country and there were a few scattering gins which had no outlet for their cottonseed. In Central and North Texas and up in the "territory," or "Nation," as Oklahoma was known then, the ginner was finding outlets for his cottonseed in the cowman who bought it cheaply to use as a fattener on his sage grass.

So to the cowman the ginner turned in West Texas, as a market for his by-product. The cowman was receptive, if not cheerful about the seed. He was tallying fewer and fewer cattle each year, finding more carcasses in canyon, coulee, and bog each spring, and less grass and water. Then, too, the banks and loan companies were sending out some pretty smart fellows to check his cattle and range. They had ideas as to how the cowman could help himself and were rather pointed in telling him what would have to be done if friendly relations were to continue.

He added half a dozen four-up teams and as many teamsters to his ever-growing overhead, for the gins were far from the ranch and the old-time wagon freighter was not interested in hauling cottonseed at the same price he did fence posts, windmills, and lumber. He bought sparingly, groaned each time he paid the teamsters, ginners, and horse feed bills. He was very unhappy on the whole, for he was actually eating his own beef, and only a dream were the days when his overhead consisted of a payroll of a dozen $25-per-month cow hands with a semiannual purchase of bacon, beans, coffee, flour, and baking powder with which to feed them.

The seed was messy to handle, requiring ricking if it was not to heat and spoil. He didn't begin feeding until late in the spring and then only to such old cows as he felt just wouldn't winter unless fed. He got little or no value from his hit-or-miss feedings, insofar as his finances were concerned, but he did learn the art of "tailing up," a new accomplishment for him and his cow hands.

For the benefit of the younger generation to whom "drifts," "die ups," and "tailing up" are but stories told by their elders, let us review the "tailing up" process, for it took heavy toll of the backs of the West Texas cowmen and cowboys and merits a place in this chronicle.

In the early spring, undernourished range cows that had been placed in the "home" pasture for feeding were called on to exert their last ounce of strength if they were to survive and conserve their unborn calves. Like humans under stress, they reached a point where nothing seemed to matter. No matter how much feed had been poured into the range cow there came a time o' cold mornings when the hoar-frost hung on her whiskers, outlined her skinny backbone and lay in patches in the hollows of her north flank, when she did not rally to the clucking of the spindles of the feed wagon wheels as they crackled and crunched on the frozen ground, nor did she arise to the lusty "who-o-oo," "who-o-oo," of its driver. Nor could the cow hand who rode with the wagon to throw stragglers into the feed line faze her by kicking her in the side, or "booger" her into getting up by stomping the frozen ground as he slapped his cold hands against his chaps.

She lay in a more or less natural position, with a stare of starvation in her eyes, which seemed to be fixed on the hides of her sisters already adorning the fences. Apparently she was holding debate with herself as to whether she should arise, and try to make "one more mile," or lie there and eventually let her hide go on the fence with her sisters. That is exactly what happened if she was not made to get up, move out a little, and get some feed inside her. Her desire to "give up the ghost" could be overcome only by the cowboy's stooping to get her tail over his shoulder and lifting. With this encouragement ordinarily she would rise to her rear feet, which is the way a cow gets up, and eventually scramble to all four feet. Sometimes, still contemplating greener pastures on high, she would refuse to cooperate and it would be necessary for feed wagon driver and cowboy to work, one at the head and the other at the tail until she was on her feet. A few old sisters, strong in the faith and a desire to attend a few more roundups, would cooperate with the lone cowboy by holding position with their rear feet when "tailed up" until he could get around to their head and set up that end.

Now, as has been said, her moral strength and will power were low.

On her feet she still debated as to the advisability of lying back down and, if frightened, would fall in her first attempts to run, after which she had to be "tailed up" again. It was not unusual for one fellow to "tail up" fifty to seventy-five head in one morning. When they were up he moved cautiously among them, for he had only one back and it was not new.

They tell of an old cowman down in the Brady country a good many years ago, who got all of his "downers" up one frosty morning and, while they were steadying down, rode over the hill to skin one he felt pretty sure had died during the night. Just after he rode over the hill he heard gun shots back in the direction of the cattle he had just left. Loping back he saw three friends from town hunting blue quail around his stack lots.

"For God's sake, don't shoot around here, fellows," he cried, riding up to them.

"Why, Lige, you told us last fall we were welcome to hunt out here whenever we wanted to. Besides, we're not going to shoot any of your cattle."

"I know you're not, fellows," replied the cowman. "That's not the idea, but when you shot a while ago fifty-five head of my old 'Nellies' tried to run and fell down and I am too danged weak in the back to tail 'em up many more times today."

The irony of a "downer" was that she stayed a "downer" and had to be "tailed up" practically every morning. When warm weather and heel flies came she generally repaid her owner for his kind attention during the winter by "high tailing" to the nearest bog when a real or imaginary heel fly attacked her. Here she usually did what she had contemplated doing earlier in the spring—"layed 'em down."

In the 1894 "convention of the Texas and Southwestern Cattle Raisers Association," a duplicate of the one held in Graham ten years earlier and not unlike the one held in El Paso last March, the cowmen discussed breeds, feeding, sales, and future prospects, and cleared the year's accumulation of dust from their throats. There was a serious vein in their talk in the convention hall, hotel lobby, and bar.

Word had come down from the packing centers—Kansas City, Chicago, and St. Louis—that the buyers were not looking with favor on the Spanish-type Texas steer being shipped in now, as they had on the same steers driven in a few years before, steers which had improved themselves and filled out their gaunt frames in grazing over the sage grass country on their way in. The packers were cutting the prices on them but paying a little premium on the better kind of cattle from Texas.

The leaders—fellows like Burk Burnett, the Waggoners, Halsells, Winfield Scott, Bill Moore of Ardmore, and others—had sensed this in 1890 and had begun experiments in feeding cattle cottonseed meal, "yeller meal," they called it. They found that a 1,000-pound steer could be developed into a 1,345-pound one in from 90 to 120 days, provided he was the right sort of steer. Bill Moore, pioneer oil-mill man and cowman from the "Nation," expressed the opinion that not enough feed could be crowded into a cold-blooded Spanish-type steer to fatten him and justify the feed bill.

They argued pro and con as to the merits of feeding steers cottonseed meal on the grass and in troughs. The farsighted among the leaders told of trips they had made to the Middlewest to visit Shorthorn, Angus, and Hereford breeders in search of better bulls with which to build up their herds. They told, also, of visits with the manufacturers of the yellow meal and how they were investing capital in oil mills to guarantee a feed supply. It was generally agreed that science was finding so many values each year in the fuzzy little cottonseed that it was only a question of time until it could no longer be bought for four, five or six dollars per ton. They proposed to protect themselves, to get in on the ground floor, and advised their fellow cowmen to follow suit, or at least prepare to breed and feed better cattle. Winfield Scott acquired interest in a mill and feed lots at Brownwood, Marion Sansome at Alvarado, and the veteran, Burk Burnett, had a working agreement with his friend Moore in Ardmore, to feed out his steers. The Witherspoons, heavy dealers in big steers in the Cherokee strip of Oklahoma, pushed far up the old Chisholm Trail, locating their own mill at Belcherville, on the Missouri, Kansas, and Texas Railroad, not far from the old trail crossing at Red River station. The Swensons, just then becoming interested in feeding, built their own mill at Stamford. Tom Trammell, operating heavily in Scurry and Nolan counties, built a mill for himself and the Newmans at Sweetwater. Mills also went in at Gainesville, Bowie, Denton, and Pilot Point. These, for the most part, were organized and partially owned by cattlemen and fed thousands of Texas steers.

The Waggoners built their own mill in their home town of Decatur and when their first draft of big steers were fat, gave a barbecue to their cowmen friends, using a meal-fed steer, which all present declared to be the best meat they had ever eaten.

While feeding for fattening had gotten under way, there was still a gap left, for the West Texas cowman needed a handy, highly nutritious food that could be hauled cheaply over long distances, stored away and fed with good results on the naturally short grasses of West Texas— entered the manufacturer who had been doing experimental work with the little seed of many virtues. He had found that the cooked slabs of cottonseed meats, from which the yellow meal was made, could be left intact, cracked into edible lumps, and sacked. It was as nutritious as the meal and was highly portable. From that time on the manufacturer was definitely in the West Texas picture and destined to follow the fortunes of nester and cowman as they solved their problems.

The cowman was not ready, however, to relinquish his interest in the manufacturing until he felt the supply was sufficient and would be available year after year. Then the manufacturer could have it and he would go back to being a full-time cowman.

To the Waggoners, Dan and his son, W. T. probably should go the credit of establishing the present modern system for guaranteeing a feed supply to the cowman and a permanent market for cottonseed to the farmer. When they came back into Texas with their cattle from the Kiowa-Comanche country they acquired the present D D D ranch in Wilbarger and Baylor counties, or added much to their holdings there. As a safeguard they acquired a cotton oil mill at Vernon. Competition for cottonseed was becoming keen throughout the South, due to the development of processes for using it and an ever-increasing demand for its products in other states and countries. The Waggoners found their supply of seed limited and threatened, and to protect themselves bought a half dozen gins in the area. Later they extended their gin development into Oklahoma. Eventually they disposed of their gin and oil-mill holdings when the industry was on a firm basis in West Texas.

Better and better cattle were developed until West Texas was providing both breeder and feeder grand champions for the national shows over the country, not "once in a blue moon," but year in and year out. Feeder calves now go to the Corn Belt in trainloads weighing nearly half as much as their three- and four-year-old Longhorn ancestors did when they were put on the first meal and hulls. They come from thousands of range mothers, carrying in their veins a high percentage of the best Hereford blood in the world. These mothers are fed on the range from the first northers in the fall until the green grass in the spring. The babies themselves, thrifty and soggy when dropped, begin eating cottonseed cake from "creeps" early in the summer they are born. They thrive throughout the year and go to the Corn Belt in the fall, thrifty, heavy, and knowing how to eat.

White farm houses dot the old cow country, many of them on the
"big flats" owned by the cowmen. Their sons and the sons' wives,
daughters of nesters, living in them are doing nicely, thank you. The
heritage is safe.

The old cow hands didn't ride toward the setting sun. A fellow passing told them a good many years ago that Colonel Littlefield was
planting the whole Pecos Valley, around Roswell, in alfalfa and that
"fodder forking" was the order of the day on the L F D's. "No use to go
to Arizona," he said, "for the thing has spread plumb to Salt River
Valley out there." As for him, he was going to get a quarter section of
land while he could, and a good nester gal for a wife, whose pa could
teach him to farm.

Railroads and highways criss-crossed the cow country. With them
went gin and oil mills to afford a day-by-day market for the product of
feed and cotton patch. The mills kept just back on the fringe and
pushed in as needed. They thought, years ago, that they had gone as
far west as necessary, but in recent years irrigation has sent them to
the Pecos and in some places west of it, into the old land of John
Chisholm and Jingle Bob. And they are now close neighbors to Roy
Bean's old shack, lower down the river.

As the trend changed from grown cattle to baby beef, the labora-
tories have worked out softer feed; and as the sheepman swung into
line on feeding, they developed a suitable sheep feed. Fortunately for
West Texas cotton growers and the oil-mill industry, there is a wide
market for cottonseed. Thousands of tons go to the Northwest for the
cowman, who before the advent of cottonseed cake, depended solely
on hay cut from the lower places on his range. Other thousands of tons
are exported or go to the fertilizer mills on the Eastern seaboard. Those
on the edge of the cow country have a highly developed feed service
that permits the cattleman to buy when needed, with delivery when
requested.

In another manner the oil mill industry is closely linked with cowman
and farmer. There is always a surplus of cottonseed hulls. In the years
when ranges are good the cowman naturally depends on grasses for
his feed. In these years the oil mills must, if they are to keep faith
with the farmer, afford the usual market for his cottonseed. This situation creates a surplus of hulls, which the oil mills can market only by
feeding cattle on their own account. In these years they become heavy
purchasers of cattle. It is not unusual for West Texas mills to have

fifteen to twenty-five thousand head on feed continuously during a feeding season.

Fortunately the industry selected early, as its executives, young men thoroughly acquainted with the area and capable of following its rapid development. They have kept a weather eye on the cowman and farmer, keen to respond to their need while widening their trade horizons in other states and countries. They have had important parts in the development of the dairy industry, the furthering of 4-H club work, and any civic matter for the betterment of West Texas.

It is not to be inferred that only cottonseed products are grown or fed in West Texas. A highly developed area on the South Plains is producing grain sorghum in quantities that permit the feeding for market of thousands of cattle and sheep, almost in the fields where it is grown. Cottonseed meal is used to make a balanced ration.

The cowman, nester, and manufacturer are just a little proud of the results of the work begun so many years ago. If you don't think so, find an old weather-beaten, shaggy-browed cowman, a nester grandfather, wise in the ways of the weather and when to plant, and a now-greying manager of one of the mills—get them together and talk it over with them. You'll see.

For the Good They Have Done

Among the "cow countries" of the nation, customs vary but little insofar as horses, men, cattle, and children are concerned. What obtains generally in one is usually applicable to all of them, with due regard to weather and seasons.

I have often felt prompted to pay tribute to a group of horses that were legion in their day and were to be found in every country where there were cowmen and cow horses. Each time I have hesitated for the reason that I felt it might sound a little Uncle Remus-like. On the other hand, these horses had a definite part in the business and the development of today's cattlemen.

I have in mind the hundreds of good old cow ponies scattered throughout the nation which were always retained from the sale when a draft of "condemned" horses were sold "down the river" to the cotton farmers and plantations, or when an outfit was sold *in toto*. Invariably, the owner alibied the retention by saying that he was "keeping him for the good he has done." Sometimes it might be a top cutting horse which had helped the owner as he bought, cut, and built up his herds.

Again, it might be an extra good river horse who had carried his owner without faltering across swollen streams spring after spring, struggling across quicksand bars or dodging swirling trees or logs as they rolled down the sand-laden streams when the river was on a "rise." Might be it was this same horse that he picked to ride for the doctor over across the river the spring night when his first-born was choking and sputtering in the throes of membraneous croup. It was a rough night and he had to swim the river twice and pilot the doctor back.

All of these happenings went to build up reasons for keeping a horse "for the good he has done," and created a sentiment toward the horse that is not generally credited to the hard-bitten cowmen of a half century ago.

There was always around the ranch a pretty good, well-built, sensible horse that was quiet and gentle in its manner. He was thoroughly reliable and could be depended upon to let you walk up and catch him in the pasture on the morning after the night horse had escaped from corral or trap, leaving the outfit afoot; or when the boss drove in unexpectedly to find no one at home and no horses in the pen. In a pinch, if one of the buggy team had a touch of colic or a thorn in his foot, old reliable could be hooked up and, in his awkward way, would hold up his end of breast yoke or tongue and keep the tugs tight until you could do better. You could carry a roll of wire, a post, feed, a dogie calf, or a sack of wild plums on him without his objecting. Perhaps he was not a top cow horse, but he was always just as essential.

If, after the young cowman married, the wife wanted to look the nearby pastures over with her husband, he saddled this horse for her, with no fear of his running away or cutting up; and when he was away from the ranch for a full day he left him in the trap as sort of a safeguard, for he knew she could catch and saddle him in an emergency.

Probably there was, and is, no happier moment in the life of the young cowman-father than when his wife handed their first-born son up to him in the saddle to ride on this same gentle horse from front gate to saddle house or corral. To him it marked the beginning of the training for a future cowman. He had plans for him—plans that call for a thorough training in cow work and a good education—better than he had been able to get. When the boy had gotten the education he hoped that he would come back to the ranch to take up the burden when his father got too old to carry on, or that he would get him a little outfit of his own. The father could not figure that there was any better profession for him than to be an up-and-coming young cowman.

He could hardly wait until the kid was old enough to understand what he was telling him. By the time the little fellow was a couple of years old he had had a good many rides sitting between the saddle horn and his father with the loose ends of the reins in his hands, or behind the saddle with his fingers twisted into the saddle strings. When the boy was four or five years old and began to play out of doors, his father was watching to see if he got a bunch of corncobs on which he ran brands with an iron fashioned from hay wire. If he did, the father felt that the education was coming along nicely.

When he was six to eight years old the father bought him a three-quarter rigged saddle, red blanket, and new bridle. If the mother did not object, he may also have gotten a pair of store boots (it was too early to get shop-made ones that he would outgrow). The saddle went on the same old horse. Mother and father knew that if junior should fall off, the horse would stop in his tracks and avoid stepping on the child if he could help it.

The elementary training continued when the father took the boy on long rides in the pasture. As they rode along he told his son of the ways of horses, cattle, and men. He told him how the men before him trailed their cattle into other "countries," and of their successes or failures and how each time when disaster threatened their herds or industry, they "bowed their necks" and kept going. He taught him how to spot from afar an animal that had screwworms, and how circling buzzards would lead him to a dead cow that might have left an orphan calf. The boy learned from him the danger of getting too near old bulls that were fighting each other, because one could never tell at what moment the larger bull, apparently the victor, might give up the fight to turn and run regardless of who or what might be in his path. During the working season the boy followed the roundups near home, still riding the steady old horse, and picked up knowledge around the branding pen. The father was proud when the boy was large enough to brand his first calf and watched to see if he flinched when the hot iron sent a cloud of acrid smoke into his face.

In all of his riding, training, and play, the boy rode that same reliable old horse. Time went on, and with the years there grew up a bond of affection between the family and the horse, even though there might be a hundred or more as good or better horses on the place. This bond of affection cannot be described, but it will be appreciated by many a middle-aged cowman who will tell his grandchildren how he learned to ride.

Junior and his brothers had outgrown the ranch schoolhouse or governess, and the folks decided to "build" in town. "Building" meant on a block of town lots, with sheds, barns, and windmill enough for ranch headquarters, despite the fact that there was only a Jersey milk cow and a ranch team to be cared for.

The boys were kind of lonesome in town and missed the activities of the ranch and the companionship of their horse. Besides, there was danger that the younger ones might grow up without knowing how to love and appreciate a good horse.

So father and mother decided to bring "Old Faithful" in and allow him to carry on his educational work for the boys. He would help them to know, love and care for a horse. He would also keep them hardened up, so that they would not be so soft when they went to the ranch in the summer. He was beginning to show his age a little, and his teeth had worn off until the oats and corn he could get in town would be good for him. If the horse got out occasionally, he grazed around on vacant lots, and always showed up at feeding time.

The change from country to town did not bother the horse much. For a few days he would get nervous every time the passenger train would rush past or when they were switching in the yards west of the house. He soon realized, however, that he was among friends, and would nicker long and loud, morning and night, when he saw the boys come out the back door.

His duties were light, and consisted in the main of trips to the post office and grocery store, where he bore the boys, most of the time bare-back, and sometimes with only a rope around his nose in lieu of a bridle. Due to the absence of telephones, there was also a demand for young fellows with ponies to carry notes from their beaux to the young ladies of the town, for which the boys received fees varying from fifteen to twenty-five cents, depending upon how long they had to wait for an answer. Herding the town's milk cows on the "town section," was also a source of additional revenue.

When a herd came in for shipping from some of the ranches, junior would ride out on the open section north of the stock pens, Saturdays and evenings after school, and "make a hand" while they were cutting and penning. Carloads of purebred bulls were coming in pretty regularly. As often as he could, he helped the three or four men who had come in from the ranches to turn these off the "town section" and get them started on their long trek home. With others of his kind similarly mounted, he would prowl the creek country, talk cattle and ranch, and chase a few nester calves and Jerseys, by way of practice. The father, on his trips to town, calculated the boys' education by the care they took of the horse and the things they had to tell of herds they had helped pen and bulls they had helped turn out. There were some pretty serious talks occasionally if it did not look as if the horse was being fed and watered as regularly as he should.

I have said that customs vary but little in the cow country, and on that basis I shall use my home town to describe this type of horse, feeling that what I say will be applicable to all similar towns. Our old horse was Old Nig, a coal black pony we had acquired in Indian Territory. He was about fifteen hands high, and was possessed of more than the average amount of good horse sense and a distance-eating fox trot and running walk. He was very easily "kept" and was always fat. In his prime and before the days of ranch buggies and matched teams, he served my father on his long buying trips in search of yearlings. In a pinch, you could do a fair job of cutting on him; but in common with most horses having a saddle gait, he could not break from it into a run without "spraddling" out or getting pretty rough before he hit a run. He was possessed of all the attributes and qualifications I have listed heretofore. He and my daddy went through some pretty tight spots. There was the time the steer herd ran, down in the Bill Washington country, and Old Nig brought my father and himself up against a wire fence at full speed. Old Nig sensed it and stopped before any damage was done to either of them, other than being badly hammered up by the steers, which were crowding them pretty closely. Horse and man seemed to understand each other and worked in perfect harmony. He was turned over to us kids about the time I was nine years old. I recall riding him on many twenty-five–mile trips from the Honey Creek Ranch in the Arbuckle Mountains to our home in Ardmore.

In Texas, we retired him as sort of a handy horse about the ranch, and eventually he came to us in town after we had moved in. As times changed, a two-seated surrey was added to our equipment and Old Nig, because of his good sense, was promoted to the honor of family buggy horse, a duty which he performed faithfully until the advent of the first automobile. The smell and noise of them aroused a hysteria that he could never overcome. One time he and the buggy were hitched in front of the house when one passed, causing him to break away and overturn the surrey. We never held these derelictions against him, feeling that it was not his fault. Eventually, to relieve him of his

fears, we gave him to an old ranch boss of ours who had a quarter
section north of town in the sand, and, for that reason, well out of
the area used for automobiles. The former ranch boss had known and
loved Old Nig in his younger days and was glad to get and take good
care of him, as a means of getting his youngsters to school. Old Nig
died at the ripe old-horse age of twenty-three years. About half of his
life had been spent in ranch service and the other in the education and
care of children. He had earned the right to be "kept for the good he
had done."

Mart Byrd was an old-time cowman who ranched in the early
days as a free-range man in the Indian Territory and Panhandle of
Texas, later going to the Portales country in New Mexico. He had
three sons, Will, Brownie, and Dick, whom he wanted educated, and
whom he wanted to see become creditable cowmen. So from the New
Mexico ranch he sent in two middle-aged dun horses—Blue Dog and
Dunny—to equalize the educational problems, and they did an excellent job of it and were a worthy addition to our town *remuda* of horses
which were being "kept for the good they had done." Two of the Byrd
boys, Will and Dick, got the edge on the balance of the town boys
one spring, when Blue Dog and Dunny carried them and their camp
equipment safely from Quanah to the ranch below Portales, a distance
of some 250 miles. They left Quanah, went to the Matador Ranch, and
from there struck out across the then unsettled plains for the New
Mexico line, passing but one or two other ranch houses until they arrived at the home ranch. Mrs. Byrd came in for some severe criticism
for allowing the boys to make the long, lonesome trip. Being a pioneer
ranch woman, she told the mothers who questioned the wisdom of it
at a club meeting one day that "if the boys haven't got sense enough
to get there, Blue Dog and Dunny will get them there." The boys and
horses were of about equal age—ten and twelve years. Mart Byrd, in
his later years, still seeking open range moved into Old Mexico, where
during the revolution he and his family were badly abused by bandits,
and his son Will killed, in defense of their cattle.

Old Choc was the town horse of the Ledbetter family, pioneers of
Oklahoma ranching days. He was a small, chunky Indian pony they
had acquired in the Cheyenne country. He was almost too small for
a cow pony, but served his time on the ranches as a night or "rustlin'"
horse in the Indian country; and in his later years he came to town
from the Pease River ranch for the use of the Ledbetter boys, John
and Thurmond. Both boys are dead now, and Old Choc died many

years ago, fat and happy, on a section they owned just west of town.

Cy Kendall's boys owned a little brown horse called "Brown Jug." He was chunky, smart, and a general pet among the boys. Cy was caught in the breakup of the old-time cow business, and as the Kendall boys were beginning to follow other lines of endeavor, it was decided to raffle Brown Jug off. The raffle was arranged and quite a few tickets sold, but at the last moment Cy weakened and purchased enough of the tickets to guarantee his winning the horse for himself. Eventually the horse passed into the hands of a kindly feed-store man, who kept him until he died.

Jim McAdams had a good, big ranch in Foard County. He was one of the old order of cowmen, and a good one. His sons, so long as the ranch existed, were all good cowmen. His eldest son, Leslie, was a particularly good one, and is now a prominent rancher, oil man, and stock farmer on a portion of their old ranch in Foard County. One son, Melvin, is an inspector for the Texas and Southwestern Cattle Raisers Association at Lubbock. Another son, Con, is a prominent ranchman at Quanah. Their education, as I recall, was taken care of in town by a small sorrel lightweight pony branded with a wheel, and another larger sorrel called Tom Thumb. The McAdams boys were among the leaders of our town crew.

Crit Clark, now a prominent cattleman in the San Angelo area, had a fat, gentle, old flea-bitten grey horse that contributed much to his early horse education. Crit's mother, Mrs. Clark, also had a good, big ex-cow horse which pulled the family's Haynes surrey. Occasionally, boys outside the industry became owners of a horse "being kept for the good he had done," by virtue of some cowman without children making a gift of such a horse. There were probably fifty head in our town kept on a similar basis, the names of most having escaped my memory. Among the boys, there was no lending or abuse of the horses. Each considered his horse a special charge and responsibility. About the best an outside boy could do was to "mooch" a ride double, once in a while. The boys knew the limitations of their horses' age and used them accordingly, which was one of the things that their elders wanted them to know.

I have lived in several cow-towns in my time, in widely scattered sections, and have found that about the same conditions existed for this type of horse in one as in the other.

In Ardmore, the James boys, sons of Arthur James, a prominent cowman of his day, had a small bay pony which at some time had had the cartilage of his nose pierced by a bullet, and one could see daylight through it. I do not know that this had anything to do with his retirement to town. You did not inquire too closely as to the origin of bullet holes in the Territory in those days.

The McClish boys, sons of Richard McClish, prominent in Territorial and Chickasaw tribal affairs, had their retired pony, and their tank in their small pasture east of town was a gathering place for most of us mounted men in the nine-year age bracket.

I recall that once my father sent a new hand from the mountain ranch into Ardmore on Old Nig. As he rode the Main Street, he attracted the attention of a hardware man and the grocery merchant who supplied the ranch. They got their heads together and decided that someone should question the fellow's right to the horse. They argued, "That is old man Hendrix's 'Old Nig.' I know, because of the heart brand on his left hip, and I know that he has not sold him to anybody, and is not going to, because he thinks too much of him. Spec, we had better talk to Marshal Hammer about it and see what he is doing with him." Marshal Hammer questioned the fellow and found beyond a reasonable doubt that he had been sent to town on an errand on the horse and was not getting away with him. I mention this to verify the fact that those days the general public knew the name and color of horses "being kept for the good they had done," and protected both them and the owners' rights, as far as possible.

Uncle Joe Harris, who ranched in the Ringgold country half a century ago, had two such horses—Old Comanche, a solid white snip-nosed Indian pony, the favorite mount of his youngest daughter, and a little sorrel called Big Enough, the top horse of a favorite son who died at an early age. Both horses died in a Ringgold wagon yard in the midst of plenty.

Charles Tompkins, of El Reno, Oklahoma, who knows the long trail to Wyoming and Montana through having followed X I T herds there in the late 80's, tells of working for a number of years on the T Diamond Ranch of Colonel Wash Bryant, in Stonewall County, whose son "W. J." still lives in Abilene, Texas, at a ripe old age, and is probably the only survivor of the first graduating class of Texas A & M in 1879. "W. J." gave up the ranch years ago to study and engage in the practice of law. When he came to this decision, rather than sell or leave his entire mount of horses to the mercy of strangers, he gave them to Tompkins, with whom, he was confident, they would be well used and well cared for.

When the Witherspoons broke up their 9 outfit in the Wichitas, the ultimate disposal of saddle horses and ranch equipment fell upon Ed Bomar, who had run the outfit for many years. Most of the best horses went to Luther Clark's outfit, and others to various people, until there was left only one old cutting horse—Old Mac—who had long been a favorite with Bomar. He had a little age on him and it was not hard to keep from selling him with the balance. Bomar kept him in the background until the last horse had been sold, and then turned him over to Dick Hill, a former employee of the ranch, who lived west of Crowell, who took him to teach the children to ride and to get them to school and back. One of the children, Clifton Hill, is a prominent and successful stock farmer at Paducah, Texas. At one time Dick Hill had no less than half a dozen such old horses which had been entrusted to his care because of the love he had for good old horses.

Many a top cutting horse in his prime has been given to the consistent purchaser of an outfit's steers because the owner would not sell him at any price, preferring to give him to a friend, thereby incurring an obligation on the part of the recipient to keep him as long as he lived "for the good he had done." A fair example of this is old JY, a big, brown cutting horse which Price Maddox, of Colorado City, presented to R. M. Simmons, of the Sweetwater Cotton Oil Company, who fed and kept him in the pink of condition until the day he died.

So, in these days of quarter horse and palomino registration, I can't help but believe that if a register (mostly from revived memories) were to be started on the horses who were "kept for the good they had done," its number would be legion and would represent some of the best cow horse blood of the entire nation; too, it would bring out a sentiment on the part of old-time cowmen heretofore unpublished.

Come and Get It

Probably no two items of subsistence have contributed so much comfort and satisfaction, first and last, to the range people of the Southwest as black coffee and red chili. The former, until the advent of the radio and its highly specialized commercials, was ordinarily referred to as "Javy" because of the fact that it was popularly supposed that all coffee including Arbuckle's and XXXX came from that far away country, Java. Black coffee has always, so far as cattle history is recorded, been a staple item around chuck wagons and cow camps, where it was, and is, consumed in prodigious quantities early and late by those who worked around them from "see to see" and sometimes when they couldn't "see," except by the lightning flashes as they rode night guard over cattle on trail or en route to the railroad.

Around an outfit of eight or ten men, anything less than a three- to five-gallon coffeepot was not considered standard and if the coffee brewed therein was not made by the time-honored recipe of one handful of ground coffee to each cup of water there were likely to be grumbling and rumblings about the cook's ability. If he failed to leave a full pot bedded down in the coals before he went to his "hot roll" each night, you could figure that before too long the pressure would get so heavy that the boss would have to give him his time.

This last omission was considered particularly serious by trail outfits holding their herds under guard, for the hard-riding cowboy took his coffee both in forward and reverse. If he was called to go on guard at, say, midnight, he wanted a cup of hot coffee to wake him up. When he came in a couple of hours later he wanted another cup of it to warm him up so he could drop off for a little sleep before the cook called him and the balance of the hands out three hours later to catch horses; the first thing he wanted then was another cup to wake him up again. Speaking of cups of coffee in this connection, it might be well to bear in mind that a "cup" is not to be classed as the conventional table tea-cup or demitasse. More often the cups were corn or tomato cans with the tops melted out, if the cook had lost or been forced to cast off too many of the pint-size tin cups because of too much usage, lost handles, and so forth. In either case the receptacle was as hot as "the hinges of hell" once it had been filled with boiling coffee. There was no tempering of its fiery heat with cream, canned or otherwise; it just wasn't done. The cowboy so long as he worked with wagon or in batch-ing camp had an aversion to milk and cream, especially in his coffee. Perhaps my last visit with Doc Ellis, long a Spur and S M S wagon boss, will exemplify their aversion somewhat. I met him on the streets of Spur a few months before he died. We "passed the time of day" and he inquired as to what I was doing now. I replied that I was doing some publicity work for a statewide dairy organization. "Better be careful, John," he warned me, "you'll be drinking the damn stuff before you know it and your old friends will quit having anything to do with you."

Truth of the matter is that most of the camp and headquarters boys were afraid that if milk was in general use around the place or if they showed too much interest in milk and butter, it might lead to a milking job and that would mean "moving on" for most of them; for few, if any, cowboys, would milk for themselves, much less for pay, at least so long as they could find anything else on earth to do—even digging postholes or heading maize. They were inconsistent, however; I have seen the same fellows drink glass after glass of either buttermilk or sweet milk in some nester shack when it was being ladled out by a yellow-haired nester daughter. That made a difference.

Practically all of the real old-time hands took their coffee without sugar. There was reason for that, too. It was not until after the turn of the century that all of the outfits provided sugar for camp or wagon. Therefore, the old-timers had perforce formed a liking for it without sugar. The latter-day boys who had become used to sugar at home didn't take to coffee straight so readily and grumbled around a good deal about it. I recall being with a little outfit about 1903 that was delivering its cattle to the loan company at Childress for shipment and to clear up debts. The folks in our country, knowing the owner's financial condition, each sent a hand and a mount of horses to help him. He had a reputation for not feeding any too good and providing no sugar at all, even though it was selling at twenty pounds for a dollar at the time. A boy, whom I knew well, came up to the wagon to unpack his bedroll. When he opened it to my surprise there rolled out two old brown Levi Garrett snuff bottles.

"Didn't know you dipped snuff," I commented.

"Hell, it ain't snuff," he replied. "It's sugar. I like my coffee, but I just can't take it without sugar."

The coffee habit originated in South Texas, from the Louisiana influence, no doubt. Over in that country you never know whether to eat or drink your coffee, it is so thick and ropy. As the trail outfits moved north and northwest, they spread the coffee-drinking habit until it met up with fellows in Montana who actually drank tea around their outfits, no doubt a Canadian influence. The Southwesterners made the Northwesterners like black coffee, but the latter never were able to make tea drinkers of the Texans.

The further away you get from South Texas the more likely you are to note moderation in coffee drinking. West of Fort Worth you will find cowmen and businessmen who can "drink the stuff or leave it alone;" in South Texas you won't find any who can "leave the stuff alone;" boss, cowboy, *vaquero,* businessmen, or banker. When you drive up to your host's wagon or camp, he grabs you and makes for the coffeepot. As soon as a drive of cattle are penned and ready for branding, the hands all break for the wagon and coffee. As soon as the irons are hot and by the time the dust is fogging good and the sweat is beginning to get in their eyes, the cook comes waddling down to the pen with a huge bucket of coffee on one arm and another of tin cups on the other. A man will brand a calf, put his iron back in the coals and gulp a cup of coffee quicker than a tomcat can perform his favorite ablution. He will do this, too, almost every third calf until they have finished the job at hand after which he will go to the wagon or camp house and really drink some coffee.

On the outfits that employ Mexican cowboys you have little or no option as to sugar in your coffee. All Mexicans love it in common with any form of sweets. To put it out in conventional sugar bowls would bankrupt the average outfit or mean that the first man or two who got the bowl would be the only ones to get sugar in their coffee as they would pour it all into their cups and add enough coffee to make it a sort of uncooked candy mess. So to avoid labor trouble the cooks boil the sugar into the coffee in moderate quantities. Some South Texas cooks add cinnamon bark which makes a tasty cup when you have gotten used to it.

Stop at the bank in most any South Texas cow-town and ask for the president or cashier. If he is not in sight or out of town, someone will tell you he has gone for coffee and will be back in a minute. If he is there, it won't be two minutes until he will take you out to get it. In Victoria, which has almost as many millionaire cowmen-oilmen as it had government workers during the war, you can always find a majority sitting at the long counter in one favorite cafe, discussing cattle, oil, and the state of the nation with a half consumed cup of coffee before each. Pull in at the curb anywhere within three blocks of the cafe and inquire if anyone has seen Bill Jones lately and some kindly by-stander, without resorting to words, will incline his head toward the cafe, and unless Bill has slipped out the back way, nine times out of ten the kindly bystander knew what he was talking about.

Coffee drinking from a business and "augurin'" standpoint really came into its own in the Southwestern cow-towns about the time prohibition became prevalent via the local option route. Heretofore it had been all right to sit out along the sidewalk in front of your favorite saloon with your cronies to talk and trade, volunteering about every so often to "buy." Times were changing, however, and it didn't do a fellow too much good to be seen too often coming out of a saloon sucking a sliver of lemon peel or chewing a coffee bean or clove. The children were growing up, too, and it wasn't good for them to see their Pa coming out of the "Chain Harness Saloon" every time Ma sent them to the grocery store or meat market. Then prohibition became almost universal and the coffee shop came into its own as a meeting place and trading ground. It is estimated that more thousands of head of cattle and sheep and acres of land have changed hands over cups of black coffee in Southwestern coffee shops than in any other organized places of business in that vast area.

The war brought trouble to the coffee drinkers. The cafes and coffee shops, overcrowded with customers and short of help, began to look askance at the boys who would file in to spend fifteen or twenty minutes over a nickel cup of coffee, while the $1.50 customers awaited their places at counter or table. They tried raising the price to a dime but it didn't help any. Some few told the boys plainly that they could take their coffee business elsewhere but these were few and far between. The scars won't heal soon either. With VE and VJ days, things automatically righted themselves and the boys lined up at the counters once more to stir, saucer, and blow as of old.

Chili, as it is known to us today in the better homes and in the tiled and highly decorated Mexicans inns and Mexican-style eating places at twenty-five to thirty-five cents per bowl, is popularly supposed to have had its origin in Mexico or in far away Spain. That this is not true will be almost as much of a shock to the present generation as learning that chop suey, chow mein, and other Chinese dishes sold in equally decorative places and cafes is as foreign to the land of Generalissimo and Madam Chiang Kai-Shek as hog jowl, turnip greens, and corn pone. This does not mean that the viands dispensed in these establishments are not wholesome, piquant, and tasteful. It is merely a matter of getting the record straight. The origin of chili in the Southwest and along the Mexican border of the United States does, as a matter of fact, trace back to the land south of the border. On the menus of the cafes and Mexican eating places north of the border it is listed as "chili con carne." In the greasy spoon joints it is "chili," and after a fashion both are right. The chili portion of the listing in either place is a shortening of the Mexican word *chilipitine,* which are those small and hellishly hot peppers used so generously by the people of Mexico as a seasoning. They use them generously in cooking meat whether the meat be ram, lamb, or ham. Chili is used extensively by the Mexican cow outfits and those living along the border. I have eaten it in sheep camps along the border and in far West Texas. You can eat it as the Mexicans do, provided you are camped near water.

Chili, like black coffee, made its advent into Texas and up along the trails through the medium of the cow outfits, chuck wagons, and cow camps. The cow hands couldn't take it straight, however, so the cooks began cutting down on the amount of pepper, adding melted tallow, cuminseed, and garlic—which tempered it to the average outdoor man's taste and made a really piquant dish of it. Food grinders had not come into general use around the camps and the first of the chili had its meat finely chopped with butcher knife or cleaver rather than finely

ground as we know it now. It was to be found more in the permanent
camps than as an item of chuck wagon diet because it was messy and
inconvenient to prepare around a wagon that was making two moves
a day.

In its denatured form it found favor throughout the entire cow country. In the wake of the last of the trail wagons there came into existence
a new form of catering to meet the demands for chili on the part of
cowboys who, with the passing of trail driving, had become more or
less stationary. In their earlier days these were known as "chili joints"
and were usually sandwiched in between the cow-town's more pretentious high-fronted emporiums which dealt for the most part in
barbed wire, salt side meat, beans, Arbuckle's coffee, and other ranch
supplies. The average length of the old-time chili joint was about
twenty-five feet and its width about half of its length with a small
space in the rear partitioned off to screen the cook stove and hide the
lack of sanitation. Front-end equipment consisted of a counter built of
one by twelves, half a dozen high stools and a few yards of red and
yellow oil cloth to cover the counter. Linen and utensils consisted of a
very few red and white checked napkins, a couple dozen soup bowls
(the deep kind), and enough tin or imitation silverware spoons to
match the bowls, with a few extra for rush times. Possibly the entire
investment represented less than $100.00, based on values of that day.
The owners for most part were ex-chuck wagon cooks or cowboys who
foresaw an end of "straight ridin' jobs" and were casting about for
something that didn't require too much work. These owners had an
advantage because the regular cafes and hotel dining rooms did not
serve chili; it was messy, the dishes were hard to wash when the grease
got cold on them, and the garlic smelled the whole place up. Besides,
for all they knew, it was just a fad and wouldn't last long. The chili-
joint man, though, knew his onions as well as his garlic, so he roughed
him out a sign on the big piece of cardboard that he found inside the
first box of crackers he opened—"Chili – 5¢"—and built him up a fire
in the second-hand cook stove in the rear, and put his pot to boiling.
Meat that went into it was from the neck or flank of a grass-fat beef,
mostly lean, but a little cheaper than the better cuts. If he was a good
enough customer the market man threw in what tallow or suet he
needed. If he was in a country where they liked it that way, he cooked
frijoles into his chili; if not, he cooked them separately and gave the
customer the benefit of "with or without." When the customers began
to come in and find that they were getting a big dish of the highly

seasoned food which provided both warmth and nourishment, along with a double handful of crackers, the big old square kind known then as soda crackers, and all the water they could drink for a nickel, business began to pick up not only from the cow hands but from bosses and businessmen as well. Before too long they were coming in the front door to holler, "Give me one in the red without."

The chili-joint man had this, too, in his favor; men become chili addicts to almost the same extent they become coffee addicts. They want it fairly regular and the year around. Despite its fiery nature, they crave it in July as well as in January, which guaranteed a year-around patronage. It teams up nicely with black coffee, too, for if you eat it slowly or do considerable "augurin'" it falls below room temperature and the grease in it has a tendency to "get sleepy" and cling to the roof of the mouth. A cup of hot black "Javy" will break the bottleneck and add to the pleasure and nourishment of the chili.

The early proprietors stayed strictly with chili and coffee as a rule. Occasionally one would add "ham and" for the convenience of his customers. One old ex-cowboy in my home town was urged to add pies to his stock in trade. Rather indifferently he told the town's baker to bring him a half dozen next time he was passing. The baker placed them on the shelf and pulled the mosquito netting down over them without taking time to tell the proprietor what kind they were. Soon a customer dropped in and inquired, "What kind of pie you got up there?" Raising the netting the fellow behind the counter gave them the once over and came back in the only language he knew with "I got 2-Bar, 3-Bar, Cross-Bar, and Open Face."

Business for the chili joint grew apace, for cowmen and cowboys hitting town would head for the chili place to take on a chili before they went on down the street to eat a real meal, then stay to eat another and to learn that they had lost interest in the big steak and French fries they had been planning on all the way in. A new source of business was coming to them also; the schoolboys of the town, having been there once with their daddies, became more or less surreptitious patrons. There wasn't anything wrong with their going into a chili joint or eating chili, but it had not found its way into the homes yet and was referred to by mothers as "that stuff." As I recall, I was about eleven years old when the local confectionery lost my patronage and my spending money, augmented by a few quarters, nickels, and dimes acquired by selling feed sacks and carrying "notes" for the local swains, began going into the till of the chili joint. I got by at home for quite a while until my mother discovered my dereliction in the same manner she found that I was chewing tobacco, by certain stains—red in this case—on my only white shirt.

Over a long period chili at five cents per bowl constituted, in my opinion, the greatest food value our country has ever known. When you were flush it was worth the money for the sheer joy of eating it; in hard times it could make a few dollars of summer wages go farther for eating than any other food that you could buy and allow a little over for smoking tobacco and other pleasures.

The chili addicts themselves were responsible for inflation in the chili market. Some of them found that chili could be made a little better by liberal doses of tomato catsup which the chili-joint owner by this time kept on the counter for his "ham and" customers. He began to look askance at his regular chili customers as they spurted a fifteen-cent bottle of catsup into a nickel bowl of chili. He retaliated by cutting down on the number of crackers and exchanging the big old square ones for oyster crackers and finally by removing the catsup from the counter. But the customer kept calling for it, so in self defense he finally raised the price to ten cents a bowl, which caused more or less consternation among his kid customers and those who were trying to cut their eating money as thin as possible.

By this time chili was finding its way into the better homes, and the cafes and hotel dining rooms were keeping a pot of it on the back of the stove. The old-fashioned chili joint was giving way to the more modern chili parlor. Food processors and canners were realizing its food value and were turning out fairly good canned chili that required only a few minutes warming to make it edible. Then came "brick" chili, highly edible and meeting the taste of the chili addicts almost as well as the old kind. It found its way into the drug stores where it became a "must" item when the white aproned-white jacketed counter-man was figuring his daily requirements. Through added demand and cost of service in the chili parlors, cafes, and drug stores, prices shot up—to an unheard of high of twenty cents per bowl—the bowls diminished in size, and the crackers began to come in saltine style, enclosed in cellophane envelopes. These innovations and prices had long since marked the end of the old-time chili joint with its cowboy proprietor who acknowledged the fact that the buffalo had been killed off, trail driving was over, and cow punching, as he knew it, just about over. He met the new condition gracefully by accepting the position of second cook or dishwasher at the Aztec Cafe down the street. With their passing went a great and noble bunch of fellows who had contributed much to the welfare and nourishment of their kind in their day.

There is this about chili; like wine, it improves with age. First-day chili is never so good as it is three or four days later; it has a raw taste when first made and its color is not the deep, almost black red that it assumes after the seasoning has had time to thoroughly permeate the meat. Chili eaters don't like too much soup with their chili; it kind of cuts it down in strength and virtue. Most of them like it "with," meaning with beans. It is all right to eat a couple of bowls of it as an appetizer or while your steak is cooking, but regulars, after long years of trying, have found that it doesn't mix with liquor. You can lay the ensuing sickness after trying it to either the chili or the liquor, as your conscience dictates. The safest thing in my humble opinion and as one who has tried both, is to keep your chili warm with black coffee rather than with red liquor. You will feel better the next day.

Of all the foods found on the range in the period prior to canned picnic meats, sandwich spreads, Uneeda biscuits, malted milks, and Coca-Colas, perhaps canned tomatoes will arouse the greatest feeling of nostalgia among the old cow hands. Many were the merits and delights of this canned product, which offered to them from one container appetizer, food, drink, and dessert. While in those days they knew little and cared less about appetizers and vitamins, their systems needed and craved these nevertheless. The canned tomato with its tangy taste and acid content automatically cared for a need now provided for by citrus juices and easily available fresh fruits and vegetables.

The rich, red pulpy meat of the tomatoes with the addition of salt and pepper, or with sugar, made a satisfying meal on which one could ride far. Its juices were equally satisfying as a thirst quencher, having a more lasting effect than the same amount of water. In batching camp or with chuck wagon a few cans of tomatoes to which had been added some left-over biscuits and plenty of sugar made a tasty stewed dish always popular with the boys.

Ranch owners realized the merits of canned tomatoes and bought them liberally for their outfits and quibbled not at the quantity cooks and men used. They were comparatively cheap if their merits were weighed, and a plentiful supply available when a man felt the need for them made for a satisfied outfit. It was custom when a man dropped into camp or wagon, for him to "cut" a can of tomatoes, most of the time without asking anyone's permission. The chuck-wagon cook, ordinarily noted for his grouchiness or cussedness, accepted this custom and raised no kick when the cowboy or horse wrangler, in for a brief visit or to get matches and smoking tobacco, mounted the wheel of the wagon to scratch around among the stores in back of the chuck box for a can of tomatoes.

Ofttimes the lone cowboy in a batching camp which was plentifully supplied with ranch provisions, riding in after a long day along the fence lines and among the cattle, would eye his larder, take into consideration time and effort necessary to prepare a meal and wind up by eating a can of tomatoes and a few cold biscuits left over from the last meal. Then next day, if his work was to carry him afar, he would tie some cans into his slicker or cram them into his saddle pockets as provender until he got back to camp. In the countries where drinking water was scarce and of poor quality he often carried them in lieu of a canteen.

There would be mornings sometimes, during his rare visits to town, when he would awaken, even as his town brother, with a woefully weak stomach and a roaring head. Where the town brother would ring for tomato juice, Worcestershire, and lemon, he would work his way to the back end of the grocery store where the outfit traded to "cut" a can of tomatoes into which he poured a bottle of pepper sauce and plenty of salt and pepper. To say this mixture got the job done is putting it mildly.

Tomatoes may have been considered poisonous and called "love apples" a comparatively few years ago, but not within the knowledge of the old-time cowboy. If he had been told these things after cutting the first can he would have gone on eating and liking them just the same. They balanced his rations without his knowing such balance was necessary or being done.

Sometimes there was a bunch of cattle to be moved ten or fifteen miles, not far enough to use the wagon and a little too far to make it back to the ranch before the boys got so hungry, as they expressed it, "that their bellies would think their throats are cut." If they were not to be near a town or country store where salmon, sardines, cove oysters, or cheese and crackers could be had, or if the trail did not lead by some friendly ranch or nester house by noon, the headquarters lady would fix each of them a package of lunch that would be rolled up in his slicker or tied on to his saddle. When noon came they would let the cattle graze or fill on water while they dropped into the shade to eat their lunches. The packets would contain a couple of sandwiches made from big biscuits and fried steak, if the outfit happened to have a beef hung up, or bacon or ham. There was likely to be a fried peach or apple pie, the kind that folds over the ends and carries well if you don't cut it in two with a saddle string in tying the package on. It is a cinch that there would be in each package one or two biscuits that had been heavily buttered, covered with sugar, and pressed back together. It is just as good a bet that when the last of this delicacy had been eaten the oldest one of the boys would say, as he wiped the last grain of sugar from his mouth, "Gosh-dang, that was good. Ma used to always put them in my dinner bucket when I was a kid going to school down in the piney woods."

A fondness for barbecued meats and the pleasure of preparing them for those they love or those whose friendship and good will they seek is inherent with Texans. Barbecue and barbecues as social, political, and economic factors are in the very weave and warp of the state they call their own. They are as much a part of Texas as its mighty capitol building, the hallowed Alamo, ten-gallon hats, or good beef cattle.

They served colonial Texans as a medium of entertainment and relaxation among themselves and as a way to welcome uncles, aunts, and cousins come a-visiting from "The Old States" and to introduce them to plantation owners, ranchmen, and families from up the Brazos, Trinity, and Colorado, or from along the bayous and creeks running inland from the Gulf Coast.

Equally well they served to welcome sons and fathers home from the wars and to perpetuate the memories of those who did not return. Troths have been plighted in their blue smokes and full many a blushing bride and happy groom speeded from them on their way to build new homes and raise future Texas heroes, statesmen, industrialists, and fair daughters.

The barbecue has ever been the Texan's method of extending welcome and courtesy to the stranger, whether his visit be social or in the interest of industry. Its influence has been felt in Texas architecture, for the selecting of a site and landscaping of the average Texas country home depends on availability of a shade tree or two or even a small grove and running stream to provide proper setting for the inevitable barbecue pit. This is not true only of the more pretentious homes, since a large per cent of the modest city ones boast some sort of barbecue pit. True it may serve a greater portion of the year as a trash incinerator, but come spring it can be cleaned out in a very few minutes, and a bed of coals accumulated against the "coming in" of neighbors in the cool of the evening to enjoy whatever you may barbecue—from hot dogs to choice beef briskets, yellow-legged fryers, or pork ribs. It is small wonder that Texans are connoisseurs of the outdoor roasting of meats and the concocting of piquant sauces which ultimately decide the merits of the meat. Neither is it a matter of particular wonder that the average group of Texans, if given their choice of holding a function in a banquet room under soft lights, with a special menu, napery, and shining silver, or meeting in a grove to eat barbecue with their fingers while the blue, acrid smoke stings their eyes, will choose the latter.

The influence of the barbecue has been even more keenly felt in the political arena than from the social standpoint. When Texas was in her formative period counties could be organized, county seats selected, and a full slate of political candidates ranging from constable to governor selected and ratified, over a few hundred pounds of barbecued beef, half a bushel of onions, a keg of pickles, and plenty of light bread and black coffee, with everyone going home satisfied, loving his fellowman, and in high good humor. Scarcely a statesman of the many Texas has produced but owes his first success and start upward to some address made at a Fourth-of-July barbecue.

A barbecue has been Texas' way of getting her people together to sell them on an idea, whether it be to buy lots at a townsite auction, raise more bonus and right-of-way for the railroad threatening to pass three miles east of town, vote in the herd law, clean out the courthouse, or purchase a town bull. Texans figured that what they couldn't do over a good portion of barbecue wasn't worth doing.

While Texas was still in her swaddling clothes economically the barbecue served a function similar to that of the present-day Chamber of Commerce. Even to this good day these groups, with their graphs, charts, plotted curves, comparative and potential figures, realize the merits of a good old-fashioned barbecue, and fall back on it when the going gets rough. The forty-, thirty-, and twenty-beef free barbecues of half a century ago served the same purpose in developing an area as that now performed by the regional Chambers of Commerce, each of which owes its origin to a barbecue called to consider its organization. I recall attending two of these, one in Longview for the East Texas Chamber of Commerce, the other in Sweetwater, at which time initial plans were made for organizing the West Texas Chamber of Commerce. Smaller barbecues in an area's new and growing town served the function now performed by the local Chambers of Commerce, that of bringing the people together once a year to relax, visit, trade, and learn from each other possible solutions for their local problems.

Merchants and proponents of a new town used barbecues as a means of expressing their good will toward their trade territory and attracting its custom to their town and away from their nearest competitors. They were about 60 per cent business and 40 per cent social, this type of barbecue. They were held on July 4th to commemorate Independence Day and because that was the time of year when crops were "laid by," and folks had time to "project around" a little. (If held before or after that date they were invariably known as Old Settlers or Old Confederate Reunions.) The 4th was also a favorable date and place for candidates to announce for public office, to meet the folk, and to get in a few good licks against the fall election. There were no primaries then.

Many of these were gigantic affairs which attracted people by rail, covered wagon, horseback, or "private conveyance," from a wide radius. Those from farthest away came early, camped along the creek, did their trading and picnicked until it was over and the last of the beef eaten. The picnicking consisted of drinking enormous amounts of red lemonade, playing the knife board and doll racks, weighing, and riding the merry-go-rounds, either steam or mule powered. The itinerant "medicine show," with its high-hatted doctor and its black-faced singer and comedian, was always a top attraction. Once in a while even yet, when an old-timer gets excited or in a hurry, his yell of "More medicine, Doc" will quickly establish him as an early devotee of Doc Blair's Medicine Show.

I have before me an old hand-bill announcing one of the best of these barbecues under date of July 4, 1896. The invitation, in part, reads, "COME ONE! COME ALL! FREE BARBECUE! 30 FAT BEEVES! ALL THE TRIMMINGS! PLENTY OF ICE WATER AND SHADE! ALL FREE!" In smaller type is mention of certain sure-fire attractions: matched baseball game, balloon ascension, greased-pig and sack races, and greased-pole climbing, with prizes for all winners. There is also announcement of an address to be made by the Honorable Joseph Weldon Bailey, with time given to all candidates for public office. It also states that Molly Bailey will be on hand with her Dog and Pony Show for four performances. This latter attraction and the fact that Joe Bailey will speak mark this as one of the big ones. Aunt Molly did not take her family and her little wagon show over the long dusty Texas roads unless she loved the people where she was going and was sure they loved her and needed her show to make their event a success. Joe Bailey was a mighty popular man in those days and his presence was guarantee of a good crowd. The old bill is signed and vouched for by "The Committee," which, in effect, embraced every merchant and professional man in town, as well as all parties running for public office that year.

These big barbecues required a lot of work and food. Until the railroads fingered out over the western portion of the state it was necessary to haul by wagon freight from the nearest railroad point everything that went into a barbecue except the beef. Recently I talked to a gentleman who for years had charge of the feeding arrangements of the annual barbecue held on July 3, 4, and 5 at Ozona in West Texas. Among the items that he could recall off-hand, as necessary daily to feed the crowd which came from as far south as the Rio Grande and from as far north as the Salt Fork of the Brazos, was 30 pounds of red beans, 50 gallons of pickles, 500 to 700 loaves of bread, 300 to 500 pounds of onions, 125 pounds of coffee, and from 125 to 150 head of goats and calves.

The beef for the most of these affairs was donated or purchased very reasonably from funds which had been raised to defray the expense thereof. Out in the cow country getting the beef free was no problem— many of the cowmen lived in town and if it was too far to bring beef in from the ranch they either "paid in" or bought from local traders. Ofttimes the committee would start the town's local freighter out with a trail wagon outfit to call on the ranches for the promised beef. It was always good beef, too, for the cowman donating it did not want people to think that he was "short" or that his cattle were on the "lift" as they would if he sent in an old "rannie" cow or dogie yearling. All labor except the butchering and barbecuing was donated. Actual cutting up and serving of the meat was done by local merchants and town leaders who were anxious to have the visitors see them in the role of hosts.

It required a chief barbecuer and about twenty helpers to get the big batch of beef on the fire, cooked, and ready to serve around noon on the day of the Fourth. To accomplish this fires had to be lighted in the pits around the middle of the afternoon of the third. By sundown the pits were a glowing bed of coals and not until they were did the cook dare begin laying his meat on the fire. He did well to get all his meat on by 10:30 or 11:00 o'clock that night. Extra fires were kept burning and coals from them added to the pits from time to time to maintain an even heat.

After the meat was on and beginning to take heat nicely the barbecuer and one or two helpers began basting it with a sauce, the ingredients of which the barbecuer alone knew. It was made up in five-gallon lots and applied with a mop made from a flour sack tied on to a green stick. Other crews kept the meat turning over with pitchforks and as it began to get done, stacked it toward one end of the pit, leaving the rare meat for extra cooking. If everything went well the meat was pretty well done toward 11 o'clock on the day of the Fourth, at which time the local butchers, as their donation, began cutting it up into chunks which went into galvanized tubs to be placed back on the pits and kept warm until the marshal of the day yelled "Come and get it." Come they did, with everything from a dishpan to a washtub, for it was the custom to carry the meat away to where you were camped or where your friends were congregated. I do not doubt that more good barbecue has been thrown away than has been eaten because people's eyes were bigger than their bellies and because it was all free.

While the type of barbecue described here leaned a little to the commercial side, such affairs had their merits in bringing people of an area together to renew friendships, talk over old times, show last year's crop of new babies, and discuss fifteen-cent cotton and other problems that beset their existence. It also afforded opportunity for the country man to see that his patronage was appreciated by the town man, as evidenced by the time, hard work, and money the latter put into it to the end that the country man and his family might enjoy themselves for one or two days of the year.

Time was when they didn't barbecue anything in Texas but beef. Then some Negro found that barbecued pork ribs could be eaten with relish. Someone else discovered that chickens could be barbecued nicely and that goat could be made into edible meat via the barbecue.

Each community had its barbecue expert, who merited the title after long experience with mop and long-handle fork during which time he had never "cut a gut." In the Ozona country it was Bob Cook, who lives yet at Sanderson out in the Big Bend country, and occasionally does barbecuing for his friends. Up around Quanah it was Ben Johnson and Bill Marlin; in the Amarillo country John Snider, an ex-cowboy, was and is still considered tops. A few years ago he and the tools of his trade, along with a good supply of Texas beef, were transported to Washington, D.C., when a delegation of West Texans wanted to entertain certain interests in the capital city in good Texas style. Over in the Sweetwater country Horace Wade, an enterprising livestock commission man, has for years been dean of the barbecue pits. Ton upon ton of good red Texas beef has had his attention at the many Hereford auctions held in that section. Down in the Uvalde country high claims are made for J. H. Denmark, than whom, according to Dolph Briscoe, there is none better.

Their technique in actually cooking the beef varies but little, but when it comes to the matter of sauce they vary widely, each claiming a secret process which makes his mixture far superior. Perhaps so, but I have at times purchased supplies for most of the best of them and found that the list of ingredients varies but slightly. Might be that they use some sort of secret incantation as they mix it. I must admit that some sauces are better than others, but they are all good. Basic ingredients for the sauce are vinegar, butter, black and cayenne pepper, salt, cooking oil, and tomato catsup.

There is also a wide variation and discussion as to the best kind of wood to be used in barbecuing. The East Texas experts claim it a waste of time and meat to barbecue with anything but seasoned hickory; the Cross-Timber fellows hoot at the idea that hickory is any better than dry post oak, while the Cap-Rock boys are sure they can do an equally good job with hackberry and mesquite grubs. I have eaten it cooked with each kind and could tell little or no difference. I doubt not that an equally good job can and has been done by the Plains fellows with a cow chip fire.

They were and are legion, these good barbecuers. It is impossible to mention them all by name for there are experts in every section of the state. The Brazos, Trinity, and Colorado bottoms abound with them, both white and colored. In the brush country of South Texas there are Mexican cow cooks, who can make savory and highly edible barbecue from either a javelina hog or an aged Brahman bull. These "experts" have added to the color and flavor of Texas and made it the "out barbecuingest state" in the union. George Sessions Perry, in his excellent and best selling book, *Texas: A World within Itself,* takes cognizance of Texans' love for barbecue with the statement, "Down in Texas we barbecue anything we can get to stand still." They have passed their art on to the younger generation until practically every home in Texas boasts an expert, who, despite burned fingers, red eyes, soiled sport clothes, and a greasy oniony sort of smell over the week-end, still claims he is best and is raring to go when the folks want to run out to the lake (artificial) in the cool of a Saturday evening with a few pounds of beef, a side of ribs, or half dozen chickens. The meat may assume the appearance of a burnt offering or it may be served done on the outside and raw on the inside before the evening is over, but it will be barbecue and everyone will swear that it is the best yet.

As the state settled up, new towns came into existence to share trade territory with the old ones. Roads (the dirt and graded kind) and railroads enabled people to move about more freely, "trade" oftener, and visit more. The big barbecues were on the wane, but not the people's love of barbecue and the good fellowship it portended. They merely came down in size to smaller affairs catering to the people of the county and those living on the "town" section. The number of expert barbecuers increased, each claiming to have learned under the old masters of the area. Slowly but surely the public or mass barbecue was being pushed back into the rural section. Out there a "cemetery working" or re-roofing the school house was always ample justification for a small barbecue. The older folks' standard form of invitation to each other became, "Bring the folks and come over some time—if you will we will throw a piece of meat on the fire."

Then the breaks began to come right along for the barbecue again. The state was growing by leaps and bounds industrially. Smokestacks, other than those of the gin, oil mill, and railroad pump station, were beginning to raise themselves throughout the state: cement mills, cotton mills, sawmills, and the like. The managers for these, nearly all new to the country, found they were not getting along any too well with the help, but just couldn't put their finger on the trouble. They sought counsel from the older native heads and because the managers by this time were becoming their sons-in-law they gave them benefit of their experience and allowed that a good barbecue had always been a means of settling things in Texas by filling the folks up and then allowing them to talk over their troubles. The managers took heed, "threw" a barbecue, and found that it worked. The sales manager happened to be there, ate of the barbecue, watched the results, then yelled loudly, "Why don't somebody tell me about these things, if it will work on the employees it will work on the customers." It did, and the barbecue tendered "the trade" became an annual event even larger than the employees' affair.

About this time the automobile became a part of Texan home life, which called for a system of highways. The state's fine system of highways with its roadside parks and the rest places may well be said to have been evolved around a series of barbecues which extended through the periods when counties were called upon to vote bonds for the construction of their county road systems. Most of these elections were the result of county-wide rallies and barbecues held to present the matter to the voters. Sometimes it took two or three of them per county to get the job done and convince various and sundry reactionaries that the road just couldn't pass in front of every man's house. Later when the state took over the matter of building state highways the agency through which this was accomplished, the State Highway Commission, was tendered barbecues by every section of the state wanting new designations or bigger and better river bridges. Later the opening of each highway or bridge, sometimes called a "ribbon cutting," was the occasion for a second barbecue. One commission under which much good was accomplished was composed of excellent trenchermen of the old Texas school who appreciated good barbecue and good fellowship. That each of the state's wayside parks includes one or more barbecue pits is a stone and mortar monument to barbecue and this fine commission.

No class of people get more pleasure and good out of a barbecue than Texas ranch folk. To use their own expression "it is right down their alley," meaning they raise beef, love it themselves, and want as many others to like it as possible. A barbecue is their method of telling their fellow cowmen, bankers, and town friends that they don't owe a dime to a dang soul and that they have plenty of grass all over the place, and every tank and water hole is brimming full. So when a Texas cowman invites you to a barbecue at his home you may know without him telling you (for he won't) that all is well with him and his affairs. Perhaps it will signal the fact that he has completed a breeding and culling program on his cow herd which will guarantee a uniform crop of heavy calves each year that will be attractive to the Corn-Belt buyer. It may be the completion of the ranch home he and his wife have dreamed of through the dry hard years it took to bring them to the point where they felt they could afford it. It is his way of expressing what grass and cattle have meant to him and his.

The best of these I can recall was that three-day affair given by Bill Richards in 1903 at the hackberry grove over in his west pasture. Twenty choice 3 D two-year-old heifers were slaughtered and turned over to Ben Johnson for cooking. Bread, pickles, onions, ice water, soda pop, and a baby grand piano were hauled out from Quanah by wagon, a distance of fifty miles. For three days 250 to 300 people ate, danced, and reminisced; and when it was over there was beef enough left on the pits to have fed them another three days. Everyone knew that Bill was proud of the fact that he had not only paid out his 3 D outfit but had acquired the adjoining Moon Ranch as well. It is pleasant to recall that during the three-day celebration not one untoward incident arose to mar the pleasure for those present; not one man to my knowledge was carrying a gun for another, nor was drinking in evidence except the soda pop and lemonade, which were free. It was at a time, too, when the order was changing and there still prevailed semifeuds and misunderstandings over brands, fences, and waterholes, which time had not wholly healed. Acceptance of the invitation, however, served as an automatic truce and to my knowledge few of these were ever revived after the barbecue. It is of record that in Texas feuds have been settled and killings averted by a timely barbecue given by those desirous of seeing an end put to such foolishness. So far as I am able to ascertain, there is no record of a killing or cutting scrape at a barbecue in my section of the state. Occasionally the barbecuer worn out and red-eyed after a night over the coals might slap the whey out of a helper, but that was in the line of duty.

The Texas Hereford breeders have found the barbecue an almost necessary adjunct to the many auction sales which are held by them throughout the state each year. These are prepared on an elaborate scale. Ofttimes the beef used for barbecue is of the same quality as that being offered in the auction ring. The feeds are held just prior to the opening of the sale and serve to put everyone in a good humor and make them ready to bid when the auctioneer starts the sale.

Down in the sheep and goat country between Sonora and Rocksprings the state maintains a livestock experiment station which is host every two years to West Texas ranchmen. On these occasions state veterinarians tell the gathered ranchmen things they have learned about bitter weed, loco, sore mouth, and other things and pests which bother their herds. A big barbecue each day provides meat for those who are camped in and around the station or visiting it for the day. I think that it must have been at one of these affairs that George Sessions Perry got the idea for his statement that down in Texas we barbecue anything that holds still. I have seen overflow crowds show up at the last minute, which taxed the supply of barbecue already on the tables. When this happens fifty or seventy-five extra goats are killed, dressed, and thrown on the fire in short order. Sometimes the rush is so great that the goats can hardly be said to be standing still when they go on the fire.

The average ranch barbecue of today assumes somewhat the proportions of a combination chuck wagon dinner and barbecue at which there are extra trimmings in the way of red beans, son-of-a-gun, dried stewed fruit, and cobblers of various kinds. This has been brought about largely through the many rodeos to which the cowman brings his chuck wagon to feed his own outfit and as many of his friends as he can accommodate.

In attempting to explain why Texans love their barbecue I have taken as my cue the definition given in Webster's dictionary, which says, "A barbecue is a social or political entertainment at which animals are roasted whole with appropriate surroundings." I have been able to follow the text fairly well until it came to the matter of a whole roasted beef. Big as Texas is, and with as many cattle as it has and generous as its people are you just couldn't provide each person with a whole beef and have anything left at all to sell.

Texas has gone further in demanding barbecue as a regular diet than any other state in the union. The influx of newcomers to the state who have been recipients of barbecue on their arrival have swelled the ranks of barbecue addicts until the matter of supplying it for them between barbecues is fast becoming a problem. This has given rise to a new industry—the barbecue joint, saloon, or place, as you choose to call it, to meet the demands of the barbecue-hungry. These are to be found along the highways and byways and in the hearts of the cities themselves. They range from tin shacks with dirt floors and open pits in the rear from which a greasy savory odor arises, where you stand on the sawdust-covered floors to munch your daily portion, to tile-lined palaces in the business section of town where you may sit at ease to eat a plate of just-fair barbecue cooked over a charcoal fire in a mechanical contraption which does its own salting, saucing, and turning. Every town has its favorite spots—Jack's, the Big Apple, or Mexican Joe's. There is one in Austin, up a back alley, where a Mexican barbecues Fredericksburg sausage and yams, and serves them with a fiery sauce. In my home town, Fort Worth, there is Bailey's, housed in a small sheet iron building only a few steps from the heart of the city's financial and shopping district. There is sawdust on the floor and the smoke drifts in from the pits to settle on the hair and collars of the town's leading merchants each day from 12:00 until 1:30. It is truly a barbecue place serving nothing but barbecued beef. Your only choice is whether you prefer it brown or just medium done. Recently one of the town's leading department store managers took an exclusive Eastern salesman to Bailey's for lunch. The next day the salesman took the manager, and on the third day chided him because the barbecue place didn't serve breakfast.

Time has given rise to a number of methods in preparing barbecue. In some sections they build small tin houses about the size of and resembling in architecture the well-known Chic Sale structure, in which the meat is suspended over coals in a concrete firebox. In other sections an enormous pit is dug, fires burned in it overnight and withdrawn early in the morning before the barbecue is to be used in the late evening. The meat is then sewn in burlap sacking, placed in the hot pit and covered with warm dirt and ashes. The meat is allowed to remain until time to use it when it is dug from the pit and the wrapping removed. This system cooks the meat very nicely, leaving the juices in it, but it no more resembles real barbecue than buzzard does turkey.

In recent years the major packing companies have been turning out a fair grade of barbecue which they make of good meat, seasoned well, and delivered where wanted in fireless cookers. Their type of barbecue is in heavy demand at industrial affairs and political rallies, and by organizations that do not have facilities of their own to properly barbecue meat. Several companies are building small barbecue wagons of chromium and nickle, fired by charcoal, to be wheeled into the patio by the butler when madame signals. Charcoal has been a boon to the home barbecuer as it can be purchased in small lots at the corner grocery store where you buy the meat you are to barbecue. It may offer a solution to the wood question, because it can be made from many of the woods favored by the old experts; but it is a cinch there isn't any cow chips charcoal—it just won't make it.

A better way to cook barbecue is to dig a pit 5 or 6 feet long and about 2½ feet deep, then get an armful of old Ford axles, a few short lengths of gas pipe and a piece of sheep fencing long enough and wide enough to cover the pit. Fill the pit up with any kind of wood available, old fence posts, goods boxes, paper cartons, or cow chips, if available. While it is burning down to steady coals with a white covering of ashes over it, trim your meat into two or three pound chunks, salt well, and rub with black pepper. When the meat begins to heat evenly, make a sauce of the following ingredients:

½ cup melted butter
¼ cup of sugar
¼ teaspoon red pepper
½ teaspoon mustard
½ pint Wesson oil
12 ounce bottle catsup
½ bottle Lea & Perrin sauce
2 or 3 cloves of garlic
1 grated onion, large
juice of 1 lemon
tabasco to taste
2 to 3 tablespoons "liquid smoke"

Mix well—the more the better—it keeps well, so make lots and use lots.

The above recipe is sufficient for one medium-sized goat or a half dozen thick steaks or chickens. To obtain best results it should be applied with a mop made by wrapping a portion of the dish towel around a green limb. Baste almost constantly as meat is turned. Should you plan a larger barbecue increase the ingredients proportionately. When meat is finished and ready for serving, pour any leftover sauce over it; it makes an excellent gravy or sauce. Don't be afraid of making up too much sauce. It will keep almost indefinitely. It is a little more expensive to prepare than the old vinegar kind, but it is well worth the difference for a small barbecue.

There are a few things it is well to remember in barbecuing: the better the meat the better the barbecue. Choice beef briskets are desirable, they cook nicely, slice evenly, and are considered very good for barbecuing. Do not put your meat on until you are sure there is no danger of blazing up. Use care in applying sauce not to apply it so fast that it will drip on the coals causing a blaze. Don't get scared if your fire looks like it has gone out entirely, your meat is just cooking good then, for the pit is hot and the ashes have heat enough to finish the job. No more meat should be cooked than can be consumed at one time for warmed over barbecue is not good. The ingredients used in the sauce are inclined to "sour" the meat when cold and it is impossible to revive the flavor in warmed-over meat.

An ideal small barbecue may be had by using a small milk-fat kid if available, split it up the back-bone into halves then take off shoulders and hams which will give you four excellent pieces of meat and two plates of ribs and can be cooked in from 3½ to 4 hours.

In building up a case for Texans and barbecue I have attempted to show that they love it because it was the meat of their forefathers and the dish around which they built their social structure. I have also tried to show its effect on the economic and political life of the state but there still must be other reasons why it alone exceeds chili and hot tamales as the state's favorite viand. Perhaps it is (1) because Texas is a beef-producing state, (2) because Texans like their meats well done, crisp and brown, with highly seasoned sauces, (3) because barbecues are outdoor affairs affording a tang and zest not to be found indoors, (4) because they are invariably given as a gesture of good will or friendship, (5) or because they are free.

Maybe just because the durn stuff is good!

Meat shortages, actual or impending, hold no terrors for South-westerners. For that matter neither did sugar rationing, insofar as desserts were concerned. One might even go so far as to say that a shortage of the highly advertised vitamins A, B, and C would cause no particular consternation nor debilitation.

The Southwesterners do not fear these shortages, nor look upon them as hardships. They, like their forefathers, have an ace in the hole insofar as food, dessert, and body building essentials are concerned. The hole card with them is their "beans." Give them all they want of the kind they like, cooked as they like, and they will not only "winter" good but will "slick off" early each spring and then go on eating beans the rest of the year.

To outlanders these will sound like strong statements and must be verified. In substantiation, I give you the entire oversize outdoor-living population of the Southwest and any portion of the more sedentary who have become bean addicts. In further evidence, I give you (name on request) the statement of one of our eminent West Texas physicians who has been nationally acclaimed for his success in fighting the ravages of tuberculosis, that beans are indispensable as food and that he recommends and uses them for curing and rebuilding the bodies of thousands whom he returns as cured.

As to the matter of dessert, the hostess will find that if beans in sufficient quantity are available, the guest will wholly overlook dessert, and feel fortunate that there was nothing sweet to clutter up the meal. Speaking of hostess, guests, desserts, and the like, the bean does really have a place in the political, financial, and social life of the cow and sheep country. At the scores of purebred auction sales held each year where contentment and a full stomach are conducive to higher bidding, beans are the *pièce de résistance* of the barbecue luncheon served stockmen, visitors, and guests just prior to the opening of the sale.

If the gathering should be a political rally, there will usually be a lot of beans—for they are cheaper and just as soul-satisfying as the barbecued beef. One politician went so far as to tell prospective attendents that he would guarantee more than one thousand good things to eat—adding in an undertone, "all beans."

The bean appears in ultra society frequently when madame serves from the rubber-tired barbecue luncheon wagon which is rolled into the patio where the guests are seated.

Now, just any old bean will not do. Didn't we just say it must be the kind they like and cooked as they like them? Southwesterners are

funny that way about their beans. The bean to which I am referring
is not the snap or string bean of the northern section, nor the portly
butter bean to be found on the tables of the central portion. True, the
butter bean offers much in quantity, but not so much in quality.
Neither do I refer to the navy bean, which had its fling along the old
Chisholm Trail before better beans were discovered, a fair bean in
its time but as lacking in strength as 3.2 beer is to the real beer of
the 90's. The bean I am referring to is the strong, heady red bean—
sometimes referred to as frijole, and sometimes as pinto, but known
always as "red beans." These are beans which have nursed the Southwest through its cow days and given strength to the nester grubbing
the doughty mesquite that he might broaden his productive acres, the
bean that has seen the sons and daughters of the Southwest through
its drouth periods and times of low prices and that has brought them
out strong and eager to break more sod and build bigger and better
towns.

When I say strong I mean just that—for the Southwest turns its
men out big. Look at the next general convention you attend and pick
them out by their height and girth. If you are still not convinced take
their boots and hats off and they will still top the meeting for size.

The bean pot has been a symbol of nourishment and encouragement
to Southwesterners through the cow days and until this day. The tired
cow hand riding up to his wagon at midnight to find the outfit asleep
in their tarps knew that he would find the bean pot with coals and
ashes drawn around it simmering away, offering nourishment and
cheer. The tired nester coming to his dug-out or shack after a day
of grubbing, fencing, or tanking smelled its savory odor from afar and
quickened his steps. Juan, the sheep herder in his lonely camp after
his charges were safe in the brush corral for the night, offers a prayer
to his patron saint for the *buenos frijoles* as he stirs to life the embers
under his simmering bean bucket. The clerk in the counting house or
store, when the clock strikes twelve, takes his hat and coat from its
peg and remarks tersely, "It's bean time."

Ever humble, the red bean has never commanded the price of real
delicacies, but is ever on hand when hard times make beef scarce and
groceries high, selected because of its nourishing qualities and because
pioneer transportation methods demanded the most food for the least
space.

When we say properly cooked, we do not mean prepared by chefs
in suits of white and towering caps, nor do we mean cooked in vessels

of burnished copper, but in pots of iron by cow cooks with run-over boots and feed-sack aprons (if any), or by nester mothers in calico who learned the art from the cow cooks. For the benefit of outlanders who have not eaten red beans cooked Southwestern style, we are giving herewith the recipe handed down from the army of chuck-wagon cooks who, when cattle roamed the open range, drove the creaking chuck wagons from roundup ground to roundup ground, cussing their four-mule teams singularly and collectively, damning the weather be it fair or foul, always spoiling for a scrap, but turning out food that made real he-men.

Soak 5 pounds of red beans overnight, drain off water next morning (pick out small rocks), cover with cold water, and place on slow fire. While beans are coming to boil, cut 3½ pounds of dry salt bacon into cubes an inch square and drop into pot. When beans are nearly done or have become so soft that you can't pick up one with a fork, add a couple of No. 2 cans of tomatoes, stirring them well into the beans, then add 3 large sliced onions, salt, and pepper (plenty), with a dash of cayenne pepper. Chop three buttons (not pods) of garlic as finely as possible into the pot. Then soak 3 or 4 pods of Mexican chili pepper in warm water until seed can be removed. Make pulp of pods and stir into beans.

Red beans to be cooked properly should stay on the fire not less than five hours. As a matter of fact, they can cook for ten hours and be better. Cooked in this way, red beans become bread, meat, and dessert, and afford the same nourishing qualities as these dishes to those who work in the open and work hard. Men in the milder walks of life have become red-bean addicts and resort to almost unbelievable tactics in cadging invitations to homes where red beans are being served. The beans are supposed to be eaten in the conventional manner with the fork, but if the hostess is not looking, they may be eaten with a large spoon. They are better that way.

The recipe given above is for an average cow outfit of nine men who arise at daybreak, ride in twenty-mile circles and flank three-hundred-pound calves in a branding pen all day. If your family is small—cook about the same amount, for what you don't eat the first, second, or third days, you will finish on the fourth, when you will put a new batch on to soak. The longer you keep them and warm them over, the better they get—gaining in strength and virtue after each warming.

There are sections in the Southwest where the chuck wagon is used yet. Due to the character of the country, there will be chuck wagons there until a substitute for good red beef is found. These outfits have found out, at the cost of some loss of time and added expense in the way of grocery bills, that society is interested in the chuck wagon, and likes its highly seasoned and wholesome food. One of the big cowboy reunions features at its annual gatherings a camp of chuck wagons sent in by half a dozen neighboring ranches. During the reunion each of these wagons becomes headquarters and provides meals for the outfit's friends. Hundreds are fed each year, and the camp is one of the most popular attractions of the entire show. This invasion of the sacred domain of the Ancient and Honorable Order of Cow Cooks is causing some querulous comment from the wagon cooks, both active and retired.

Most of the well known old-time chuck-wagon cooks have taken off their flour-sack aprons and cleaned the dough from their fingernails for the last time. The few living are too old for active work. Occasionally one of these can be prevailed upon to preside over the rear end of his old company's wagon at the reunion. He does it not so much for pay as for the opportunity of trying his hand again with the skillets and ovens and mingling with friends "who knew him when." Locate one of these and you find food fit for the gods and lots of homey philosophy as well.

The afternoon had been long and hot, and as the steer riding was announced I left my place along the arena fence and headed for the wagons. I was full-up on red soda pop and I knew I would find a barrel of tank water cooled by a hunk of ice in the front end of one of the wagons on the camp ground. As I passed the chuck-box end of the Block wagon I saw squatted on the ground under its fly Ab Evans, veteran cook of half a dozen outfits, one whose cooking I had eaten as a boy. He was unraveling flour sacks which would eventually become dish towels and aprons. As I climbed upon tongue and doubletree and pushed the wagon sheet off the water barrel, Ab said, "When you get your drink come around and augur with me awhile."

As I didn't care anything about the steer riding I slipped under the fly and dropped down to lean against a wheel. "Are you going to have a big crowd for supper—maybe I should say dinner?" I inquired of Ab.

"No, just the boys from the ranch that are ropin' and ridin', but we are goin' to have a hell of a dinner tomorrow at noon providin' I can get them two button-head boys that are supposed to help me off that arena fence long enough to do sumpin'." he replied and continued, "The old man said we'd have two or three hundred tomorrow on account that the Lions and Rotary from Fort Worth was comin' out."

"Can you tell me," continued Ab, "why it is that people who could go to a restaurant and put their feet under a table and eat a meal of good victuals want to come out to these wagons and get beans and gravy all over themselves tryin' to squat down and eat like us boys do? It's worse every day both at these reunions and at the ranch. You can't plan a day's cookin' any more. When you camp your wagon you don't know whether to make a salad or cook a son-of-a-gun. Like as not if you fix for eight or ten cow hands, you'll have a couple of carloads of women folks or the old man's daughter and her graduatin' class will run in on you.

"I seen this comin' on thirty years ago when cowmen begin movin' their families into town. First the old man would go in once a month on horseback with his old clothes on and come back the same way. Then he got a side-spring buggy and begin goin' in every Friday. He'd come out about Monday or Tuesday with his good clothes on and while he was changin' he'd tell us about playin' cards at parties and learnin' to eat olives. I know'd it was comin'.

"After the women folks moved into town, when we would be in there shippin', the old lady would round up all the other ranch women and drive out to the wagon in their surreys and phaetons.

"I never will forget what happened to the fellow that was cookin' for Ben Hattox when he was runnin' that big outfit down in the Wichitas. They came in to Quanah with a herd to ship and camped the last night out in the edge of the 'Nesterments' and the milk pen calves ate the cook's clothes up while he was takin' a bath in Riley Wheat's tank. The only surplus clothes in the outfit was a pair of chaps that one of the boys had in the wagon. This coosie climbed into them and got his breakfast and dinner and then pulled into town and camped at the railroad tank near the stock pens and got his fire to goin' and his supper started. He hadn't more than got started good when Mrs. Hattox and a surrey full of women folks drove up to see Ben and eat supper at the wagon. You can imagine how that poor boy felt cookin' a meal of victuals, tendin' his fires and all without ever turnin' his back on them women folk.

"With them and the commission men, train crews, and chuck riders, it kept you humpin' to feed all of 'em. Then when the railroads built out into our country and we just used the wagon when we was brandin', the old man's boys used to bring their college friends out in the summer and it was plum tryin' sometimes. They all wanted to ride and eat, and there wasn't a one of them that didn't ride up in ten feet of the wagon before they stopped which usually made my dough look like a chocolate cake.

"When the towns began to grow up around us and the Lions and Rotary was organized, some of our outfit belonged and we'd have the clubs once a year for Ladies' Night. Don't know as I blame anybody, though, that has to eat as many canned peas and mashed potatoes as them club members do, for wantin' a change once in a while."

Ab rose, and after favoring the foot that had gone to sleep on him, took his pot hook and hobbled over to rake the coals up around the pots that simmered on the fire in front of the wagon. Coming back, he resumed, "Then come these reunions; they ain't so bad, for the old man always gives me plenty of help, such as it is. I git to see and talk to fellers that I ain't seen in thirty-five years and that's sumpin'.

"Course, I ain't kickin' for I expected to work when I hired out, and I ain't begrudgin' them what they eat, for you know it would make me and the Old Man both sore as hell if we thought any man, woman, or child ever come to our wagon and didn't get their bellies full before they left. I just don't understand what it's all about."

"You just don't savvy this generation, Ab," I said. "It isn't beef and beans alone they're coming for. They have missed the glamor and romance of the cow country. You have lived it and you and these wagons are the last stand of the old order. It is color and romance they are looking for."

"I'll do anything I can to help 'em find anything they've lost," replied Ab as he rolled the ravelings from the flour sacks into a ball and pitched them over his shoulder into the chuck box, "but I had a dang sight rather be back about thirty years cookin' for a straight cow outfit and cussin' the hoss wrangler for rustlin' green wood.

"In the spring soon as we killed a fat calf I'd build the boys up a son-of-a-gun that would make the world look level. Some of them would come in with their shirts full of wild plums and I'd cook 'em a cobbler that would keep 'em from wantin' to go to town until fall."

"Speaking of a son-of-a-gun," I said, "hasn't society coming to the wagons about caused that noble old dish to lose its real name? You don't dare call it by its real name or discuss the ingredients around these crowds, do you?"

"Generally speakin', yes it has," replied Ab, as he dusted the last crumb of smoking tobacco from a sack into the brown paper he held in his hand. "Over in our country which covers a part of three counties, and is populated mostly by old-timers and fellers who work for the outfit, we've solved the problem pretty well. Few years back old Tib Ellison, who taught school over in the nester settlement, run for congressman-at-large. He got himself elected by promisin' every man and most of the women folks a government job. When he got to Washington he found out that he didn't have any jobs to put out except a couple of shinnery post offices, both of which got mail twict a week. This left the other four or five hundred of his constituents pretty sore. Some time during the year, all of them ate at our wagon. When I know they are comin', I generally cook up a pot of son-of-a-gun and by common consent and agreement when one of them wants more of the dish, they have a little more of Congressman Ellison. Everybody nods in approval and knows that the old dish is being called by its rightful name without embarrassin' any ladies that might be present.

"When you stop to figger it though, there ain't nothin' so bad about a son-of-a-gun except its name and the yarns that has been told about it," said Ab meditatively. "It has always been told around that the dish is made up of a little bit of every part of a new-killed beef even to a little of the hair. I never made any that way nor never saw a cook that did. That recipe must have been figgered by some of the old cooks that worked for the outfits that trailed up through the Nation where the Indians used to hang around the wagon to beg coffee, sugar, or canned goods, and clean up where the outfit had killed a beef. Up in the Otoe or Sac and Fox country they had bunches of Indians they called 'gut eaters' to separate them from the better class ones. You could kill a beef, around a bunch of them and if you didn't hurry, you couldn't find enough of the insides to make a son-of-a-gun with five minutes after it quit kickin'.

"I figured some South Texas cook got sore at a bunch of the 'gut eaters' and mixed them a stew seasoned with cayenne pepper and them Indians tended to the namin'. The son-of-a-gun the boys liked best was made up of the liver, heart, sweetbreads, marrow guts, and brains of a fresh-killed beef. Everything but the brains was cut into fine pieces and put in the pot to stew. You had to be careful in proportionin' the liver or you would get it too bitter. When the meat parts were done, we stewed the brains in a separate pan with enough flour to make them pretty thick. When they had cooked until they were beady lookin' they were added to the stew pot as thickenin'. Salt and pepper were the only seasonings added—plenty of pepper. When it was all done, it was a grey lookin' dish with the pepper showin' plum plain against the thickenin'. It didn't look so hot to an outsider, but a bunch of hungry hands could sop up one and holler for more before you could say Jack Robinson. Everybody would like it if it wasn't for the marrow guts and the fact that its name rhymes so well with witch."

The shadows had grown long and the crowds were streaming out from the arena and still Ab talked. "I been wonderin'," he said, "if we was to go back to usin' a pack mule if as many of these romance hunters would gather around it as they do these new-fangled chuck wagons with flies as big as Mollie Bailey's old show tent, ice water, and canned goods. There ain't near as much romance settin' around an old red pack mule eatin' bread you cooked by wrappin' the dough around a green stick and holdin' it over the coals while you fished greasy sow belly out of a fryin' pan with your pocket knife with the other hand.

"Maybe if some of these outfits would buy groceries like they used to when fortunes were being made in the cow business, it would slow the romance hunters up some and help the business. First few years I cooked the shoppin' consisted of so many pounds of flour, so many pounds of Arbuckle, a sack of beans, a sack of salt, a few pounds of black pepper, and five gallons of kerosene for the lanterns. We had a little sow belly to season the beans but we did all of our fryin' in tallow for we was raisin' the beef and tallow ourselves.

"Never will forget what old Ab Blocker told the city feller when he asked him how he accounted for his good health and old age. Says Ab, 'I always et a big beef steak once a day. The meat keeps you strong and the taller keeps your guts greased up so they work good.' Yes, sir, give an outfit plenty of good beef and even fair bread and you won't have much gripin'," added the old cook as he put an oven lid on the fire.

"Some of the outfits went to furnishin' sugar sooner than ours did; it was long in '95 before our outfit would let me buy any sugar."

The last of the crowd had left the grandstand. Over across the road at the dance platform, the fiddlers were tuning up for a square dance that would run until the east was red. Ab rose, stamped to shake his pants leg down and remarked, "It's dang near dark, I guess them $30.00-a-month cow hands have gone into town to fill up on 3.2 and hamburgers. I'm going over to that dance and shake a leg—maybe—if there are any widders over there." He added as he started away, "There's biscuits in the big oven and some beans in the pot, git you a cup of coffee and by-the-way, there's a bucket of mighty good lick there in the box—ribbon cane that the Old Man sent out special for this reunion. Help yourself and when you git through put up the chuck box lid and hook the snap through the staple."

As he climbed through the fence that enclosed the encampment, he called back to me, "If you've got any friends from Fort Worth, Dallas, or Austin, that hasn't ever et at a chuck wagon, bring 'em around; love to have 'em."

Any discussion of chuck wagons will bring out a dozen stories on the alleged cussedness of the old-time chuck wagon cook. It is doubtful if a third that number would be developed in behalf of the fine old fellows who moved a wagon with bedding and cooking outfit enough for a dozen men twice a day, and had three hot meals ready when the outfit came in. About the best the defense could get would be: "He was a danged good cook, but contrary as hell."

Perhaps it would be fair then, to present here, a couple of stories, one tending to show the attitude of the cook as to the sanctity of the circle he reigned over—from the tip of the wagon tongue to the chuck-box lid—the value he placed upon it, and his utter indifference to criticism, even from the boss. The other may serve to pierce the hard shell with which the old wagon cook seemed to have been armored.

Over in Foard County Dick Hill cooked for an outfit until he was looked upon as one of the family. One summer the outfit was split up to brand calves and receive small bunches of yearlings that were being bought up from nesters and "little men." To serve both crews the wagon was camped in the Blue Hole country. A long-aged brindle milk-pen yearling took up with the wagon, using it for shade and salting himself by chewing on the work team's collar pads. No amount of scaring or liberal application of hot water could persuade him to stay away from the wagon. One afternoon when the dishes were washed up Dick walked down along the creek and returned to the wagon with a half-dried beef hide, a dozen empty tomato cans, and a ten-pound lard bucket half-filled with smooth washed gravel. With awl and stay wire he fringed the hide with the cans, placing a little gravel in each and squeezing the tops together to prevent the gravel from dropping out.

From the supply of mule feed in the front end of the wagon, he poured a generous portion near the right front wheel and invited the yearling to eat, at the same time tying the loose end of a stake rope around his neck and securing it to a wagon spoke. As he ate, Dick, with the aid of more wire, attached the can-fringed hide to the year-ling's tail, not loosely, but wired firmly to the burr-infested bush. While

the yearling was enjoying the last of his feed Dick reached into the
tool box on the front end gate to bring forth a pint bottle of turpentine
and a long red cob. As the yearling finished, Dick applied the turpen-
tine-soaked cob—with pressure—where it would be most effective,
slipped the stake rope off, and headed the brindle yearling out across
the flats.

A couple of miles out the yearling ran through the day's branding
which was being loose herded until cows and calves got together.
These he scattered to the four winds, and passed on over the ridge
to the beef pasture, where a thousand or more prime beef steers
awaited the few days when the market would steady and they would
be sent to town. The brindle made an opening in the fence where he
struck it and began to slow down with the idea of joining his fellow
creatures. He was a pariah among them. They fled at his approach.
Not only did they flee before him that night, but for days and nights
they circled the beef pasture, stopping neither for food nor drink lest
the rattling terror overtake them.

The Old Man came out to ride through the beef and estimate his
profits. These he found badly shrunken, due to the brindle. It took a
day to work the beef pasture and get the remainder of the hide and
cans off the yearling and another three to get the nervous steers back
to eating. The day the job was finished, the Old Man rode into the
wagon early with the idea of administering, privately, a mild rebuke to
the cook. Easing around to where the latter was working his dough
he began, "Dick, that prank you played with that brindle yearling—
You hadn't oughta done that—It's cost me four days time—I'll bet
them beef steers have run off four or five dollars apiece—Wouldn't be
surprised if that danged foolishness didn't cost me five thousand
dollars."

Dick said nothing. His eyes strayed toward the out-stretched wagon
tongue where four new yellow collar pads hung in good array, then
swept the sacred circle around the wagon to find no sign of recent
bovine occupancy. Between thumb and forefinger he pulverized the
one small lump that his unerring fingers found in the otherwise fault-
less batch of dough. As he dissolved this he observed—not to the Old
Man, but to the world in general, "By God, it was wuth it to me."

Probably George Patullo, brilliant young Canadian writer who came
to the Cap-Rock country years ago to work with its cow outfits and
write stories of them that are not equaled, caught the soft side and
truer inner feeling of the old-time chuck-wagon cook in his story, "Old

Sam." Sam was night wheeler in the chuck-wagon team of a Canadian River cow outfit years ago. In a soft moment, the cook, noted for his contrariness and efficiency, had dropped into the habit of feeding him bread scraps around the chuck wagon, probably because when the going got hard in the sandy streams that abound along the Canadian he knew he could reach down with his boot heel, kick Old Sam on the rump, and get an extra thousand pounds on the doubletree. Then, too, as men do who work alone, he had fallen into the habit of discussing his past, present, and future with him and enjoying it because Old Sam never talked back nor disagreed with him.

One evening when the move had been long and supper was likely to be late, the cook, while the dough was rising in the pan, walked to the creek for a bucket of water. Returning he found Sam with the entire batch of dough entangled in tooth and lip, trying to disengage it by rubbing it into the dirt. Exasperated, with the aid of pot hook and language thrice as hot as his oven lids, he boogered the old mule far out into the flats, where he was swept into a band of passing mustangs.

All summer long the cook mourned his loss and worked a half-broken cow horse to replace Old Sam. When the wagon pulled in that fall, he packed a little grub in a flour sack along with a few oats, and started afoot to the range of the mustangs to "walk" Old Sam down. After he located them, there followed a week in which he kept the mustangs from watering or grazing. He came upon the band in the moonlight at the end of the week, gaunt and leg-weary—unable to go another foot. Old Sam, scenting the cook, walked dejectedly, with flopping ears, toward him to nuzzle his shoulder. As a finale, Patullo pictures the old mule with the cook's arm over his neck. As they start the long walk back to headquarters, he pats him affectionately and says, "You pore old devil, you ought to a-knowed I wasn't half as mean and mad as I made out like I wuz."

The Sweetwater Wagon

The Chuck Wagon—rolling kitchen and traveling home of the old-time cowboy, successor to the pack mule of South Texas "cow hunts," now nearly out of the picture as a necessity—is not forgotten and will not be forgotten as long as the guard of old bowlegged boys who called the Wagon "home" from the late 70's to the early 90's live and can find one to gather around.

To a layman, a wagon is a wagon, and as such means only a method of transportation, whether it be used to haul wood, feed, water, or what not; but to a shaggy-browed old-timer, the Wagon meant his capitol and his home.

The outfit might have a freight wagon, wood wagon, bed or calf wagon, each bearing its proper prefix. But when one was called the Wagon, it meant fire, food, dry clothes, companionship, and to it the cow hand pledged his allegiance once he had thrown his bedroll into it and put his calomel, quinine, or black draught into one of the cook's handy drawers. The companionship, it is true, might be marred by the

general cussedness of the cook, whose efficiency as such was gauged
by his contrariness. My own daddy, an old-timer now gone, left unfinished an argument of years' standing with his old friend Luther Clark
as to which assayed highest in general cussedness, an old-time stagecoach driver or an old cow-camp cook. I know that this is still a moot
question among all old-timers. But let the cook be cranky, just as long
as he was clean, a good cook, and always had it ready when the boys
got in. Some of them always saw to it that he got away to town when
his turn came; and nobody could pick on him. Many a good cow hand
selected the outfit he wanted to work for by the reputation of its Wagon
more than for the matter of pay, for, as I have said before, it was his
home, his politics, and his destiny. His Wagon was always referred to
as "*the* Wagon" or "*our* Wagon," while neighboring outfits were referred
to as the "O X Wagon," or "3 D Wagon," but never as the "O X or 3-D
Chuck Wagon."

Forty-three years ago Jake Raines cast his lot and bedroll with the
Spur Wagon, and twenty years later when the Wagon, land, cattle, and
horses were sold to the Swenson Land and Cattle Company, Jake went
with the Wagon, and is with it now, possibly the oldest cow hand in
the point of continuous service with one Wagon in the state. Then there
is "Scandalous" John Selman, who has been boy and man with the Spur
and S M S Wagons since he could ride alone, but that and how he
acquired the name of "Scandalous" John is another story. There are
many more whose records nearly equal these two, and there is no
record of how many men have died in service with the Wagon and
outfit they started out with.

That this sentiment toward the Wagon existed and still exists among
real old-timers is evidenced by an organization in California known as
the Old Time Chuck Wagon Trailers, which has a membership of over
500 old-time cowboys who meet near Los Angeles twice a year, and by
an organization in our own state known as the Sweetwater Chuck Wagon
whose membership consists of some 175 old-time and active cowmen.

Sweetwater, in the late 80's and early 90's, was a mecca for Wagons
and cowboys, and was the home of a great many cattlemen prominent
in their day, and some still active in the cattle business and other lines.
While no Wagons roll along its paved streets now, or pull up to Myres'
Saddlery or Connell's General Store to load up with the sow-belly and
red beans, so essential to a chuck wagon, descendants of these cattle
kings of a few decades ago, many of whom as children ate, slept, and
spent such time as they were not in school at daddy's Wagon, and in

mature years, assumed places with their daddy's outfit, live here and cherish memories of the days when Sweetwater was a cow-town.

There is another group of graying, bowlegged, old men who were in their prime in Sweetwater's Wagon days, most of whom at some time were employees of ranch owners living in or near Sweetwater, or who at some time were stray men for some of the company-owned ranches north and south of Sweetwater, who, with the general break-up of the cattle business, elected to stay here and pick up a new line of endeavor. Some have become wealthy and now enjoy every comfort in their old age by dint of thriftiness and that resourcefulness always characteristic of a cow hand. Others acquired small farms, while some, not quite so fortunate, still work at day labor or small jobs as opportunity affords, but an old-timer can spot one of them as far as he can see him, whether he be on a horse, in a Packard, or laboring on the streets, for to one who knows his stuff, they bear a brand as indelible as was ever burned on a steer.

It is a blending of these two groups, sprinkled with a few active younger cattlemen and honorary members entitled to such distinction through some connection or achievement in the past with the cattle industry, that have formed the organization I am telling you of, known as the Sweetwater Chuck Wagon, whose by-laws state that the purpose of the organization is to preserve the traditions and customs of the old-time cow outfit and Chuck Wagon, and who cover the matter of dues with a single line—"The hat will be passed from time to time as necessity demands." I imagine, in writing this part of the by-laws, somebody had in mind that it would give a more affluent member an opportunity to drop in an extra dollar for some less fortunate old cow hand whom he had worked with or for in the old days. For around this Wagon there is no discussion of wealth or present values; when they are together, they are once more just an outfit living in the past. That the organization might operate along well ordained lines, they elect a wagon boss, wrangler, cook, and hoodlum, and from among their members an outfit of nine men to handle their affairs and say when and where the Wagon should be camped.

That the organization might have the proper equipment and historical background, the Newman brothers, Cap, Auti, and Mose, sons of the late Jim Newman, pioneer cattleman, sheriff, and breeder of some of the world's finest race horses, tendered the use of the chuck box and equipment used by Newman senior on his D Z Ranch at Sylvester, Fisher County, Texas, and later on the South Plains and in New

Mexico. Cap Newman, eldest son of Jim Newman, says that the box was built at Sylvester in 1884 at the time his father was moving a portion of his cattle from Fisher County to the South Plains, to what later became the Yellow House Division of the famous X I T Ranch. Jim Newman, on arriving there, gave buffalo hunters, whom he found already on the ground, $60 for the dugout they were occupying and the privilege of using as much of that portion of Texas as he wanted to. Later, when the state traded land to the Capitol Syndicate Company for the building of the present state capitol, the D Z headquarters were moved to near where Portales, New Mexico, is now located, better known as Salt Lake then, where it continued to operate until 1896, when the ranch and cattle were sold to the Curtis brothers, who operated it for several years, Newman bringing his Wagon, horses, and boys back to Fisher County. The Newman brothers are still actively engaged in the cattle business on the original Newman Ranch in Fisher County. The box in use has been encamped with such Wagons as the X I T, V V N, L F D, and Turkey Tracks—cow outfits who have contributed much to cattle history and the settlement of a vast empire. A wagon of age and in keeping with the box was secured, and when the equipment of water barrels, *morales,* branding irons, hobbles, and stake ropes were added, the Wagon is as complete as any which went on a work or up the trail.

In addition to the spring and fall meetings held each year somewhere near Sweetwater, the Wagon visits any convention or celebration in West Texas where cowmen are to be found. It assisted with the Golden Jubilee at Wichita Falls, providing a Chuck-Wagon dinner for hundreds of old-time cowmen, Kiowa and Comanche Indians, Texas Rangers, and buffalo hunters. It was placed in the lobby of a leading hotel in Fort Worth for a week during the Cattle Raisers' Convention, and to it as they do at the big Stamford Cowboy Reunion each year, came riders and range bosses of the 70's and 80's to meet and renew the friendships of what is considered by a great many writers the most romantic age of the cattle industry.

The Wagon box bears dozens of brands of old-time and active cow outfits. When it is camped, a running iron is kept in the fire at all times, and old-timers are invited to burn their own or their outfit's brands upon it.

When at its headquarters in Sweetwater, the association, its Wagon, and equipment are often hosts to the boys 4-H Clubs, or any organization that tends to develop the cattle industry.

The original organization consisted of some sixty-five active and ex-cattlemen, but as time goes on, eligible members from Montana to the Texas Coast are being added. Among the interesting members are former Ranger Captain Tom Hickman; Clyde Burnett, owner of the 9 9 Ranch in Knox County; Claude Jeffers, thirty-two years with the Matador Wagon, and now its wagon boss. Among the honorary or advisory members are: J. E. Boog-Scott of Fort Worth, J. Ealy Moore, a former trail boss for the Capitol Syndicate (X I T) Ranch; J. Frank Dobie of Austin, and W. G. Swenson of the S M S Land and Cattle Company.

Among the real patriarchs of the organization are Julian Moody, former range boss for the Worsham Land and Cattle Company's R 2 Ranch; Walter Trammell of the old 9 R Ranch; Jim Chinn, a former O S Wagon boss; R. A. Weatherby of the 1 8 Ranch; Ben Jones, who came from Fort Griffin to Sweetwater killing buffalo when the first cowboys arrived; and Tump Thornton, of whom an oil painting graces the lobby of the Stephen F. Austin Hotel in Austin, Texas, bearing the inscription "The Most Typical Old Time Texas Cowboy."

And so in the spring and fall, when the Sweetwater Wagon is camped along the creek whose name it bears or along Trammell Lakes, and the evening shadows have grown long, tall tales are told of old days along the Cap Rock, Double Mountain, or Croton breaks, and around the firelight old hands like Julie Moody, Ealy Moore, Jim Chinn, Walter Trammell—all veterans of the Montana and Wyoming Trail—tell stories of Tascosa nights, stampedes, and swollen streams, and recount the prowess of pet cutting, roping, and circling horses. And always Julie Moody tells a tale of his top cutting horse and R 2 pony named Gotch, acclaimed the best cutting horse of his day. Gotch's greatest achievement came at a roundup near where Chillicothe, Texas, now stands, where Julie, as Wagon boss, was trimming up a herd for the trail. In bringing a two-year-old heifer down alongside the herd in a run toward the cut, he crossed the path of another two-year-old heifer being brought out of the herd. Gotch jumped completely over the outbound heifer without losing sight of his own quarry, or, for that matter, without losing his stride.

Just out in the shadows, on stake rope, in hobbles, or with dragging reins, there grazes a phantom mount of Gotches, O X Yellows, Black Nigs, Arbuckles, and Brown Jugs, each with an ear cocked toward the Wagon as if to see if they are being properly credited with their achievements.

The Association

Falling as it did just before the "rise of grass" in Texas, when the Texas cowman had had a chance to inventory his cattle as to number and condition and to plan his spring work—branding, delivery dates, and usual matters of ranching business—the three-day Texas and Southwestern Cattlemen's Association convention always came at a time when people were most relaxed. Men who worked day and night without intermission for twelve months out of the year, with no break other than a visit to town every two weeks looked forward to convention week as a time of relaxation and an opportunity to rub shoulders with their neighbors and old-timers whom they had not seen since trail-driving days. The long winter was about over, their cattle had wintered and required no special attention, and they were trusting to the Lord that rains would come when they were due.

The convention enabled the Northwestern buyer to get his requirements "laid in" for his year's business. The steers, yearlings, two- and three-year-olds were sold by the head with a 10 per cent cut. Thousands upon thousands of these were shipped each May and early June in fulfillment of trades made in the hotel lobbies during the convention. Sales were of two classifications: "straight mark and brand," which meant the entire steer output of the ranch or brand; and "put up" herds, sold by traders and speculators who made up their offerings from the smaller bunches of cattle owned by "little men." In the case of the former, the buyer seldom went to the seller's ranch more than one time to see his cows and range. After that, he bought the herd at the convention "sight unseen," depending wholly on the seller's integrity and his own knowledge of range conditions which had prevailed during the year. In the case of "put up" herds, the purchaser exercised more caution because such herds varied greatly in ages and uniformity.

Sales at the convention each year invariably set prices that would prevail for that season on steers. In addition to the activities outlined above, the convention served as a meeting place for a more local trade, fellows who "went to Kansas each year" with a string of steers or Texas and Oklahoma fellows who ran steers on their ranches, buying them as yearlings and selling them as two- and three-year-olds. Many large strings of South Texas stock cattle changed hands to stock the North Texas and Panhandle pastures which had not as yet reached their maximum of cattle. A great many of the larger ranches themselves changed ownership as a result of trades made during the conventions.

The fact that the Association had expanded its activities to cover the entire state gave added interest to the convention as it brought the Southwest Texas cowman and the "coast fellows" as they were referred to in those days, into closer contact with the North Texas and Plains fellows to trade and participate in Association activities.

The conventions had a social as well as business significance for the cattle industry. To them came the cowmen's families, wives, sons, and daughters, to visit, shop, and be entertained by the ladies of the host city on a lavish scale while their men folk talked of cows, prices, and the politics of the organization. Local department stores, aware of the purchasing power of the visitors, made special preparations by filling their shelves and cases with fashion's latest modes in coats, gowns, and millinery. Eastern fashion manufacturers sent their top sales people to assist their local accounts and to book orders for future delivery. The Southwest's leading jewelers and manufacturers sent consignments of diamonds, pearls, and manufacturer's art to be put on display in hotel lobbies. Who could tell—romance might develop, as if often did, between the sons and daughters of the Southwest cattle people, or the "old man" might suddenly decide to take "Mama" something "pretty nice" if he had left her at home or to "fix her up" as good as the best if he had her along.

Preparations to meet the demands of the male contingent of visitors were not so varied: a few additional Stetson hats, perhaps, and a goodly supply of the salt-and-pepper suits much in favor with the cowmen of those days. An ex-saloon keeper of that era told me here in Fort Worth a few days ago that he always ordered a straight carload of rye and bourbon liquor in advance of the convention. He added, somewhat to their credit, that the cattlemen were not such heavy drinkers but there were "such a helluva' lot of them." He further stated that there was little or no demand for fancy mixed drinks, most of them taking it straight or in the form of "toddy."

The late Leon Gross, who for more than a half century was connected with Washer Brothers, as clerk, manager, and finally president, probably knew as many southwestern cattlemen as any man in America. Before the days of highly specialized reservation services and Chamber of Commerce convention visitors' bureaus, Gross served in these capacities as a favor to his cowmen friends, making hotel reservations for them in advance of the convention dates, securing theater tickets, cashing checks, or assisting in any way possible. On one occasion shortly before his death, he told me that as nearly as he could figure more than three million dollars of cowmen's checks had passed through his hands for purchases or had been okayed by him for customers who needed identification. Of this amount he does not recall that a single one of them ever "bounced back" on him. Until the time of his death a few months ago, he took great pride in maintaining a list of the present generation of cowmen to whom he had sold their first long trousers and Stetson hats. Nothing gave him more pleasure than to have these men visit the store and recall that fact to him. I am indeed proud that my name is among them. Fathers sending their sons to Fort Worth alone for the first time would advise them that if they ran short of funds or found themselves in need of advice or in a "jam," they should hunt up Mr. Gross. He was a loyal supporter of the Association, beloved by all of its members. Insofar as I know, he never owned a single cow, but certainly for the love he held for the southwestern cowmen and their families and the many favors he did for them over a long period of years, he is entitled to honorable mention in any chronicle of their activities.

With the men folk, especially the stags who attended the convention, the entertainment was planned on a much broader scale than that provided for the lady visitors. Let's drop back for a moment and analyze this type of visitor. The "big fellows" came early and established themselves in the hotels; these maintained a certain amount of dignity by virtue of their position in the industry and their mellowing ages, but before the end of the convention their breaths all smelled alike. Some of them maintained homes in the convention city which gave them some advantage over the outsiders in the matter of entertaining visiting friends and serving as co-hosts with the local entertainment committee.

From the back country came a host of "little men" to hobnob with the leaders and "sorter get an idea of what yearlings are gonna' go at this year" and to seek advice and counsel from the "big fellows" who had achieved success. Many of the so-called "little men" had in other years worked as "hands" for the bigger fellows, and relied heavily on their judgment. I have made some distinction here between the "big fellow" and the "little man." This difference in station was never apparent during convention; in fact, the contacts were of a most democratic type. The bigger the man, the more he seemed to take pride in the fact that the smaller fellow and his success was partly of his making. This was more pronounced in those days than at the present time.

For a week before the convention, throughout the cow country the fellows had been "fixin' up" at home, with a new suit, hat, boots, and at least one good necktie in anticipation of the trip. I recall that when I was about thirteen years of age, I accompanied my father to the leading department store in our little cow-town when he was bent on his annual "fixin' up" preparation for attending the 1899 convention in Fort Worth. En route to town, he gave considerable and serious thought to whether or not he should purchase a pair of shoes for the occasion. "If I do," he argued, "it will be the first time I have owned a pair of them since I came to Texas from Ohio in 1876. I was married to your ma in a good pair of shop-made boots that old man Jordan made for me in Ardmore." As I recall, he compromised finally on a pair of low-topped bootees with elastic in the sides which were just coming into vogue at the time as a boon to old cowmen who had taken to riding buggies more than they did horseback. By the way, I have an acquaintance who, man and boy, has ridden and handled cattle by the thousands all of his life and has never owned a pair of boots (name on request).

Friends would pair off weeks in advance in and around the town's local "bull pen" or along the shady side of the First National and plan what they would do when they got to the convention. Two old cronies from my home town always started their planning with an agreement to confine their drinking to splitting a quart of bourbon each time they felt the need of a drink. Back in the "bull pen" after the convention was over, they admitted a little sheepishly that the plan worked all right until about "three hours of the sun" the second day when they went to splitting a bottle of white soda pop.

Trains poured the cowmen into the convention city by the hundreds and the hacks and streetcars did a thriving business getting them to the hotel serving as convention headquarters. In the hotel they found representatives of the commission companies and old friends who greeted them heartily—so heartily in fact that had one of them attempted to whisper a confidence the listener would have had to have been at least two blocks away for his statement to have borne any semblance to a whisper. The visitor's first chore was to hunt up the Association desk, register, pay his dues, and receive his convention badge—an ornate affair of white satin ribbon topped by a gilded steer's head, with necessary convention data printed on the satin badge. No more had he left the desk than he was supplied with an equally ornate badge pinned on him by representatives of the city seeking the next year's convention. Almost equally nice ones were given him by contenders for the meetings two and three years hence. Add to these some pretty nifty offerings in the nature of lapel buttons and more steer heads provided by representatives of the commission companies and river markets, and he could put to shame a returned veteran of the Pacific campaign who has been awarded all the decorations that a grateful government and its people can bestow upon him. (Incidentally, at the Stamford Cowboys' Reunion a few weeks ago, a very, very dear old-time friend of mine told me, more than half seriously, that his nephew had been awarded a decoration for valor with four bunches of "shinnery.")

Catching sight of himself in a bar mirror which reflected him in all of his splendor, the cowman would be reminded that he needed a shave and that his boots needed "blackening," so he repaired to the barber shop to join others of his kind in looking over the current issue of the Police Gazette with its lurid cover and intimate pictures as he awaited his turn. Once in the barber chair, at the barber's insistence, he threw caution to the wind and told the barber "to give him everything," which in those days included shave, haircut, shampoo, and plenty of tonic. This was before the days of marcelled and highly persuasive lady manicurists. Rather sheepishly he submitted to having his straw-colored mustache "blackened" a little—75 per cent of the men had hirsute adornments in those days, varying in color from a corn yellow to the deepest of black, most of them beginning to be streaked with gray. None of these was of the eyebrow type in vogue today. His eyebrows, closely clipped, received the same color treatment. He sort of hoped that all this would wear off before he got home, for the stay-at-homes would sure "cod the hell out of him" if it didn't.

With these preliminaries attended to, he followed the crowd to a local auditorium—"hall" it was called in those days—where the convention was in session. He was a little late for the opening session, having missed the mayor's address of welcome which had included a great many pseudo cow-camp terms, but which was none the less hearty and which conveyed the fact that the town was theirs to have, hold, and use as they saw fit. It also hinted at certain entertainment to be provided for their edification that the mayor felt sure would meet with their hearty approval. The cowman was kinda' proud of the way old Jim Callan answered the mayor and got right back at him with a good story. He listened attentively to the president's address and to the fellows who followed him to talk intelligently and knowingly of the problems confronting the cowmen—freight rates, ticks, Texas fever, cottonseed cake, the packers, and the trend toward improved range cattle. Particularly interesting to him was the secretary's report covering the finances of the organization, the work of the inspectors, and the number of new members added since the last meeting. Equally interesting was the Association attorney's report on the number and value of cattle returned to their owners, and the thieves apprehended and convicted during the past year. He expressed the opinion to his seat neighbor that "if we fellows will stay back of the Association and Old Sam, they'll break up stealing and send the last one of them damn cow thieves to the pen."

He and his partner straggled back to the hotel lobby, which by this time had taken on the atmosphere of a Board of Trade or Grain Exchange session. Most of the buyers and sellers had finished their sparring and word of deals, such as "the Pitchforks bought Jim Mc-Adams' yearlings at $16.00 and Bill Richards sold the 3 D yearlings to John Molesworth for $17.00," begin to get about. This set prices on two classifications for one area. After listening around a bit for news of deals showing the trend on South and Southwest Texas cattle, as well as those from the Midland, El Paso, and Davis Mountain countries, the cowmen began trading in real earnest, with commission men working overtime between buyer and seller. Many of the deals between the larger buyers and sellers were negotiated privately, between themselves. Many not too old-timers will recall the genial Pat Paffrath, who as a commission agent in Fort Worth, made the conventions in Texas over a long period of years. Equally well known was Bill Davis, Fort Worth livestock commission man, who for a number of years served as the city's mayor, thereby earning the sobriquet of "Cowboy Mayor." On hand always, as long as they lived, were the veterans, George W. Saunders and Lee Russell of Menard, who annually handled thousands of steers on his own account. To the credit and integrity of both buyer and seller at the conventions it may be said that thousands upon thousands of cattle whose value ran well into millions of dollars were contracted and delivered without a scrap of paper, guarantee, or deposit to bind the deal—just a man's hand-shake and word that he would deliver or receive as agreed.

It will be recalled that the mayor in his address of welcome had indicated that there would be entertainment on the second evening for the visitors. For the ladies this took the form of open houses or soirees as they were sometimes termed in those days. These were either held progressively in the homes of local cowmen or at the town's country club, which with its golf course was a comparatively new institution to the Southwest. They were elaborate affairs, well in keeping with social requirements of the time. They brought together the elite of the cattle country femininity and were productive of much good will and widening of acquaintance. It is well to remember that due to travel limitations, household duties, and the tendency to raise larger families then than now, feminine attendance was much smaller than in the present day of automobiles, buses, and air travel.

This naturally left the "stags" or unencumbered men in the majority. These were provided entertainment of such robust nature that it left little to be desired in the opinion of those in attendance. Usually this took the form of a "smoker" held in some convenient beer garden—in Fort Worth the gathering was held in one occupying the site of the present Texas Electric plant just north of the courthouse. Once inside the park, the visitors wended their way along an avenue flanked by foaming kegs of beer presided over by a score or more of Negroes in white coats who drew and served the foaming beverage to passers-by as though their very lives and hopes of future success depended on how much of the beverage they could force on the visitors. The avenue led to long tables on which were piled heaps of sandwiches of every variety, flanked by huge platters of every conceivable food that might fit into the menu of beer and "what do you like with it." Negroes serving these viands worked with the same nervous energy as those serving the beer. Incidentally, the beer servers had been moved to a new vantage point and plied their vocation at a battery of beer kegs (full) adjacent to the food with the same zeal they had along the avenue leading to the table. They had added the passing out of cigars to their efforts. These they pressed upon the visitors in large quantities, even urging "boss" to "put a few in your pocket for tomorrow." By this time the affair had reached a state justifying its name of "smoker"; so dense was the cigar smoke that it made the pale and flickering gaslights almost indistinguishable.

When food, beer, and smoke had settled somewhat, and the visitors had also settled on seats improvised from two-by-sixes and beer kegs, a near master of ceremonies took over to announce that a program would be presented. The roar of conversation and laughter which would have rivaled half a dozen highlines in a seventy-mile wind subsided to a mere hum in anticipation of what might be in store. A couple of local lads, introduced in due and ancient form, boxed a few rounds; by private agreement neither was knocked out, maimed, or injured in any way. Followed a battle royal, participated in by eight husky Negro boys who, also by private agreement on the part of seven of them, doubled up on the eighth and mauled him until the referee stopped them. Efforts of both boxers and battle royalists were received with boos, shouts, and advice to the contestants as how to best maim, murder, or dispose of his or their rivals. Needless to say, many of the remarks and much of the advice would be classified as unprintable in these blasé days. These events disposed of, a hush fell upon the audience as the master of ceremony announced that a young lady classical dancer, who had appeared before the crowned heads of Europe as well as in the harems of practically all the sultans of record, would now entertain them with interpretative dances. That old beer garden in the Trinity bottoms may not be the place where Salome danced, but the little red-headed gal with six of her seven veils missing who pinch hit for her sure filled in the gap. Her appearance on the platform was not greeted by the highly cultivated whistle effected by soldiers and sailors of today, but with lusty cow yells that had long rung throughout the Croton, Cuba, and Cap-Rock breaks and had rolled over the Great Staked Plains since the earliest roundups. Interspersed among the yells could be heard expressions such as "red-headed filly" and "catch her out for me," these being about the mildest that can be recalled at this late year. With this kind of encouragement from out front, probably augmented by a couple of shots of rye taken in back just before she entered, she proceeded to do her interpretative dance in a manner that would have put Salome to shame and have caused dismay to the Little Egypts of the eastern world. She did a strip tease in minutes less than it takes Gypsy Rose Lee to achieve the same thing, she added wiggles and twists that surpassed any effort heretofore seen at similar occasions. When she finally dragged her veil and herself from the stage, she had given them everything she had, but her victory was complete for if she was exhausted by her efforts her audience was equally exhausted and hoarse from twenty-five minutes of continuous yelling and back-slapping. The meeting gradually broke up after disposing of any beer left on hand, and it was generally agreed that a good time was had by all. The men who had succeeded in slipping away from their better halves gave as reason for their prolonged absence that they had been talking to "old man Akers who kinda' made out like he wanted to buy our outfit." The smoker was one of the things that the fellows didn't tell their home folks much about when they got back.

There may be some who if they read this article will recall the convention in Fort Worth some thirty-five years ago when they were initiated into the ranks of the "Knights of Bovina," and had the brand of that order "burned" onto their right hip as they struggled, bellowed, and begged like a "sleeper calf."

This particular year entertainment was apparently lagging a little. A few visitors with the idea of livening things up fell upon the idea of forming the organization. Headquarters were opened in a couple of rooms in the old Worth Hotel, since destroyed by fire. Word of the Order was passed around the lobbies with the hint that no loyal cow-man could exist and expect to do well if he did not become a member; candidates were plentiful. They appeared at the room designated as headquarters and were immediately accepted for membership, after which they were escorted into a second room designated as the "brand-ing pen" and bearing visual testimony that to all purposes and intents it was real corral and had been recently used as such—the evidence was there on the floor, along with a strong odor of burned hair.

Upon entering the room they were seized by a husky crew of bull-doggers who blindfolded, stripped, and threw them to the floor face down, but not until they had had opportunity to see a portable black-smith forge going full blast with half a dozen red-hot "B" branding irons showing in the coals. When they were stretched in approved branding-pen style with one man holding the head down and a couple more on the legs, the boss sang out "hot iron." There was considerable business of speeding the blower up and handing the iron to the boss who held it just near enough to the bare right hip of the victim to assure him that in reality it was a hot iron, after which it was exchanged for one that had been packed in ice until it was as cold as the other was hot. The cold iron was pressed firmly against the flesh of the victim while the hot iron was pressed into a bacon rind or piece of hide to get the proper odor and sizzling effect. To the victim the illusion was perfect, and he writhed and groaned in more agony than was ever experienced by a calf under the iron. Fortunately the illusion was not carried to the point of using the knife on his ears or elsewhere. Upon being released he made a beeline for the lobby, not in search of his mother but in search of a victim whom he might bring into the fold so that he could witness the "initiation." They were no respecters of person for the "big man" as well as the "little one" along with a fair number of town fellows who clamored for associate membership fell victim to the arguments advanced by charter members and earlier victims of the iron. It was horseplay pure and simple, but they loved it and indulged in it much as the cowman of today likes to "touch up" the railroad livestock agent or commission man with the electric prod pole when he gets in the way around the loading chutes.

They were great days, those old convention days, and I have digressed to add this chapter thinking it might be of interest to a few old-timers to whom it may recall memories long forgotten. Too, it is an epoch in the seventy-year life of the organization; a sort of cross section of its work in both a commercial and social way. I have made no attempt to describe any particular convention or convention city. What has been chronicled here has had its counterpart in Fort Worth, San Antonio, Dallas, Oklahoma City, or Corpus Christi. Men didn't get around so much in those days and they wanted to have a hell of a good time when they did—after business had been attended to.

Never Again

Each issue of cattle magazines and trade journals chronicles the passing of one or more old-time cowmen. When the last of them has gone, never again will the world know their like. Many of them have died in peace and plenty, surrounded by children and grandchildren, but more of them have died broken both in heart and finance.

It was tragic struggle for them to draw themselves in from an unfenced world where men did business on courage and faith, to barriers of barbed wire and the baffling intricacies of percentage, protein, adding machines, and modern efficiency.

Soon will be gone the last of the bluff, hearty cowmen who rode by the bank in the early spring to holler in the window to the portly, yellow-mustached cowman-banker with the Henry Clay collar and string tie (yeah, I am thinking about Uncle Dick Worsham of Henrietta), "I've got grass for about fifteen hundred more cattle than I'm runnin', and I'm goin' out and buy 'em. I don't know how much money I've got, but I'm goin' to check on you and when I'm through I'll come in and 'fix up'."

The banker, without pressing any buttons, summoning any clerks, or looking at the ledger, waved him on, for he knew that if he bought the needed cattle and every hoof and horn died before they reached the home pasture, he would come in and "fix up" just the same. The banker never sent out an inspector, either.

Some died on the ranches where they lived their lives, but most of them moved to town and "built" when the girls grew up and had to go to school. They ran their ranches from town, going out Monday morning and coming in Saturday night.

Those who lived in town foregathered in the saddle shop or along the south side of the First National to talk their own language, for theirs was not the language of the nester nor the implement dealer.

In the little cow-town between Red and Pease rivers where I grew up, there lived dozens of these old fellows. When one of them died, or, as his kind would say, "laid 'em down," they would put three or four of us boys on horses to go different ways into the Catfish, Hooley Ann, and Medicine Mound country with instructions to tell the cowmen who still lived on their ranches, and those out from town working, that "Old Mr. Jim Clements has died, and the buryin' will be at three o'clock tomorrow."

By noon next day, the street in front of and along the side of Mr. Jim Clements' house would be filled with saddled horses, Haynes ranch buggies, hacks, and buckboards, with a sprinkling of town surreys and phaetons. As a new arrival would drive up, hitch, and help his wife from buggy or hack, he would escort her to the front porch where she would join the women folks inside who were consoling Mis' Clements, and he, with the aversion of all cowmen for tears or show of emotion would join a dozen of his kind along the south side of the house. After answering the general inquiry from all present as to how his "stuff" had wintered and how his grass and water was, he would squat on his boot heels and drop into the general silence that prevailed.

On the upper end of the line, an old man with wrinkled face and eyes of blue would pause in his work of drawing the Moon brand in the dust with a broom weed, to observe, "I first knowed old man Jim when he brought his Swingin' C cattle in on the head of Squaw Creek in '78. I was holdin' a little bunch of cows there, and we throwed in and wintered together." After further meditation, he might add, "He was a real cowman, and an honest-to-God hand."

After another period of meditation, the little, old, bowlegged fellow with the run-over boot heels and the five cords on his hat band sweated together, would finish his job of tracing the Turkeytrack brand to say, "I had a little outfit that joined him on Salt Fork. He was a good neighbor and one man that never eat a bite of beef that he didn't own or pay for."

There followed a silence while three or four old fellows on the outer edge gave thought to this last statement, and fell to wondering silently which way the Heavenly cutting gate would send them if they were too particular about little things up there.

Rolling a brown cigarette at the lower end of the line, a fellow whose blue overalls and shoes placed him in the laboring class, but whose bowed legs and expressions catalogued him as a "hand" who had spent his life working with cattle, for other people, never acquiring any for himself, said, "I worked for him twenty years off'n on, and never heard him say a hard word about any man, or seen him whip a horse over the head." Pausing while he waited for his match to get into full flame, he added, "I helped pick his boy, Tom, up when he was killed over on the Lone Tree roundup ground. The old man never was the same after that."

Another, rising from the middle of the line to gaze west toward the blue hills of the Pease River Breaks, as though in fancy he could see a winding snake of cattle narrowed down for counting, passing between two men who "put their finger" on each one as it passed, dusted off his trousers, and stamped to shake a pants leg down that had risen above his boot top, addressed no one in particular, "I sold him my yearlin' steers for ten years hand runnin', and he took my count every time. I never asked him for a forfeit, for his word was as good as his bond."

Subdued rustling from within the house, and the soft strains of "In the Sweet Bye and Bye" gave notice that the services in the house had begun. As the group mounted the porch to stand with bared heads, the local banker, falling in step with old man Dodson from down on Mule Creek, said "It's fine for a man to die and leave his family provided for like old Jim did. He didn't owe a livin' man a dime and had money in the bank."

After a song or two, pallbearers made up of cowmen friends and town fellows that had come to know and love old man Jim, would carry the casket out to be taken to the church that the old man and his kind had helped build in the years when the grass was lush and beef was high. In the church, Brother Clark would tell the newcomers of the deceased's sterling qualities and what he and his kind had contributed toward the settling and upbuilding of the country.

After he had offered words of consolation to the widow and children, and while the ladies of the choir were singing "There Is a Land That Is Fairer Than Day," the old fellows who had sat outside Jim's would rise and march down the aisle, their old Stetsons touched to their left breast and their boot heels beating a requiem on the wood floor as they filed by for their last look and farewell to a good cowman, a man who never spoke a hard word to anyone, whose word was as good as his bond, and who left his family well provided for.

Index

Aberdeen, Scotland: cattlemen from, 232
Abilene, Kansas: 56, 217; red-light district of, 35; 80 John Wallace in, 164
—, Texas: 196; cattle drive to, 9; rustlers near, 21; railroad through, 38; cotton gin in, 66; W. J. Bryant of, 261
Ada, Oklahoma: 199
Adair, Joe: in Colorado City, 51; shipping of cattle by, 62. SEE ALSO Carey, Adair, and Solomon.
Adams, Judge: at Colorado City, 53
Adams, (rancher): and 3 D Ranch, 130
Adams, Andy: *The Log of a Cowboy* by, 186–187
Adirondack Mountains: E. P. Swenson's home in, 127
Adobe Walls, Texas: fight at, 224
Africa: wool production in, 96; Dick Walsh in, 103
agencies, Indian. SEE reservations, Indian
agriculture: effect of, on springs, 22; on Plains, 27; near Colorado City, 34; by nesters, 66; Tom Burnett on, 78. SEE ALSO farming
Akers, Old Man: 309
Alabama and Texas Cattle Company: 43
Alamosa Camp: of Waggoner Ranch, 85–86
Albright, Fred: with Waggoner Ranch, 86
Alice, Texas: 80
Alley, R. T.: with Matador Ranch, 135
Alvarado, Texas: 250
Amarillo, Texas: railroad to, 48; mail service to, 51; as cattle shipping point, 61, 65; development of, 67; Englishmen in, 103; Fred Horsbrugh in, 103; John Arnot in, 104; Bud Arnett in, 131; Francklyn Land and Cattle Company near, 215; cemeteries near, 229; barbecue in, 277
America, South: John Molesworth in, 94, 110; Dick Walsh in, 103; use of horses in, 187; cattle dip from, 223
Anderson, John: in Greer County, 215
Andrews County: in Colorado City trade area, 41
animals, wild: on Cap Rock, 27; on

Mosquero Ranch, 90; on Hendrix and Royer Ranch, 201–202
Anson, Billy: and British Army horses, 106
Anson, Texas: "Cowboys' Christmas Ball" at, 54
Apache Indians: 197; at Hueco Tanks, 15; raids of, 34; sale of cattle of, 77–78; in San Simone Valley, 115
Arbuckle Mountains: springs in, 17; Hendrix and Royer Ranch in, 198, 199, 258
archeologists: on Hueco Tanks, 15
Archer County: Waggoner Ranch in, 85; E. H. East of, 211; cattle from, 215
Ardmore, Oklahoma: 203, 304; Sig Simons in, 65; Hendrix and Royer Ranch near, 198, 199; cottonseed oil mill in, 199; Federal courts in, 209; Bill Moore in, 250; Hendrix home in, 258; horses in, 260
Argentina: John Molesworth's trip to, 110; cattle dip from, 223
Arizona: ranching in, 4, 6, 115, 119, 135, 197, 212; boot-hill cemeteries in, 228; farming in, 252
Arizona Breaks, Little: 27, 31
Armour Company: 232
Army, British: officers of, in San Antonio, 98; horses for, 106; Major de Maud in, 128
—, United States: and Double Mountain, 33; and sale of Indian cattle, 78; polo team of, 99; surrender of Geronimo to, 115
Arnett, Bud: with 6 6 6 6 Ranch, 77, 120, 131; Horace Bryant as son-in-law of, 131; at Bill Richards' dance, 159
Arnett, D. W.: with Spade Ranch, 68
Arnot, John: 104; and LX cemetery, 229–232; as president of Old Time Panhandle Cowpunchers Association, 230
arsenic: in cattle dip, 223
Aspermont, Texas: ranching near, 68
attorneys: at Colorado City, 53

326

Diamond Tail Ranch: 107

Dickens County: cattle outfits in, 18, 42, 131; in Colorado City trade area, 41; frontier stores in, 42; wagon bosses in, 124; J. P. Cole in, 132; Al Yantis from, 220

"die-up": 34; effect of, 61–62

distemper: among horses, 180, 187

distillers: the Tilfords as, 45

District Court, Burnet: and automobile, 195–196

Doan's Crossing (Red River): monument to trail drivers at, 119

Dobbins, J. R.: as county judge, 35, 36

Dobie, J. Frank: A Vaquero of the Brush Country by, 6; and Sweetwater Chuck Wagon, 300

Dockum's, Texas: mail line to, 51

doctors: in Colorado City, 35, 52–53; and nesters, 238

Dodge, General: 221

Dodge City, Kansas: 38, 40, 56, 217, 230; red-light district of, 35; hotel in, 53; freight hauled from, 58; 80 John Wallace in, 164; trail drives to, 214; boot-hill cemetery in, 228

"Dodge City of the Southwest": Colorado City as, 35

Dodson, Old Man: 313

Dodson, Oscar: ranch of, 219, 227

dog and pony show: at barbecues, 275

"doghouse": definition of, 167

dogies: increase in, 246

dogs: handling of cattle with, 31

Donley County: ranches in, 102, 107, 112

Dooling, Pat: 221

Double Mountain: 18, 68, 300; ranches near, 18, 41–42; near Colorado City, 33; women near, 35; as cattle country, 41, 67, 68; F. Theodore Cookson near, 46; shipment of cattle from, 65

Douglas, Arizona: John Hollicott in, 104

Drace, W. J. (Will): with Matador Ranch, 135

drag line: building of tanks with, 89

dripping springs. SEE springs, dripping

Dripping Springs Pasture: on O X Ranch, 17, 78, 216

drive, cattle. SEE trail drives

—, trail. SEE trail drives

drouths: effects of, 34, 44, 63–64, 66

DuBose, John D. Sr.: and Longhorn weathervane, 117

Duck Creek: 26, 167

dugouts: as ranch headquarters, 13, 16–17, 35, 71, 124; as home of nester, 19, 236, 238; near Colorado City, 38; G. Backus lives in, 130; of claim jumpers, 132; building of, 236–237, 238

Dunn, A. W.: as county treasurer, 35, 37; store of, at Colorado City, 36–37, 48; account of, 37; advertising by, 37; home of, in Colorado City, 51

Dunn-Coleman Company: in Colorado City, 48

Dunn's store. SEE Colorado City, Texas; Dunn, A. W.

Dunny (horse): of Byrd boys, 259

Dutchman Creek: 159

Dyer, A. E.: and Swensons' Ranch, 125

D Z Ranch: of Jim Newman, 298

Earle, Joe: killed by Indians, 214; funeral of, 214; monuments for, 227

Earnest, Judge: at Colorado City, 53

Easley, Ben: at Bill Richards' dance, 159; and Jim McAdams, 216

Easley, Frank: at Bill Richards' dance, 159; and Jim McAdams, 216

East, E. H.: sale of cattle to, 211

East, Jim: in Arizona, 104; and John Hollicott, 232

East, Mrs. Jim: 231

East, Tom: on Tom Burnett, 75

East Texas. SEE Texas, East

East Texas Chamber of Commerce: formation of, 274

Eddleman, Elzy: in Greer County, 215

Edinburgh, Scotland: communication with, 50

Edmondson, Colonel R. E.: auction sales conducted by, 225

Edwards, C. O.: and T Bar Ranch, 47; ranching by, 68

Edwards Plateau: springs on, 20

Egypt, Little: 309

1 8 Ranch: of A. W. Dunn, 37, 56; R. A. Weatherby with, 300

8 0 outfit: of Clay Mann, 41

328

Flat Top Ranch (S M S Ranch): location of, 126; John Selman with, 127
Flippen Creek Camp: of Waggoner Ranch, 85–86
Florida: sale of polo ponies to, 101
flour sacks: use of, on cattle ranch, 171
Flowers, Will: ranching by, 68
Floyd County: in Colorado City trade area, 41
Fly, Milt: 117
Foard County: 146; springs in, 15–16; Burnett Ranch in, 78, 80, 81; Waggoner Ranch in, 85; O X Ranch in, 108; wagon bosses in, 124; Joe Johnson in, 124; Ed Bomar as sheriff of, 125; Witherspoons Ranch in, 125, 216; 3 D Ranch in, 130, 158; Leslie McAdams' ranch in, 136; cattle outfits in, 216; H A T Ranch in, 216, 260; formation of, 219; nesters in, 241–242; Dick Hill in, 293
Forsyth, Major: and O X Ranch, 132
Forsyth, Ed: cattle owned by, 38
Fort Chadbourne, Texas: ranching near, 42
Fort Clark, Texas: Las Moras Springs near, 14
Fort Concho: 18; ranching near, 42
Fort Elliott: doctor in, 230, 231
Fort Griffin: 37, 56, 300; freight hauling from, 42; Tige Avery at, 162
Fort Lancaster: ranching near, 42
Fort Sill: 76, 77; driving of Indians to, 41; Tom Burnett at, 73, 75; sale of Indian cattle at, 77–78
Fort Sumner: boot-hill cemetery at, 228
Fort Stockton: history of, 14; Comanche Springs near, 14–15, 22
Fort Union: trail drive to, 39
Fort Worth, Texas: 33, 54, 203; Gordon Witherspoon of, 22; railroad building from, 37, 214; freight hauling from, 42; Lon Barkley as postmaster of, 42; C. O. Edwards in, 47; ladies' fashions in, 49; opera house at, 49; cowmen live in, 51–52; Colvin in, 52; I. H. Burney at, 53; "Hell's Half Acre" in, 55; Harvey Means in, 57; Winfield Scott in, 65; Captain M. B. Loyd in, 72; the Burnetts in, 73, 76; Horace Wilson in, 75; rodeos in, 78; Guy Waggoner in, 85; oil

west of, 91; John B. Kennedy of, 111; John C. Burns of, 131; Furd Halsell of, 136; Johnnie Jones in hospital at, 135; Hugh Moore of, 209; packing house in, 221; cattle dipping in, 222; livestock shows in, 226; barbecue in, 282; Cattle Raisers convention in, 299, 307–309, 310; Sweetwater Chuck Wagon in, 299; J. E. Boog-Scott of, 300; Bill Davis as mayor of, 307; Pat Paffrath of, 307
Fort Worth and Denver Railway: 48, 51, 219; building of, 37–38, 65, 214; and Burnett Ranch, 71, 73; shipping of cattle on, 73, 86, 103, 221; and Waggoner Ranch, 84, 86; and cowtowns, 210; and location of Quanah, 214; Arthur Walker with, 221; Pat Dooling with, 221
Four Corners Camp: of Waggoner Ranch, 85
Four Lakes Ranch: on Mescalero Springs, 22
Francklyn Land and Cattle Company: 215
Franks, W. C.: and Longhorn weathervane, 116–117
Frederick, Oklahoma: 76
Fredericksburg, Texas: sausage from, 282
freighters: 34; in red-light district, 58
freight hauling: to ranch headquarters, 35; from Colorado City, 35, 42, 44, 58; from San Antonio, 42; prices of, 58; by nesters, 66; by John Molesworth, 97, 99; from Quanah, 220
Frenkel, Joseph: opera house of, 49, 54
frijoles. SEE beans
Frisco Railroad: SEE Santa Fe and Frisco Railroad
From Cowboy to Cotton Patch: by Don H. Biggers, 55
Fry, Bud: at Bill Richards' dance, 159
Fulda, Texas: cattle shipments from, 86
Fulton, ———: John Molesworth meets, 97

Gage, Alfred: and John Molesworth, 110–111
Gage Estate: 111
Gages, the: 110
Gail, Texas: mail lines to, 51

Moore, Hugh: sale of Hendrix and Royer Ranch to, 209

Moore, J. Ealy: and Sweetwater Chuck Wagon, 300

Moore, Prinkle: 68

Moore, W. R.: Lanc Ranch owned by, 47

Moras Springs, Las: 14

More, Robert L.: as manager of Waggoner Ranch, 87, 90–91, 92; on effect of mesquite, 88; and oil, 91; nature of, 91–92

Morgan horse. See horses, Morgan

Morris, C. W. (Charley): with Matador Ranch, 135

Morton, ———: killing of, 21

Mosquero, New Mexico: Waggoner Ranch land near, 85

Mosquero Ranch (Waggoner Ranch): Guy Waggoner at, 85; cattle on, 86; improvements on, 89

"Mother City of West Texas": Colorado City as, 35

motion pictures: J. Ellison Carroll in, 193

Motley County: Matador Ranch in, 18, 42, 143; in Colorado City trade area, 41; wagon bosses in, 124

Mott, Charley: death of baby of, 231

Mound Station: 227

Muldoon, Tom: and John Molesworth, 97, 99

Mule Creek: Old Man Dodson from, 313

Murchinson, John: in Colorado City, 51

Mushaway Peak: 145

Myers, Fred: boots made by, 50

Myres' Saddlery: 297

Nama (Indian): as Quanah Parker's wife, 76

Nation. See Indian Territory

Navajo Mountain country: 218

Nave, ———: visits of, to Colorado City, 51–52

Nave-McCord Cattle Company: Square and Compass Ranch owned by, 43

Neal, Billy: ranch of, 219, 227

Nebraska: trail drive to, 39; sale of horses in, 99; storm in, 163

Necktie (horse): and J. Ellison Carroll, 192

Neeley, Charley: ranch of, 219

Neel S (horse): races by, 225

Negro cowboys. See cowboys, Negro

Negroes: as cowmen, 51

nesters: dugouts as homes of, 19, 236, 238; and springs, 19–20, 22; at Colorado City, 34; character of, 62, 233, 234; in West Texas, 65, 66, 234–235; and cowmen, 66, 120, 194, 236, 238, 240–241, 243, 244–245, 246, 247, 251, 253; freight hauling by, 66; cutting of fence posts by, 66; selling of bones by, 66, 238; agricultural efforts of, 66, 241, 242, 247; selling of claims by, 85, 239, 241–242; and range bosses, 119, 120; and wagon bosses, 120; and R 2 Ranch, 124; and Joe Erricson, 126; and J. P. Cole, 132; move of, into Greer County, 193; and cutting up of ranches, 212–213; definition of, 233–234; classes of, 234, 235; source of name of, 234–237; horses of, 235; location of land of, 236, 246; clearing of land by, 237; mesquite fences of, 237; on Pease River, 237; hauling of water by, 237; purchases by, 238; lack of money of, 238; and doctors, 238; hunting of rabbits by, 239, 247; and bankers, 240, 241; and merchants, 240, 241; growing of wheat by, 241; and Pete Scroggins, 241; and Spur Ranch, 241; in Foard County, 241–242; improved conditions of, 242; feed grains raised by, 242, 247; raising of cotton by, 242, 247; and manufacturers, 243, 253; hardships endured by, 246–247; and beans, 286. See also farmers; immigrants; settlers

nesterments: 289; development of, 236, 238, 241. See also settlements

Nevada: John Sparks in, 123

Nevil, R. L.: William Patton works for, 162

Newlin, Texas: T. M. Pyle's ranch near, 108

Newman, Auti: and Sweetwater Chuck Wagon, 298

Newman, Cap: and Sweetwater Chuck Wagon, 298

Newman, Jim: and Sweetwater Chuck Wagon, 298